The Decline and Fall of Civilisations
by
Dr Kerry R Bolton

The Decline and Fall of Civilisations
by
Dr Kerry R Bolton

Copyright © 2017 Black House Publishing Ltd

All rights reserved. No part of this book may be reproduced in any form by any electronic or mechanical means including photocopying, recording, or information storage and retrieval without permission in writing from the publisher.

ISBN-13: 978-1-910881-96-5

Black House Publishing Ltd
Kemp House
152 City Road
London
United Kingdom
EC1V 2NX

www.blackhousepublishing.com
Email: info@blackhousepublishing.com

Contents

Foreword by Mark Dyal	3
Introduction	9
Part I - Tradition	11
Traditional Historical Outlook	13
The Axis	13
The Wheel	15
Universality of Cyclic Outlook	21
Time and Tradition	27
The Golden Age	27
Expanses of Time	28
Traditional Perspective of Time	29
Time As An Organism	31
Ebb & Flow of History	37
Progress & Its Dissidents	45
Society as an Organism	75
The Value of Tradition	85
Part II - Ethnos	89
Race and Ethnos	91
The "Race-Forming Idea"	99
Spengler on Race-Formation	105
Carl Jung on Race-Formation	107
Place and Land in the Making of Culture	115
"Environmentalism" and Communism	121
Race as Historical Destiny	125
Phenotypic Plasticity	127
Epigenetics	135
Liberal Reaction	142
Behavioural Epigenetics	149
Morphic Field Theory	151
Formative Causation	151
Soil and Race Formation	161

Contents

Part III - Rise and Fall	**165**
I.Q. and Creativity	167
Inspirare	172
Assumptions About Miscegenation	175
Modernist Versus Traditional Interpretations of History	177
Civilisations That Died	189
Mesopotamia	189
Persia	193
Greece	195
Sparta	198
Rome	200
The Collapse of Rome	204
No More Romans	205
India	212
The Real Meaning of *Varna*	*213*
The Indus Valley	216
Maurya	220
Gupta India	222
Egypt	224
Arabia	228
Hebrew	235
Mesoamerican and Andean	239
Inca	242
Japan	247
Afrikaner	254
China	260
Chiang Kai-shek attempts a Resurgence	270
"Harmonising" Elements	274
Liberalism and Communism	275
Is China the Future?	279
Birth of The West	287
Romanesque & Gothic Styles	294
Comparative Culture Styles	298
Western Science	302

Decline of The West	307
Decay of the Megapolis	315
Demographic Suicide	322
Degenerative Culture	325
Cultural Pathology as Geopolitical Strategy	331
Rise of Russia	337
The Soul of Russia	339
"Russian Socialism"	341
Taras Bulba	341
Tension of Polarities	344
Russia the *Katechon*	*345*
Russo-European Symbiosis	351
Conclusion	355
Bibliography	359

"On the world's loom Weave the Norns doom
Nor may they guide it nor change"
— Richard Wagner, *Siegfried Act III*

"The essence of history does not reside in recorded facts but in the thoughts, emotions, ideas and aspirations of the human beings who have made it... Facts are only the outer shell... History is life itself, and, like everything else that is alive, it has both a cyclical rhythm and a linear tension... The great cycle which has been in evidence throughout history like a giant wheel of destiny revolves around the sequence leading from *Culture* to *Civilisation*".
— Amaury de Riencourt, *The Soul of China*, xvii.

"Turning and turning in the widening gyre
The falcon cannot hear the falconer;
Things fall apart; the centre cannot hold;
Mere anarchy is loosed upon the world,
The blood-dimmed tide is loosed, and everywhere
The ceremony of innocence is drowned;
The best lack all conviction, while the worst
Are full of passionate intensity".
— W. B. Yeats, *The Second Coming*

Foreword

We are men and women living at the end of history. We are American vagabonds, relishing the promise of a horizon beyond which to pass. We are autochthonous Europeans, proudly defending what is left of our inheritance. Some of us are socially conservative, while others of us are violently revolutionary. Some pine for stasis and gentility, others burn for action and primitivism. Some of us are waiting to embrace a messiah, others of us to ambush him in a rhododendron thicket. Some have a God, others Tyler Durden – and still others little more than the sensation of a chilly early-Fall breeze as we pause to watch a spider patiently devour a futilely struggling bumblebee.

But we are all here ... together. Well, not really. We are a collection of "places without a place," too amorphous to be *concentrated*, but too autonomous to create a counter-power to the neo/post-liberal State and Capital.[1] We struggle to detach ourselves from the epistemography and ontology of a form of life to which we relate with nothing but mutual disdain. And yet, for most of us, as things continue to fall apart around us; as the State becomes the dystopia that only our most pessimistic and paranoid writers could have imagined; as even the sick, maimed, mediocre, scared, bored, herd animals that we have become begin to recognize the bounds of our rangelands – for most of us, for the too helplessly modern, perhaps, there will never be enough reasons to decide to fight our enemies to the death.[2]

Perhaps, though, having reasons – more precisely, *reason* – is what is holding us back and keeping us forever acted upon and never acting ourselves; keeping us stuck in the redundancy of being rational modern citizens and never immersed in the duration of becoming something else.[3] For life is flow. It is constant change. There is perpetual energy and vitality, and there is stasis and death. As Dr. Kerry Bolton demonstrates

---

1   Franco "Bifo" Berardi, *After the Future* (Edinburgh: AK Press, 2011 – Kindle edition), loc. 536.
2   Friedrich Nietzsche, *The Gay Science* (Cambridge: Cambridge University Press, 2001), #352, pg. 210.
3   Georges Sorel, *Reflections on Violence*, ed. by Jeremy Jennings (New York: Cambridge University Press, 1999 – Kindle edition), loc. 658.

herein, energy, vitality, stasis, and death come to define the boundaries of all living things – including, and especially, cultures and civilizations.

With the light touch of an expert archaeologist, Dr. Bolton uncovers the remains of the various known civilizations that have fallen to the axe of time. One by one, Mesopotamia, Persia, Greece, Sparta, Rome, India, the Indus Valley, Arabia, Mesoamerica, Japan, Afrikaner South Africa, China, and others rise and fall; becoming unique and powerful expressions of human will, ingenuity, and problem creating and solving, that, for all of their power and the value of their values, disappeared. And as we pause in the light of Bolton's words, we think about what the end must've been like, what life became in the colorless shadow of their demise. But only for a moment, as both Bolton, and the miserable comfort of our lives remind us with glaring and unblemished clarity that we are living at the end of our own unique and powerful civilization, itself falling to the axe of time.

But time alone is not enough to fell something so powerful, so lasting, and so important. No, we are not so lucky that "the somber and spurious judgment of objective forces" alone acts to defeat what we die to create, for time gets a helping hand from human weakness, perfidy, greed, and righteousness.[4] These human traits do not always manifest themselves in Bolton's narrative in ways that will comfort many of his readers, though; for his analyses conclude that it was not simply immigration or miscegenation that precipitated civilizational collapses, but instead the becoming-mediocrity and decadence of imperial nobles – via the contagion of leisure, luxury, and affluence, which themselves unleashed destructive forces of spiritual and cultural chaos.

But while boundaries are one thing, potentials – and the fact of actually *living* the death of civilization – are another. Things fall apart, Bolton tells us, but rarely do they do so of their own accord. And that is where we come in. The axes of this book are formed by civilizational creation and destruction, on one plane, and race and contemporary epistemography and politics, on the other. The nexus is the individual and his or her genetic, historical, situational - in short, epigenetic - potential as inheritors and guarantors of whatever the West was and, unfortunately, has now become.

---

[4] Irving L. Horowitz, *Radicalism and the Revolt Against Reason* (London: Routledge, 2009 - Kindle edition), loc. 320.

The Decline and Fall of Civilisations

As Western Civilization continues to confirm the vision of ancient and (counter)modern thinkers of civilizational birth and death – yes, Spengler, we are indeed doomed! – and, as we become experts at dystopic living, actually perusing magazines devoted to post-civilizational home furnishing strategies while breathing air thick with mediocrity, vulgarity, and the ignominy of our weakness in the face of death by asphyxiation, what, we ask, are we to do?

Thankfully, the pessimism of Bolton's cast of characters does not engender defeatism as much as a renewed will to defiance of the captain and crew that continue to hunt bigger and sharper ice burgs into which our already sinking ship may be ever more destructively steered. While dismantling the corrosion of materialism – and more importantly outlining the myriad symptoms of its ideational and conceptual power (from notions of progress to teleologies of development and evolution; from Marxist critiques which merely bolster the necessity of *homo economicus* to neoliberal globalists intent to impose a singular morality of consumption on each and every living thing on Earth; from zoological racists to anti-race racists) – Bolton gives us the keys to reformulating our relations to and with the tiger we are riding.

He does so by providing a space in which to ponder the need for new tactics, images, and myths – not to forestall the inevitable but instead to begin to create something of our lives that will be important and useful to future generations. In so doing – whether we do so or not, really – we will be playing our role in the building of whatever grows from the ashes of the West. For races, he tells us, are dynamic, ever changing, and never static, like people, peoples, and all living things. They can be changed, destructively or constructively, over generations, strengthening or debilitating individuals and stocks, being eugenically and dysgenically influenced by behavioral norms and political codifications.

Dr. Bolton clearly relishes explaining these behavioral norms and political codifications. Just as he swings away at the modern totems of the racial materialists, so too does he attack the epistemological foundations of those who might still harbor a soft spot for the State as an example of Western greatness. In fact, in his explanation of American politogenesis[5], which is now the hegemonic model of liberal

---

5   Peter Gelderloos, *Worshiping Power: An Anarchist View of Early State Formation* (Chico, CA: AK Press, 2016), 17.

Foreword

state development, it is the same materialism that allows quantity to reign as the essence of the modern world that points to our demise in a sea of *demos* – mere population as a vulgar political entity – specifically designed to obliterate the *ethnos* (and *ethnoi*) of our forbearers.

The individual, even as a metaphysical collective, is not just a cog but also a potential wrench thrown into the wheel of the inevitable. We have possibilities far beyond those given us by our present predicament. If we choose submission, so be it: we will bequeath the freedom "to live and think like pigs" to the future.[6] But if we choose to fight, then the fun is just getting started. Who and what do we fight at this point? Do we strengthen our enemies today so as to hasten the fall tomorrow? Do we weaken our enemies in order to forestall the inevitable? Do we push along the collapse, then, helping an already terminal creature to its passing?

Although we are certain that the answers to these questions depend on our relationships with the techniques of the contemporary elite that are driving along our demise: capitalism – which organizes our bodies and lives for labor and consumption; the State – which provides us the ecology of laboring and consuming; universities – which provide the required specialized skills for participation and advantage within that ecology; and media – which buttresses the university's work of creating a liberal intelligentsia by promoting such a creature as the optimal face of the West; they also depend on our abilities to identify creative and tactical opportunities in both the State's ecology and the decaying West that feeds it.

Perhaps the most important development in recent dissident thought is that thinkers of the Right are identifying the State and capitalism as enemies of our people. Dr. Bolton is, by now, quite comfortable demonstrating that the post/neo-liberal State is dysgenic. It is an agent of our demise. It is actively weakening each and every one of us, ensuring that our progeny inherits little beyond obedience, flaccidity, and a desire to be canalized by the whims of revenuers and profiteers. "You are awaiting the apocalypse? Man, *our lives* are the apocalypse."

Our lives. Your life. Your life that is already always overdetermined and organized – at this point by our enemies. We don't start with nothing, but with everything; it is the State's incessant overcoding and canalizing that

---

6   Gilles Châtelet, *To Live and Think Like Pigs: The Incitement of Envy and Boredom in Market Democracies* (New York: Urbanomic/Sequence Press, 2014).

regulates our potentials. As Dr. Bolton explains, the body is not purely biological but also cultural, historical, and political. It will become what is demanded of it, and through each demand, a power of life is affirmed. So we must ask ourselves as we sit in the twilight of an extinguishing civilization – witnessed in the flickering hum of a television or computer screen – with "empty head in captive hands,"[7] is it the West that is exhausted, or is it us? Is it civilization that has become unable to realize alternate possibilities or is it us, who can no longer even possibilize the destruction of the cultural, historical, and political habits that ensure our defeat and the imprisonment of our children.[8]

The State will not save the West, but instead will erase it along with you. So, without it, what do we have? Men, women, and will. This isn't a call for wild-eyed dreaming or mass-suicide-by-cop. This is neither romantic nor pretentious. It is instead a herald to begin creating a new ontology – a new way of living and of thinking life – and to recognize that our bodies – their rhythms, thoughts, functions, and abilities – are the fields upon which the final battles will be fought.

Dr. Bolton shows that we have been here from the beginning: in all civilizations there have been dissidents who fought on the side of strength, wisdom, and spiritual nobility.

We must become stronger, wiser, and nobler. We have virile, sublime, heroic work to do – not to save the West, but to save our children and ourselves. This is not a reason. It is not reason. It is instead a myth: a guiding sense, a purity of conviction, not to change the world but to reform our wills, to change us![9] The West might well be doomed, but we all have something to do about it. Things fall apart but rarely of their own accord.

Mark Dyal, Ph.D.

---

[7] Gilles Deleuze, *Essays Critical and Clinical* (Minneapolis: University of Minnesota Press, 1997) pg. 155.

[8] Deleuze 1997, pg. 152.

[9] Sorel, 1999, loc. 1608.

Mark Dyal, Ph.D. Anthropology, City University of New York, has taught African-Amercian Studies, Race History and Race Theory, Anthropology of Western and of Southern Europe; Anthropology of Violence, of the State, and of Revolution, and North American and European New Right Thought, at Ohio State University. He blogs at "Cultural Anthropology from a Derelict Space": https://markdyal.com

Introduction

That so many cultures in such disparate times and places have a similar outlook on the rise and fall of societies suggests a common source of inspiration. Whether this is of divine origin, as suggested by what is called the perennial tradition[1]; or the intuition and observation of those who lived close to nature and the organic cycles of birth, life, and death, is secondary for our study. Philosopher-historians such as Dr. Oswald Spengler presented empirical evidence for their historical analysis, Hindu and American Indian mystics intuited from divine inspiration. Both empiricists and mystics, centuries apart, rejected what is today called the "progressive" approach that regards history as an onward marching line from "primitive to modern".

The traditional (or "conservative", if you prefer) historical outlook is *cyclic*. This is at odds with the "modernist" approach to history. This modern historical outlook was formulated as the "Idea of Progress" during the French Revolution by the Marquis de Condorcet, a leading philosopher of the "Enlightenment". It was given impetus in the 19th century by Darwin's theory of evolution. The biological theory was applied to history, politics, economics and sociology, as "social Darwinism". It gave scientific validity to Free Trade economics. The Darwinian myth justifies revolutionary upheavals in society as "progressive". Those opposing change are ridiculed as "regressive", against "progress" or, to use the Leftist term, "reactionary". Such a dichotomy obscures historical realism: that notions regarded as "modern" and hence "progressive", are nothing unique to our epoch, nothing resulting from an "enlightenment" special to our age: they are symptoms typical of the Late epoch of a civilisation. The traditionalist rejects such notions of "progress". For the traditionalist "progress" is a dangerous spectre.

All manner of decay is justified in the name of "progress." A sage from corresponding periods of decay in Rome, India, Egypt, Greece, or Arabia would find the corruption of today's Western civilisation familiar. He might say, "Here we go again", and would be ridiculed as "old fashioned," and "reactionary".

---

1 "Perennial" insofar as there are concepts that seem timeless yet eternally relevant because they reflect the laws of the cosmos.

Introduction

Here we will examine the historical perspectives of a number of traditional cultures. The traditionalist approach is based upon a religious perspective, a feeling or intuition for the numinous at work; the belief that society is in balance when it maintains a nexus with the Divine. This sacral nexus is maintained through ceremonies and the ordering of society to reflect a cosmic order. Traditional societies are hierarchical rather than egalitarian, and their ethos is spiritual, not materialistic.

What is required is an overcoming of the Age of Materialism. This looms over the entirety of the world, obliterating the few vestiges of tradition with its cultural pathogens. The contention here is that man must reconnect with the divine. Those who rebel against the present Zeitgeist or Spirit of the Age, generally oppose its symptoms, but not the root cause which is of a spiritual character. They are themselves caught up in the materialistic quagmire. Like Karl Marx, their solutions therefore become mirror images rather than those of transcendence. Hence, "races" are defined in materialistic terms. Measuring physiological indices does not tell anything about the élan of a "race" any more than statistics on the gross national product inform about the élan of a nation other than from an economist's viewpoint.

Conclusions are drawn about why civilisations fall that are fallacious and deflect from the actual reasons. Such assumptions also lead to a preoccupation with secondary symptoms of decline, such as immigration, and again causes are obscured. Additionally, by neglecting to consider whether the very notions of "progress" and "evolution" are even legitimate, the contagion of the Age is accepted and those who revolt against the symptoms of decay put themselves on the defensive by accepting the assumptions of the opposition. Race-materialism implies the acceptance of evolution and the illusion of "progress". By accepting such assumptions there is an implicit acceptance of the liberal, positivist, and universalist ideologies that are part of the process of decay. Posited here instead is a total rejection of the modern world under the thrall of the spirit of mammon.

Part I

Tradition

Traditional Historical Outlook

A culture ceases to be "traditional" when it no longer feels its relationship with the Divine.[1] Baron Julius Evola[2] described this traditionalist outlook as the "metaphysics of history."[3]

High Cultures have structural features in common, expressed in different ways because each represents a different spiritual outlook. This structural commonality transcends time, race and geography. The same broad structures of organisation in High Cultures have existed as far apart geographically and ethnically as the Germanic, Egyptian, Aztec, Japanese and Vedic-Indian. They possess castes as the basis of social order reflecting the cosmic order on Earth, hold the ruler to be literally of divine origin, a priest-king and often a God-King. They consider their own culture as part of a cosmic-divine cycle. The God-King is not only the ruler of his own civilisation, and a direct nexus between the human and the divine, he is also the "King of the World", and his capital is the centre of the world; the *axis mundi*.

The Axis

Traditional societies revolve around a symbolic axial point. Each civilisation has had a holy centre, where the terrestrial and the celestial bisect. The axis might be physical or mythic. The Germanics had the World Column *Irminsul*, the Norse the World Tree *Yggdrasil*. The Gate of the Sun was the axis of the Tiahuanaco-centred civilisation in Bolivia. The Teotihuacan civilisation of Mesoamerica had the Temple of the Sun. The Hindus and Buddhists have Mount Meru; Mount Olympus for the Greek Civilisation; the Mount and Temple of Jupiter Optimus Maximus Capitolinu for the Roman; Al Kaaba Al Musharrafah at Mecca for the Arabic; Mount Fuji for Japan; Mauna

---

1 Two particularly cogent expressions of the traditionalist outlook are the Hindu *Bhagavad-Gita*, and in our Western Civilisation the poems of W. B. Yeats.

2 Julius Evola (1898-1974) wrote on historical cycles from a traditionalist outlook. His perspective might most readily be compared to the Ancient Vedic, with a focus on the divine origins of caste, and on the "cosmic" or dharmic duty of the warrior caste. Evola was the Italian translator of Oswald Spengler (*The Decline of the West*).

3 Julius Evola, *Revolt Against the Modern World*, Foreword, xxxvii.

Traditional Historical Outlook

Kea for Hawaii; various mountains, rivers and legendary migratory canoes that symbolise the divine nexus for Maori tribes throughout New Zealand; Jerusalem for the Jewish, and for the Western Gothic High Culture.

The Khmer Empire, extending from Cambodia over most of Southeast Asia, and into Laos, Thailand and southern Vietnam, was founded in 802 A.D. by King Jayavarman II, who was regarded as the *chakravartin*, or King of the World, the God-King *Deva Raja* in Sanskrit. He was ritually sanctified on Mount Mahendraparvata.[4]

The Chinese Temple of Heaven, designated in their characters as the "altar of heaven" (天壇) was the point where emperors, embodying the nexus between heaven and earth, performed rituals and prayed for the maintenance of right order. The Chinese expressed the cosmic axis ethically as *Tao*. Behaviour not in accord with the standard of morality which, in Chinese, is denoted by the two characters *Dao De*, meaning "Tao" and "Virtue" respectively, was said "not to follow the principle of Tao." Peasant uprisings raised banners proclaiming "achieve the Way on behalf of heaven". Lao Zi (6th Century B.C.) credited with being the founder of Taoism, wrote:

> "There is something mysterious and whole, which existed before heaven and earth. Silent, formless, complete, and never changing. Living eternally everywhere in perfection, it is the mother of all things. I do not know its name; I call it the Way. Man follows the earth, the earth follows heaven, heaven follows the Tao, and the Tao follows what is natural".[5]

An emperor who failed to harmonise with heaven was said to have lost the "mandate of heaven", his dynasty would fall, and be replaced by another "dynastic cycle". The *Tao* is changeless, hence the universe is ordered. By respecting the *Tao* mankind also lives harmoniously. Everything in traditional Chinese culture revolved around this concept, prior to Communism.

---

4   Benny Widyono, *Dancing in the Shadows*, 56.
5   Lao Zi, *Dao De Jing*, Chapter 25.

The Decline and Fall of Civilisations

The Wheel

The wheel is a motif in many cultures representing the cyclic nature of life, for the individual, society and entire civilisations. The spiralling motion represents the action of the cosmos itself. The wheel symbolises the axial foundation of cultures.

The Medieval world of Western High Culture had its "Wheel of Fortune", *Rota Fortunae*, with eight spokes of opposites reminiscent of the Buddhist *Wheel of Dharma*. The Wheel of Fortune was a feature of Medieval churches, hanging from the ceiling, and used as an oracle.[6] It is depicted on the 10th Major Arcana of the Tarot oracle, which is of Medieval origin.

The Greek Boethius, writing in Rome during the 6th century A.D., on the chaotic cusp between Roman ruin and Western birth, composed his *Consolation of Philosophy* as a Socratic dialogue between *Fortunae* and himself. Here the Roman goddess of good fortune is transformed into a principle of cyclic time in the service of the Christian God, who will just as likely bring collapse as favour in the unfolding of fate. Her symbol is the wheel. Her spinning of the fortune of kings and peasants alike is as inexorable as that of the seasons and the tides. She replies to Boethius:

> "Or am I alone kept from exercising my right? Heaven is permitted to reveal bright days and to conceal the same with dark nights; the year is permitted to redeem the face of the land at one time with flowers and fruits at another to confound it with clouds and frosts; it is right for the sea at one time to charm with a level surface at another to tremble with storms and waves: is incessant human greed to bind us to a consistency alien to our morals?

> "This is our power; we play this continuous game: we turn the wheel in a revolving cycle, we like to change the lowest to the highest, the highest to the lowest. Ascend if it pleases, but choose it, only if you will not think it an injury when the procedure of my game requires you to descend".[7]

---

6   D. Phillips, "Wheel", *Man, Myth & Magic*, Vol. 7, 3014-3015.
7   Boethius, "Fortune Pleads Her Case", II: 2. Chaucer edition, circa 1382.

Boethius' *Consolation of Philosophy* became one of the most influential texts of the Western Medieval epoch, translated and read throughout Europe.

Carmina Burana, a corpus of poems by monks, was another text of the Western medieval epoch that included the cyclic motif as a wheel:

> The wheel of Fortune turns;
> I go down, demeaned;
> another is carried to the height;
> far too high up
> sits the king at the summit -
> let him beware ruin!
> for under the axis we read:
> Queen Hecuba.[8]

The Jains[9] hold that time is endless, and is represented by a wheel

---

8 *Carmina Burana*, (2) Fortune Plango Vulnera ("I Bemoan the Wounds of Fortune").

9 The Jains derive from the same roots as Buddhism and Sankhya Hinduism, confined to India with 1,700,000 adherents, but traces its founding "saviour" to Parsva ca. 743 B.C., the first of a series of "saviours", the last being Mahavira, contemporary to Buddha, ca. 540 B.C. Jainism is marked by a severe asceticism. C. Furer-Haimendorf Von. "Jains", *Man, Myth & Magic*.

of twelve spokes. Like the Medieval West's *Rota Fortunae* and the *Dharmic* wheel, the Jain wheel represents polarities of life, divided into pairs of six. It is a specifically cyclic motif. One set represents a descending cycle in which good things gradually give place to bad, and the other an ascending cycle. The Jains state that the present cycle is the fifth spoke of the descending cycle.[10]

Apart from the Celtic Cross, a variation of the Norse Sun Wheel, the Celts had the *Triskele*, a curved three armed cross, radiating from an axial point; an intermediate motif between the Sun Wheel and the Swastika, representing the three cycles of life, both physical and metaphysical. The *Triskele* was a common motif in Celtic art particularly between 5th century B.C. and 8th century A.D. It represents with its three spiralling arms the importance of the Triad in the Celtic outlook. The *Triskele* represents the three cycles of *life, death and rebirth* within the three primary elements, Land, Sea, Sky, and also represents the interaction between the three physical spheres and the spiritual realm. As the arms spiral from an axis, we again see the traditionalist motif of life radiating from a central – cosmic-axis, which W. B. Yeats alluded to in *The Second Coming*, where he describes the end cycle of this Civilisation: "everything falls apart; the centre cannot hold". The three aspects, life, death, rebirth, revolve and return to the centre, the divine or cosmic pillar or axial point, analogous to the Teutonic World Column *Irminsul*, the Norse *Yggdrasil*, and the Hindu Wheel.

Another widespread motif of the cyclical nature of life relates to the Fates weaving Time. Fate is derived from Latin *fatum*, meaning decrees of the Gods, which we can call destiny, both individual and collective. Traditionally even the Gods are subjected to Fate, like the Norse Gods meeting this death at Ragnarok; a necessary cyclic sacrifice.

Nemesis is the Greek Goddess of Fate who punishes those guilty of *hubris* or arrogance towards the Gods through their wealth or power. It is a reminder that mortals are subject to the cosmic laws of time, the relentless motion of the cosmic wheel, as destiny is spun according to those laws. Fate became represented by the Triple Goddess *Moirai* among the Greeks, and *Parcae* among the Romans. Hesiod records their names as Lotho, spinner of destiny; Lachesis, weaver of the web

---

10   Graham Phillips and Martin Keatman, 1993.

Traditional Historical Outlook

of chance or luck that sustains life; and Atropos, the inescapable, who cuts the thread of life.[11] The Three Fates sat among the Gods, and Zeus himself was often considered to be subject to them.[12]

In the Germanic tradition Fate is represented again by Three, known collectively as the *Norns*. Like the Greek Fates, they also weave destiny at a spinning wheel. They are named Urd, past; Vervandi, present; and Skuld, future.[13]

The Norse World Tree *Yggdrasil* has its three roots fed by Urd, the past. Here again the traditional cultures are based on the belief that society is sustained by its nexus with its divine origins, which when cast asunder lead to the collapse of that cycle. It is notable that *Yggdrasil* is being continuously gnawed at and interfered with by a serpent, a reminder of the precarious position of a culture's foundations.

Urd, the past, is the cause of both present and future. Vervande, present, also means becoming. Therefore the present is not static, but is seeded with the possibilities of the future (Fate). These two Norns, past and present, create the third, Skuld, future, which is defined as something owed. What is owing is the *restoration of balance* from the interaction of Urd and Vervande. The *Voluspo* states:

> Thence come the maidens mighty in wisdom,
> Three from the dwelling down 'neath the tree;
> Urt is one named, Verthandi the next,-
> On the wood they scored,- and Skuld the third.
> Laws they made there, and life allotted
> To the sons of men, and set their fates [14]

This Germanic concept of Fate, like the Hellenic, was symbolised by Three sisters at a spinning wheel. It has come down to us in Wagner's *Siegfried:*

---

11 Basil Ivan Rakoczi, "Fate", *Man, Myth & Magic*, Vol. 3, 918.
12 Ibid., 920.
13 Ibid.
14 *Voluspo*, verse 20.

The Decline and Fall of Civilisations

On the world's loom
Weave the Norns doom
Nor may they guide it nor change.[1]

In Arthurian legend it is three mysterious maidens in white who take the body of Arthur to Avalon, where he is not dead, but asleep, and will return to rally the British from the depths of decline. Arthur fulfils the role of the Norse Baldur who awaits the allotted time to return after Ragnarok to preside over a new heaven and a new Earth, and other mythic figures often represented in Messianic terms. The Arthurian legend has the primary elements of tradition: the assumption to power of Arthur as a youthful regenerative force amidst a land sunk into decay, the Holy Grail as the axis around which the warrior caste maintains its connection to the divine, the round table itself as a symbol of cyclicity, and the cyclic return to decay, with Arthur awaiting to return to set in motion a new cycle.

The Indian flag is instructive as to wheel symbolism. The 24-spoked wheel on the flag is the *Ashoka Chakra*. Dr. S. Radhakrishnan speaking before the Constituent Assembly, which adopted the flag in 1947, explained:

> "The Ashoka Wheel in the centre of the white is the wheel of the law of dharma. Truth or satya, dharma or virtue ought to be the controlling principles of those who work under this flag. Again, the wheel denotes motion. There is death in stagnation. There is life in movement".[2]

The cosmos is subjected to constant change, but also founded on unchanging cyclic laws (*dharma*). The Akosha Wheel is derived from the Sanskrit *Dharma Chakra*, meaning literally the "wheel of the law", the cosmic law of cyclic motion.

The same concept of the "wheel of time" is held by the Q'ero Indians in Peru, and the Hopi of Arizona. The Hopi conception of time is cyclic. Benjamin Lee Whorf, the American linguist, stated that the Hopi "has no general notion or intuition of time as a smooth flowing

---

[1] Richard Wagner, *Siegfried*, Act III.
[2] S. Radhakrishnan, Constituent Assembly, 1947, "Flag Code of India," http://web.archive.org/web/20060110155908/http://mha.nic.in/nationalflag2002.htm

continuum in which everything in the universe proceeds at an equal rate, out of a future, through a present, into a past".[3] This cyclic concept is manifested as a wheel that is spinning in one place without forward momentum, producing an eternal recurrence explained in seasonal terms, reminiscent of the way Spengler explained cultural morphology. This produces the cyclic eternal recurrence of the same sequence of seasons, which are never accumulated into years and decades, or "the tape measure of Western linear time". More familiarly known as the Hopi Medicine Wheels, the designs of stone with spokes emanating from an axis are based upon the teaching of cycles. This is associated with the "hoop dance": "The hoop is symbolic of 'the never-ending cycle of life'. It has no beginning and no end. Tribal healers and holy men have regarded the hoop as sacred and have always used it in their ceremonies. Its significance enhanced the embodiment of healing ceremonies".[4]

The Wheel is a universal, archetypal motif of civilisations across time and space, attesting to the cyclical perspective common to traditional societies. What the centre of a wheel symbolises is the *axis mundi*, or world axis, the Tree of *Genesis*, *Yggdrasil*, *Irminsul*, and many others. The priest-King or God-King, another universal motif, is the human representation standing at the *axis mundi*. With the turning of the epochal cycles the spokes separate with decay, and everything falls apart from the *axis mundi*, in the way poetically described by Yeats.

---

3   James B. Carroll (ed.), *Language, Thought, and Reality: Selected Writings of Benjamin Lee Whorf*, 57.

4   D. Zotigh, "History of the Modern Hoop Dance".

Universality of Cyclic Outlook

"The whole cosmic order is under Me. By My will it is manifested again and again, and by My will it is annihilated at the end."
— *Bhagavad Gita* [1]

Because traditionalists are attuned to the cosmic rhythm of life, depicted by the Dance of Shiva, by the Buddhist Wheel of Life, the universality of the Swastika, and the related Sun-Wheel of the Celts and Norse, they are aware that history is comprised of the ebb and flow of great expanses of time within which civilisations are born, mature, grow old and die, like any living organism. Within these great expanses of time are cycles, the "Great Year" of the Chaldeans and Hellenes, the Etruscan and Latin *Saeculum*, the Iranian *Aeon*, and the Hindu *Kalpas*.

The Egyptians were bound to the unchangeability of their rites and prayers because of their role in sustaining the cosmos. The hieroglyphs were the "words of god" that gave expression to the divine in the world. Rites required precise repetition. The sacred does not change, so the symbolic expression of the sacred cannot change. Rites and recitations reflected "cosmic life and the cyclical recurrence of its natural phenomena: day and night, summer and winter, the motions of the stars, the inundations of the Nile, sowing and reaping, decay and regeneration".[2]

"The purpose of this ritual mimesis was dual: first, it was designed to incorporate the decline and decay with a chance of regeneration… second, it served to sustain cosmic life itself in its circularity, not merely to 'keep' time by observing its calendrical progress, but actually to generate it".[3]

---

1   *Bhagavad-Gita,* 9:8.
2   J. Assmann, 2002, 72.
3   Ibid.

Universality of Cyclic Outlook

The calendar stabilised the cosmic that it represented. The cyclical stability of the cosmos was continually threatened, and the permanence of ritual and recitation maintained its stability. Cultural order sustained cosmic order. "The world is commemorated in order to counterbalance the perpetual drift towards decline, inertia, entropy and chaos".[4]

The Greeks and Romans referred to four eras named after the four metals: gold, silver, bronze and iron. Between the Bronze and Iron cycles was an intervening Heroic cycle, where the Heroes resist encroaching Chaos. The Hindus also have four cyclic divisions: *Satya Yuga*, *Treta*, *Dvapara* and *Kali*, a demon not to be confused with the goddess Kālī, the Kali Yuga being the Dark Age of decline and chaos. The Persians had four cycles named after gold, silver, steel and "an iron compound".[5] The Chaldean view was similar.

The Mayans had solar cycles[6], with a fifth Heroic cycle in which giants are fought. Each world in a cycle of creations had its own Sun. The presiding God preceding the present cycle was Vucub Caquix ("Seven Macaw") who was a usurper presiding over humans that had been carved as effigies from wood. From the descriptions of the *Popul Vuh* creation myth, these "humans" were noted for their cruelty and disregard for animals and nature, and this world was destroyed by the Gods. The false "Sun God", Vacub Caquix, was the "antithesis of all behaviour and values held dear by the Maya". He was destroyed by the Hero Twins.[7] These Hero Twins represent the beginning of a new cycle. It is notable that the legend arises immediately after the disintegration of the Olmec civilisation, indicating the birth of a new culture cycle under a new leadership.[8] It is evident that these worlds were destroyed, according to the myth because, like Sodom and Gomorrah and the civilisation of the Noah legend, they were thoroughly degenerate, and this was the prelude to a new culture cycle.

---

4   Ibid.

5   Julius Evola, *Revolt Against the Modern World*, 177-78.

6   According to the Creation Myth, the Popul Vuh, the First Cycle or "Sun" fell with the "heat of heaven blowing mist into their eyes..." All wisdom and knowledge of the beginning was destroyed. Christensen (translator), Popul Vuh.

7   Coe, *The Maya Vase Book*, 163,

8   Coe, Ibid., 164.

The Decline and Fall of Civilisations

The Hopi of Arizona state that there have been three prior "world cycles" or "Suns".[9] According to the Hopi lore related by an elder, this cycle will end "If people do not change their ways." The "spirit of the world will become frustrated." The elder believed that the world had worsened since he was told of the lore by his grandfather during the early 20th century. "There are no values at all any more – none at all – and people live any way they want, without morals or laws. These are the signs that the time has come".[10] The only chance is "that the Hopi do not abandon their traditions", and that they impart their tradition to the rest of the world. He explained that all is fated according to divine law.[11] The Hopi are a remnant of a truly traditional culture.

In the *Book of Daniel* the rise and fall of civilisations are depicted on a statue with a head of gold, chest and arms of silver, stomach and thighs of brass, legs of iron, and feet of iron and clay, symbolising four civilisations[12]

Islam states that there is a succession of "prophetic cycles", each ending in corruption, and the nexus with the divinity restored by a new prophet. For example the cycle initiated by the Prophet Jesus was corrupted by teaching that he was the "son" of God. Muhammad serves as the final Prophet.[13]

Chinese tradition recounts ten former Ages called *kis* that have died in succession. The Chinese have an historical perspective based on "dynastic cycles". The Buddhists have "Seven Suns" or epochal cycles, including the present.[14]

Norse cosmology is recorded in *Voluspo*, where the seeress explains to Odin the creation and destruction of the cosmos. She states that prior to the present there had been Nine Worlds:

---

9   Graham Hancock, 213.
10 Ibid., 532.
11 Ibid., 533.
12 *Book of Daniel*, 2.
13 M. D. Coogan, 95.
14 Graham Hancock, 213.

Universality of Cyclic Outlook

> Nine worlds I knew,   the nine in the tree
> With mighty roots   beneath the mold".[15]

The present or tenth cycle ends with the death of Baldur the sun god, and the dark forces representing chaos are unleashed to do battle with the gods in the cataclysm called *Ragnarok*.[16] Norse cosmology shows that even the gods are subject to the cycles of history. They meet their death at *Ragnarok*, but this is their *Wyrd*, of which they are conscious. The cycle preceding *Ragnarok* is, like the Hindu, one of chaos among mortals. In particular there is a sundering of family bonds and infidelity becomes common place:

> Brothers shall fight   and fell each other,
> And sisters' sons   shall kinship stain"[17]

This passage depicts the moral rot typical of the end-cycle of a civilisation. As can be discerned there is nothing "progressive" or "new" about the present West's "permissive society". It is also a time of violence:

> Hard is it on earth,   with mighty whoredom;
> Axe-time, sword-time,   shields are sundered,
> Wind-time, wolf-time,   ere the world falls;
> Nor ever shall men   each other spare".[18]
> Yggdrasil shakes,   and shiver on high
> The ancient limbs"[19]

The forces of chaos, the world serpent Iormungandr, the Fenrir Wolf, Garm the Hel Hound, Surtr with a flaming sword, and their hordes are loosened upon the worlds of gods and mortals.[20] The earth staggers, the sun dims, stars fall, fire engulfs the cosmos itself, and entwines the "Life-supporter", the World Tree.[21]

---

15   Voluspo, verse 2.
16   Ibid., 33-60.
17   Ibid., 45.
18   Ibid., 45.
19   Ibid., 47.
20   Ibid., 50.
21   Ibid., 59.

The Decline and Fall of Civilisations

Following the cataclysm a new cycle begins:

> Now do I see   the earth anew
> Rise all green   from the waves again"²²

Baldur returns as the principal God of the new cycle.²³ This ushers in a new Golden Age of virtue, joy and serenity "during long ages."²⁴ Hence another civilisation begins further cycles of life and eventual death.

> In wondrous beauty   once again
> Shall the golden tables stand mid the grass,
> Which the gods had owned in the days of old"²⁵

It is notable that Baldur is the founder-god of this new civilisation on the death of the old; he embodies the spark of the prior civilisation that is used to reignite a new civilisation. Evola counselled a new generation youth, for whom he was a guru in Italy, that one can no longer defend Western civilisation, which is in an inexorable cycle of death. The best that can be done is to "ride the tiger", adopting an Eastern term, during the present era, and lay the foundations of the next civilisation. This is the new generation's cosmic duty, or *dharma*.²⁶

---

22 Ibid.
23 Ibid., 62.
24 Ibid., 66.
25 Ibid., 61.
26 Evola, 2003, passim.

Time and Tradition

The Golden Age

In contrast to the lineal view of history, the traditional perspective sees humanity as having *declined* or "fallen" from a Golden Age, rather than evolving.

The Golden Age was at the beginning, from whence proceeds a gradual stagnation and decline, and a return to chaos, as the nexus between man and the divine breaks through descending cycles. There is a reflection of this belief in the Hebrew myth of Adam and Eve representing primordial human perfection and the *Fall* from this state.[1]

Jesus can be seen in this traditional context in heroic terms as having sacrificed Himself to restore the connection between man and God, as well as being at the head of an army which militarily defeats its foes at the end of a decadent cycle that is analogous with the Hindu Kali Yuga, and the Norse Wolf Age.[2]

The primordial Golden Age is called *Satya Yuga* by the Hindus (*Satya* = Being), in Latin *Saturn* presided over the Golden Age.[3] In Egypt the first Cycle, *Zep Tepi*, was the Golden Age, ruled directly under a dynasty of the gods. The Mayan civilisation refers to its Golden Age as a time of great knowledge, which has been lost, including the ability to have "measured the round face of the earth." The Golden Ages of the traditional cultures are times when humanity was one with the gods, maintained by the performance of rites, and enforced by a warrior caste, under the rulership of priest-kings.

Evola in explaining a universal general decline, asked how the "higher can emerge from the lower", "greater from less"?[4] The traditionalist rejects evolution whether in social, historical, or biological forms.

---

1   Book of Genesis 2-3.
2   Book of the Revelation of St. John, 19: 11-15.
3   Hancock, 403.
4   Evola, 1938.

Expanses of Time

According to Plato's account of the dialogue between Solon and the Egyptian priests, the priests stated:

> "Oh Solon, you Greeks are all children, and there is no such thing as an old Greek. You are all young in kind; you have no belief rooted in old tradition and no knowledge hoary with age. And the reason is this. There have been and will be many different calamities to destroy mankind... so these genealogies of your own people... are little more than children's stories".[5]

The Egyptian priests were describing Atlantis as having existed 9,000 years before their own civilisation. Such an account is impossible under our own era's darwinian linear historical paradigm. However there are many archaeological anomalies which do not accord with the darwinian time frame, which may show technologically advanced civilisations not only well before our own but which make the fabled Atlantis very "young".

A large amount of data on anomalous archaeology has been assembled by Michael Cremo and Dr. Richard Thompson, which despite the heretical nature of the subject, has received critical acclaim by a number of eminent academics. Cremo and Thompson provided many examples of anomalous artefacts indicating that civilisations may have been rising and falling well before our present common assumptions. Anomalous artefacts such as a gold thread found in a stone at a depth of 8 feet, identified as being 320-360 million years old; and the inscribed coin found in Illinois 114 feet underground in deposits between 200,000 and 400,000 years old, may point to the antiquity of civilisations of high technical achievement that have risen and fallen millions of years prior to our own time.[6]

Many such archaeological anomalies question the assumed age of homo sapiens by evolution. Leif A. Jensen marshals science to refute darwinism from a Vedic traditionalist perspective.[7] He quotes astrophysicist Carl Sagan that "the Hindu religion is the only one of

---

5   Ignatius Donnelly, 6-21.
6   Michael A. Cremo, and Richard L Thompson, 1999.
7   Leif A. Jensen, 2010.

the world's great faiths dedicated to the idea that the Cosmos itself undergoes an immense, indeed an infinite number of deaths and rebirths. It is the only religion on which the time scales correspond to those of modern scientific cosmology".[8] As we have seen, Hinduism is not the "only" such religion, but it is an extant traditional religion that remains significant to much of the world.

Traditional Perspective of Time

Traditional man lives in continual communion with the divine and his society maintains its reverence for the sacred. Professor Mircea Eliade in his seminal study[9] on the time-conceptions of sacred and profane societies examined many cultures across distances of both history and geography. He drew the distinction between societies that are "sacred" and "profane", like Julius Evola referred to societies as "traditional" and "modern". The sacral view of time, wrote Eliade, did not see life as a straight line leading to death, but as something that could be renewed by reconnecting with creation through the annual performance of rites. The balance of the cosmic with the terrestrial was sustained and renewed, lest chaos return and engulf the world. The distinction between sacred time and mundane is that profane time was bridged by the religious character of society. While our modern rational mind baulks at such "superstition", this continual communion with divine origins ensured that the foundations of the culture were reaffirmed. The rites were – and in some places still are – a reminder of one's place in the cosmos:

> "For religious man time too, like space, is neither homogeneous nor continuous. On the one hand there are the intervals of a sacred time, the time of festivals (by far the greater part of which are periodical); on the other there is profane time, ordinary temporal duration, in which acts without religious meaning have their setting. Between these two kinds of time there is, of course, solution of continuity; but by means of rites religious man can pass without danger from ordinary temporal duration to sacred time".[10]

---

8   Carl Sagan, 2002, 258.
9   Mircea Eliade, 1959.
10   Ibid., 68.

Time and Tradition

The sacred quality of the world at its godly origin is re-enacted through rituals that restore the primordial quality to the mundane world, and sustain the nexus with the divine. To the Hindus this is one's *dharma* – cosmic duty – performed through right-action in accordance with the obligations of one's caste. As we have seen the Hopi Indian performs his ritual to sustain the world, without which chaos and world destruction descend. Annually the Chinese emperor, in his role as priest would ascend the temple platform within the Forbidden City and perform the rites necessary to maintain universal order. Eliade continues:

> "One essential difference between these two qualities of time strikes us immediately: by its very nature sacred time is reversible in the sense that properly speaking it is a primordial mythical time made present. Every religious festival, any liturgical time, represents reactualization of a sacred event that took place in a mythical past, 'in the beginning.' Religious participation in a festival implies emerging from ordinary temporal duration and reintegration of the mythical time reactualized by the festival itself. Hence sacred time is indefinitely recoverable, indefinitely repeatable. From one point of view it could be said that it does not 'pass,' that it does not constitute an irreversible duration. ... In other words the participants in the festival meet in it the first appearance of sacred time, as it appeared [originally]. For the sacred time in which the festival runs its course did not exist before the divine *gesta* that the festival commemorates. By creating the various realities that today constitute the world, the gods also founded sacred time, for the time contemporary with a creation was necessarily sanctified by the presence and activity of the gods".[11]

Sacral society is based on a sense of eternity that time is cyclical insofar as through right-action – *dharma* – including the correct rites, cosmic balance can be renewed. It is time that is "circular", "reversible and recoverable, a sort of eternal mythical present that is periodically reintegrated by means of rites".[12] Eliade stated that this difference in time-perception is what primarily distinguishes "religious from nonreligious man". Traditional man refuses to live in what the

---

11   Ibid., 71.
12   Ibid.

modernist calls the "historical present"; he attempts to "regain sacred time" and a sense of eternity.[13] When Evola counselled "ride the tiger", live in the world but remain detached, this is a primary lesson of the *Bhagavad Gita*. Christians were counselled similarly: "And be not conformed to this world: but be ye transformed by the renewing of your mind, that ye may prove what is that good, and acceptable, and perfect, will of God".[14] Here also is the theme of inner "renewal" for the "religious man", and the rite performed is that of the Holy Communion, literally a communion with God.

For "modern" "non-religious man", time is measured by the drudgery of his work, which he interrupts with "celebrations and spectacles"; what Eliade calls "festal time". Non-religious man seeks escape from "the comparatively monotonous time". Some escape allows modern man to experience "a different temporal rhythm from that which he experiences when he is working or bored".[15] Eliade gives the examples of listening to music or waiting for a loved one as experiences that change time-perception for modern man. Our "modern" epoch of Western civilisation, having broken the sacred nexus, attempts to relieve the monotony of profane time by ever more crass levels of distraction.

The more Western time is detached from the Eternal the more depraved or trivial the distractions. The prophets and sages of all the civilisations have lamented these epochs. Those civilisations at a certain point in their life-cycle stopped adhering to the traditions of their forefathers, or reformed them, moderated them, "modernised" them. For Western civilisation the finale of this disconnection was Vatican II (1962-1965) when fundamental reforms "modernised" the Catholic Church, the last vestige of tradition in the West.

Time As An Organism

The traditional perception of society and of history was organic and hence cyclic, or "seasonal". Diverse cultures performed rituals for the return of the Sun, and hence a new beginning of a cycle of life: the Egyptian Atum and Ra, Mesopotamian Shamash, Hindu Surya, Greek Helios, Slavic Svarog, Germanic Sol, Norse Baldur, Cetlic

---

13 Ibid.
14 Romans 12: 2.
15 Mircea Eliade, 72.

Time and Tradition

Lugh, Aztec Tonatiuh, Roman Sol Invictus, Chinese Rigong Riguang Pusa, Buddhist Sūryaprabha, Japanese Amaterasu, Maori Tamanuiterā, Massai Ngai, Australian Aboriginal Yhi, and many others.

The Soyal Solstice Ceremony symbolising the renewal of life is the main rite of the Hopi Indians. For Persians, continuing to celebrate the ancient traditions, the rite of Shab-e Yalda is performed for the victory of Mithras, the Sun Father, later adopted by the Roman Legions as Sol Invictus, the conquering sun. With the adoption of Christianity by Constantine, Sol Invictus became the conserving "Son" (Christ), and the Solstice celebration became his birthdate. The Church Father Ambrose (339–397), called Christ the true sun, alluding to Christ as the "morning light", the "rooster's call", "light … upon the senses",

> Eternal maker of all things
> Of day and night the sov'reign King,
> Refreshing mortals, You arrange
> The rhythm of the seasons' change.[16]

Note even here at the foundation of what became the faith of the West that Ambrose referred to the "rhythm of the seasons' change". Returning to Eliade, he states that in North American Indian dialects,

> "the term world (= Cosmos) is also used in the sense of year. The Yokuts say 'the world has passed,' meaning 'a year has gone by.' For the Yuki, the year is expressed by the words for earth or world. Like the Yokuts, they say 'the world has passed' when a year has passed. This vocabulary reveals the intimate religious connection between the world and cosmic time. *The cosmos is conceived as a living unity that is born, develops, and dies on the last day of the year, to be reborn on New Year's Day.* [Emphasis added] We shall see that this rebirth is a birth, that the cosmos is reborn each year because, at every New Year, time begins *ab initio*.[17]

"The intimate connection between the cosmos and time is religious in nature: the cosmos is *homologizable* to cosmic time (= the Year) because they are both sacred realities, divine creations.

---

16   Ambrose, Aeterne Rerum Conditor.
17   Mircea Eliade, 74.

Among some North American Peoples this cosmic- temporal connection is revealed even in the structure of sacred buildings. Since the temple presents the image of the world, it can also comprise temporal symbolism. We find this, for example, among Algonquins and the Sioux. ... Their sacred lodge represents the universe; but at the same time it symbolizes the year. For the year is conceived as a journey through the four cardinal directions, signified by the four doors and four windows of the lodge. The Dakotas say: 'The Year is a circle around the world' - that is, around their sacred lodge, which is an imago mundi".[18]

Eliade also raises a significant point, which we shall consider in the chapter on the "Birth of the West"; that architecture reflects the spiritual outlook of a people. Eliade refers to the sacred lodge as constructed to reflect the cosmic outlook of the North American Indian, no less than the Gothic spire of the Western, or the domed Mosque of the Islamic.

Eliade refers to the Hindu fire altar as "equivalent to a repetition of the cosmogony". The fire altar represents the year with 360 bricks of the enclosure corresponding to the 360 nights of the year, and the 360 *yajusmati* bricks to the 360 days. Eliade comments:

"This is as much as to say that, with the building of each fire altar, not only is the world remade but the year is built too; in other words, time is regenerated by being created anew. But then, too, the year is assimilated to Prajaparj, the cosmic god; consequently, with each new altar Prajapati is reanimated - that is, the sanctity of the world is strengthened. It is not a matter of profane time, of mere temporal duration, but of the sanctification of cosmic time. What is sought by the erection of the fire altar is to sanctify the world, hence to place it in a sacred time".[19]

There was a similar cosmological symbolism of the Temple at Jerusalem. Citing the Jewish historian Flavius Josephus[20] the twelve loaves of bread on the table signified the twelve months of the year and the candelabrum with seventy branches represented the decans

---

18 Ibid.
19 Ibid., 75.
20 Flavius Josephus, Antiquities of the Jews (circa 93 A.D.), III, 7, 7.

(the zodiacal division of the seven planets into tens). The Temple was a world-image, *imago mundi*; "being at the Center of the World, at Jerusalem, it sanctified not only the entire cosmos but also cosmic life – that is, time". [21]

Cosmic time for the religious man is symbolised by the course of the year "imagined in the form of a circular course". "The year was a closed circle; it had a beginning and an end, but it also had the peculiarity that it could be reborn in the form of a new year". The New Year, symbolising a new cycle, and was "pure" and "holy", "because not yet worn".[22] That is the important distinction between the traditional perception of cycles and the profane perception of lineal history. When the Persian priest-king commemorated the New Year, Nawroz, he proclaimed, "Here is a new day of a new month of a new year; what time has worn must be renewed". Eliade comments:

> "Time had worn the human being, society, the cosmos – and this destructive time was profane time duration strictly speaking; it had to be abolished in order to reintegrate the mythical moment in which the world had come into existence, bathed in a 'pure', 'strong', and sacred time. The abolition of profane past time was accomplished by rituals that signified a sort of 'end of the world'".[23]

To "modern" man the ritualised "renewal" of the cyclic life, which was such an important function of the priest-king, is nothing but superstition. He can only see "progress" ahead in a straight line towards an horizon, without comprehending that beyond that horizon might be a cliff edge. Traditional man understood that his culture was subject to decay, but could be renewed by reiterating the ethos on which it was founded. Therefore, religion and myth were far more than the superstition condemned by Marx as an "opiate" and scoffed at by our rationalists: it was the basis for renewal. Eliade states that with each New Year "the fabulous time of Creation" was being "reintegrated".[24]

---

21   Mircea Eliade, 75.
22   Ibid., 77.
23   Ibid., 78.
24   Ibid., 80.

The Decline and Fall of Civilisations

We might now understand how prophets such as Jeremiah and a few of our own historians such as Oswald Spengler, Julius Evola and Rene Guénon, could warn that their societies were in the process of decay, when tradition was being forgotten. These often ridiculed doomsayers were the few who had a higher perspective above the masses of the ignorant and the smug. Hence the wide denigration among academia of Oswald Spengler by those who are too immersed in the present *Zeitgeist* to understand what is happening around them, while most of our esteemed modern historians such as Francis Fukuyama and Arnold Toynbee can only see the continuing "march of progress" towards a universal democratic millennium. The response of academia is epitomised by the dogmatic assertion of Robert Nisbet that,

> "No one has ever seen a civilization die, and it is unimaginable, short of cosmic disaster or thermonuclear holocaust, that anyone ever will. Nor has anyone ever seen a civilization – or culture or institution – in literal process of decay or denegation, though there is a rich profusion of these words and their synonyms in Western thought from Hesiod to Spengler. Nor, finally, has anyone ever seen, as we see these things in plants and animals – growth and development in civilizations and societies and cultures... We see none of these in culture, death, degeneration, development, birth".[1]

While Dr. Nisbet, typical of most modern academics, albeit lauded as a great "conservative" sociologist,[2] can only see a jumble of unrelated facts, Spengler discerned a pattern. Dr. Nisbet assures us that this is not possible. One of those who saw what was going on about him, who was ridiculed and vilified for his warnings, retorted: "Hear now this, O foolish people, and without understanding; which have eyes, and see not; which have ears, and hear not".[3]

---

1   Robert A. Nisbet, 3.
2   Gilbert S. Sewall, "Robert Nisbet's Conservativism". Nisbet was a libertarian, not a conservative; an example of the careless use of such terms. He saw history in terms of the individual; hence his aversion to the organic, morphological approach to sociology and history.
3   Jeremiah, 5: 21.

Ebb & Flow of History

"I see in place of that empty figment of ONE linear history... the drama of a number of mighty cultures, each having its own life; its own death... Each culture has its own new possibilities of self-expression which arise, ripen, decay and never return. I see world history as a picture of endless formations and transformations, of the marvellous waxing and waning of organic forms... The professional historian on the other hand, sees it as a sort of tapeworm industriously adding to itself one epoch after another". — Oswald Spengler. [1]

While each civilisation has characteristics particular to itself, its own type of art, architecture and mathematics, they have analogous cycles of birth, flourishing, decline and death. Typically, the cycle of decline is marked by religious scepticism, seen as scientific or progressive, materialism, and the rise of the merchant class with its money ethics, over traditional classes based on birth and with obligations to duty. Family and children are seen as a burden rather than as assuring continuity of one's lineage.

The Hindu text *Visnu Purana*, describes the Kali Yuga in terms that could just as well have been written by a contemporary critic of Western society:

"Wealth (inner) and piety (following one's dharma) will decrease day by day until the whole world will be entirely depraved. Then property alone will confer rank; material wealth will be the only source of devotion; passion will be the sole bond between the sexes; falsehood will be the only means of success in litigation...

"Earth will be venerated for its mineral treasures...

"He who gives away much money will be the master of men, and family descent will no longer be a title of supremacy...

---

1   Spengler, *The Decline of The West*, Vol. 1, 21-22.

"Men will fix their desires upon riches, even though dishonestly acquired".[1]

Hesiod wrote of ages of culture, and the predominant human type of each age, as a degenerating fall from Divinity to lower levels of being:

"Or if you will, I will sum you up another tale well and skilfully - and do you lay it up in your heart, - how the gods and mortal men sprang from one source.

"First of all the deathless gods who dwell on Olympus made a golden race of mortal men who lived in the time of Cronos when he was reigning in heaven. And they lived like gods without sorrow of heart, remote and free from toil and grief: miserable age rested not on them; but with legs and arms never failing they made merry with feasting beyond the reach of all evils. When they died, it was as though they were overcome with sleep, and they had all good things; for the fruitful earth unforced bare them fruit abundantly and without stint. They dwelt in ease and peace upon their lands with many good things, rich in flocks and loved by the blessed gods.

"But after earth had covered this generation - they are called pure spirits dwelling on the earth, and are kindly, delivering from harm, and guardians of mortal men; for they roam everywhere over the earth, clothed in mist and keep watch on judgements and cruel deeds, givers of wealth; for this royal right also they received; - then they who dwell on Olympus made a second generation which was of silver and less noble by far. It was like the golden race neither in body nor in spirit. A child was brought up at his good mother's side a hundred years, an utter simpleton, playing childishly in his own home. But when they were full grown and were come to the full measure of their prime, they lived only a little time in sorrow because of their foolishness, for they could not keep from sinning and from wronging one another, nor would they serve the immortals, nor sacrifice on the holy altars of the blessed ones as it is right for men to do wherever they dwell. Then Zeus the son of Cronos was angry

---

1 Vishnu Purana, 310.

and put them away, because they would not give honour to the blessed gods who live on Olympus.

"But when earth had covered this generation also—they are called blessed spirits of the underworld by men, and, though they are of second order, yet honour attends them also—Zeus the Father made a third generation of mortal men, a brazen race, sprung from ash-trees; and it was in no way equal to the silver age, but was terrible and strong. They loved the lamentable works of Ares and deeds of violence; they ate no bread, but were hard of heart like adamant, fearful men. Great was their strength and unconquerable the arms which grew from their shoulders on their strong limbs. Their armour was of bronze, and their houses of bronze, and of bronze were their implements: there was no black iron. These were destroyed by their own hands and passed to the dank house of chill Hades, and left no name: terrible though they were, black Death seized them, and they left the bright light of the sun.

"But when earth had covered this generation also, Zeus the son of Cronos made yet another, the fourth, upon the fruitful earth, which was nobler and more righteous, a god-like race of hero-men who are called demi-gods, the race before our own, throughout the boundless earth. Grim war and dread battle destroyed a part of them, some in the land of Cadmus at seven-gated Thebe when they fought for the flocks of Oedipus, and some, when it had brought them in ships over the great sea gulf to Troy for rich-haired Helen's sake: there death's end enshrouded a part of them. But to the others father Zeus the son of Cronos gave a living and an abode apart from men, and made them dwell at the ends of earth. And they live untouched by sorrow in the islands of the blessed along the shore of deep swirling Ocean, happy heroes for whom the grain-giving earth bears honey-sweet fruit flourishing thrice a year, far from the deathless gods, and Cronos rules over them; for the father of men and gods released him from his bonds. And these last equally have honour and glory.

"And again far-seeing Zeus made yet another generation, the fifth, of men who are upon the bounteous earth.

"Thereafter, would that I were not among the men of the fifth generation, but either had died before or been born afterwards. For now truly is a race of iron, and men never rest from labour and sorrow by day, and from perishing by night; and the gods shall lay sore trouble upon them. But, notwithstanding, even these shall have some good mingled with their evils. And Zeus will destroy this race of mortal men also when they come to have grey hair on the temples at their birth. The father will not agree with his children, nor the children with their father, nor guest with his host, nor comrade with comrade; nor will brother be dear to brother as aforetime. Men will dishonour their parents as they grow quickly old, and will carp at them, chiding them with bitter words, hard-hearted they, not knowing the fear of the gods. They will not repay their aged parents the cost their nurture, for might shall be their right: and one man will sack another's city. There will be no favour for the man who keeps his oath or for the just or for the good; but rather men will praise the evil-doer and his violent dealing. Strength will be right and reverence will cease to be; and the wicked will hurt the worthy man, speaking false words against him, and will swear an oath upon them. Envy, foul-mouthed, delighting in evil, with scowling face, will go along with wretched men one and all. And then Aidos and Nemesis, with their sweet forms wrapped in white robes, will go from the wide-pathed earth and forsake mankind to join the company of the deathless gods: and bitter sorrows will be left for mortal men, and there will be no help against evil".[2]

The Revelation of John has a similar account of the end cycle of a world-encompassing civilisation, descriptive of today's "modern civilisation". Using the analogy of a prior fallen civilisation, the figure of the Whore of Babylon is evoked to describe a world system that has amassed great power and wealth, that is devoid of a spiritual nexus and that is in the throes of collapse. "Babylon the great is fallen," exclaims the prophet. The "habitation of devils and of every foul spirit, and a cage of every unclean and hateful bird."[3] John of Patmos was declaring that the future world civilisation he was visualising, a civilisation based on wealth and power, is spiritually and morally bankrupt. It is the end

---

2   Hesiod, "The Story of the Ages of Man", Works and Days, ca. 700 B.C.
3   Revelation of John, 18:2.

cycle of a civilisation when outward glamour, wealth, excess, and hedonism predominate. St. John sees this Late civilisation in terms of a world power to which all pay tribute. There have been fanciful interpretations, especially by Pentecostals, in calling this The Vatican, or the European Union. Contemporary political observers might today see this world empire as being manifested in the world outreach of the USA. That this end cycle manifests as a world empire is shown by John's *Revelation*: "For all the nations have drunk of the wine of the wrath of her fornication, and the kings of the earth have committed fornication with her, and the merchants of the earth are waxed rich through the abundance of her delicacies".[4]

Here John sees this world empire as receiving the homage of most nations ("the kings of the earth"), and as being the basis of a world financial and economic system ("the merchants of the earth…"). The nexus around which this "civilisation" is based is therefore described as being that of money rather than Divinity. In keeping with the traditional outlook, John's *Revelation* foresees the crumbling to decay and death of this godless empire, with plagues, death and mourning, "utterly burned", with the "kings of the earth" who have ingratiated themselves with this empire lamenting its end, along with the merchants.[5]

John reminds us that the basis of this *neo-Babylonian* civilisation in its end cycle is that of *commerce*. The merchants lament its demise because the commerce will no longer be conducted in gold and silver, precious metals and the symbols of opulence.[6] John's *Revelation* states that it is the merchants who rule this world empire, just as Spengler said that mercantile values dominate civilisations in their "Winter" cycle. John described the merchants in this civilisation as "the great men of the earth" who rule the earth, "for by their sorceries were all nations deceived".[7] This end-system is plutocracy. The banking system on which it is based has been described as "sorcery". After the apocalyptic end of this civilisation John foresaw a new thousand year civilisation. One is not compelled to believe in the Christian faith to recognise

---

4   Ibid., 18: 3.
5   Ibid., 18: 8-10.
6   Ibid., 18: 12.
7   Ibid., 18: 23.

the efficacy of John's "prophecy"; any more than one must accept Hinduism or Norse paganism, to see the exactitude of their prophecies on end-cycles. John understood the unfolding of history from a traditional perceptive, as did the sages of other faiths and cultures, and his descriptions accord precisely with the present situation.

The Chinese dynastic cycle (朝代循環) states that each dynasty, after reaching a political, economic and cultural peak, falls through moral corruption, losing the Mandate of Heaven, and is succeeded by a new dynasty, which goes through the same cycles:

> A new ruler unites China, founds a new dynasty, and gains the Mandate of Heaven.
> China, under the new dynasty, achieves prosperity.
> The population increases.
> Corruption becomes rampant in the imperial court, and the empire begins to enter decline and instability.
> Natural disaster hits the rural population, and famine ensues because of corruption and overpopulation.
> Famine causes rural rebellion and civil war.
> The Emperor loses the Mandate of Heaven.
> The population decreases because of the violence.
> Epoch of warring states.
> One state emerges victorious.
> The victorious state is the focus for a new empire.
> The new empire gains the Mandate of Heaven.
> The cycle is repeated by the succeeding dynasty.

A Chinese proverb summarises the dynastic cycles: "After a long split, a union will occur; after a long union, a split will occur" (分久必合，合久必分). Sinologist Dr. John K. Fairbanks wrote of this:

> "China's two thousand years of cornered politics have produced apparent rhythms and pulsations.... Anyone who seeks historical uniformity, or who makes societies and civilisations his units of study, will find the Chinese chronicles inexhaustible".[8]

Sima Guang, commissioned to write a voluminous history of China,

---

8   John K. Fairbank, 100-101.

Zizhi tongjian ("Comprehensive Mirror for Aid in Government"), which taught the lessons of right statecraft, saw the key to returning to the Golden Age and the overcoming of the "dynastic cycles" as being the revival of tradition, including ritual in achieving harmony and equilibrium, in the sense that Eliade describes. The word *Li* can mean specific rites and ceremonies, the courtesies of social interaction, an aspect of personal cultivation, political and social institutions, and "culture" in a broad sense, indicating that interconnections between all of these aspects of life. As in other civilisations, Sima looked on the Golden Age of the ancestors as the ideal for the present:

> "The Way of the ancients was always wide and never narrow. They always concentrated on the profound and never the superficial. Their words were always high-minded and never low. ... Even if they passed their days in bitter poverty, the customs and achievements they bequeathed still serve as examples after hundreds and thousands of years".[9]

Sima saw human nature and the character of the cosmos as constant. What was valid for the ancestors continues to be so. It is a departure from tradition that causes decay.

> "Are there any differences between the Heaven and Earth of antiquity and those of today? Were the ten thousand things then different from today? Did people then have different natures and emotions than today? Heaven and Earth are unchanged, sun and moon are the same. The ten thousand things are as always, and human nature and emotions have not been altered. Why should the Way alone have changed?"[10]

Sima defines "The Way" as based on "filial piety, compassion, humanity, righteousness, loyalty, trustworthiness, ritual, and music"; the function of music being that of "harmony". The changes that occur are either superficial and have not touched the essence of "The Way" or they are deviations. While changes in material culture are superficial, what subverts "The Way" are changes in beliefs, including, according to Sima, Buddhism, Daoism, and "perverted practices" such as geomancy.

---

9 Sima Guang's Collected Works as Transmitted in His Family, quoted by Philip Clart, 239.

10 Sima, cited in Clart, 240.

When influential at the imperial court Sima opposed any changes in customs and beliefs.[11] He was an avid Confucian.

The Golden Age of the Zhou dynasty, based on ritual order, was subverted by King Weilie of Zhou in 430 B.C., undermining imperial authority and leading to the fall of the Zhou. The "dynastic cycles" of rise and fall were caused by the inability of successive dynasties to recover the harmonious social order of the early Zhou, defined by and operating through correct rituals. Sima writes in *Zizhi tongjian* that "among the emperor's duties there is none greater than ritual".[12]

Influenced by Buddhist cyclic principles, the Samurai ethic refers to the "flow of time" in the ethical treatise *Hagakure*, by Jocho Yamamoto (1659-1719). In his commentary on *Hagakure* for the present, the Japanese literary figure Yukio Mishima, alludes to this *cyclicism*. Mishima states: "Lamenting as he does the decadence of his era and the degeneration of the young samurai, Jocho is also a realistic observer of the flow of time…" Resisting the flow of time rarely produces desirable results, he states.[13] Citing Book Two of *Hagakure* Mishima quotes: "The climate of an age is unalterable. That conditions are worsening steadily is proof that we have entered that last stage of the Law".[14] Jocho employed the analogy of the seasons, reminiscent of Spengler, in describing the historical cycles: "However the season cannot always be spring or summer, nor can we have daylight forever". According to Jocho's advice, one should not look to nostalgia and the return of obsolete forms, nor to the superficiality of what is "up to date" while "detesting the old fashioned", but should "make each era as good as it can be according to its nature".[15]

---

11   Clart, Ibid.
12   Ibid., 241.
13   Yukio Mishima, 81-82.
14   Ibid., 83.
15   Ibid.

"Progress" & Its Dissidents

The assumption that there is a line of human ascent was given intellectual legitimacy by the Enlightenment philosopher, the Marquis de Condorcet, a primary influence in the French Revolution, who served as secretary of the Paris Assembly, albeit dying in a Jacobin jail in 1794. Condorcet has remained an influential figure in the prevalent notion that history is one of "progress" through science. *Sketch for a Historical Picture of the Progress of the Human Mind* was Condorcet's *magnum opus* that has had a seminal influence on "modern" thinking. Condorcet assumed an "unbroken chain" of human history.[1] He assured his readers that historians no longer need make assumptions about the past; all is now clear and man's past, present and future can be mapped out with confidence by "collecting and arranging facts". This has formed the basis of "modern" history ever since. Condorcet wrote:

> "From the period that alphabetical writing was known in Greece, history is connected by an uninterrupted series of facts and observations, with the period in which we live, with the present state of mankind in the most enlightened countries of Europe; and the picture of the progress and advancement of the human mind becomes strictly historical. Philosophy has no longer anything to guess, has no more suppositious combinations to form; all it has to do is to collect and arrange facts, and exhibit the useful truths which arise from them as a whole, and from the different bearings of their several parts".[2]

The triumph of progress is assured and will usher a universal state of equality through the supremacy of the rational mind. Despite precisely those "Enlightenment" doctrines having brought Condorcet to a Jacobin prison and to his death, we are assured that mankind is "perfectible", even if a liberal use of the guillotine might be required along the "progressive path" of human perfection, based on "the constancy of the laws of nature". In triumphal spirit Condorcet assures us history teaches that mankind will reach Utopia:

---

1 Marquis de Condorcet, *Sketch for a Historical Picture of the Progress of the Human Mind* (1794), "Introduction".

2 Ibid.

"There remains only a third picture to form,—that of our hopes, or the progress reserved for future generations, which the constancy of the laws of nature seems to secure to mankind. And here it will be necessary to show by what steps this progress, which at present may appear chimerical, is gradually to be rendered possible, and even easy; how truth, in spite of the transient success of prejudices, and the support they receive from the corruption of governments or of the people, must in the end obtain a durable triumph; by what ties nature has indissolubly united the advancement of knowledge with the progress of liberty, virtue, and respect for the natural rights of man; how these blessings, the only real ones, though so frequently seen apart as to be thought incompatible, must necessarily amalgamate and become inseparable, the moment knowledge shall have arrived at a certain pitch in a great number of nations at once, the moment it shall have penetrated the whole mass of a great people, whose language shall have become universal, and whose commercial intercourse shall embrace the whole extent of the globe".[3]

Here we see the doctrines of the American Founding Fathers and of Karl Marx alike: of our "modern" democracy, socialism, liberalism, communism and capitalism; and of precisely the doctrines that the USA has tried to impose on the world, whether by Hollywood or by bombs. This universal Utopia would be ushered by an enlightened elite, who knows best how to organise humanity to ensure its "happiness". Condorcet wrote of this elite: "This union having once taken place in the whole enlightened class of men, this class will be considered as the friends of human kind, exerting themselves in concert to advance the improvement and happiness of the species".[4] How this happiness is to be achieved, wrote Condorcet, is through "commercial intercourse" embracing the whole world.

To these sweeping philosophical assumptions from the Enlightenment, a more "scientific" façade was applied with the use of evolutionary theory the following century. There was an optimism of the 19th century with the introduction of the Machine Age as the ultimate in human potential and of infinite duration. This optimism among

---

3 Ibid.
4 Ibid.

the highest intellectual circles was cogently expressed by leading 19th century evolutionist Dr. A. R. Wallace in a book optimistically entitled *The Wonderful Century* (1898):

> "Not only is our century superior to any that have gone before it but... it may be best compared with the whole preceding historical period. It must therefore be held to constitute the beginning of a new era of human progress. ... We men of the 19th century have not been slow to praise it. The wise and the foolish, the learned and the unlearned, the poet and the pressman, the rich and the poor, alike swell the chorus of admiration for the marvellous inventions and discoveries of our own age, and especially for those innumerable applications of science which now form part of our daily life, and which remind us every hour of our immense superiority over our comparatively ignorant forefathers".[5]

Perhaps few passages more succinctly expresses the antithesis between the modern and the traditional. Dr. Wallace epitomises the darwinian outlook, of which he was the primary proponent alongside Charles Darwin, not just in terms of biological evolution, but in terms of how this evolutionary doctrine is applied to history and society. We "moderns" see history and society as evolutionary. Our era is regarded as the apex of history, with all other civilisations as preludes. It is hubris and egotistical blindness. Never mind that the ruins of prior civilisations such as that of the Roman, Chinese, Incan, Egyptian, or Aztec attest to periods of history millennia ago that had technical grandeur every bit as magnificent as that of the "modern" world, and one day some civilisation millennia hence, will be excavating the ruins of New York City.

As for the present state of historical scholarship, Francis Fukuyama, when deputy director of the U.S. State Department's policy planning staff, delivered a lecture at the University of Chicago in 1989, subsequently printed in *The National Interest*, and expanded as a book in 1992, tellingly called *The End of History*. Fukuyama's influential treatise is that there is nothing beyond liberal-democracy, and that this will achieve universal supremacy. Fukuyama sees the collapse

---

5   Quoted by Asa Briggs (ed.), 29.

of the Soviet bloc and the end of the Cold War as ushering a new dispensation. He sees the universal order of liberal-democracy as "the triumph of the West":

> "The triumph of the West, of the Western *idea*, is evident first of all in the total exhaustion of viable systematic alternatives to Western liberalism. In the past decade, there have been unmistakable changes in the intellectual climate of the world's two largest communist countries, and the beginnings of significant reform movements in both. But this phenomenon extends beyond high politics and it can be seen also in the ineluctable spread of *consumerist Western culture* in such diverse contexts as the peasants' markets and color television sets now omnipresent throughout China, the cooperative restaurants and clothing stores opened in the past year in Moscow, the Beethoven piped into Japanese department stores, and the rock music enjoyed alike in Prague, Rangoon, and Tehran.
>
> *"What we may be witnessing is not just the end of the Cold War, or the passing of a particular period of postwar history, but the end of history as such: that is, the end point of mankind's ideological evolution and the universalization of Western liberal democracy as the final form of human government.* [Emphasis added].
>
> "For better or worse, much of Hegel's historicism has become part of our contemporary intellectual baggage. The notion that mankind has progressed through a series of primitive stages of consciousness on his path to the present, and that these stages corresponded to concrete forms of social organization, such as tribal, slave-owning, theocratic, and finally democratic-egalitarian societies, has become inseparable from the modern understanding of man".[6]

Fukuyama's "triumph of the Western idea" cannot distinguish between "Beethoven piped into Japanese department stores, and the rock music enjoyed alike in Prague, Rangoon, and Tehran". The epitome of Western civilisation is "consumerist Western culture" spread to every corner of the globe, to every hill-tribe and Amazon forest dweller, Asian peasant

---

6   Francis Fukuyama, "The End of History?", 1989.

and Siberian villager. This is the culmination not just of Western achievement, but of history. What Marx saw as the "march of history," of "progress" culminating in the "end of history" with the triumph of Communism over the world, Fukuyama sees for liberal-democracy, which he regards as the ideological foundation of "consumerist culture". It is the messianic aim of the USA as the carrier of a culture-pathogen throughout the world, as expressed approvingly and in similar terms by another U.S. strategist Colonel Ralph Peters, considered in a closing chapter. For now, we are tracing the historical origins of the "Idea of Progress" that is itself a symptom of Western decline. Fukuyama, as heir to the European Enlightenment that engulfed the remnants of Europe's traditional society through revolution, sees "human history" as a linear evolution through a "series of stages", as did Marx. He misses the ebb and flow of history, the rise and fall of cultures, each with their own analogous epochs of birth, flowering, decay and death, succeeded by the birth of another High Culture. To Fukuyama and the progressives, the meaning of all history is just a prelude, a series of footnotes to the end of the path: liberal-democracy and its consumer society. Alexander the Great thought the same about his own "universal civilisation".

The Western intelligentsia do not recognise that their type and their ideas have all been seen before. They are the products of an epoch of decline and death, not the heralds of a new dawn. Their "progress" is a phantom that will end in collapse. They are the harbingers of a disease that they mistake for health, with which they aim to infect all others in the name of "progress". They call this infection "liberal democracy"; in medical pathology it is called syphilis.

Before this epoch of "Enlightenment scholarship", which is based on the collection of data, as Condorcet put it, the traditional outlook was a clear perception of how history unfolded. There was a perception among Christian philosophers that putrefaction had entered the world after the Fall of Man, which meant that the social organism grows old and dies like other organisms. Man's decay walked beside his increase in knowledge. With knowledge comes arrogance, or "hubris" as the Greeks called it, and self-destruction, when man seeks to become "god". Can we not recognise this decay today alongside our "modern" technology that accompanies the primacy of matter over soul? It is Icarus ascending to the heights and falling to his death, Adam eating the fruit of knowledge and being expelled from Eden.

Amidst the flowering culture of Elizabethan England, the poet John Donne perceived that despite the greatness of his era, there was a degeneration of mankind from a formerly higher state:

> "As the world is the whole frame of the world, God hath put into it a reproofe, a rebuke, lest it seem eternall, which is, a sensible decay and age in the whole frame of the world, and every piece thereof. The seasons of the year irregular and distempered; the Sun fainter, and languishing; men lesse in stature and shorter lived. No addition, but only every yeare, new sorts, new species of wormes and flies, and sicknesses which argue more and more putrefaction of which they are engendered".[7]

Godfrey Goodman, chaplain to Elizabeth I, stated that the further something proceeds from its source the more corrupt it becomes. "And as we see decline and decay in individual parts of nature, as for instance in man, so the universe itself must partake of the nature of its parts and pass through the cycle of youth, old age, and death".[8] Ibn Khaldun, the Arab Spengler, said much the same during the 14th century.

The epochal crisis of World War I prompted a reconsideration of the West's optimism. Scientists and philosophers, including Carl Jung and Oswald Spengler, reconsidered what the modern epoch of Western civilisation had lost when materialism and science made the soul redundant and as Nietzsche said, "killed God". and despite his own aversion to Christianity saw nihilism as the result:

"The madman jumped into their midst and pierced them with his eyes. 'Whither is God?' he cried; 'I will tell you. We have killed him' - you and I. All of us are his murderers. But how did we do this? How could we drink up the sea? Who gave us the sponge to wipe away the entire horizon? What were we doing when we unchained this earth from its sun? Whither is it moving now? Whither are we moving? Away from all suns? Are we not plunging continually? Backward, sideward, forward, in all directions? Is there still any up or down? Are we not straying, as through an infinite nothing? Do we not feel the breath of empty space? Has it not become colder? Is not night continually closing in on us? Do

---

7   Quoted by Robert A. Nisbet, 100.
8   Ibid., 101.

The Decline and Fall of Civilisations

we not need to light lanterns in the morning? Do we hear nothing as yet of the noise of the gravediggers who are burying God? Do we smell nothing as yet of the divine decomposition? Gods, too, decompose. God is dead. God remains dead. And we have killed him".[9]

Carl Jung, who opposed the mechanistic, materialistic direction of modern science, including the psychiatry of his former mentor Sigmund Freud, saw in the fetish for "progress" something different from that of the darwinian optimists: that the layers of man's psyche were not keeping apace with the rapid developments of modernity, which would mean a fractured personality, suppressing those levels of the psyche that are the legacy of our ancestors. Modern man therefore denies most of what he really is.

> "A great horde of worthless people do in fact give themselves a deceptive air of modernity by skipping the various stages of development and the tasks of life they represent. Suddenly they appear by the side of the truly modern man - uprooted wraiths, bloodsucking ghosts whose emptiness casts discredit upon him in his unenviable loneliness. Thus it is that the few present-day men are seen by the undiscerning eyes of the masses only through the dismal veil of those spectres, the pseudo-moderns, and are confused with them. ... This, however, should not prevent us from taking it [proficiency] as our criterion of the modern man. We are even forced to do so, for unless he is proficient, the man who claims to be modern is nothing but a trickster. He must be proficient in the highest degree, for unless he can atone by creative ability for his break with tradition, he is merely disloyal to the past. To deny the past for the sake of being conscious only of the present would be sheer futility. Today has meaning only if it stands between yesterday and tomorrow. It is a process of transition that forms the link of past and future. Only the man who is conscious of the present in this sense may call himself modern. Many people call themselves modern - especially the pseudo-moderns. Therefore the really modern man is often found among those who call themselves old fashioned".[10]

---

9   Nietzsche, *The Gay Science*, "The Parable of the Madman", para. 125,181-82.
10   C. G. Jung, Collected Works, Vol. X, 75-76.

This crisis of Western civilisation received much attention from the German thinkers during the post-World War I Weimar period. Nietzsche was a primary influence on them, including Spengler and Jung. Unlike the British assumption of the inherent goodness of "progress", and the French "positivist" philosophers, who have had such a terminal influence on Western philosophy, the German thinkers delineated the contrasts between *Kultur* and *Civilization* with the latter representing the decadent epochs. It was Spengler in particular who explained this dichotomy. The differences between *Kultur* and *Civilization* are summarised by Jay Sherry in a doctoral thesis[11] on Carl Jung:

> "The dichotomy of *Kultur/Civilization* had become a polemical reference point during the war and was carried over into the *Kulturkampf* of the Weimar period. The following schematic list might be the best way to organize all this":

Kultur	*Civilization*
mythos – soul	logos – intellect
spiritual	materialistic
holistic	atomistic
national	international
rural	urban
aristocratic elite	mass democracy
clean – healthy	dirty - degenerate
youthful	senile
life-promoting	hostile-to-life

---

11   Jay Sherry, 58.

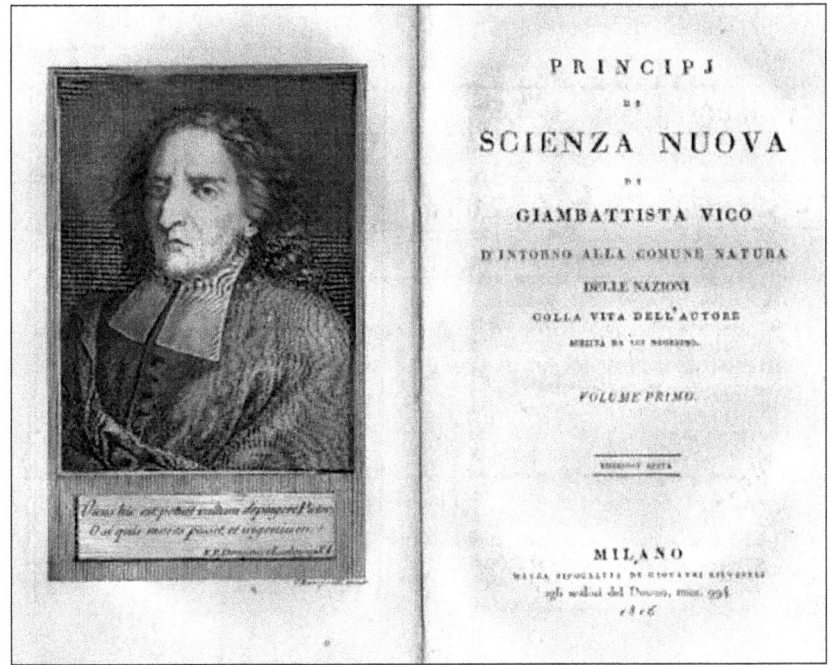

Giambattista Vico

Giambattista Vico, (1668-1744), considered the father of historical-philosophy, looked at history as something knowable by considering the human condition. At odds with the Enlightenment philosophers, retaining his Catholicism and his belief in the imminence of the divine in nature, Vico rejected the faith in unlimited "progress" that was already beginning to dominate the sciences. He also rejected the Enlightenment faith in "reason" by maintaining the importance of the "imagination" in culture. Vico, looking to antiquity, understood history not as an unfolding of infinite "progress," but as a cyclic ebb and flow that saw civilisation going through cycles represented by "poetic man," "heroic man" and "reasonable man". Vico saw religion as a necessary binding element, again being at odds with the rationalist philosophers.

As the civilisation, or what Vico called the "nation", progressed away from the poetic/imaginative and into the reasonable/rationalistic, the creative impulse is lost, and society reverts to barbarism, or what Spengler called the *Fellaheen*; historically and culturally passé and exhausted; like Hindu or Arab villagers dwelling in the shadows of ancient monuments. The epochs of Vico are analogues to those of Spengler:

Vico	*Spengler*
Poetic/imaginative	Spring
Heroic	Summer
Reasonable [Rationalist]	Autumn/Winter

Vico saw the increasing agnosticism of "reasonable man" and his loss of faith, like Spengler, as a prelude to collapse. At this epoch "man begins to think too much", that is to say, he tries to weigh and measure everything, in what Vico called the "barbarism of the intellect", and destroys the foundations on which the civilisation had been constructed over centuries. Everything is in flux. There is no sense of permanence. We see it pervasively today in the fleeting notions of culture determined consumer marketing trends. Vico identified three epochs of decay:

> I: "It [providence] first ordains that there be found among these peoples a man like Augustus to arise and establish himself as a monarch and, by force of arms, take in hand all the institutions and all the laws, which, though sprung from liberty, no longer avails to regulate and hold it within bounds.
>
> II: "Then, if providence does not find such a remedy within, it seeks it outside .... [P]rovidence decrees that they become slaves by the natural law of the *gentes* which springs from this nature of nations, and that they become subject to better nations. ... Herein two great lights of natural order shine forth. First, that he who cannot govern himself must let himself be governed by another who can. Second, that the world is always governed by those who are naturally fittest.
>
> III: "But if the peoples are rotting in that ultimate civil disease and cannot agree on a monarch from within, and are not conquered and preserved by better nations from without, then providence for their extreme ill has its extreme remedy at hand .... By reason of all this, providence decrees that, through obstinate factions and desperate civil wars, they shall turn their cities into forests

and the forests into dens and lairs of men. In this way, through long centuries of barbarism, rust will consume the misbegotten subtleties of malicious wits that have turned them into beasts made more inhuman by the barbarism of [the intellect] than the first men had been made by the barbarism of sense".[12]

Again there are analogues with Spengler. The first type of decay mentioned by Vico corresponds to the "Age of Caesarism" accompanied by a revival of faith, or "Second religiousness" over rationalism,[13] where a great leader imposes his will on a dying civilisation and provides it with an impressive finale on the world stage, rather than its slinking off to die. Here Vico uses the example of a literal Roman Caesar, Augustus.

The third form of decay is analogous to Spengler's use of the word *Fellaheen*, as a description of a hitherto great people that have become culturally exhausted and subsist as only bystanders of history. They have returned to a barbarous existence not through lack of intelligence, but through "the barbarism of the intellect", which intellectualises the founding ethos of a vibrant culture out of existence.

---

12   G. Vico, paragraphs 1104-1106.
13   Spengler, *The Decline*..., passim.

Johann Wolfgang von Goethe

Carl Jung, while a student at Basel University faculty of medicine, rejected the materialistic and mechanistic science of his teachers. From an early period he condemned academia "for having stuffed a passel of materialistic rubbish into the gaping mouths of those guttersnipes, the educated proletariat." He referred to this as resulting in "the moral instability of the upper echelons of society and the total brutalization of the working man".[14] Sherry comments that it is important to understand that Jung, like many other scientists in the German-speaking world, was schooled in a tradition rooted in the scientific works of Goethe rather than in Darwin's *Origin of Species*.[15] Here we see the fundamental difference of world-views between the German and English, with England as the harbinger of the age of materialism, of liberalism and capitalism, reflected in its science. Goethe influenced Oswald Spengler's morphology of history, and he also influenced Jung's morphology of the psyche.

Sherry states that although Goethe as a scientist was a "keen empiricist", he also "opposed the mechanistic model proposed by Bacon and employed by Newton … He rejected a mathematically abstract approach to science for one that included both the sensual reality of

---

14 Quoted by Sherry, 18.
15 Jay Sherry, 17.

the thing observed and the imaginative faculty of the observer. This technique of *Anschauung* ('direct vision') reflected Goethe's artistic-poetic temperament and was used to study Nature in a holistic, organic way".[16] While visiting the botanical garden at Palermo he had a sudden insight into the underlying character of plants, which he called the *Ur-pflanze* ("archetypal plant"). Jung's study of "archetypes of the soul"[17] is analogous to the Goethean study of the archetypes of plants and animals.

Modern science can no longer discount Goethe's plant archetypes. In recent years genetic studies of mutant flowers indicate that a single gene triggers the growth of flowers in plants, which sets off the myriad of changes needed to produce a flower. "The discovery is part of a wider series of breakthroughs in the study of flower development which have confirmed the theory, originally put forward by the poet Johann Wolfgang von Goethe more than 200 years ago, that the different organs in a flower, such as petals and stamens, are all variations on a single theme".[18] This suggests that life, including human life, has archetypal forms that unfold. It was a morphological approach that was adapted by Spengler to the study of history.

---

16 Ibid.
17 Ibid., 18.
18 Enrico Coen, Rosemary Carpenter, 1992.

Oswald Spengler

Goethe was the basis of Spengler's historical method. He is cited throughout *The Decline of The West*. Of the method of historical morphology developed from Goethe, Spengler states:

> "Culture is the prime phenomenon of all past history and future world-history. The deep, and scarcely appreciated, idea of Goethe, which he discovered in his 'living nature' and always made the basis of his morphological researches, we shall here apply – in its most precise sense – to all the formation of man's history, whether fully matured, cut off in the prime, half opened or stifled in the seed. It is the method of living into (*erfühlen*) the object, as opposed to dissecting it".[19]

This is what Spengler calls Goethe's "looking into the heart of things", "but the century of Darwin is as remote from such a vision as it is possible to be". We look in vain for any treatment of history that is "entirely free from the methods of Darwinism".[20] Spengler credits Goethe with describing the "epochs of the spirit" of a civilisation that

---

19   Spengler, *The Decline…*, Vol. I, 105.
20   Ibid.

agrees with his own, preliminary, early, late, and civilised stages,[1] which Goethe called in an 1817 essay, *Epochs of the Spirit*, the Ages of Poetry, Theology, Philosophy, and the Prosaic. They equate with Spengler's seasonal metaphors (Spring, Summer, Autumn, Winter) which he calls "spiritual epochs".

The Age of Poetry is one of myth and imagination. The Age of the Holy or the Age of Theology, is one of religion and awe before the divine. Already in this epoch rationalism enters and "reason" destroys what it is reasoning about, proceeding with the Age of Reason (Age of Philosophy) or the Enlightenment as it is called in Western civilisation. The historical life-course ends with the Prosaic Age, which is the culmination of the prior epoch in rationalising mystery to extinction. This ends in confusion as the masses, detached from all spirituality, blindly attempt to find alternatives to the shallowness of the Prosaic Age.[2]

Spengler remains the most recognised exponent of what has been persistently called German "cultural pessimism", distinct from the Anglo-American and French positivist utopian faith in perpetual progress. It is however nothing more than the "pessimism" of recognising that all organisms die, and are replaced by other organisms that go through the same life cycles, unless they are prematurely aborted by external factors such as invasion or natural disaster.

The Weimar era (1919-1933), during which Spengler wrote and lectured, starkly showed the character of *Civilization* in the degeneracy wrought by Germany's wartime defeat. There were no barriers to experimentation in the arts and morals, and society sunk into depravity comparable to the mythic Sodom and Gomorra. However, there was nothing novel about this. The depravity had been enacted many times before over millennia.

Spengler made a comparative study of the cultural epochs of the Indian, Egyptian, Chinese, Classical, Arabian, and Western civilisations. He showed that each have analogous cycles of birth (Spring), adolescence (Summer), maturity (Autumn), and decay (Winter).

---

1   Ibid., Vol. II, 37.

2   Erich Heller, 18-19.

"Progress" & Its Dissidents

At the Spring epoch the population is "rural-intuitive": "there are no great cities, but an intellectual ferment has begun". For the West this "epoch" was around A.D. 900 to 1300, and included Francis of Assisi, Thomas Aquinas, and Dante. From this proceeds the "culture-period" during which the *Kulturvolk* reach their highest stature. This corresponds to the Summer epoch. Cities are developing but they belong solely to the culture. The city has not yet become a *megapolis*, ascribed to the Winter epoch. Traditions are important at this stage. They involve the recognition of a noble élan, Faith and Church, hierarchy and dynasty, with the privileges and obligations that go with them. In art, a convention of tradition is maintained. In science, man stands in awe of God's universe, and does not strive to become God. His science unfolds God's creation, and does not try to supplant or improve it. The arts and sciences serve tradition, not as in the Winter epoch, questioning and undermining the foundations of the culture in the name of "progress". The culture has not yet been ossified by intellectualism, rationalism and materialism. This Summer epoch in the West is ascribed to ca. 1300 to late 1600s. Towards the end of this epoch there is an impoverishment of religion, which Spengler identifies with Puritanism, which gives money a religious sanctity, and sets the stage for the triumph of city over village; factory over village market; proletarian over craftsman and peasant; plutocrat and oligarch over landed-aristocrat; intellectual over priest; in a word all that we now call "modern".

The Autumn epoch, the "Age of Reason", sees the development of the great soulless cities, the city as a money-centre, intellectualism and scepticism, the time of Locke, Voltaire, Rousseau; where religion becomes rationalised and intellectualised, and the spiritual nexus is further broken, harbouring the materialism of the next epoch.

The 19th century inaugurates the Winter epoch where "population" no longer means *people/volk/ethnos*, but rootless masses: proletarians and bourgeois. The city has become a *megapolis*, a world-financial-centre with a rootless population drawn from the world, like Rome in its decline, or New York. This rootlessness and "cosmopolitanism" is lauded as superior to the "old fashioned" and "narrow-minded" parochial person who does not "keep up with the times", and "fears change". This is international-urban civilisation, where the population is "shapeless, fluctuating, irreligious", as Spengler stated. There is no sense of *ethos* or *ethnos*. The workers of the land are held in the lowest regard. Marx referred to the "idiocy of rural life", because he was not an agent for the type of historical change envisaged by Marx. The peasant is looked on as a "yokel", whereas in a healthy culture-organism he is the well-spring of a healthy *ethnos*, and the literal *sustainer* of the nation. There is a shift to the cities as industry displaces agriculture and cottage industry. "The spiritual creative force has been lost". "Abstract thinking" degenerates into the "professional scientific lecture-desk philosophy'". "In politics the whole tendency is away from the individual culture that made the people great, and towards internationalism, pacifism, and socialism" wrote Spengler.

Marx lauded the axial shift of a culture from country to city, from peasant and craftsman to bourgeois and factory worker, as part of a "progressive" dialectical process, while Spengler saw this as symptomatic of cultural decay. This was the transition from the Spring and Summer epochs of a *culture* to the Autumn and Winter epochs of a *civilisation*. Marx wrote of this:

> "The bourgeoisie, by the rapid improvement of all instruments of production, by the immensely facilitated means of communication, draws all, even the most barbarian, nations into civilisation. The cheap prices of commodities are the heavy artillery with which it batters down all Chinese walls, with which it forces the barbarians' intensely obstinate hatred of foreigners to capitulate. It compels all nations, on pain of extinction, to adopt the bourgeois mode of production; it compels them to introduce what it calls civilisation into their midst, i.e., to become bourgeois themselves. In one word, it creates a world after its own image.
>
> "The bourgeoisie has subjected the country to the rule of the towns. It has created enormous cities, has greatly increased the urban population as compared with the rural, and has thus rescued a considerable part of the population from the idiocy of rural life. Just as it has made the country dependent on the towns, so it has made barbarian and semi-barbarian countries dependent on the civilised ones, nations of peasants on nations of bourgeois, the East on the West.

"The bourgeoisie keeps more and more doing away with the scattered state of the population, of the means of production, and of property. It has agglomerated population, centralised the means of production, and has concentrated property in a few hands. The necessary consequence of this was political centralisation. Independent, or but loosely connected provinces, with separate interests, laws, governments, and systems of taxation, became lumped together into one nation, with one government, one code of laws, one national class-interest, one frontier, and one customs-tariff".[3]

Where Spengler saw decline into decay and death for a culture-organism, Marx saw the march of "progress", as do the present day ideologues of "American Exceptionalism".

---

3   Karl Marx, *The Communist Manifesto*, "Proletarians and Bourgeois".

Amaury de Riencourt

Amaury de Riencourt came to similar conclusions on the character of culture, civilisation and the rhythmic cycles of historical life. Like Spengler he went beyond viewing the sum total of history as a lineage of "facts", without having a feel for the "thoughts, emotions, ideas and aspirations" of those who make history. "Facts are only the outer shell", he wrote, "the crystallization and materialization of ideas and emotions". History is "life itself" and has, like other organisms, both a "cyclical rhythm and a linear tension". While the West focuses on history as a lineal unfolding, on the other hand the pulse of historical rhythm shows "a definite pattern of recurrences which is clearly visible in all human societies: they are born, they grow and they die – and often enough they are followed by other societies in formation who feed off their rotting corpses like maggots – the Persians in Babylon, the Classical Greeks in Egypt, the Germanic hordes in the Roman Empire".[4]

> "What we have to discover is the grand cycle of history, that which takes into account the whole of a particular society's life – its arts, sciences, religions, philosophies, politics, economics, all of which are intimately connected and interrelated. It has to be all-inclusive".[5]

---

4   Amaury De Riencourt, xvii.

5   Ibid.

De Riencourt, having intimate knowledge of the Orient, referred to the "giant wheel of history", and like the German historical thinkers, distinguished between the epochs of *Kultur* and *Civilization*:

> "Those now familiar words we are now going to use in an unfamiliar fashion, in the periodic sense of youth followed by maturity, in the sense of organic succession. Instead of coinciding in time, Civilisation follows and fulfils the Culture which was tending toward it during the life span of a particular society. In this sense, each organic society has 'its' own culture and 'its' own Civilisation".[6]

---

6   Ibid., xvii-xviii.

Rene Guénon

H. T. Hansen in his introduction to Evola's *Revolt Against the Modern World* describes him as "Guénon's leading Italian representative". Evola cited Guénon throughout *Revolt Against the Modern World*, the title itself being reminiscent of Guénon's *Crisis of the Modern World*, published in France in 1927. It is Guénon who wrote of the concepts of the "axis of the world", and the "Tree of Life" as the way for the return to the Absolute. It was Guénon who provided a spiritual analysis for the crisis of the modern world.

Guénon was born in Bloise, France, in 1886. He was initiated into the tradition of Shiva by a Hindu sect. Troubled by the anti-religious agitation of the French intelligentsia, he became an initiate of Sufism, although regarding Hinduism as the best means of reviving a lost spirituality in the West, particularly since Hinduism remains a living tradition. Because of the ultimate kinship of Europeans with the Indo-Aryans, he regarded Hinduism as more amenable to the Western psyche.

Guénon moved to Cairo in 1930, where he remained until his death in 1951. He wrote numerous books on tradition and on the need of the West to reconnect to the Absolute.[7] This connection he saw

---

7   The basis of Sufism is the renunciation of the material world and of the ego and the pursuit of union with the Godhead via asceticism and gnosis.

running through all traditions (hence, the "*Perennial* Tradition"): the Hindu concept of *yoga*, the Buddhist *nirvana*, the Sufi *tahaqquq* (self-realisation in God), and the Catholic *deificatio*.

Dr. Martin Lings[8] who became part of Guénon's household in Cairo and is the English translator of Guénon, summarised his doctrine:

> "The Mysteries and especially the Greater Mysteries are explicitly or implicitly the main theme of Guénon's writing, even in *The Crisis of the Modern World* and *The Reign of Quantity*. The troubles in question are shown to have sprung ultimately from loss of the mystical dimension, that is, the dimension of the mysteries of esotericism. He traces all the troubles in the modern world to the forgetting of the higher aspects of religion. He was conscious of being a pioneer, and I will end simply by quoting something he wrote of himself, 'All that we shall do or say will amount to giving those who come afterwards facilities which we ourselves were not given. Here as everywhere else it is the beginning of the work that is hardest'".[9]

Guénon, although an ascetic and a hermit did not counsel a resigned fatalism, but like Evola called for an "elect" to prepare for the aftermath of the cyclic "cataclysm":

> "If the elect of which we spoke could be formed while there is still time, they could so prepare the change that it would take place in the most favourable conditions possible, and the disturbances that must inevitably accompany it would in this way be reduced to a minimum; but even if they cannot do this, they will still have before them another yet more important task, that of helping to preserve the elements which must survive from the present world to be used in building up the one that is to follow. Once one knows that a re-ascent must come, even though it may prove impossible to prevent the downward movement first ending in some cataclysm, there is clearly no reason for waiting until the

---

8   Dr. Martin Lings taught for many years at the University of Cairo before becoming Keeper of Oriental Manuscripts at the British Library. He has authored many books including *The Eleventh Hour*, *Symbol and Archetype*, and *Muhammad: His Life Based on the Earliest Sources*. Lings was an authority on tradition and particularly on Sufism.

9   M. Lings, "Rene Guénon".

The Decline and Fall of Civilisations

descent has reached its nadir before preparing the way for the re-ascent. This means that whatever may happen the work done will not be wasted: it cannot be useless in so far as the benefit that the elect will draw from it for themselves is concerned, but neither will it be wasted in so far as concerns its later effects on mankind as a whole".[10]

---

10   Rene Guénon, *Crisis of the Modern World.*

Julius Evola

Evola's political, philosophical and historical teachings were motivated by his traditionalism as a manifestation of what he termed the "revolt against the modern world". While adhering to the cyclic conception of history Evola added to this the concept of a *duality* of civilisations categorised as *traditional* and *modern*. Evola saw the end cycle of Western civilisation, the beginning of which he ascribed to the Late Medieval period, as the start of the super-cycle of the *modern*. All those civilisations that had come and gone before were still within the context of the *traditional*. Evola wrote of the cycles of decline:

> "Recently in contrast to the notion of progress and the idea that history has been represented by more or less continuous upward evolution of collective humanity, the idea of a plurality of the forms of civilisation and of a relative incommunicality between them has been confirmed. According to this second and new vision of history, history breaks down into epochs and disconnected cycles. ... A civilisation springs up, gradually reaches a culminating point, and falls into darkness and, more often than not, disappears. A cycle has ended...."[11]

Evola considered this revived cyclic approach to history as "a healthy reaction to the superstition of history as progress", which was a product of Western materialism. He offered this added dualist dimension

---

11   Julius Evola, *The Hermetic Tradition*, 13.

however, and cautioned that Spenglerian cyclicism did not offer the entire story. In addition to "a plurality of civilisations", an historical "duality" should be recognised. "Modern civilisation stands on one side and on the other the entirety of all the civilisations that have preceded it." For the Western civilisation he put the end of the traditional phase and the beginning of the modern super-cycle as the "late Middle Ages", when the point of rapture with tradition was complete. Since that time, "modern civilisation" has completely cut itself off from the past. "For the great majority of moderns, that means any possibility of understanding the traditional world has been completely lost".[12]

In 1938 Evola wrote a synopsis on the traditional approach to history, where he defined traditional and modern civilisations:

> "On the one hand there are the traditional cultures… The axis of these cultures and the summit of their hierarchical order consist of metaphysical, supra-individual powers and actions, which serve to inform and justify all that which is merely human, temporal, subject to becoming and to 'history'. On the other hand there is 'modern culture', which is actually anti-tradition and which exhausts itself in a construction of purely human and earthly conditions and in the total development of these, in pursuit of a life entirely detached from the 'higher world'".[13]

While Evola joined the debate over the meaning of "race" in Fascist Italy, when racial zoology suddenly gained momentum as official policy with the publication of the "Manifesto of Race" in 1938, ironically the same year he wrote in a German (that is, "Nazi") publication an article explaining the traditionalist approach to the question of why civilisations decay. He contended that the "degeneration" of civilisation is not caused by race-crossings, which Hitlerism regards as axiomatic, but rather through the *spiritual* corruption of the culture-hierarchy from the top down.[14]

Evola begins by repudiating the modernist idea of "progress", stating that man is not ascending (evolution) but descending from a primordial

---

12   Ibid., 14.
13   Julius Evola, "On the Secret of Degeneration".
14   Ibid.

higher state. One does not go from lower to higher forms. Hence, as we have seen, the widespread belief – or memory - across times, places, and cultures, in the "fall" of man from a mythic "Golden Age", ascribed to the arrogance of man in defying the Godhead.

> "Anyone who has come to reject the rationalist myth of 'progress' and the interpretation of history as an unbroken positive development of mankind will find himself gradually drawn towards the world-view that was common to all the great traditional cultures, and which had at its centre the memory of a process of degeneration, slow obscuration, or collapse of a higher preceding world. As we penetrate deeper into this new (and old) interpretation, we encounter various problems, foremost among which is the question of the secret of degeneration".[15]

Of the theories that have been considered Evola, writing for the Germans, alludes to the classic work of Comte Arthur de Gobineau, *The Inequality of the Human Races*, pioneering the doctrine that civilisations collapse through race-mixing. Evola quickly disposes of this by giving a passing nod to the theory, proceeding with a consideration of "a higher order of things" than blood admixture. Evola in reality does more than "expand" de Gobineau's race-theory with "a few observations"; he disposes of it by pointing out that race-impurity does not explain the unremarkable state of present day Nordic states that have retained their race-purity:

> "We can thank the Comte de Gobineau for the best and best-known summary of this problem, and also for a masterly criticism of the main hypotheses about it. His solution on the basis of racial thought and racial purity also has much truth in it, but it needs to be expanded by a few observations concerning a higher order of things. For there have been many cases in which a culture has collapsed even when its race has remained pure, as is especially clear in certain groups that have suffered slow, inexorable extinction despite remaining as racially isolated as if they were islands. An example quite close at hand is the case of the Swedes and the Dutch. These people are in the same racial condition today as they were two centuries ago, but there is little

---

15   Ibid.

to be found now of the heroic disposition and the racial awareness that they once possessed. Other great cultures seem merely to have remained standing in the condition of mummies: they have long been inwardly dead, so that it takes only the slightest push to knock them down. This was the case, for example, with ancient Peru, that giant solar empire which was annihilated by a few adventurers drawn from the worst rabble of Europe".[16]

On the other hand there are cultures that Evola refers to as being outwardly motivated by modernism, yet retaining their inner traditional substance. Japan remains the prime example of such a state. One might also say that of Israel. There are also certain Buddhist states in Southeast Asia that have materially prospered through the adaptation of modern techniques but have maintained a traditional nexus, as has India, despite these cultures having gone through the full cycles of rise and fall. A remnant lives, and might yet re-enter history in symbiosis with a post-Western civilisation.

Evola sees history unfolding within the great cosmic ages or *yugas* over vast expanses of time, and all the civilisations known to modern man as only decaying remnants of a long lost primordial civilisation. Hence, the history we know today is that of the fall of man over cycles of decline, interrupted by civilisations that have sought to maintain the cosmos connexion, but still subject to cyclic decay. Hence there are cycles of rise and fall within a great cosmic cycle; wheels within a great cosmic wheel. This outlook differs from the historical morphology of Spengler and others who work within more ordinary time-frames, yet both have broad features in common.

Evola sees "the whole of history as degeneration", repudiating the notion of both historical and biological evolution, and the chimera of "progress". Rather, the course of history is one of "involution":

> "From the standpoint of the latter, the whole of history is degeneration, because it shows the universal decline of earlier cultures of the traditional type, and the decisive and violent rise of a new universal civilization of the 'modern' type. A double question arises from this."

---

16   Ibid.

"First, how was it ever possible for this to come to pass? There is a logical error underlying the whole doctrine of evolution: it is impossible that the higher can emerge from the lower, and the greater from the less. But doesn't a similar difficulty face us in the solution of the doctrine of involution? How is it ever possible for the higher to fall? If we could make do with simple analogies, it would be easy to deal with this question. A healthy man can become sick; a virtuous one can turn to vice. There is a natural law that everyone takes for granted: that every living being starts with birth, growth, and strength, then come old age, weakening, and disintegration. And so forth. But this is just making statements, not explaining, even if we allow that such analogies actually relate to the question posed here."

"Secondly, it is not only a matter of explaining the possibility of the degeneration of a particular cultural world, but also the possibility that the degeneration of one cultural cycle may pass to other peoples and take them down with it. For example, we have not only to explain how the ancient Western reality collapsed, but also have to show the reason why it was possible for 'modern' culture to conquer practically the whole world, and why it possessed the power to divert so many peoples from any other type of culture, and to hold sway even where states of a traditional kind seemed to be alive (one need only recall the Aryan East)."

"In this respect, it is not enough to say that we are dealing with a purely material and economic conquest. That view seems very superficial, for two reasons. In the first place, a land that is conquered on the material level also experiences, in the long run, influences of a higher kind corresponding to the cultural type of its conqueror. We can state, in fact, that European conquest almost everywhere sows the seeds of 'Europeanization,' i.e., the 'modern' rationalist, tradition-hostile, individualistic way of thinking. Secondly, the traditional conception of culture and the state is hierarchical, not dualistic. Its bearers could never subscribe, without severe reservations, to the principles of 'Render unto Caesar the things that are Caesar's' and 'My kingdom is not of this world.' For us, 'Tradition' is the victorious and creative presence in the world of that which is 'not of this world,' i.e., of the Spirit, understood as a power that is mightier than any merely human or material one".[17]

---

17 Ibid.

The Decline and Fall of Civilisations

Although Evola was writing in 1938, this "modern world" is now a global hegemony, reaching every corner of the globe. The World War which came a year later resulted in the triumph of decadence over the remnants of tradition. Now we see the present "clash of civilisations", as it has been called by American geopolitical theorists, where the remnants of a long *fellaheen* – historically passé - Islam trying to resist encroachments on what remains of their cultures. As we shall see near our conclusion, American policy-makers are overt in seeing America as having a world-mission in destroying all vestiges of tradition in the name of "progress".

> "This is a basic idea of the authentically traditional view of life, which does not permit us to speak with contempt of merely material conquests. On the contrary, the material conquest is the sign, if not of a spiritual victory, at least of a spiritual weakness or a kind of spiritual 'retreat' in the cultures that are conquered and lose their independence. Everywhere that the Spirit, regarded as the stronger power, was truly present, it never lacked for means - visible or otherwise - to enable all the opponent's technical and material superiority to be resisted. But this has not happened. It must be concluded, then, that degeneracy was lurking behind the traditional facade of every people that the 'modern' world has been able to conquer. The West must then have been the culture in which a crisis that was already universal assumed its acutest form. There the degeneration amounted, so to speak, to a knockout blow, and as it took effect, it brought down with more or less ease other peoples in whom the involution had certainly not 'progressed' as far, but whose tradition had already lost its original power, so that these peoples were no longer able to protect themselves from an outside assault."[18]

The Late Western perspective of history is that of a line of evolution from primitive to modern, culminating in the "end of history" when the world adopts liberal-democracy and free trade. The traditional perspective sees history as the waxing and waning of civilisations, each self-contained, going through analogous life-cycles of rise and fall. The two outlooks are reflections of differences in perceptions of time; the "modern" linear, the traditional cyclic. Traditional societies are premised on maintaining a connexion with the divine. The modern

---

18   Ibid.

outlook sees this as superstition, but "progress" has become as much a religion as any form of mysticism. The "modern" road to "utopia" is through universal happiness achieved by material prosperity, and man need look for no higher purpose, state apologists such as Fukuyama. The traditional society saw human purpose not as the achieving of an elusive "happiness" based on fads but the fulfilment of one's cosmic duty (*dharma*) as an integral part of a holistic order.

Society as an Organism

Tradition peoples look on society as an organism as they looked on cultures in recognising the cyclicity of time. This outlook in the West reached its apex in the Gothic era, when guilds were the basis of the socio-economic order that was like all else premised on one's duty and obligations. The craftsman had his obligations – and his rights – as did the knight, the priest and the noble, integrity into a hierarchy that was considered a reflection of the divine cosmic order. This organic conception of society endured in vestige right up until the French Revolution which, in the name of "the people" and in the interests of the merchant class, abolished the guilds by the Chapelier Law of 1791. That the Left abolished the guilds in the interests of commerce, indicates how muddled today's definitions of "Left" and "Right" (the terms originating in the French National Assembly) are, when it was the Left that imposed capitalism on the remnants of a traditional society that until then had a regulated economy intended to keep economic interests in subordination to social obligations and duties.

The traditional society was structured as an organism; a body, hence the Roman word for the guild as "corporation", from *corpus*. Each individual served the social organism in an analogous manner to a cell. The guild constituted an organ of the social organism. Each had a duty to maintain the health of their profession by obligations to ensure the excellence of their craft, punish miscreants for such crimes as the adulteration of food or weights and measures, and ensure the training of apprentices, the lodging of members and the fair distribution of raw materials and of just wages. The trades unions that the rootless, urbanised proletariat were obliged to form after the destruction of the guilds have been a poor substitute.

The Greeks recognised the organic character of the State. Aristotle made the analogy of the State with an organism and its constituent organs:

> "Further, the state is by nature clearly prior to the family and to the individual, since the whole is of necessity prior to the part; for example, if the whole body be destroyed, there will be no

foot or hand, except in an equivocal sense, as we might speak of a stone hand; for when destroyed the hand will be no better than that. But things are defined by their working and power; and we ought not to say that they are the same when they no longer have their proper quality, but only that they have the same name. The proof that the state is a creation of nature and prior to the individual is that the individual, when isolated, is not self-sufficing; and therefore he is like a part in relation to the whole".[1]

The corporations of Sparta and of Rome were overseen by patron gods and heroes. They had their own temples, rites, holy days, feasts and games. The Roman corporations were hierarchically organised and run with a military ethos and organisation, with centuria led by a centurion, and a lieutenant (*optio*). Those who were not masters were *plebs* or *corporati*, or, like soldiers, *milites caligati*.[2] These ancient artisan guilds, most commonly dedicated to the goddess of handiwork, Minerva, combined in the *collegia opificum*. Numus Pompilius (715-673 B.C.), the legendary second king of Rome, is said to have created the corporate structure of ancient Rome, as described by Plutarch:

"But of all his measures the most commended was his distribution of the people by their trades into companies or guilds; for as the city consisted, or rather did not consist of, but was divided into, two different tribes, the diversity between which could not be effaced and in the meantime prevented all unity and caused perpetual tumult and ill-blood, reflecting how hard substances that do not readily mix when in the lump may, by being beaten into powder, in that minute form be combined, he resolved to divide the whole population into a number of small divisions, and thus hoped, by introducing other distinctions, to obliterate the original and great distinction, which would be lost among the smaller. So, distinguishing the whole people by the several arts and trades, he formed the companies of musicians, goldsmiths, carpenters, dyers, shoemakers, skinners, braziers, and potters; and all other handicraftsmen he composed and reduced into a single company, appointing every one their proper courts, councils, and religious observances. In this manner all factious

---

1   Aristotle, Politics.
2   Evola, Revolt, 105.

distinctions began, for the first time, to pass out of use, no person any longer being either thought of or spoken of under the notion of a Sabine or a Roman, a Romulian or a Tatian; and the new division became a source of general harmony and intermixture".[3]

These guilds were incorporated in the constitution of Servius Tullius, 6th king (575-535 BC.).[4] However, the Church did not rely on Greek or Roman precedence. The organic character of the Church had been explained by Saint Paul, using the analogy of the human body when writing of the body of the early Church:

> "The eye cannot say to the hand, 'I don't need you!' And the head cannot say to the feet, 'I don't need you!' On the contrary, those parts of the body that seem to be weaker are indispensable… its parts should have equal concern for each other… Now you are the body of Christ, and each one of you is a part of it".[5]

The whole of chapter 12 of *Corinthians* is an explication of the *corporatism* that was to become during the 19th and early 20th centuries the basis of Catholic social doctrine.[6] Paul writing of the organisation of the body of the Church explained that there are "differences in administration" and "diversities of operations", but undertaken under the one lordship.[7] However, every member of the Church body is a manifestation of the same spirit.[8] Within this spiritual body there is a diversity of talents, but all work within that body,[9] without resentment for not having the talents of another, since all are essential.[10] Therefore, since all are parts of the one body, if one part causes schism, the whole suffers. Therefore "the members should have the same care one for another".[11] It was the Reformation, Liberalism and Marxism that caused "schism" on the social body, fracturing the Western psyche;

---

3   Plutarch, Numus Pompilius.
4   Catholic Encyclopaedia, "Guilds".
5   Paul, I Corinthians 12: 21-27.
6   Pope Leo XIII, Rerum Novarum, 1891. Pius XI Quadragesimo Anno, 1931.
7   Paul, Corinthians, op. cit., 12: 5-6.
8   Ibid., 12: 7.
9   Ibid., 12: 8-11.
10   Ibid., 12: 28-31.
11   Ibid., 12: 25-27.

the social doctrine of Catholicism from the 19th century attempted to address these social cancers.

At the formative stage of Western culture, guilds were established in England, France and the Low Countries by the 7th century. Something of the character of the guilds can be discerned by their apprenticeship system, in comparison to the child labour of later years:

> "The apprentice had to remain from three to ten years in a condition of entire dependence under a master, in order to be qualified to exercise his trade as a journeyman. Before a master could engage an apprentice, he had to satisfy the officers of the guild of the soundness of his moral character. He was to treat the boy as he would his own child, and was held responsible not only for his professional, but also for his moral, education. On completing his apprenticeship, the young artisan became a journeyman (*compagnon*); at least, such was the rule from the fourteenth century onward. To become a master, he must have some means and pass an examination before the elders".[12]

In Germany, guilds began to flourish by the 12th century. In Saxony and Bohemia mining guilds became significant. The statutes of the mining guilds show that conditions were established for hygienic, ventilation of the pits, precautions against accident, bathing houses, working hours (eight hours daily; sometimes less), supply of the necessaries of life at fair prices, wage scales, care of the sick and disabled, etc.[13] The guilds in England were suppressed in the 16th century, being seen as a challenge to the spiritual authority of The Reformation. Of the attempts to revive the guilds during the 19th century, there was perhaps none so vehemently opposed to what he called "reactionism" as Karl Marx. The return to an organic society would have derailed Marx's historical dialectic of class struggle, and rolled back his perception of the "wheel of history", which rolls undeviatingly in a straight line over a cliff edge:

> "The lower middle class, the small manufacturer, the shopkeeper, the artisan, the peasant. All these fight against the bourgeoisie,

---

12 Catholic Encyclopaedia, "Guilds".
13 Ibid.

to save from extinction their existence as fractions of the middle class. They are therefore not revolutionary, but conservative. Nay more, they are reactionary, for they try to roll back the wheel of history. If by chance they are revolutionary, they are so only in view of their impending transfer into the proletariat, they thus defend not their present, but their future interests, they desert their own standpoint to place themselves at that of the proletariat".[14]

Among the "reactionist" efforts, Pope Leo in his *Encyclical* of 1891 addressed the antagonism between employers and employees, offering the return of the organic state as the alternative for what he saw as the equally Godless and materialistic forces of "socialism" and capitalism that were fracturing the West:

"Just as the symmetry of the human frame is the result of the suitable arrangement of the different parts of the body, so in a State is it ordained by nature that these two classes should dwell in harmony and agreement, so as to maintain the balance of the body politic. Each needs the other: capital cannot do without labour, nor labour without capital".[15]

---

14   Karl Marx, *The Communist Manifesto*, 57.
15   Leo, 19.

Society as an Organism

In contrast to the inorganic conceptions of the State by Protestantism, Marxism and Liberalism, the philosopher Paul Carus, in addressing the question of whether the State is only legitimate as a "social contract" among individuals, according to Liberal doctrines, explained that the "State" emerges from an organic development of a community of interests:

> "Common interests create a common will, and as soon as this common will becomes consciously organised by habits, traditions, and the ordinances of those who have the power to enforce them, by written or unwritten laws, by acts of legislatures, or similar means, the primitive social life enters a higher phase of its evolution: it changes into a State".[16]

The State is founded on much more than laws or economic (class) relations; it is an expression of a collective soul:

> "The State is not constituted by laws and institutions alone; the State is based upon a certain attitude of the minds of its members. The existence of a State presupposes in the souls of its citizens the presence of certain common ideas concerning that which is to be considered as right and proper. If these ideas were absent, the State could not exist".[17]

Again the situation shows that from the Medieval epoch, and the destruction of the traditional organic social order, there was a colossal deterioration. Carus critiques the Liberal dogma of the State existing to merely serve as an arbiter among individualistic interests. Carus uses the analogy of organic growth in describing the growth of the State. While he stated that the 18th century Liberal doctrine had become "obsolete", he was writing at a time (circa 1900) when the creative role of the State was being reconsidered. In the aftermath of World War II the Liberal theory has resumed its dominance until it is regarded today by its ideologues such as being on the brink of world dominance. Carus proceeds:

> "As a factor in the development of States the conscious aspiration of individuals for their ideals even, in practical life,

---

16   Paul Carus, 1904, 16.

17   Ibid.

cannot be estimated high enough; for this factor has grown in prominence with the progress of the race, and it is growing still. In the explanation of the origin of States, however, this very factor can most easily be overrated, and it has been overrated, in so far as some savants of the eighteenth century, the great age of individualism, have proposed the now obsolete view that States are and can be produced only by a conscious agreement among individuals, which, however, they grant, may be tacitly made. And this theory found its classical representation in Rousseau's book, *Le contract social*, in which the existence of the State is justified as a social contract. This is an error: States develop unconsciously and even in spite of the opposition of individuals; and it is a frequent occurrence that the aspirations of political or other leaders do not correspond with the wants of their times. Thus it so often happens that they build better than they know, because they are the instruments of nature. The growth of States is as little produced by conscious efforts as the growth of our bodies. Conscious efforts are a factor in the growth of States, but they do not create States. A State grows solely because of the need for its existence. Certain social functions must be attended to; they are attended to, and thus the State is created as the organ of attending to them".[18]

Although there have been States created through legalistic processes, such as in particular the USA with its constitutional foundations, whose "Founding Fathers" were children of the Enlightenment, Carus insisted that,

"The existence of Empires and States does not rest upon the final resolutions passed at the time of their foundation, but upon the common will of the people, which, such as it is, has been shaped in the history of national experiences. The United States developed in spite of the individualistic clauses of its founders..."[19]

Where Marx and Rousseau only saw the state as a reflection of relations between classes or individuals respectively, Carus accepts that the State is a reflection of "God", insofar as it is a part of the unfolding

---

18   Ibid., 20.
19   Ibid., 24-25.

of God's laws expressed in nature. It is a "reflection of a moral empire" that "reveals the nature of that All-power, which religious language hails by the name of God".[20] He revives the traditional perception of the State as a reflection of the divine:

> "When we grant that the State is a divine institution, we mean that its existence is based upon the un-alterable laws of nature. All facts are a revelation of God; they are parts of God and reveal God's nature; but the human soul and that moral empire of human souls called the State are more dignified parts of God than the most wonderful phenomena of unorganised nature".[21]

> "For the purified conception of Christianity is monistic; it regards natural phenomena as the revelations of God, and the voice of reason as the afflatus of the Holy Ghost. The State is a human institution, but as such it is as divine as man's soul; the State should not consist of rulers and ruled subjects, but of free citizens. And yet we must recognise the truth that the State is a superindividual power, and that the laws of the State have an indisputable authority over all its members".

Hence the state is "organic" in the sense that it is a superorganism that coordinates into one body – the *body politik* - the constituent cells (individuals) and organs (classes). Any intrusion, such as Liberalism, Marxism and Capitalism, is a social pathology. Such ideologies literally destroy the harmonious functioning of the cells and organs of the social organism, and are therefore social cancers. Carus writes that the organic State does not invariably maintain divine perfection any more than the individual soul:

> "When we say the State is divine, we do not mean to say that all the ordinances of government are, *a fortiori*, to be regarded as right. By no means. We might as well infer that because man's soul is divine all men are saints, and their actions are *eo ipso* moral. Oh, no! The State institution, as such, and the human soul, as such, are divine; they are moral beings and more or less representative incarnations of God on earth".[22]

---

20   Ibid., 40.

21   Ibid.

22   Ibid., 43.

The Decline and Fall of Civilisations

One modern economist who does capture the spirit of the Medieval era, writing of Nuremberg, states that Medieval man saw himself not as an isolated unit but as "part of a larger organism".[23] Bliss states that to the Nuremberger (or Medieval man) "competition is the death of trade, the subverter of freedom, above all, the destroyer of quality".[24] The Reformation was more disruptive as a social pathogen on the Western social organism than any political revolution.

Professor Howard Wiarda in his history of corporatism states of the Liberal, Enlightenment era that is the basis of our present epoch, that it fractured the social organism. While it is "individual rights" that were from then to the present lauded as the ultimate in human aspiration, they came at the cost of "group rights", the rights of association that had served as the social foundation of High Culture:

> "The emphasis on the individual and on individual rights accelerated in the West during the eighteenth-century Enlightenment; in the course of the French Revolution beginning in 1789, and subsequently throughout most of the rest of Europe, group rights (of the Roman Catholic Church, guilds, and other groups) were extinguished. Thereafter, at least in the West, the atomistic individual ruled supreme, while the older system of historic or natural corporatism was snuffed out".[25]

Until the French Revolution, royalist France was an organic, corporatist state.[26] A 16th century Church document explained the doctrine of the organic state where "the head is the king. The arms are the nobility. The feet are the third estate... the clergy is the heart. The three estates are members of one body, of one province which is mother to them all".[27] Professor Kennedy in his history of the French Revolution commented that "one man is seen equal to another", and that "although the members perform different functions, they are integrated organically into one body".[28] How very different was the

---

23 W. D. P. Bliss, 545.
24 Ibid., 545.
25 Howard J. Wiarda, 17.
26 E. Kennedy, 13.
27 Quoted by Kennedy, 15.
28 Kennedy, Ibid.

traditional hierarchy of the West to the money-based, greed-oriented, ego-driven ideology that has dominated Western Civilisation since the tumults of The Reformation, English Puritan Revolution, French Revolution, and Industrial Revolution, each one a phase in the continuing rise of oligarchy over the traditional hierarchy.

The Value of Tradition

Our "progressive" obsessions for change neglect to consider consequences. Change is demanded for the sake of a fad or a slogan: "equality", "democracy", "reproductive rights"... Even a word of caution is damned as "reactionary", "old fashioned", or "fascist". Traditions, customs, beliefs, are regarded as being as transient as the planned obsolescence of computers. Carl Jung made the point that Western man's psyche is not keeping pace with his technology. The levels of our unconscious are multi-layered, reaching back to primordial existence, yet Western technology has exponentially leaped ahead leaving behind any anchorage of tradition. That is called "progress". Jung wrote of this:

> "Our souls as well as our bodies are composed of individual elements which were all already present in the ranks of our ancestors. The 'newness' of the individual psyche is an endlessly varied recombination of age-old components. Body and soul therefore have an intensely historical character and find no place in what is new. That is to say, our ancestral components are only partly at home in things that have just come into being. We are certainly far from having finished with the middle ages, classical antiquity, and primitivity, as our modern psyches pretend. Nevertheless we have plunged into a cataract of progress which sweeps us into the future with ever wilder violence the farther it take us from our ranks. The less we understand of what our forefathers sought, the less we understand ourselves, and thus we help with all our might to rob the individual of his roots and his guiding instincts".[1]

Konrad Lorenz, the father of the science of ethology, the study of animal instinct, gave a warning from an ecological viewpoint, that the abandonment of customs and traditions is steeped with dangers which are likely to be unforeseen. Culture is "cumulative tradition".[2] It is knowledge passed through generations, preserved as belief or custom. The deep wisdom accrued by our ancestors, because it might

---

1   Jung, Memories, Dreams, Reflections, 235-236.
2   Lorenz, 61.

be wrapped in the protection of religions and myths, is discounted by the "modern" as "superstitious" and "unscientific". Lorenz referred to the "enormous underestimation of our nonrational, cultural fund, and the equal overestimation of all that man is able to produce with his intellect" as factors "threatening our civilization with destruction". "Being enlightened is no reason for confronting transmitted tradition with hostile arrogance", stated Lorenz. Writing at a time when the New Left was rampant, as it is today under other names, Lorenz observed that the attitude of youth towards parents shows a great deal of "conceited contempt but no understanding".[3] Lorenz perceived a great deal of the psychosis of the Left as a pathogen in the social organism, as it remains today: "The revolt of modern youth is founded on *hatred*; a hatred closely related to an emotion that is most dangerous and difficult to overcome: *national hatred*. In other words, today's rebellious youth reacts to the older generation in the same way that an 'ethnic' group reacts to a foreign, hostile one".[4]

What is of interest is that Lorenz saw this as a youth subculture that was tantamount to a separate, foreign *ethnos*, when a group forms around its own rites, dress, manners and norms. In the biological sciences this is called "pseudospeciation". With this new group identity comes a "corresponding devaluation of the symbols" of other cultural units.[5] The obsession with all that is regarded as "new" among the youth revolt was described by Lorenz as "physiological neophilia". While this is necessary to prevent stagnation, it is normally gradual and followed by a return to tradition. Such a balance however is easily upset.[6] Fixation as the stage of neophilia in the psychology of individuals results in behavioural abnormalities such as vindictive resentment towards long-dead parents.[7]

This lack of respect for tradition is aggravated by the breakdown of traditional social hierarchy, mass organisation and "a money-grabbing race against itself"[8] that dominates the Late West.

---

3   Ibid., 64.
4   Lorenz, 64.
5   Lorenz, 64-65.
6   Lorenz, 69.
7   Lorenz, 69-70.
8   Lorenz, 73.

The Decline and Fall of Civilisations

Since Lorenz wrote of these symptoms of Western decay during the 1970s the Western social organism has increasingly fractured. There are now the presence, vastly greater than in Lorenz's time, of actual *ethnoi* that have no attachment to the West, but maintain a great resentment. There is also further *pseudospeciation* among women in terms of radical feminism and "gays", possessing their own manners, rites, dress, terms of speech, and even their own flags and other symbols. They are united in their hatred of the West, which is often denigrated as "white patriarchy"; with its symbols being torn down[9] and its heroes ridiculed as "dead white males".

---

9   Such as the destruction of Confederate monuments in the USA, as this is being written.

Part II

Ethnos

Race and Ethnos

Julius Evola, while repudiating the zoological primacy of "racism" as another form of materialism, suggested that a "spiritual racism" is necessary to oppose the forces seeking to turn man into an amorphous mass; as interchangeable economic units without roots; what is now called "globalisation". Evola gave the traditional view when stating that there "have been many cases in which a culture has collapsed even when its race has remained pure, as is especially clear in certain groups that have suffered slow, inexorable extinction despite remaining as racially isolated as if they were islands". He gives Sweden and The Netherlands as recent examples, pointing out that although the race has remained unchanged, there is little of the "heroic disposition" those cultures possessed just several centuries previously. He referred to other great cultures as having remained in a state as if like mummies, inwardly dead, awaiting a push "to knock them down". These are what Spengler called *Fellaheen*, spiritually exhausted and historically passé. Evola gives Peru as an example of how readily a static culture succumbed to Spain.[1] Hence, such examples, even as vigorous cultures such as that of the Dutch and Scandinavian, once wide-roaming and dynamic, have declined to nonentities despite the maintenance of racial homogeneity.

The Khmer Empire with its Hindu foundations, underwent its crisis and a lengthy decline from the 14th century, after the Hindu foundations were replaced by Theravada Buddhism, which eliminated the Godhead of the King, meaning a collapse of the traditional social order. The epoch of the grand temples had gone.

Mount Meru is the mythic axial point of the cosmos for Hindus, Jains and Buddhists. It exists both in the visible and invisible realms and hence is the nexus and the abode of Siva and Vishnu; analogous to the Greek gods' Mount Olympus. It is Mount Meru that is the centre of the Tibetan Mandala Wheel of the cosmos, the *Kalachakra* (Wheel of Time). The end of the cosmos of this cycle according to Tibetan cosmology sees the burning up of Mount Meru in this universe, and its counterparts in other universes.[2]

---

1   Evola, "On the Secret of Degeneration".

2   Patrul Rinpoche, 40.

Seeking causes of decay and death for civilisations that might be averted by laws, is like the individual who seeks the Elixir of Life to achieve personal immortality. Reality is obscured. The mortality that is inherent in every organism is called "pessimism" paradoxically by the scientific epoch that claims to be based on reality but believes the modern era to be uniquely immortal. Tradition does not know immortality even among the gods. Odin, Tyr and Thor die at Ragnarok. Tibetan Buddhism states:

> Whatever is born is impermanent and is bound to die.
> Whatever is stored up is impermanent and is bound to run out.
> Whatever comes together is impermanent and is bound to come apart.
> Whatever is built is impermanent and is bound to collapse.
> Whatever rises up is impermanent and is bound to fall down.[3]

While Spengler and Evola eschewed zoological race, "race" was nonetheless central to their philosophies and historical analyses. "Race" as a doctrine of form against formlessness, cosmos against chaos was, for Evola, an important weapon against universalism, egalitarianism and the chaos that is unleashed by to create a nebulous mass-man in the name of "liberty, equality, fraternity". In the descent of castes, from higher to lower, that is to say, the inversion of hierarchy, the result is the disappearance of all "qualitative difference", the creation of "mineralised masses". Race is posited by Evola against all disintegrative tendencies whether from plutocrats, bourgeois or proletarians. The "race" that is posited against disintegrative forces must be "distinctly heroic and aristocratic", of "heroic soul, of a style of honour and loyalty", a "race of the soul", transcending the race of "materialism" and "zoologism".[4] This "heroic soul of style and honour" formed the warrior castes of all traditional societies, whether of Vedic India, Medieval Europe, Imperial Japan, or Zulu Africa. It was what Evola and Spengler meant by "having race".

Many assumptions have long been made on the interbreeding of races to the point of becoming the central dogma to much of the Right. The only alternative views are assumed by genetic determinists to be intrinsically Communist or some variant of the Left, or of the Ayn Rand libertarian

---

3   Ibid., 46.
4   Evola, The Elements of Racial Education, 60-63.

The Decline and Fall of Civilisations

variety that upholds the individual as a fractured atom and opposes the concept of "race" as being "the lowest form of collectivism".[5]

The traditionalist sees matters differently from any of these, whether genetic determinist, classical liberal or Marxist. The traditionalist sees the genetic determinist conception of "race" as the mirror-image to the liberal and Marxist rejection of "race", for the same reason that he sees Marxism as the mirror image of capitalism. All of these ideologies arose during the same *Zeitgeist* (Spirit of the Age): materialism. Anything that is beyond quantifying statistically is regarded as superstition. Hence, "race" becomes a matter of skull and bone measurements, and of counting genes. The Marxist and the classical liberal posit in opposition to this the measuring of man in terms of material accumulation, disposing of the divine spark in man.

The traditionalist conception of "race" was expressed especially among the German Idealists. German Idealism gave history a spiritual content; in contrast to English economic theories. Hegel and Herder gave us metaphysical concepts of history and sociology such as *Zeitgeist*, and the "spirit of nations". In the 20th century Oswald Spengler developed this conception of history as a spiritual unfolding, and Carl Jung did something similar in studying the human psyche as something more than quantifying brain structure. This is not to deny, like Lysenko in the USSR, the insights of genetics and microbiology. There are new scientific fields such as epigenetics and morphic field theory that provide added insights into nature in ways that were until recently dismissed by materialists as "superstition".

"Race" exists beyond skull measurements and gene clusters. As Spengler wrote, one cannot discern *character* by looking at bones, but rather by looking at the mien suggested by a portrait painting, or sculpture. What can one tell of the character of the Greeks by studying a skull rather than studying a sculpture; by studying the DNA rather than studying the architecture or mathematics?

Ethnos (plural *ethnoi*), is the expression of a race, or races amalgamating as an ethnos, based on common experiences forming a common outlook, with a consciousness of being distinct from others. How

---

5   "Racism is the lowest, most crudely primitive form of collectivism", Ayn Rand, "Racism", (1963), Ayn Rand Lexicon, http://aynrandlexicon.com/lexicon/racism.html

this common outlook is acquired and passed along to subsequent generations might now be explained by epigenetics, and in particular behavioural epigenetics. This psycho-spiritual formation of ethnos was perceived by the German Idealists such as Herder and Fichte, and continued into the twentieth century by Spengler and the Swiss father of analytical psychology, Carl G. Jung.

The Russian ethnologist Lev Gumilev discussed types of ethnic relations moulded by historical experiences:

- (a) coexistence, in which the ethnoi do not merge and do not imitate each other, borrowing only technical innovations;
- (b) assimilation, i.e. the swallowing-up of one ethnos by another with complete forgetting of origin and old traditions;
- (c) cross-breeding, in which traditions of the preceding ethnoi and a memory of the ancestors are retained and combined (these variants are usually unstable, and exist through replenishment by new *metises* [6]);
- (d) merging, in which the traditions of the original components are forgotten and a third, new ethnos arises alongside the two precursors, or in place of them.[7]

In regard to (a) "coexistence", Gumilev introduces an aspect of ethnic relations that is seldom considered, that of *symbiosis*. He gives the example of Bantu and pygmy in the Congo:

"In the upper reaches of the Congo, for instance, Bantu and pygmies live in a symbiosis. The Negroes cannot move in the forest, except by paths, without the help of the pygmies, while the paths are rapidly overgrown unless cleared. The Bantu can get lost in the forest, like a European, and die within twenty meters of his own home. But the pygmies need knives, vessels, and other articles of daily use. For these two ethnoi dissimilarity is the guarantee of well-being, and their friendship is founded on that".[8]

---

6   Metises: interbreeding.
7   Lev Gumilev, Ethnogenesis and the Biosphere, Chapter II, "The Properties of an Ethnos".
8   Ibid.

The Decline and Fall of Civilisations

"Complementarity" of relations between ethnoi within an "ecological niche", where different ethnoi have common interests, might form a "superethnos" to contend with common challenges and enemies, while retaining their separate identities.

With (b) "assimilation" is an ultimatum demanded by a conquering ethnos, Gumilev referring to the Irish vis-a-vis the English, but this does not mean that such subservience is a genuine internal assimilation. Such an artificial construct is a weakness, tantamount to living with a fifth column at times of conflict. One might consider the falsely "assimilated" Marranos Jews in Spain who outwardly converted to Catholicism but secretly maintained their Jewishness.

"Cross-breeding" as an attempt to synthesise the traditions of two or more *ethnoi*, is regarded by Gumilev as a cause of decline. Note that what is being discussed is the result of the mixing not of genes but the discordant merger of race souls, or archetypes, or what Gumilev calls the "stereotypes of behaviour" formed over millennia of historical experience and muddled or obliterated over a generation. Gumilev gives the quite recent example of Turkey as a state that collapsed through the corruption of the Turkish traditional ethnos by foreign elements:

> "The decline of the Sublime Porte in the seventeenth century attracted the attention in its time of contemporaneous Turkish writers. In their view *ajen-oglani*, i.e. the children of renegades, were the reason for the decline. The influx of the foreign-born spoiled the stereotype of behavior, which told in the venality of viziers, the purchasability of judges, the fall in the fighting capacity of troops, and the collapse of the economy. By the beginning of the nineteenth century Turkey had become the 'sick man'".[9]

Gumilev placed geography at the basis of *ethnogenesis*, much as Spengler placed landscape at the formation of a "race" and "people". The processes of race-formation, or as Gumilev calls it, *ethnogenesis*, are differentiated from the zoological definition of race as much by Gumilev as by Spengler. Gumilev explains the significance of ethnic

---

9   Ibid.

"rhythms", energised by the biosphere. These rhythms we might identify as life cycles subjected to cosmic rays. Gumilev's theory is not part of our enquiry however, and we will confine ourselves to his comments on the various components of *ethnoi*. What Gumilev describes is the disruption of the rhythms specific to *ethnoi* when they meet, as for example in a multicultural state. Gumilev defines ethnic "stereotypes" as inherited group-memories expressing fear, hope, life and death, around which religions and myths emerge to sustain an ethnos as unifying factors. When such differing group-memories meet one might expect the fracturing of both the individual and the culture. This fractured state is lauded as "cultural enrichment" by the zealots of multiculturalism. Gumilev refers to the role of marriage within and outside an *ethnoi*, referring to the children of mixed *ethnoi* inheriting conflicting "stereotypes".

> "Let us try to interpret the phenomenon described. If ethnoi are processes, then, when two dissimilar processes clash, interference will arise disturbing the rhythm of both components. The resulting association will be chimeric, which means unstable to outside effects and short-lived. Death of the chimeric system will entail annihilation of its components and extinction of the people involved in the system. Such is the general mechanism of the disruption of the pattern, but it has its exceptions, namely that with slackening of the original rhythms a new one sometimes arises, i.e. a new ethnogenctic inertial process. I shall not say yet what this is associated with, because this is too serious a matter to resolve as a side-issue.[10] But endogamy is clearly necessary in order to maintain ethnic traditions, because the endogamous family passes on a developed stereotype of behaviour to a child, while an exogamous one passes on two stereotypes that mutually cancel each other out. Exogamy, which is not related at all to 'social states' and lies on a different plane, thus proves to be a factor of ethnogenesis, i.e. a real, destructive factor during contact on a superethnic level. And even in rare cases when a new ethnos develops in a zone of contact, it absorbs, i.e. annihilates, both of the former ones".[11]

---

10   Gumielv was referring to what he regarded as the influence of cosmic rays from the biosphere on the rhythms of ethnoi, causing their energy levels to rise and fall.

11   Gumilev, Ethnogenesis, Chapter II.

While it appears that Gumilev is proposing a zoological outlook on race, he rejects this. Ethnos and zoological race are distinct. Hence, differences are more marked between *ethnoi* than between zoological races. It is *ethnos* that expresses a "community of fate", a sense of common past and future, built up around myths, customs and religions. Gumilev writes of this distinction between *ethnoi* and zoology, and reiterates the role played by geography in the formation of *ethnoi*:

"In conclusion, let me point out that in the example cited, and also in the overwhelming majority of cases, the racial principle plays no role. It is not a matter of somatic differences, but rather of behavioural ones, because the steppe dwellers, Tibetan hill men, and Chinese belonged to a single, first-order Mongoloid race, and it is obvious that, with closer approximation to second-order race, North Chinese are racially closer to Xiang-bi and Tibetans than to Southern Chinese. But the outward similarity of cranial indices, eye color, hair color, epicanthus, etc., has no significance for ethnogenetic processes.

"It is also obvious from the example adduced that the link between ethnos and topography, sometimes doubted, really exists. The Hunni, having seized the valley of the Huangho, pastured their cattle there; the Chinese acquired the arable, and built canals; but their hybrids, not having the skills of either cattle-herding or cultivation, predatorily fleeced neighbours and subjects, which led to the formation of long-fallow lands and restoration of the natural biocoenosis, although impoverished by the cutting down of forests and the killing of ungulates during the emperors hunts. Everything tallies.

"... [I]f an ethnos is the result of a long-lasting process of ethnogenesis, it is part of the biosphere of Earth, and since changes of terrain through the use of technique are linked with an ethnos, ethnology should be ranked among the geographical sciences although it draws its initial material from history in the narrow sense of the term, i.e. study of events in their connection and sequence".[12]

---

12   Ibid.

Race and Ethnos

Gumilev's views have been considered here, albeit only partially, because he became an influential ethnologist even within the USSR, during the later phases when conservative elements of the nominally "Communist" state were looking for doctrinal foundations beyond Marxism. With the fall of the USSR Gumilev's theories have gained widespread support, reaching into the highest echelons of the State.[13] As Russia struggles for her place as leader of a post-Western dispensation, *ethnogenesis* is likely to provide a significant contribution to the post-Western world-view if Russia succeeds in fulfilling her culture-mission.

Gumilev referred to inherited "stereotypes of behaviour" of an ethnos, "the behavioural skills" according to geographical adaptation, handed down through generations. Although Gumilev was not a Spenglerian, his "rhythms" are analogous to Spengler's life-cycles; *ethnoi* are analogous to Spengler's non-zoological conception of "race", and both considered geography as moulding ethnos. Gumilev refers to organic cycles similar to those of Spengler, based in Gumilev's system on the influences of cosmic energies in affecting the life cycles of an ethnos, in a process called the "aging of the ethnos": "Every ethnic system, like a living organism, passes the stage of adolescence (growth and expansion), maturity (maximum activity) and old age (decay and decomposition)".[14]

---

13 For the life and influence of Gumilev on both the USSR and post-Soviet Russia, see: Charles Clover, 92-148.

14 V. A. Michurin, "Glossary of terms, and concepts in the theory of Ethnogenesis of L. M. Gumilev".

The "Race-Forming Idea"

The German scholar Eric Voegelin published two books on race in Germany in 1933, the year of Hitler's assumption to Government, which repudiated the genetic determinism of English thought. These were *Race and State* and *The History of the Race Idea: From Ray to Carus*.[1] Voegelin explained the "race" concept in terms of the "race-soul" that pervades the entire body. Those who share this race-soul are members of the same "race". He was writing in the tradition of the German Idealists, Fichte, Herder, et al. It is ironic that the "Nazis" adopted the English darwinian and French positivist materialistic conceptions of "race" from Houston Stewart Chamblerain[2] and Arthur de Gobineau, rather than those of German Idealism.

Voegelin considered Othmar Spann (1878-1950), professor of economics and sociology at the University of Vienna, to have undertaken the only significant philosophical attempt at the time to examine the foundation of race as having social origins. Voegelin saw the merit of Spann's theory in seeing race not as originating with biology but with an *Idea*. This race-forming *Idea* provides unity among those who possess it and is the medium by which spirit enters the material world. Race emerges and changes as the result of spiritual, not biological, laws. This is not to say that an individual can change his race as he changes his clothes (or gender) as is the vogue today, but that races are born, and their character changes, in the spiritual experiences of communities. Voegelin quotes Spann:

> "It is the great founders of religions, sages, and rulers who impart to their peoples new religious life ..., who deeply stir up the people's feeling for life. It is they who give new impetus to racial formation and thus succeed in changing the natural species image of man (*das stammliche Artbild*). The spiritual history of archetypal humanity is primarily religious history. It was Schelling who endeavoured to explain race formation from this point of view."[3]

---

1 Erich Voegelin, *Race and State*, 1933.
2 Houston Stewart Chamberlain, 1911.
3 Voegelin, 1933, 113.

The "Race-Forming Idea"

Spann regarded ethnos or *volk*, as the basis of the organic, "spiritual community", sharing a culture that provides the social bond.

Friedrich Schelling (1775-1854), German Idealist philosopher, similarly called the ideas that form individuals into a community the community's *myth*. It is not the people, *ethnos* or race that create the myth but the myth that creates the *ethnos*. It is the ability of individuals to identify with this myth that shapes the common outlook cementing individuals into a community. Every *ethnos* has its formative myth. It is what defines that *ethnos* and what sustains it.

If there were ever an Australasian *ethnos* as there might be in future centuries, especially if conscious of common enemies in the region, the formative myth would be that of the *Anzac*. Russia's *ethnos* and state-forming myth is the battle of Kulikovo Field against the Tatars in 1380. The Hebrews have their founding myth of Abram and his spiritual progeny chosen by Yahweh, an eternal covenant with God as a "chosen people", with sustaining rites such as circumcision as a symbol of membership of the *ethnos*, and celebrations such as Passover. The Afrikaners were maintained as an *ethnos* by the myths of Blood River and "The Great Trek".

Voegelin considered that the primacy of materialism in the sciences had obscured the understanding of race. Anthropology textbooks that define race without considering spirit are inadequate.[4] Voegelin begins the *Introduction to The History of the Race Idea* with a discussion on ideas about physique. The race-idea had become dominated by the body-idea. This is a retrograde step, having replaced the theories of the German Idealists such as Herder who considered spirit. However, the study of external phenomena cannot comprehend the spiritual character of race.

Voegelin objected to the zoological materialism that dominated National Socialist race-theory in Germany. In this he was similar to other German conservatives such as Spengler. Voegelin rejected the notion that "the historical substance can be produced at will by industrious organizations for the breeding of racially pure bodies[...]. It is a nightmare to think that we should recognize the people whom

---

4   Voegelin, *The History of the Race Idea*, 22.

we follow and whom we allow to grow close to us, not by their glance, speech, or comeliness (*am Blick, am Wort und an der Gebaerde*), but by their cranial index and the measured proportions of their extremities".

Voegelin and other German conservatives rejected the materialism of National Socialist race-theory for reasons that also applied to their criticism of liberalism and Marxism. All three rejected the spiritual essence of man, although for National Socialism this was not an explicit rebellion against the spirit, and theorists continued to refer to "race souls". Alfred Rosenberg,[5] while rejecting the primacy of spirit in race-formation as proposed by Spengler and Voegelin, did not reject the existence of the race-soul. The National Socialist movement accepted something of the legacy of Fichte and Herder, although the English-led materialistic *Zeitgeist* represented by Darwin, Malthus and Galton predominated. Race was determined by callipers measuring nasal width, the cephalic index, and other physiological features.

Paul Carus (1852-1919) was, like Voegelin, a German scholar resident in the USA, who regarded darwinism and zoology as regressive methods for studying "race". He believed that the West had erred in fracturing body, mind and spirit. Carus in *The Rise of Man* from the first lines called Darwin's *Descent of Man* inadequate, being "one-sided", because Darwin "attempts only to trace the physiological connection of man with a series of lower animals".[6]

Ironically, considering Nietzscheanism is often synthesised with Social Darwinism in "Right-wing" race doctrines,[7] Nietzsche was prompted to posit his "will-to-power" as the basis of evolution, contra Darwinism, which he regarded as that animalisation of man.[8] He considered "natural selection" as more likely to produce bigger and better "brutes" than more and better artists, philosophers and saints.[9]

---

5 Alfred Rosenberg, The Myth of the Twentieth Century. The first chapter is entailed "Race and Race Soul", and refers to different race "spirits", such as the "Nordic spirit", predicated on "blood" inheritance; i.e., genes. Spengler became persona non grata in National Socialist Germany. See Bolton, "Spengler: A Philosopher for all Seasons".

6 Paul Carus, 1907, 1.

7 A primary example being Hitlerism. Also the popularity of the late 19th century polemic by Ragnar Redbeard among today's Right.

8 Bolton, *Nietzsche Contra Darwin*, 5-19, passim.

9 Nietzsche, *Untimely Meditations*, V.

The "Race-Forming Idea"

In questioning whether the Darwinian belief of "survival of the fittest" is an invariable law of evolution from lower to higher forms, Carus pointed out that "natural selection does not always favour the strongest and the best". "The ablest flyers on the island are swept by the winds into the ocean, and only the weakest survive, those who are lacking in a special virtue, not the bravest, not the strongest, not the best!" This led Carus to consider the cyclic rise and fall of nations and peoples:

> "There are also periods in history when society is radically corrupt and the spirit of the time makes it actually impossible for good men to exist and act morally. The evil influences of tyranny, of corruption or of hypocrisy sweep the brave, the courageous, the honest, the thinking out of existence and allow only the weak, the degenerate, the unthinking to remain. It is true that whatever nation falls under such a blight is doomed. Other nations will take her place, and indeed there have been a number of peoples entirely blotted out in such a way from the face of the globe. We have retrogressive as well as progressive adaptation, and in many cases adaptation is not a sign of progress either in the physical world, or the moral progress of human beings. The law of adaptation explains survival, but not progress". [10]

Carus was writing a decade before Spengler's first volume of *The Decline of The West* was published in 1918. He referred to "periods in history" within "the spirit of the time"; the *Zeitgeist* which determines the character of what unfolds during an epoch. He points out change, adaptation or what we optimistically call "progress" is not synonymous with an upward reach towards the divine, but is more likely to be the reverse, having referred to the traditional religious beliefs in the divine origin of man that were assaulted by darwinism.[11] Proper evolution, real "progress" is "tested" by the "growth of the soul." The "soul-form" is a manifestation of how the organism "feels" towards its environment. Through this evolution of soul-form we are better able to comprehend "the laws of nature, the order of the cosmos, and its divinity". "The test of progress, in one word, is the realization of truth, extensive as well as intensive, in the soul of man".[12] The more truth the soul comprehends,

---

10 Ibid., 8.
11 Ibid., 2.
12 Ibid., 11.

the more it "partakes of the divinity of its creator". "It will come more and more in harmony with the cosmos, it will more and more conform to its laws, it will be more religious, the holier, the greater, the diviner, the higher it develops and the further it progresses".[13] Rejecting the assumptions of darwinists such as Thomas Huxley who insisted that civilisation arose from the triumph of brute force and the "survival of the fittest", Carus stated that the normal state is one of mutual co-operation, manifested in family life and "social faculties".[14]

It is the animalisation of man, his reduction to savagery in a raw competition for survival, that eliminates the divine spark. We see the same atavistic urge in Capitalism and Marxism, formulated as doctrines under the same *Zeitgeist* as Darwinism, to account for history as a "struggle" of contending economic forces; "class struggle" in the case of Marxism, individual struggle in the case of the Free Trade Manchester School, but darwinesque economic struggle nonetheless. England was the home of the economic *Zeitgeist* which reached it height during the 19th century, and while Marx is regarded as one of the leading so-called "Left-wing Hegelians" of his time, he rejected the spiritual basis of Hegel's dialectics, and wrote *Das Kapital* as a resident of Britian, under the impress not of German Idealism but of English economics. Returning to Carus, who rejected such struggle as the basis of history at any level:

> "The infuriated savage may be cruel to his enemies, but we must not forget that the fury with which he takes up the combat is prompted by the love of his wife and child, or of his whole tribe, and the rise of mankind would not have taken place without a growth of the more refined sentiments of sympathy, kindness, and love".[15]

The collection of families becomes a tribe or a clan, which becomes an *ethnos*, uniting to overcome challenges, such as the taming of a river or the defeat of an enemy, to hold or take land and resources, and establish themselves in what Gumilev called the "ecological niche" that shapes and sustains an *ethnos*.

---

13   Ibid., 12.
14   Ibid., 78.
15   Ibid., 79.

The "Race-Forming Idea"

Spirit forms *ethnos* as a unit of history and culture, not zoology. The Maori race in New Zealand did not and still has not formed a *superethnos*, despite being confronted by foreign invaders. As separate *ethnoi* however, the Maori maintains his identity on traditional foundations in the midst of Western decay. These traditional premises are:

Each Maori traces his lineage to a canoe (*waka*).[16]
Each Maori identifies with a mountain.
Each Maori identifies with a river.

Hence Maori affinity is based on the inheritance of symbols. Even blood inheritance is predicated on the symbol of a canoe, regardless of genetic admixture. This elective affinity, recognised in New Zealand law in defining a Maori, draws much ridicule and criticism from those who object that many Maori are far more genetically European by zoological criteria. The ideal of many supposedly "conservative" New Zealanders of "One people, one nation, one law", in forming a *New Zealand ethnos* from disparate elements is theoretically possible, but shows minimal indication in reality since the Treaty of Waitangi in 1840, which was supposed by authority of British legal principles to make Maori and British a single *ethnos*.

Africans have not formed a *superethnos* in Africa. Tribalism predominates. Conversely, disparate races have formed *ethnoi*, such as Europeans, Indians and Africans in South and Central America. Afro-Americans have formed an *ethnos* via the shared experiences of slavery. However, "Americans" have not formed an *ethnos*. Nor has the Enlightenment liberal notion of the "social contract", expressed by the American Constitution and Bill of Rights, welded an American *superethnos* from disparate *ethnoi*. The more likely prospect is for the American Enlightenment project at nation-building to break-up into separate *ethnoi* that might not even act symbiotically unless confronted by a common enemy.

---

16 "Maori Waka:" http://www.arawai.co.nz/Maori_waka.html

Spengler on Race-Formation

Spengler rejected the zoological conceptions of "race". Spengler reiterated history, race and nation as manifestations of soul within the legacy of the German Idealists Herder, Fichte, Scheller, et al. Rootedness of families in landscape produces what Spengler called "race", which he defined as "a character of duration".[1] This "conception of a morphology of world history", "of the world-as-history in contrast to the morphology of the world-as-nature",[2] is important in considering the decline and fall of civilisations as an organic process of life cycles, which genetic interpretations overlook or discount.

Spengler in rejecting a zoological interpretation of history as well as a zoological categorisation of "race", stated that "what I for the first time have pointed out is that 'nation', like state, art, mathematics, is only a *term*, that race-forms like art-forms are determined by the style of a culture and cannot as stationery substances be made the foundation of history".[3] Spengler, like Gumilev later in regard to the "ecological niche" of an *ethnos*, stated that "races" have a "plant-like" quality, insofar as "a race has roots". "Race and landscape belong together. Where a plant takes root, there it dies also". A race is permanently fixed in "its most essential characters of body and soul" to its home. If the race can no longer be found in its home, it has ceased to exist.[4]

"A race does not migrate. Men migrate, and their successive generations are born in ever-changing landscapes; but the landscape exercises a secret force upon the plant-nature in them, and eventually the race-expression is completely transformed by the extinction of the old and the appearance of a new one. Englishmen and Germans did not migrate to America, but human beings migrated thither *as* Englishmen and Germans, and their descendants are there *as* Americans".[5]

---

1 Spengler, The Decline…, op. cit., Vol. II, Chapter V, "Cities and Peoples: (B) People, Races, Tongues", 113.
2 Ibid., Vol. I, "Introduction", 5.
3 Oswald Spengler to Hans Klöres, 1 September 1918; Oswald Spengler, Spengler Letters 1913-1936 , 67.
4 Spengler, The Decline…, op. cit. Vol. II, 119, "Peoples, Races, Tongues".
5 Ibid.

Spengler on Race-Formation

Spengler accepted the race-forming force of the landscape in changing the physiology and soul. He referred to studies that had shown that "Whites of all races, Indians and Negros have come to the same average in size of body and time of maturity, referring to the studies of American anthropologist Franz Boas that indicated the impact of environment on the change in skull shape of American-born children of Sicilian and German-Jewish migrants. Spengler stated that assumptions should not be made about race based on ancient skulls, such as those of the Etruscans, Dorians and others.[6] These views more than any other make the acceptance of Spengler problematic for Right-wing zoological materialists. Spengler wrote that "of all expressions of race, the purest is the House", expressing the "prime feeling of growth" of a race.[7] Hence, Spengler studied the meaning of Doric columns, the domed mosque, and Gothic spires, each expressing the soul of a civilisation more so than cranial angles.

---

6   Ibid.
7   Ibid., 120.

Carl Jung on Race-Formation

Carl Jung (Swiss born) developed a German School of Psychology, as there is a German School of Political Economy (Friedrich List), and a German School of Cultural Morphology (Spengler). "Analytical psychology" was Jung's answer to the materialistic "psycho-analysis" of his mentor Sigmund Freud. Jung wrote of his visit to the USA that he was struck by the metaphysical impress of the land on race-formation, referring, like Spengler, to Boas' studies:

"In 1909 I paid my first short visit to the United States… I remember, when walking through the streets of Buffalo, I came across hundreds of workmen leaving a factory. The naïve European traveller I was then could not help remarking to his American companion: 'I really had no idea there was such an amazing amount of Indian blood in your people.' 'What,' said he, 'Indian blood? I bet there is not one drop of it in this whole crowd.' I replied: 'But don't you see their faces? They are more Indian than European.' Whereupon I was informed that probably most of these workmen were of Irish, Scottish, and German extraction without a trace of Indian blood in their veins. I was puzzled and half incredulous. Subsequently I learned to see how ridiculous my hypothesis had been. Nevertheless, the impression of facial similarity remained and later years only enhanced it. As Professor Boas maintains, there are even measurable anatomical changes in many American immigrants, changes which are already noticeable in the second generation".[1]

Jung continued explaining, as did Spengler, that the impress of the landscape moulds *race*. In the footsteps of the German Idealists, Jung alluded to the spirit of the land:

"To a keen European eye there is an indefinable yet undeniable something in the whole makeup of the born American that distinguishes him from the born European.

---

1   C. G. Jung, 1930.

Carl Jung on Race-Formation

"Man can be assimilated by a country. There is an x and a y in the air and in the soil of a country, which slowly permeate and assimilate him to the type of the aboriginal inhabitant, even to the point of slightly remodelling his physical features.

"The foreign country somehow gets under the skin of those born in it. Certain very primitive tribes are convinced that it is not possible to usurp foreign territory, because the children born there would inherit the wrong ancestor spirits who dwell in the trees, the rocks, and the water of that country. There seems to be some subtle truth in this primitive intuition. That would mean that the spirit of the Indian gets at the American from within and without. Indeed, there is often an astonishing likeness in the cast of the American face to that of the Red Indian".[2]

Not only is there an impress on the physical by metaphysical forces, but there is an impact on the collective psyche, or group memory:

"The external assimilation to the peculiarities of a country is a thing one could almost expect. There is nothing astonishing in it. But the external similarity is feeble in comparison with

---

2   Ibid.

the less visible but all the more intense influence on the mind. It is just as though the mind were an infinitely more sensitive and suggestible medium than the body. It is probable that long before the body reacts the mind has already undergone considerable changes, changes that are not obvious to the individual himself or to his immediate circle, but only to an outsider. Thus I would not expect the average American, who has not lived for some years in Europe, to realize how different his mental attitude is from the European's, just as I would not expect the average European to be able to discern his difference from the American. That is the reason why so many things that are really characteristic of a country seem to be merely odd or ridiculous: the conditions from which they arise are either not known or not understood. They wouldn't be odd or ridiculous if one could feel the local atmosphere to which they belong and which makes them perfectly comprehensible and logical".[3]

Jung proceeds to describe the *national spirit*.

"Almost every great country has [what] one might call its genius or *spiritus loci*. Sometimes you can catch it in a formula, sometimes it is more elusive, yet nonetheless it is indescribably present as a sort of atmosphere that permeates everything. ... In a well-defined civilization with a solid historical background, such as for instance the French, you can easily discover the keynote of the French *espirit*: it is an '*a glorie*,' a most marked psychology in its noblest as well as its most ridiculous forms.

"The old European inheritance looks rather pale beside these vigorous primitive influences. Have you ever compared the sky-line of New York or any great American city with that of a pueblo like Taos? And did you see how the houses pile up to towers towards the centre? Without conscious imitation the American unconsciously fills out the spectral outline of the Red Man's mind and temperament.

"There is nothing miraculous about this. It has always been so: the conqueror overcomes the old inhabitants in the body but succumbs to his spirit. Rome at the zenith of her power

---

[3] Ibid.

contained within her walls all the mystery cults of the East; yet the spirit of the humblest among them, a Jewish mystery society, transformed the greatest of all cities from top to bottom. The conqueror gets the wrong ancestor spirits, the primitives would say: I like this picturesque way of putting it. It is pithy and expresses every conceivable implication". [4]

While German Idealism, through Johann Gottfried von Herder (1744-1893) gave Western philosophy the notion of *Zeitgeist*, or the "Spirit of the Age," and *volkgeist* or "spirit of a people," Jung refers here to the "spirit of a loci." Since that time the Jewish culture has given a pervasive Jewish countenance to American culture, in addition to Negroid rhythm and Indian nomadicism. Of the Negro influence Jung observed:

> "Another thing that struck me was the great influence of the Negro, a psychological influence naturally, not due to the mixing of blood. ... The peculiar walk with loose joints, or the swinging of the hips so frequently observed in Americans, also comes from the Negro. American music draws its main inspiration from the Negro, and so does the dance".[5]

The USA has an inner primitivity behind the façade of Western technology. This difference between the inward substance and outward form of a culture Spengler referred to as *pseudomorphosis*,[6] borrowing the word from geology. This bastardous chaos is celebrated throughout Western civilisation as "cultural enrichment", and expressing a "common humanity", but what occurs, when a synthesis cannot be reached giving impetus to something new and stronger, such as occurred with the Christianisation of Europe that created Western High Culture, is a culture-abortion, not a birth or rebirth. Of this fetish for the alien, Jung said, "This craving for things foreign and faraway is a morbid sign".[7] Jung continues:

> "[T]he American presents a strange picture: a European with Negro behaviour and an Indian soul. He shares the fate of all

---

4   Ibid.
5   C. G. Jung, "Mind and Earth," 1931.
6   Spengler, The Decline..., Vol. I, 209-214, 228.
7   C. G. Jung, Letters, Vol. I, 40.

usurpers of foreign soil. Certain Australian primitives assert that one cannot conquer foreign soil, because in it there dwell strange ancestor-spirits who reincarnate themselves in the newborn. There is a great psychological truth in this. The foreign land assimilates its conqueror. But unlike the Latin conquerors of Central and South America, the North Americans preserved their European standards with the most rigid puritanism, though they could not prevent the souls of their Indian foes from becoming theirs. Everywhere the virgin earth causes at least the unconscious of the conqueror to sink to the level of its indigenous inhabitants".[8]

Jung regarded the American White as different in both look and mentality from the European. He stated that Europeans find it difficult to tell what race a White American is when dressed in Indian garb, and Indians dressed as Whites. He believed this to be observable in other nations too, commenting that "Man can be assimilated by a country". "That would mean that the spirit of the Indian gets at the American from within and without".[9] Jung saw the mind as being continually "moulded by earthly conditions". He stated that a large population of Europeans transplanted to a strange soil and climate can be confidently expected to undergo psychic and perhaps bodily changes in the course of a few generations, without the admixture of "foreign blood". Jung stated that this is observable in the differences among Jews, moulded by different localities, in spite of the similarity of race. Although difficult to define, the differences are readily felt by acute observers of human nature.[10]

Jung stated that the "greatest experiment" in modern times was the settlement of a predominantly Germanic population to North America. Admixture with Indians did not play any role in the race-formation of the "Yankee", yet Jung observed on his first visit to the USA, as cited above, that White Americans appeared so similar to Indians he had assumed there had been wide-scale racial admixture. He understood the "Indianisation" of Americans many years later when he analysed large numbers of American patients. "Remarkable differences were revealed in comparison to Europeans", in terms of psyche.[11]

---

8   Spengler, op. cit.
9   G. Keith Parker, 19.
10 C. G. Jung, 1964, 93.
11 Ibid., 94.

The other influence on forming the "Americans" has been the Negro, again not through miscegenation; particularly on the emotions, and most apparent in the way that an American laughs, the loose jointed way of walking and the swinging of the hips. Negro influence could be seen already by Jung on American music, dance, the phenomenon of the "revival meeting" that was popular then, and other manifestations of religious feeling, the "ceaseless gabble" expressed in the manner of American newspapers, "more like the chattering of a Negro village" than the character of Germanic forebears. "The almost total lack of privacy and the all-devouring mass sociability remind one of primitive life in open huts where there is complete identity with all members of the tribe", the open doors and the lack of hedges.[12] Interestingly, because the Negro is a minority and did not threaten to engulf the White, as in Africa, Jung did not regard the Negro influence as necessarily negative, unless one had "jazz phobia". Whether Jung would still be of the same opinion, with the excess primitivity that now dominates American culture, and its reach across the world, is another matter. Jung opined that while the Negro influence is shown on outward behaviour, the Indian influence impresses on the inner life of the psyche.[13]

While the Negro manifested in the most superficial levels of the psyche in American patients, it is "only in very deep analysis" that Indian symbols appeared. This was so for example in the archetype of the "hero-motif" as an Indian.[14] The "hero" archetype is man's highest ideal. Jung compared the rigours of American sports training, in contrast to the European, to that of Indian initiation. He held the American virtues to be Indian virtues: tenacity and endurance towards goals.[15]

Jung also saw the influence of the shaman (conjuror and medicine man) in American religious experiences such as Spiritualism and Christian Science, popular at the time, as manifestations of this Indian influence on the psyche. Both were forms of exorcism, the latter the exorcising of sickness.[16] The "power word", the magic of words expressed in advertising, was seen then by Europeans as peculiarly

---

12   Ibid., 95.
13   Ibid., 95.
14   Ibid., 98, 99.
15   Ibid., 101.
16   Ibid., 101.

American, which Europeans then "laughed at". Jung commented: "It is yet to be seen what America will do with it". [17] "Thus the American presents a strange picture: a European with Negro behaviour and an Indian soul".[18]

The magic of words is now used to control the world. The "words of power" include "democracy, "human rights" and "progress", which when uttered can strike the opposition mute.

The impress of the land on the American character has been reflected in a certain American nomadism, observed in high levels of geographic mobility. Over the period of 1999-2000 43.4 million Americans moved house. Elazar saw a nomadic character in such mobility; "a compulsion to move about" that has created "a nation of restless wanderers unlike any in the world", "scornful of that attachment to place that restrains the European".[19]

As Jung commented, such attachment is not only a restraint, but also a bond with the land, to form an *ethnos* moulded and sustained by group-memories and symbols, or what Jung called *archetypes*. Of these archetypes the British psychologist William McDougall wrote:

> "... each race and each people that has lived for many generations under or by a particular type of civilization has specialized its 'collective unconscious', differentiated and developed the 'archetypes' into forms peculiar to itself ... He [Jung] claims that sometimes a single rich dream has enabled him to discover the fact, say, of Jewish or Mediterranean blood in a patient who shows none of the outward physical marks of such descent..."[20]

Count Hermann Keyserling, an important philosopher of Weimar era Germany, in close contact with Jung, writing of the "psychology of nations", likewise asserted, at a time when the Hitlerites were on the rise, that "In Germany anyone who places the accent mark on blood rather than spirit is in the deepest sense of the word a racial alien and

---

17   Ibid., 102.
18   Ibid., 103.
19   Daniel Elazar, 73.
20   William McDougall, 125-27, quoted by Jay Sherry, 60-61.

not the person in whose veins Nordic blood flows". Jay Sherry states in his thesis on Jung that "Keyserling saw race as just one factor in the formulation of a philosophy of humanity that also included the spirit and the environment".[21] Keyserling, in critiquing National Socialist philosopher Alfred Rosenberg's *Myth of the 20th Century*, wrote: "Rosenberg's book made clear to me that National Socialism is, in its present form, basically hostile to the spirit."[22]

---

21 Hermann Keyserling, 399; quoted by Sherry, 69.
22 Quoted by Sherry, 117.

Place and Land in the Making of Culture

G.W.F. Hegel, the philosopher-historian, wrote of the "World Spirit" which manifested through nature as peoples and nations, infused with a "soul" whose unique character is shaped by geography. Explaining the "geographical basis of history", Hegel wrote:

> "Contrasted with the universality of the moral Whole and with the unity of that individuality which is its active principle, the natural connection that helps to produce the Spirit of a People, appears an extrinsic element; but inasmuch as we must regard it as the ground on which that Spirit plays its part, it is an essential and necessary basis. We began with the assertion that, in the History of the World, the Idea of Spirit appears in its actual embodiment as a series of external forms, each one of which declares itself as an actually existing people. This existence falls under the category of Time as well as Space, in the way of natural existence; and the special principle, which every world historical people embodies, has this principle at the same time as a natural characteristic. Spirit, clothing itself in this form of nature, suffers its particular phases to assume separate existence; for mutual exclusion is the mode of existence proper to mere nature. These natural distinctions must be first of all regarded as special possibilities, from which the Spirit of the people in question germinates, and among them is the Geographical Basis. It is not our concern to become acquainted with the land occupied by nations as an external locale, but with the natural type of the locality, as intimately connected with the type and character of the people which is the offspring of such a soil. This character is nothing more nor less than the mode and form in which nations make their appearance in History, and take place and position in it. ...."[1]

Hegel listed three primary geographical features that shape the soul of a people:

---

1   G.W.F. Hegel, 96-97.

Place and Land in the Making of Culture

"(1) The arid elevated land with its extensive steppes and plains.

"(2) The valley plains — the Land of Transition permeated and watered by great Streams.

"(3) The coast region in immediate connection with the sea.

"These three geographical elements are the essential ones, and we shall see each quarter of the globe triply divided accordingly. The first is the substantial, unvarying, metallic, elevated region, intractably shut up within itself, but perhaps adapted to send forth impulses over the rest of the world; the second forms centres of civilization … ; the third offers the means of connecting the world together, and of maintaining the connection".[2]

The first, arid plains and steppes, are the abode of the Mongols, conducive to nomadism, although similar regions exist in Arabia and South America. The horse is central to the Mongols, for both nourishment (milk) and war.

The valley plains traversed by rivers in such locations as Babylonia, Egypt, China and India. Here great states are formed, based on agriculture, in contrast to the nomads of the arid steppes and plains.

The lands of coasts and rivers allow for ready communication and travel. Hegel refers to the character of coastal peoples in a manner that Spengler was to call "Faustian" for Western man:

"The sea gives us the idea of the indefinite, the unlimited, and infinite; and in feeling his own infinite in that Infinite, man is stimulated and emboldened to stretch beyond the limited: the sea invites man to conquest, and to piratical plunder, but also to honest gain and to commerce. The land, the mere Valley-plain attaches him to the soil; it involves him in an infinite multitude of dependencies, but the sea carries him out beyond these limited circles of thought and action. Those who navigate the sea, have indeed gain for their object, but the means are in this respect paradoxical, inasmuch as they hazard both property and life to attain it".[3]

---

2   Ibid., 105-106.

3   Ibid., 108.

The Decline and Fall of Civilisations

Here we see the character of the merchant-soldier-adventurer who built the empires of Western civilisation through both trade and heroism; the antithesis of the haggling market traders of the Orient and Levant. Hegel commented that "This is what exalts their gain and occupation above itself, and makes it something brave and noble".[4] The soul of the Westerner bordering the oceans is in contrast to that of Orientals likewise bordering oceans yet confined to land. One looks on the ocean as a challenge, the other as a hindrance:

> "This stretching out of the sea beyond the limitations of the land, is wanting to the splendid political edifices of Asiatic States, although they themselves border on the sea — as for example, China. For them the sea is only the limit, the ceasing of the land; they have no positive relation to it".[5]

Observing the differences within states of peoples according to the impact of upland and lowland geography, Hegel stated of the Persian, Chinese and Indian:

> "First as to Geographical position, we see China and India, exhibiting as it were the dull half-conscious brooding of Spirit, in fruitful plains — distinct from which is the lofty girdle of mountains with the wandering hordes that occupy them. The inhabitants of the heights, in their conquest, did not change the spirit of the plains, but imbibed it themselves. But in Persia the two principles — retaining their diversity — became united, and the mountain peoples with their principle became the predominant element".[6]

An ethno-psychology is formed by the land, sea and mountains, deserts, steppes and plains, which cause differences in temperament between *sub-ethnoi* within a *super-ethnos*. What gives unity to a people by *synthesis* or *symbiosis* of such varying *ethnoi* are the perceptions of common challenges, history, and enemies. Such common experiences transcend primitive tribal blood ties and form a "people", whose collective experiences are passed along by mechanisms which are only recently being discovered to become a race-soul.

---

4   Ibid.
5   Ibid.
6   Ibid., 193.

Place and Land in the Making of Culture

D. H. Lawrence came to similar conclusions as Jung and the German Idealists, referring to the "spirit of place". Lawrence wrote:

> "Every continent has its own great spirit of place. Every people is polarized in some particular locality, which is home, the homeland. Different places on the face of the earth have different vital effluence, different vibration, different chemical exhalation, different polarity with different stars: call it what you like. But the spirit of place is a great reality. The Nile Valley produced not only the corn, but the terrific religions of Egypt. China produces the Chinese, and will go on doing so. The Chinese in San Francisco will in time cease to be Chinese, for America is a great melting pot.

> "There was a tremendous polarity in Italy, in the city of Rome. And this seems to have died. For even places die. The Island of Great Britain had a wonderful terrestrial magnetism or polarity of its own, which made the British people. For the moment, this polarity seems to be breaking. Can England die? And what if England dies?"[7]

Lawrence sought out a more genuine existence for the White race by looking at the surviving traditions of the non-white races, in particular the American Indians. This is the theme of *The Plumed Serpent*[8] and *The Woman Who Rode Away*.[9]

Lawrence regarded the liberty and equality of the modern world as detaching modern man from the rhythms of the cosmos, which traditional peoples such as the Hopi attempted to maintain amidst the onslaught of a superficial civilisation. He wrote of the proffered freedom, the basis of American democracy that retards the American from finding an inner depth:

> "Men are less free than they imagine; ah, far less free. The freest are perhaps least free. Men are free when they are in a living homeland, not when they are straying and breaking away.

---

7   D. H. Lawrence, *The Spirit of Place*, Chapter I.
8   D. H. Lawrence, *The Plumed Serpent*.
9   D. H. Lawrence, *The Woman Who Rode Away and Other Stories*.

Men are free when they are obeying some deep, inward voice of religious belief. Obeying from within. Men are free when they belong to a living, Organic, *believing* community, active in fulfilling some unfulfilled, perhaps unrealized purpose. Not when they are escaping to some wild west. The most unfree souls go west, and shout of freedom. Men are freest when they are most unconscious of freedom. The shout is a rattling of chains, always was".[10]

The "freedom" that is a dogma of the Late West, called "democracy", and "human rights", is the freedom to escape from duty, identity, purpose, family, home, homeland, community; in the pursuit of the most superficial layers of the ego. The result is not ego-fulfilment, but dissatisfaction in trying to find an elusive yearning for meaning in what ultimately is selfishness, atomisation, and increasingly in the West leads to suicide, depression, and addiction.

---

10 D. H. Lawrence, *The Spirit of Place*.

"Environmentalism" and Communism

One of the primary misconceptions from those who oppose Liberal and Leftist theories on history and human nature is that they are dogmatically based on "environmentalism". Liberals and Marxists are assumed to insist that human nature can be changed at will by changing the environment without regard to genetics. The example is that of Lysenko, the Soviet Russian agronomist who theorised that the characteristics of plants could be changed by altering the environment, and that the changes would be conveyed to subsequent generations. Because such theories rejected the laws of genetic inheritance they were elevated to the status of Soviet dogma in the fight against "fascist science". The Amercian-Jewish anthropologists Franz Boas, who had numerous Left-wing affiliations, considered the landscape to be of such impact that it could change the skull shape of first generation Sicilian and Jewish immigrant children born in the USA. This is condemned by the Right as typically communistic yet, as we have seen, the conservatives Oswald Spengler and Carl Jung had similar views regarding the impact of landscape on race and cited Boas' studies. For this they are criticised by Right-wing genetic determinists.

This Right-wing characterisation of Liberal and Marxist theories on environmentalism is inaccurate. Rather, "environmentalism" has been vehemently rejected by the Left precisely because it affirms rather than negates the influence of "biologism". This is also why "epigenetics", as will be seen, is problematic for the Left.

The Liberal and Marxist dogmas insist that humankind is, uniquely, totally divorced from nature, including geography. Although Lysenko's plant environmentalism was imposed as official state dogma in the USSR because it taught that genetics is irrelevant to plant breeding, it was not claimed that this proved human characteristics were also changed geographically. Such a notion implied there are biological laws at work that transcend laws of social production. Classical Leftist theory states that the laws of social production – Marxist "dialectal materialism" – are *solely* responsible for shaping history and human characteristics. While Marx was one of the primary "Hegelians of the Left", this Hegelian Leftism required the repudiation of two primary

"Environmentalism" and Communism

elements of Hegel's philosophy: "spirit" as the animator of nature, and nature as the animator of race and history. History is only impelled by changes in social production, according to Marxism. Marx wrote of this:

> "In the social production of their life, men enter into definite relations that are indispensable and independent of their will; these relations of production correspond to a definite stage of development of their material forces of production. The sum total of these relations of production constitutes the economic structure of society — the real foundation, on which rises a legal and political superstructure and to which correspond definite forms of social consciousness. The mode of production of material life determines the social, political and intellectual life process in general. It is not the consciousness of men that determines their being, but, on the contrary, their social being that determines their consciousness. ..."[1]

The genesis of an *ethnos* through the collective overcoming of the geographical challenges of oceans, rivers, steppes, mountains, deserts, jungles, cannot be accepting as the driving force of history by Marxism, because these factors render social production subsidiary rather than determinative. While Marx saw capitalism as being responsible for what he called a "metabolic rift" between man and nature, which has recently provided justification for a belated Marxist entry into the "green" movements, the theory does not relate to the environmental role in race-formation and history. What is called "Marxist geography" examines geography again from the viewpoint of social production.

Since the implosion of the Soviet Union, the geographical formation of race has become a significant influence on scholarship and politics. However this *ethnogenesis* had been established as a field of research during the Soviet years by Dr. Lev Gumilev. He endured considerable opposition despite his references to Engels and use of occasional Marxist terminology.

The Communists critiqued *ethnogenesis* as a form of *biologism* that undermined dialectical materialism. F. V. Konstantinov, a leading

---

1 Karl Marx, "Preface", 1859.

The Decline and Fall of Civilisations

Soviet philosopher, wrote that humankind was not subject to the laws of the natural world:

> "Human society is the highest link in the general chain of development of the material world. It represents a specific part of the material world with its special laws of movement and development that apply to it alone... The movement of society is subject to laws that are different from the laws of the natural world".[2]

Joseph Stalin rejected the geographical impact on history, because social development is "incomparably faster" than geographical changes, and cannot be the "principal cause for directing social development".[3] "Geographical materialism", like genetics, was condemned as the science of "geopoliticians", "fascists", and "imperialists". In the 1930s geography was divided into "economic" and "physical" branches, to separate the studies of social laws and environment. Nature was seen as the enemy of human development, and something that must be reconstructed. This was the doctrine behind the massive construction projects regardless of ecology. The aim was the creation of a "new Soviet man".[4] Although Gumilev tried to frame his theories in Marxian terms, his premise is fundamentality different: It was "the *ethnos* that was shaped by the geographical environment and adapted to it, and not the other way around". The *ethnos* was "a natural part of... an ecological niche". He attempted to bypass his problems with Communist dogma by conceding that the *ethnos* reshapes the landscape for its needs. Nonetheless the premise remained that it is "the landscape that defines the possibilities of the ethnic collective at the moment of its creation".[5]

Where the German Idealists refer the national-soul or race-soul, Gumilev formulated the concept of the *passionarnost*,[6] a kind of human photosynthesis for converting energy from the "biosphere" that

---

2 F. V. Konstantinov, Istoricheskii materialism 32, 34; cited by Mark Bassin, 119.
3 Stalin, Marksizm i voprosy iazykoznaniia cited by Bassin, 119.
4 Mark Bassin, 121-122.
5 Gumilev, "Pomni o Vavilone", cited by Bassin, 127.
6 Bassin, Ibid., passim.

vitalises an *ethnos*, which declines when it is entropically expended.[7] This ethnic *passionarnost* might in its character, if not its origins, be considered as the collective equivalent to *libido*, Jungian "psychic energy", or the élan vital of Bergson's philosophy.

---

[7] Jung referred to "psychological entropy".

Race as Historical Destiny

Historical "race" formation is contrary to reliance on genetics. The genetic determinism of the "Right" can be as dogmatic as the economic determinism of the Left.

We have considered various theories that are often at odds with the scientism of the 19th to 21st centuries, and even prior to that with the fracturing of knowledge during the Renaissance and Enlightenment eras by philosophers and scientists such as Decartes. What is the "modern mind" to make of such metaphysical concepts as archetypes, *zeitgeist*, the spirit of nations, race-soul, and the discredited theories of Lamarck and Lysenko on the "inheritance of acquired characteristics", that seem to be a throwback to superstition?

In recent years there has been a questioning of the materialistic, mechanistic assumptions of "modern science". Credible scientists are looking at subtleties in the cosmos that have been obscured, and even dogmatically stifled. Some of these theories and hypotheses on the nature of the cosmos provide added dimensions of perception that might be applicable to "race" and "ethnos" beyond the zoological, while giving "race" a depth that repudiates those who, in the name of what is "modern", claim that there are no "races" because of the zoological unity of the nebulous mass called "humanity". While there is an underlying unity of all life, there are those who for ideological reasons seek to take that unity to lengths that would ultimately make life amorphous.

The antagonism between those who regard zoological races as being of prime significance in history and culture, and those who regard race as a "social construct" both appeal to genetics. The "anti-race" advocates state there is more genetic variation among "races" than there is between "races;" that there are no specific genes that determine "race." The zoological materialists, on the other hand, advocate genetic determinism, and state that there are crucial genetic differences. Both rely on mechanistic assumptions.

The metaphysical basis of "race" expounded by Spengler, Herder, Jung, and others, considers the matter from another perspective, and challenges the materialism that has dominated questions of race even prior to Mendel's discovery of the laws of hereditary. These concepts are regarded as un-scientific, and rendered obsolete by Mendel and Darwin. However, as in much else, modern methods of empirical evidence are re-discovering the knowledge that has been discarded as superstition when it does not accord with the materialistic paradigm.

Phenotypic Plasticity[1]

Oswald Spengler [2] and Carl Jung referred to Franz Boas on the impact of the environment on the formation of race. This seemingly communistic, Lamarckian and Lysenkoan espousal of environmentalism, and the repudiation of Mendelian genetics was used by the Left to undermine the race consciousness of Caucasians, especially in the USA. Yet both Spengler and Jung reaffirmed the reality of "race".

Franz Boas, regarded as the father of modern anthropology, claimed that the skull shape of immigrant children is changed by the new land in which their parents settle. Therefore one of the most important identifiers of "race" – skull shape – does not seem to be as fixed as hitherto assumed.[3] Boas and Spengler refer to the pioneering statistical studies of the physiology of White, Indian and Negro soldiers conducted for the U.S. military after the Civil War.[4]

Boas leaves the question open as to whether changes in head-form among Hebrew infants might be caused by methods of cradling, but this does not apply to Sicilian infants. Neither does this apply to "Bohemian" infants who showed a change of face width.[5] Boas did not claim to have solved the problem as to why the changes occur, only that head-forms change without a change of descent.[6]

Those who repudiate the impact of environment on phenotype state that genes are not altered in such a manner by the environment, and such changes cannot be passed along to subsequent generations. They object that Lysenko spent decades in the USSR trying to prove a similar theory. This controversy about the "inheritance of acquired

---

1   Phenotype: outward, physical manifestation of the organism. Anything that is part of the observable structure, function or behaviour of a living organism.

2   Spengler, *The Decline* ..., Vol. II, 119, "Peoples, Races, Tongues".

3   Franz Boas, "Changes in Bodily Form of Descendents of Immigrants", 530–562.

4   J. H. Baxter, 1875. B. A. Gould, 1869.

5   Franz Boas, "Changes in Bodily Form", 554.

6   Ibid.,, 562.

characteristics" raged for decades into the 20th century.[7] One of the most notable challenges was by August Weismann who cut the tails from hundreds of mice for twenty-two generations to show that the lack of a tail would not be inherited by subsequent generations.[8] Conversely, Boas, in a study for the U.S. Immigration Commission on the physical assimilation of races, found that the first generation of European immigrants (in this study Sicilians and Jews) showed significant changes in skull shape within the first generation. The East European Jews became longer headed, and south Italians shorter headed, within the first generation, even when the parents are new arrivals. William Ridgeway, professor of archaeology at Cambridge, considered the anthrometric findings on skull form and other physical factors indicated that "the whole bodily and mental make-up of immigrants may change", under the impress of the American environment.[9]

Boas presented his findings in 1911 to an academic conference on race in London. He began by raising the assumption about hereditable I.Q. differences among European races, and questioned whether far-reaching changes might occur not only through social but also geographical environment.[10] He suggested that race types might not be as fixed by heredity as assumed. Boas, without being dogmatic, referred to the hypothesis of William Ridgeway, stating:

> "It would seem, however, that besides the influences of more or less favourable environment which affect the form of the body during the period of growth, a number of other causes may modify the form of the body. Professor Ridgeway goes so far as to think that the stability of human types in definite areas and for long periods is an expression, not of the influence of heredity, but of the influence of environment; and that, on the other hand, the modifications of the human form which are found in the Mediterranean area, in Central Europe, and in North-western Europe, are due to the differences of climate, soil, and natural products. It does not seem to me that adequate proof can be given for modifications of the human form as far-reaching as

---

7   Loren Graham, 15-100.
8   Ibid., 20.
9   William Ridgeway, Vol. II, 293.
10 Franz Boas, *The Instability of Human Types*, 1912, 99–103.

those claimed by Professor Ridgeway, although we must grant the possibility of such influences. We have, however, good evidence which shows that the various European types undergo certain changes in a new environment. The observations on which this conclusion is based were made by me on emigrants from various European countries who live in the city of New York, and on their descendants".[11]

Among the changes summarised by Boas on his study were that "American-born descendants of immigrants differ in type from their foreign born parents. The changes which occur among various European types are not all in the same direction.[12] They develop in early childhood and persist throughout life".[13]

There have been claims that Boas' findings are incorrect or minor.[14] When Boas' report was released it was scrutinised for statistical inaccuracies, which Boas addressed at the time.[15] Recently his results have been re-evaluated. One such re-evaluation, using new methods of analysis, states:

"As Boas hypothesized, our results show that children born in the U.S. environment are markedly less similar to their parents in terms of head form than foreign-born children are to theirs. This finding thus corroborates Boas's overarching conclusion that the cephalic index is sensitive to environmental influences and, therefore, does not serve as a valid marker of racial phylogeny."[16]

Gravlee et al state that their use of analytic methods not available to Boas, "provide stronger support for Boas's conclusion". Boas and

---

11   Ibid.
12   That is, in Sicilians the heads form shorter, in the Jews the heads form longer, suggesting a convergence to an "American" head-form.
13   Boas, "Changes in the bodily form", 530.
14   Corey Sparks and Richard Jantz , 14636–14639.
15   Boas, "Changes in the bodily form", 533.
16   Clarence C. Gravlee, H. Russell Bernard, William R. Leonard, 123–136. For a discussion of this see: Gravlee, Bernard, Leonard, "Boas's Changes in Bodily Form: The Immigrant Study, Cranial Plasticity, and Boas's Physical Anthropology", American Anthropologist , 105: 2, Jun 4 2003, 326–332; http://nersp.osg.ufl.edu/~ufruss/documents/boas.paperII.pdf

generations of anthropologists that were influenced by him, were Leftists who had an ideological stake in repudiating the role of genetics on human behaviour and race formation. Boas is often regarded in tandem with the 18th century French biologist Lamarck, and the Soviet agronomist Lysenko. The latter, alluded to above, attempted to show that inheritance in plants can bypass the laws of genetics, by what he called "vernalization", to convert winter wheat to spring wheat. The experiments did not work.[17] While Lysenko was trying to disprove Mendelian genetic laws, Boas did not discount their significance. The extent of changes caused by environment are limited.[18] However, the significance is summarised by Gravlee et al:

> "As we argue in our earlier article, the significance of the immigrant study must be understood in historical context. At the time Boas conceived the study, the prevailing view among physical anthropologists was that humankind consisted of a few, unchanging races or types—'permanent forms which have lasted without variation from the beginning of our modern geological period up to the present time'.[19] Boas's immigrant study is significant because it treated this assumption as an empirical matter. The most important result was that the cephalic index, which had 'always been considered one of the most stable and permanent characteristics of human races',[20] was sensitive to the environment. Given the prevailing faith in the absolute permanence of cranial form, Boas's demonstration of change—any change—in the cephalic index within a single generation was nothing short of revolutionary". [21]

Boas was not dogmatic in his assertions, and did not claim to have reached conclusions as to the reasons why skull form changes among migrant children, other than to suggest that skull form is not as fixed as supposed. Professor William Ridgeway went further than Boas was willing to go in suggesting that changes in skull and body form among different migrant races towards a mean average might

---

17 Zhores A. Medvedev, 155-157.
18 Gravlee, et al., 330.
19 Boas, Race, Language, and Culture , 35.
20 Boas, Changes in Bodily Form ..., 5.
21 Gravlee, et al., 331.

give rise to an "American type". The adaptability of "various races" coming to America within the first generation indicated that "widely varying nationalities and races" might form "what may well be called an American type".[22] It is this "American type" that Jung believed he observed as a consequence of the impress of the American soil, and psychologically under the impress of the *genius loci*.

Recent studies of face shapes among the Turkman from central Asia and the native Fars in northern Iran indicate that geography impacts on phenotype within a relatively short time; less than a century. The dominate face shape of native Fars and Turkman females is *euriprosopic* (broad); of males of both races *mesoprosopic* (round). It has been concluded from studies in various parts of Iran of different racial and ethnic groups that "the geographical factor similar to the ethnical factor can affect the form of the face".[23]

In studies of ear length (EL) and health, geographic clusters transcend race. There are differences in ear length between Chinese according to geographic origins: Taiwanese and Singaporean Chinese babies have longer ears than Hong Kong Chinese babies. "Even within the same ethnic group, EL appears to be impacted by country of origin".[24]

A more definitive study of change of bodily form by geography was undertaken by anthropologists H. L. Schapiro and Frederick Hulse whose subjects were Japanese immigrants to Hawaii, Japanese born in Hawaii and Japanese in the villages in Japan from whence the immigrants came. Twenty-one indices were measured on thousands of subjects. Japanese born in Hawaii differed from Japanese immigrants to Hawaii and both differed from those in Japan. The cephalic index differed between those born in Hawaii and the immigrants by 2.6 points; a significant six times the standard deviation. The differences emerged within a short time; the longer an immigrant lived in Hawaii the greater the divergence.[25]

---

22 William Ridgeway, 291.

23 M. Jahanshahi, "Ethnicity and Facial Anthropometry", 2535-2542, in Victor R. Preedy, 2012.

24 Wee Bin Lian, "Anthropometry in Ethnic Groups and Cultural and Geographical Diversity: Auricular Anthropometry of Newborns: Ethnic Variations", in Preedy, 2523-2533.

25 H. L. Shapiro and Frederick Seymour Hulse, 1939.

Phenotypic Plasticity

In 1943 Marcus Goldstein, a founder of the science of dental anthropology, undertook studies in regard to the differences of head-form between Mexicans, immigrant Mexicans in Texas, and their Texas born offspring, and like Boas found significant differences in head-form.[26]

The Left have always used Boas' studies to show that races are too fluid to matter, and the "Right" has condemned him on the same basis. However, Boas unequivocally stated, "against the characterisation of 'Boas' theory as environmental-economic', I protest as based on a hopeless muddle of two distinct problems that have no relation whatever, namely that of a selection of immigrants according to economic conditions, and that of the changes in bodily form of the descendants of immigrants".[27] This is a repudiation of the communistic dogma of economic determinism.

Phenotype is not as fixed by genetic inheritance as was once thought. A re-examination of Boas' data has shown that skull formation has a plasticity according to environmental factors. Phenotypic plasticity describes the change of bodily form even at the molecular level, including the "remodelling" of the brain by external stimuli.[28] Having assumed that the physiology of the human body was genetically determined, scientists did not fully appreciate the significance of phenotypic plasticity until the late 1960s, when seeing how physical performance could be improved by physical training.

> "Exercised muscles responded to the stimulation, and remodelled to improve performance. In the intervening years, scientists have characterised many physiological aspects of this phenomenon across a range of tissues, and with the advent of modern molecular tools, it has proved possible to uncover some of the mechanisms that underpin the phenomenon.[29]

> "Although the effects of phenotypic plasticity in muscle can be physically dramatic, the effects in the brain, although less visible,

---

26   M. Goldstein, 1943.
27   Boas, Changes in Bodily Form, 553.
28   Kathryn Phillips, 2006.
29   Ibid., i.

are no less spectacular. Brains constantly remodel in response to a relentless barrage of physiological and environmental factors, allowing us to encode information by remodelling synaptic interactions".[30]

Such changes in phenotype caused by outside stimuli, such as stress and diet can then become an inherited trait passed to subsequent generations to become part of a genotype.[31] The eminent British geneticist and embryologist C. H. Waddington discussed this question at an early period, suggesting how an adaptation to a temporary environmental stimulant as an "acquired characteristic" might become an inherited trait of subsequent generations, even when that environmental stimulus is no longer present.[32]

The hypothesis here is that a race or *ethnos* might be formed and maintain what Spengler called "the duration of character," not through a fixed zoological genotype but through a myriad of factors including the stresses of conflict and challenges of environment. It is suggested here that history, or shared experiences, form "race". How a group responds to challenges enables the "inheritance of acquired characteristics". We shall now examine how such acquired changes in both physiology and psychology through shared experience – culture and history - might be passed on to subsequent generations, thereby forming a race or *ethnos*.

---

30   Ibid., , ii.
31   Genotype: The inherited genetic code.
32   C. H. Waddington, 1953, 118-126.

Epigenetics

C. H. Waddington coined the word "epigenetics". He showed how acquired characteristics can be inherited, with the example of the Drosophila fly that does not possess a crossvein on the wings. The trait of crossveins emerges when the fly is treated with heat. After several generations the trait occurs without heat treatment, having becoming an inherited acquired characteristic. Waddington stated that the characteristic had become "genetically assimilated", and is regarded as an example of the plasticity of phenotype. Epigenetics, from the Greek *epi* (over, outside of), refers to changes in phenotype that might be caused by switching genes on and off through environmental factors, without changing the DNA sequence. Although Waddington coined the word in 1942 epigenetics has had considerable interest particularly since the 1990s. As explained by Professor Loren Graham, both advocates and critics often confuse epigenetics as a form of Lysenkoism. The comparison is erroneous as epigenetics, unlike Lysenkoism, does not repudiate genetic laws, but shows how outside stimuli might influence genes. Professor Chris Faulk describes "epigenetics":

"Not all heritability is genetic, and humans, like all animals, have the ability to adapt to the environment. One of the main mechanisms for altering gene expression is through epigenetics, literally 'above the genome'. Epigenetics has been in the news lately for its potential impacts on human health, and has even been touted as requiring a complete overhaul of the modern synthesis of evolutionary theory. The basic premise of epigenetics is that chemical marks (DNA methylation, histone modifications, and bound non-coding RNAs) can result in gene expression changes and can be passed down through cell division without changes in a cell's DNA. If these changes are passed down through the generations, they are considered non-Mendelian, since they do not follow the law of genetic segregation. Practically, epigenetics means that the environment can impact your physical characteristics, your phenotype, and potentially even be passed on to your offspring".[1]

---

1   Chris Faulk, "Lamarck, Lysenko, and Modern Day Epigenetics", School of Public Health, 2013.

Epigenetics

In attempting to explain cardiovascular and other health disparities between Blacks and Whites in the USA, C. W. Kuzawa, Professor of Anthropology at Northwestern University, and E. Sweet, describe the mechanism of epigenetics and the expression of genes:

> "The durability of the effects of early environments on multiple biological systems raises the question of what biological mechanisms underlie them: if early environments influence adult biology and health, where in the body are the 'memories' of these early experiences stored and maintained? The contributions of several developmental processes have been documented, each corresponding to axes of biological variation independent of one's genotype. ...
>
> "In addition to such modifications in the number of cells present, there is growing evidence that epigenetic changes in the pattern of cellular gene expression are also key to the long-term impacts of early environments. Although ascribed with numerous meanings since Waddington coined the phrase in 1942, epigenetics is increasingly being reserved to refer to the study of processes that modify patterns of gene expression without changing the nucleotide sequences of the DNA. The genome is inherited at conception and, other than somatic mutations acquired during cell division, remains unchanged in most body cells across the lifecycle. The 'epigenome', in contrast, is the product of a gradual commitment of cell lineages to more constrained patterns of gene expression. The epigenome is a result, in part, of the genome interacting with the environment, and can be viewed as the molecular basis for cellular differentiation and development over the life-course".
>
> "Unlike the nucleotide bases that form the genetic code, the 'epigenetic code' predominantly involves chemical modifications to the structure of the chromatin that scaffolds the DNA within the chromosome. If fully stretched, the chromosomes in a single human cell would be roughly 6 feet in length; thus, a complex process of folding is required to package the complete genome into each cell nucleus where the genes reside and are expressed. In the nucleus, chromosomes must be unwound locally to allow transcription factors to gain access to a gene. How the DNA is packaged within

the chromatin influences how easy or difficult a gene is to access and thus, whether and how much it may be expressed in that cell. Epigenetic markings have thus been likened to volume controls for genes, and they play an integral role in the normal process of cellular differentiation. As cells divide, epigenetic markings present in the parent cell are maintained through mitosis and thus heritable to both daughter cells. Through a complex series of bifurcations at which patterns of gene silencing and amplification are progressively acquired, the single totipotent 'stem cell'[2] formed at conception is capable of creating a body with roughly 200 cell types that vary in structure and function, despite the endowment of each of these daughter cells with an identical genome".

"An important class of mechanisms of epigenetic gene silencing involves localized chemical modifications to the chromatin and its protein constituents, which alter how tightly the DNA is packaged in the region of specific genes. The attachment of an extra methyl group (methylation) to 'CpG islands' (regions of DNA rich in cytosine and guanine linked by a phosphodiester bond) within the promoter region of a gene typically impedes expression of that gene in that cell. The histone proteins that the DNA fibers are wrapped around can also be modified to alter the tightness of DNA packing, and thus the accessibility of that stretch of DNA to enzymes and transcription factors. Methylation of the histone generally impedes gene expression, whereas acetylation loosens the chromatin and promotes gene expression"....[3]

Kuzawa and Sweet state that epigenetics as an explanation of how phenotypes can be altered is a "revolution in biology that is gathering momentum". "By demonstrating one important way that the impact of a gene on the phenotype can be modified by the environment, this new understanding of epigenetic processes is helping shed light on this issue".[4] Epigenetic inheritance of health problems can be caused by stressors including "psychosocial stress" during pregnancy, and "can perpetuate changed biological settings to offspring".[5]

---

2   Totipotent *stem* cells have the potential to develop into any cell found in the human body.

3   C. W. Kuzawa and E. Sweet, 2008, 4-5.

4   Ibid., 6.

5   Ibid.

Epigenetics

Applying this epigenetics "inheritance of acquired characteristics" to how races and *ethnoi* are formed, we might hypothesise that epigenetic changes to the phenotype could impress on the shared experiences of groups, and that "psychosocial" stressors can have both positive and negative impacts that encompass not only individual experiences, but collective experiences. Hence, such hitherto unexplained concepts as "race memory", "race soul", "national soul", etc., dismissed by rationalists as superstition, might be explained by epigenetic experiences that become collectively acquired characteristics. Such "race traits" might be reinforced through the continuation of those shared experiences, such as continuity of landscape, climate, nutrition, wars, challenges and achievements.

Kuzawa and Sweet contend that epigenetics challenges the inflexibility of race and explains the mechanism for Boas' data on the flexibility of racial phenotypes:

"As emphasized by Boas (1912) a century ago, the contingency of the adult phenotype on environmental conditions experienced during growth and development poses a fundamental challenge to essentialist concepts of race. Current research on developmental and epigenetic contributions to adult health disparities is updating Boas' argument. Not only are traditional racial categories poor predictors of gene frequencies, a fact that has been appreciated for decades, but developmental and epigenetic processes help to clarify why genes do not determine biological fates in any simple fashion. *Genes rarely 'determine' phenotypes but instead set the range of outcomes that a biological system may create as it interacts with and responds to the developmental environment.* Humans inhabit highly variable and socially stratified ecologies; it follows that systems that coordinate adaptation to these realities should come equipped with a capacity to organize in response to local patterns of stress and opportunity".[6] [Emphasis added].

The relation of epigenetics to race and "ethnicity", has proceeded apace among scientists because of the importance it has on identifying health risks to ethnicities. Hence, the significance of the formation of

---

6   Ibid., 10.

ethnoi cannot be avoided. One detailed study by a multidiscipline team from the medical and biological sciences, begins by stating that:

> "Race and ethnicity are social constructs; that is, they are not necessarily defined biologically. However, shared ancestry will produce genetic links between members of a group. In addition, members of an ethnic group often share a culture or environment that may influence their risk of disease. For example, the 'Mediterranean diet' inspired by the dietary habits of Southern Italians has been shown to reduce the risk of heart disease, diabetes and cancer".[7]

In considering the epigenetic and environmental factors impacting on ethnicity and disease the study posits that,

> "...*racial and ethnic categories also reflect the shared experiences* and exposures to known risk factors for disease, such as air pollution and tobacco smoke, poverty, and inadequate access to medical services, which have all contributed to worse disease outcomes in certain populations. Thus, it is unclear whether defining groups through genetic ancestry can capture these shared exposures. In this work we seek to explore the contributions of genetically defined ancestry and social, cultural and environmental factors to understanding differential methylation between ethnic groups".[8] [Emphasis added].

Where such researchers refer to environmental pollutants etc. as having epigenetic influences on "certain populations", our interest is in the epigenetic influence of "shared experiences" (i.e. history) and a multiplicity of other factors in shaping a "race" however one calls a "certain population" clustered with common traits. The primary point is that "racial and ethnic categories also reflect the shared experiences…"

> "The discovery of methylation quantitative trait loci (meQTL's) across populations … established the influence of genetic factors on methylation levels in a variety of tissue types, with meQTL's explaining between 22% and 63% of the variance in

---

7 Joshua M. Galanter, et al., 2017.
8 Ibid.

methylation levels. Multiple environmental factors have also been shown to affect methylation levels, including endocrine disruptors, tobacco smoke, polycyclic aromatic hydrocarbons, infectious pathogens, particulate matter, diesel exhaust particles, allergens, heavy metals, and other indoor and outdoor pollutants. Psychosocial factors, including measures of traumatic experiences, socioeconomic status, and general perceived stress also affect methylation levels".[9]

Psychosocial factors affecting the "methylation quantitative trait loci across populations" represents the shared historical experience of a population which might comprise more than one *ethnos*, and hence, form from originally diverse elements a *super-ethnos*. This is typically maintained by a common mythos, whether based on fact or fantasy, or a mixture, and often assuming religious status, which might sanctify "traumatic experiences, socioeconomic status, and general perceived stress". Hence, the mythos or religion sustains over subsequent generations epigenetic inheritance. Judaism epitomises this effect with its focus on perceived levels of stress and trauma ("persecution"), while perhaps contributing to higher rates of hysteria, neuroses, and paranoia among Jewish populations.[10]

In examining different Latin American groups Galanter et al stated that "even after adjusting for ancestry, significant differences in methylation remained between the groups at multiple loci, reflecting social and environmental influences upon methylation".

> "Our findings have important implications for both the use of ancestry to capture biological changes and of race/ethnicity to account for social and environmental exposures. Epigenome-wide association studies in diverse populations may be susceptible to confounding due to environmental exposures in addition to confounding due to population stratification. The findings also have implications for the common practice of considering individuals of Latino descent, regardless of origin as a single ethnic group.

---

9   Ibid.

10 Raphael Patai, The Jewish Mind. Studies by L. Srole indicated that the rate of neuroses and character disorders among Jews is "three times as high" as that of Protestants and Catholics. (416).

"We conclude that systematic environmental differences between ethnic subgroups likely play an important role in shaping the methylome for both individuals and populations".[11]

"...It is also possible that environmental exposures correlate with ancestry and that participants with certain ancestral backgrounds may have been more exposed to *in utero* tobacco smoke than those of other backgrounds. Several studies have shown correlations between genetic ancestry and environmental exposures, including socioeconomic status, overweight and obesity, and birth site and country of residence".[12]

Certain traits acquired from the environment including those to which pregnant women are subjected, generation after generation, are inherited as acquired characteristics. These become race characteristics for good or ill, physiologically, psychologically, morally, spiritually, and culturally. The Galanter study comments:

"...[W]e find that CpG[13] sites known to be influenced by social and environmental exposures are also differentially methylated between ethnic subgroups. These findings called attention to a more complete understanding of the effect of social and environmental variables on methylation in the context of race and ethnicity to fully understanding this complex process".[14]

A race or *ethnos* becomes the conveyer of traits that are acquired epigenetically. Race is dynamic rather than static because situations are forever changing. Epigenetic changes can have destructive or constructive results over generations and help to explain why cultures collapse for reasons other than miscegenation, where the race might have remained stable as a phenotype, but epigenetically it has been destabilised.

What is of additional interest is that liberal and Marxist notions of race-denial can have adverse impact upon those *ethnoi* that such

---

11   Galanter, et al.

12   Ibid.

13   CpG sites: regions of DNA nucleotide sequences, changes of which result in epigenetics.

14   Galanter, et al.

ideological crusaders claim to champion in the fight against "racism". Dr. Esteban Burchard of the University of California San Francscio, commented on the implications for medicine:

> "The future of medicine, Dr. Burchard argued, carefully considers genetic ancestry, race, ethnicity and culture all at the same time. He published research back in 2011 showing how far the medical research establishment is from factoring in the nuances of race and ethnicity. That 2011 research showed that 94 percent of study participants in modern genetic studies are white, Dr. Buchard said. 'We study whites a lot, and then we try to generalize that to Sri Lankans, blacks, Asians, and other racial groups. That's not just socially unjust, it's bad science and bad medicine'".[15]

One might say in this context that liberalism and the enforced dogma of universal equality to create a nebulous mass humanity, can be literally bad for one's health.

Liberal Reaction

What is of concern to liberal-activist academics is that the concept of genetically fixed races might be replaced by the concept of epigenetically-formed races. Epigenetics might be used to validate not only Boas and his more dogmatic left-wing protégés and heirs, but also "reactionaries" such as Jung and Spengler.

Becky Mansfield, Associate Professor of Geography at Ohio State University, sees epigenetics as an exciting new science that can be both "anti-racist" but also used as a new theory of race-formation. She claims that "racism forms race" epigenetically. As in other liberal theories, the dynamics of history are ignored. Epigenetics is a means by which history forms race.

Nietzsche had prefigured epigenetics in defining "race" in 1886, writing:

---

[15] "Culture etched on our DNA more than previously known, research suggests", CBS News 11 January 2017; http://www.cbsnews.com/news/culture-etched-onto-our-dna-more-than-previously-known-research-says/

"That which his ancestors most liked to do and most constantly did cannot be erased from a man's soul... It is quite impossible that a man should not have in his body the qualities and preferences of his parents and forefathers, whatever appearances may say to the contrary. This constitutes the problem of race".[16]

Further on, Nietzsche elaborates on this race-forming process and what is at the foundation of differences among the aggregates of people that form races and peoples:

"What ultimately is common sense? - Words are sounds designating concepts; concepts, however, are more or less definite images designating frequently recurring and associated sensations, groups of sensations. To understand one another it is not sufficient to employ the same words; we have also to employ the same words to designate the same species of inner experiences, we must ultimately have our experience *in common*. That is why the members of *one* people understand one another better than do members of differing peoples even when they use the same language; or rather when human beings have lived together for a long time under similar conditions (of climate, soil, danger, needs, work) there *arises* from this a group who 'understand one another', a people. In every soul in this group an equivalent number of frequently recurring experiences has gained the upper hand over those which come more rarely: it is on the basis of these that people understand one another, quickly and ever more quickly ... it is on the basis of this quick understanding that they unite together, closely and ever more closely ...".[17]

Here a people (volk) is defined not by frequency of genes, but by frequency of experience, and "groups of sensations". Nietzsche also points to the importance of language in expressing the soul of a race, and the fundamental incommunicability between different peoples even when the race of another is learnt. Rudyard Kipling poetically rendered such incommunicability that explains more than any number

---

16 Nietzsche, *Beyond Good and Evil* (264), 184.
17 Ibid. (268), 186.

Epigenetics

of clichés on multiculturalism and the "oneness of humanity", that today, in contrast to Kipling's time, every people except the Westerner understand:

> The Stranger within my gate,
> He may be true or kind,
> But he does not talk my talk-
> I cannot feel his mind.
> I see the face and the eyes and the mouth,
> But not the soul behind.
> The men of my own stock,
> They may do ill or well,
> But they tell the lies I am wanted to,
> They are used to the lies I tell;
> And we do not need interpreters
> When we go to buy or sell. [18]

Nietzsche's outlook, while at odds with the Nazi race doctrine that attempted to misappropriate him, is consistent with Spengler and Jung, both of whom he influenced. Nietzsche is stating that "race" is formed by ancestral experience, or what we might call "history", and forms the race soul that Jung called the archetypes of the collective unconscious.

In the liberal's use of epigenetics, if the patriarchal white ruling class treats Blacks in a certain manner then Blacks will acquire those characteristics projected onto them, which are epigenetically conveyed to subsequent generations. "Race" is thereby reduced to being a concept by which a ruling class that lacks melanin oppresses individuals who do have melanin, and a "non-white race" is thereby formed. Presumably, all white *ethnoi* are mental projections of white-skinned ruling classes. What can one make of white-skinned poor? Do they epigenetically become another race on account of how they are regarded and treated by their white ruling class? Or is it only possible for non-whites to be exploited, while the most economically dire whites are regarded as somehow sharing in the legacy of the "white patriarchal system"? What is being defined is an economic class, not a race. The Leftist must resort to economic reductionism; to Marxist banalities that reduce history to the forces of production, as we have seen.

---

18   Kipling, *The Stanger*.

The Decline and Fall of Civilisations

In a draft paper on epigenetics and the toxicity of fish in the diet of Blacks, Professor Mansfield, in a muddled style, laments the "intensification of racialization" that might be caused by the epigenetic theory, which otherwise should be harnessed to the "anti-racist" cause:

> "What I will show is that, far from making race meaningless, epigenetic biopolitics marks a transformation and even intensification of racialization. To the extent that biology is mutable, then evidence that childbearing women of color fail to properly manage their individual and collective bodies doubly proves that race exists, and exists on the body. First, through their improper management, they show that they are indeed different: incapable of being the rational, liberal subject, always implicitly racialized as white. Secondly, this incapacity remakes their bodies and those of their children: difference becomes quite material, in the form of altered neurodevelopment. This is the process of making race a biophysical difference from a white norm, written not in practices but in the structure of the brain, the working of the body, and the remaking of the reproductive system".[19]

By treating Blacks differently, even in warning Blacks as to the effects of a toxic diet on pregnancy, U.S. health authorities are perpetuating stereotypes about Blacks that will be epigenetically acquired and become transmitted race traits. This can make a social construct or "fiction" into a biological reality. A pregnant Black woman is encouraged to feel a certain way about herself, and that outlook is epigenetically passed along to her offspring, and it seems subsequent generations, thereby becoming a racial characteristic.

> "Whereas race may have started as a fiction—a social construction—through epigenetic biopolitics it is made quite material, not just in phenomenological embodiment, but in the molecular-environmental development of individuals. ... In this epigenetic biopolitics, in which the aim is to affect cellular processes of the developing fetus, it is the always already the pregnant woman who is racialized and who, through her actions, produces embodied race".[20]

---

19   Becky Mansfield, 2017.
20   Ibid.

Epigenetics

Professor Mansfield is addressing health authority programmes aiming to warn races on the toxicity of methylmercury in their diet, and in so doing reinforcing race, which is apparently to be regarded as a negative outcome. The liberal seems to be in a no-win situation:

> "Risk analysis has recast the problem and solution in ways that make race more rather than less salient, and that could even lead to new biophysical differences among people of purportedly different 'races.' A woman's abnormal, racialized diet is written on her child's brain. Suddenly, racial differences in intelligence - long one of the key axes of racialization - become real. The reality of such racial differences would be especially apparent, as 'truth,' when measured as populations: methylmercury might only affect a small slice of, say, black people, yet still be measurable on a population basis, so that it might be possible to find significant differences in intelligence among 'blacks' and 'whites.'"[21]

While Professor Mansfield seems to be an "activist academic" of the Left, who hopes to see epigenetics used to counter "racism", she sees the other course being the "intensification of racialization". She sees white "racism", even if well-intentioned in warning about the toxicity of diet, as epigenetically reinforcing racial stereotypes. Yet epigenetics is not a man-made construct any more than Mendelian genetics, or the law of gravity. Epigenetics shows much more than how "racism" can impact on race-formation in a negative manner. History exists beyond how Blacks in the USA might be treated by the "patriarchal white ruling class". Epigenetics explains how history, challenges of landscape, and a myriad other factors, can be passed along through generations to form a race-type. To assume that this is negative, to aim at its elimination behind the banner of "anti-racism", is to try to end history and impose a global, static uniformity to create a nebulous mass called "mankind". Even differences in landscape would have to be obliterated. Ecological interaction ranging from New York Jews to Amazon Amerindians would have to be made uniform to eliminate the epigenetic curse of race-formation. All experiences, both positive and negative, would have to be somehow made uniform to achieve the same epigenetic results in creating a raceless mass.

---

21   Ibid.

Maurizio Meloni, Senior Research Fellow at the Department of Sociological Studies, University of Sheffield, likewise sees a bright new liberal hope in epigenetics, but also laments that it might result in the revival of eugenics, which he calls "some worrying signs":

> "Epigenetics is generally considered to be a basis for a better, more progressive, liberal and inclusive social policy. If the environment is much more important than we thought in shaping our fate, there seems to be much more space to attack inequality at its root... But is that the whole truth? To understand the darker implications of epigenetics, just think back through human history. There certainly is no shortage of war, famine, exploitation, destruction, epidemic and trauma. Knowing that some of this can leave a biological trace in our genes – which can even be transmitted to future generations – could be problematic. Even in the 1920s, some believed that the environment could influence inheritance. Some focused on the fact that we could inherit the best of our civilisation and become better humans, while others argued that certain populations had been exposed to various pathogenic environments (alcoholism, poverty, promiscuity, hot climate) for too long, becoming irreparably damaged... Around 1910, English physician, writer and maverick supporter of eugenics, Caleb Saleeby, for example, spoke about 'racial poison' to describe the destructive effects toxins such as alcohol could have on entire populations ('race'). The implication was that some races, or social groups, had an acquired inferiority to others".[22]

Hence, the problem for the liberals is that while there is a widespread assumption that "epigenetics will lead to a more liberal and egalitarian society", it can also lead to new insights on race and history.

Epigenetics has the potential to explain of how responses to landscape, the impact of wars, famine, revolutions, disease, diet, climate, etc., can mould a "race". Such shared experiences are reinforced when of long duration and inter-generational, thereby establishing a race-type.

---

22 Maurizio Meloni, 2016.

Behavioural Epigenetics

Epigenetic studies on mice by Randy Jirtle of Duke University showed that "when female mice are fed a diet rich in methyl groups, the fur pigment of subsequent offspring is permanently altered. Without any change to DNA at all, methyl groups could be added or subtracted, and the changes were inherited much like a mutation in a gene". Moshe Szyf, molecular biologist and geneticist, and Michael Meaney, neurobiologist, both with McGill University, Montreal, hypothesised whether severe stressors could epigenetically cause neuron changes in the human brain? This marked the beginning of a new branch of science: "behavioural epigenetics".[1]

Dan Hurley of *Discover* magazine writes of what we might term race-history:

> "According to the new insights of behavioral epigenetics, traumatic experiences in our past, or in our recent ancestors' past, leave molecular scars adhering to our DNA. Jews whose great-grandparents were chased from their Russian shtetls; Chinese whose grandparents lived through the ravages of the Cultural Revolution; young immigrants from Africa whose parents survived massacres; adults of every ethnicity who grew up with alcoholic or abusive parents — all carry with them more than just memories".[2]

To the last comment, it might be add that "just memories" could be *racial memories*, or what Jung called the "collective unconscious", which has levels specific to races, as well as levels that are so primal as to be common to all humans. While it is predicable that the writer refers to "every ethnicity" but only refers to Jews, Chinese and Africans, to these might be added the experiences of the Highland Clearances of the Scots; the Civil War and the Reconstruction era of American Southerners, and the Great Famine of the Irish. Such epigenetic inheritance would be reinforced by incorporation into myths and folk-tales.

---

1   Dan Hurley, 2013;
2   Ibid.

Behavioural Epigenetics

Judaism is a living tradition that sustains the Jewish ethnos across time and locality by incorporating myths and experiences as shared memories. The newest mythos of "The Holocaust" has become as much part of this sustaining tradition in Judaism as Purim and Passover. In regard to the epigenetic impact of this on the Jewish collective unconscious, or race memory, a recent genetic study of 32 Jewish men and women who had experienced trauma during World War II, and of their children, compared with Jewish families who had lived outside of Europe during the war, concluded that there is "an association of preconception parental trauma with epigenetic alterations that is evident in both exposed parent and offspring, providing potential insight into how severe psychophysiological trauma can have intergenerational effects".[3]

> "Cytosine methylation within the gene encoding for FK506 binding protein 5 (FKBP5) was measured in Holocaust survivors (n= 32), their adult offspring (n= 22), and demographically comparable parent (n= 8) and offspring (n= 9) control subjects, respectively. Cytosine-phosphate-guanine sites for analysis were chosen based on their spatial proximity to the intron 7 glucocorticoid response elements".[4]

The only way by which such behavioural epigenetic "intensification of racialization", so lamented by liberal academia, other than when it sustains the positive self-identity of Jews, Blacks, and Asians, could be eliminated is by obliterating collective race memories, both positive and negative. This is precisely what is being undertaken in trying to impose historical forgetfulness on European *ethnoi*. An recent example is the campaign to prohibit the Confederate flag, reinforced by a guilt complex instilled in Southerners in identifying their heritage as founded on nothing other than slavery.

---

3   Rachel Yahuda et al., 372–38.
4   Ibid.

Morphic Field Theory

To the rationalistic modern Western mind, concepts like "race memory", *zeitgeist*, "spirit of the nation" etc. are akin to the astral plane of occultists, the abode of angels, devils, gods, hidden masters, and spirits. Carl Jung as a scientist saw the existence of *archetypes*, the recurrent symbols common to races, *ethnoi*, and the human species, within the collective unconscious, in dreams. Dr. Rupert Sheldrake's theory of morphic fields and morphic resonance provide theories applicable to such concepts. Sheldrake is an eminent researcher in biochemistry and cell biology. While eminently qualified in the empirical sciences,[1] his theories challenge materialist assumptions. Sheldrake questions the dogmatic primacy materialism has been assumed in science:

> "Committed materialists are committed precisely because they believe that materialistic explanations will be found in the future. They put their trust in what they hope for — in what is not yet known. The philosopher of science Karl Popper called this attitude 'promissory materialism,' because it involves issuing undated promissory notes for future discoveries. Promissory materialism is a faith".[2]

Formative Causation

Sheldrake's revolutionary theory of "formative causation", first proposed in 1981, "postulates that organisms are subject to an influence from previous similar organisms by a process called morphic resonance".

> "Through morphic resonance, each member of a species draws upon, and in turn contributes to a pooled or collective memory. Thus, for example, if animals learn a new skill in one place, similar animals raised under similar conditions should subsequently tend to learn the same thing more readily all over the world. Likewise, people should tend to learn more readily what others have already learnt, even in the absence

---

1   http://www.sheldrake.org/about-rupert-sheldrake

2   "Sheldrake's response to Michael Shermer", http://www.thebestschools.org/sheldrake-shermer-materialism-science-responses/

of any known means of connection or communication. In the human realm, this hypothesis resembles C.G. Jung's postulate of the collective unconscious. The hypothesis also applies in the chemical and physical realms, and predicts, for example, that crystals of new compounds should become easier to crystallize all over the world the more often they are made. There is already circumstantial evidence that this actually happens".[3]

Does Sheldrake's theory of "formative causation" offer an explanation as to how there can be collective memories across time and space, among a species? If "similar animals raised under similar conditions" contributed by experience to a "collective memory", then, as Jung contended with the collective unconscious, not only are these applicable to the human species in general, but to the visions of races and *ethnoi* within that species. In regard to the human species, and the races and *ethnoi* within, we call the learning and conditions "culture" and history. "Formative causation" provides an added factor in the process of race formation by history, as does epigenetics. Sheldrake sees epigenetics as an allied area of research.[4]

Although the human species has an underlying unity through common learning and experiences when traced back to the most primordial of beginnings, expressed at the most primitive levels of hominid life, there are also differentiations among the races and *ethnoi* that have developed over millennia. Perhaps Sheldrake has not reached this conclusion, although Jung, as seen, did in postulating that each race has its own psychology. At least, it seems, there is an implied "race memory" in Sheldrake's morphic resonance theory, when he states: "One of the most striking implications of morphic resonance concerns memory. Morphic resonance depends on similarity. The greater the similarity, the stronger the resonance".[5]

In summarising "formative causation", Sheldrake describes the manner

---

[3] Rupert Sheldrake, "An Experimental Test of the Hypothesis of Formative Causation", Rivista di Biologia - Biology Forum 86 (3/4), 1992, 431-44; 86 (3/4), 431-44, (1992); http://www.sheldrake.org/research/morphic-resonance/an-experimental-test-of-the-hypothesis-of-formative-causation

[4] Sheldrake, "Epigenetics and Soviet biology", http://www.sheldrake.org/about-rupert-sheldrake/blog/epigenetics-and-soviet-biology

[5] "Sheldrake's response to Michael Shermer".

The Decline and Fall of Civilisations

Dr Rupert Sheldrake

by which acquired characteristics could be inherited through repetition of behaviour and become a predominance trait. The forms of an organism are predetermined by a pattern that exists at a morphogenetic field. A morphogenetic field is itself formed by the cumulative influence of similar fields that have been built up. A form has been established through the repetitive experience of "the ancestors of that organism". A pattern has been established from which to build and has been fixed in a morphogenetic field. Like epigenetics, the hypothesis offers an explanation for the formation of an organism beyond the Darwinian evolutionary hypothesis of random mutations. Sheldrake writes:

"I have recently developed a hypothesis, called the hypothesis of formative causation, which takes as its starting point the idea that morphogenetic fields are indeed physical. ... This hypothesis proposes that specific morphogenetic fields are responsible for the organization and form of material systems at all levels of complexity, not only in living organisms but also in crystals, molecules and atoms. These fields order the systems with which they are associated by affecting events which, from an energetic point of view, appear to be indeterminate or probabilistic; they impose patterned restrictions on the energetically possible outcomes of processes of physical change.

"If morphogenetic fields are responsible for the form and organization of material systems, they must themselves have characteristic structures. So where do these field structures come from? The answer suggested is that they are derived from the morphogenetic fields associated with previous similar systems: the morphogenetic fields of all past systems become present to any subsequent similar system; the structures of past systems affect subsequent similar systems by a cumulative influence which acts across both space and time. According to this hypothesis, systems are organized in the way they are because similar systems were organized that way in the past. For example, the molecules of a complex organic chemical crystallize in a characteristic pattern because the same substance crystallized that way before; a plant takes up the form characteristic of its species because past members of the species took up that form; and an animal acts instinctively in a particular manner because similar animals behaved that way in the past.

"The hypothesis is concerned with the repetition of forms and patterns of organization; the question of the origin of these forms and patterns lies outside its scope. This question can be answered in several different ways, but all of them seem to be equally compatible with the suggested means of repetition. A number of testable predictions can be deduced from this hypothesis which differ strikingly from those of the conventional mechanistic theory. Two examples will suffice. The first concerns the inheritance of form, which according to the hypothesis of formative causation depends both on recognized genetic factors and on a direct influence from similar past organisms.

"The larger the number of similar past organisms, the greater should be this influence. Thus, for instance, in first-generation hybrids produced by crossing plants of two varieties, A and B, the form of the variety which has had the largest number of past individuals should generally tend to be dominant. If both varieties have had similar numbers of past individuals, the hybrids should generally be of intermediate form. Now if hybrid seeds produced in such crosses are kept in cold storage while very large numbers of one of the parental types, say B, are grown, and then if these seeds are taken out of storage and sown, the form of the resulting plants should resemble the parent B type more strongly than in the original hybrids, even though they were grown from identical seeds. Thus in the hybrids the dominance of one parental form over the other should change even though the genetic constitution of the seeds remains the same. The second example involves changes in the rate of learning of new patterns of behaviour. If an animal, say a rat, learns to carry out a new task, which can be specially devised for the purpose of this experiment, there should be a tendency for all subsequent similar rats (of the same breed, reared under similar conditions, etc.) to learn more quickly to carry out the same pattern of behaviour. The larger the number of rats that learn to perform the task, the easier should it be for any subsequent similar rat to learn it.

"Thus, for instance, if thousands of rats were trained to perform a new task in a laboratory in London, similar rats should learn to carry out the same task more quickly in laboratories everywhere else. If the speed of learning of rats in another laboratory, say in New York, were to be measured before and after the rats in London were trained, the rats tested on the second occasion should learn more quickly than those tested on the first. The effect should take place in the absence of any known type of physical connection or communication between the two laboratories. Such a prediction may seem so improbable as to be absurd. Yet, remarkably enough, there is already evidence from laboratory studies of rats that the predicted effect actually occurs. This hypothesis leads to an interpretation of many physical and biological phenomena which is radically different from that of existing theories, and enables a number of well-known problems to be seen in a new light. Its value will be uncertain until some of its predictions have been tested experimentally. But for the time being, it may serve to show that a specific organismic hypothesis is at least conceivable".[6]

Rejecting the materialistic and mechanistic world-views that have been dominant in Western biology since the 1920s, Sheldrake suggests that the universe is "more like an organism than a machine". Sheldrake, having been eminent in the field of genetic research, nonetheless departs from the current dogma and states of DNA:

"However, there is a big difference between coding for the structure of a protein - a chemical constituent of the organism

---

[6] Rupert Sheldrake, 1981, Part III: Organicism, 308-309.

Morphic Field Theory

- and programming the development of an entire organism. It is the difference between making bricks and building a house out of the bricks. You need the bricks to build the house. If you have defective bricks, the house will be defective. But the plan of the house is not contained in the bricks, or the wires, or the beams, or cement".[7]

The DNA is the same in all the cells of an organism; the same for arms and legs, etc., and does not account for the differences of form between an arm and a leg. Mechanistic biology still does not even claim to understand what is involved. *Morphogenesis* contends that the form of an organism is shaped by morphogenetic fields both in and around the organism. Sheldrake writes: "As an oak tree develops, the acorn is associated with an oak tree field, an invisible organizing structure which organizes the oak tree's development; it is like an oak tree mould, within which the developing organism grows".[8] The existence of morphogenetic patterns is suggested by the ability of fractured organisms to reconstitute themselves back to their form-pattern:

"One fact which led to the development of this theory is the remarkable ability organisms have to repair damage. If you cut an oak tree into little pieces, each little piece, properly treated, can grow into a new tree. So from a tiny fragment, you can get a whole. Machines do not do that; they do not have this power of remaining whole if you remove parts of them. Chop a computer up into small pieces and all you get is a broken computer. It does not regenerate into lots of little computers. But if you chop a flatworm into small pieces, each piece can grow into a new flatworm".[9]

Organisms, chemicals, and crystals are physical expressions of preexisting forms that are within a morphic field. Plato stated that *Form* expresses the actual substance of an object beyond the physical, material aspects. Goethe as a naturalist postulated a similar theory. A basic explanation of Plato's *Forms* states:

"A form is an abstract property or quality. Take any property of

---

[7] Rupert Sheldrake, 1987, 9-25.

[8] Ibid.

[9] Ibid.

an object; separate it from that object and consider it by itself, and you are contemplating a form. For example, if you separate the roundness of a basketball from its colour, its weight, etc. and consider just roundness by itself, you are thinking of the form of roundness. Plato held that this property existed apart from the basketball, in a different mode of existence than the basketball. The form is *not* just the idea of roundness you have in your mind. It exists independently of the basketball and independently of whether someone thinks of it. All round objects, not just this basketball, *participate* or *copy* this same form of roundness.[10]

Aristotle thought that an object is the organisation of matter by Form. He sought to explain Plato's doctrine of Forms in regard to the organisation of matter. A basic explanation states:

"Take as an example a child playing with building blocks. The child could use the same blocks to first build a wall, and then tear it down and build a house. The material or matter in each case would be the same, the blocks. Yet, the house and the wall have the matter arranged in different ways. They have different forms. The house is still just one material object; yet it has two different aspects, its form and its matter. All objects then have matter, or the material of which they are composed, and form, the way the matter is arranged. It is the form of a thing, however, that makes a thing what it is. When the child knocked down the block wall, the blocks or matter remained. The wall no longer existed, however, because the blocks no longer had the arrangement or form characteristic of a wall. It is the form of an object that makes it the particular object that it is".[11]

The soul is the *Form* of some organisms, and God is the cause. Such a theory accounts for the causality that is regarded as essential to the rational Western mind, while recognising the role of God and soul that have been destroyed by Western rationalism. Saint Anselm, the 11th century theologian who helped to disentangle Christianity from Levantine magic and mysticism and re-create it as the religion of

---

10 "Plato's Theory of Forms", Saint Anselm College, http://www.anselm.edu/homepage/dbanach/platform.htm

11 "Some main points of Aristotle's thought", Saint Anselm College; http://www.anselm.edu/homepage/dbanach/arist.htm

Western High Culture, by considering such questions as the existence of God and soul from logic, causal perspective, using his so-called "ontological argument" for the existence of God. Sheldrake, who alludes to Aristotle and Plato, approaches similar questions from the perspective of empirical science in the Western tradition. He alludes to *Form* in describing morphic fields and their role in the manifestation of both species and individuals:

"Each species has its own fields, and within each organism there are fields within fields. Within each of us is the field of the whole body; fields for arms and legs and fields for kidneys and livers; within are fields for the different tissues inside these organs, and then fields for the cells, and fields for the sub-cellular structures, and fields for the molecules, and so on. There is a whole series of fields within fields. The essence of the hypothesis I am proposing is that these fields, which are already accepted quite widely within biology, have a kind of in-built memory derived from previous forms of a similar kind. The liver field is shaped by the forms of previous livers and the oak tree field by the forms and organization of previous oak trees. Through the fields, by a process called morphic resonance, the influence of like upon like, there is a connection among similar fields. That means that the field's structure has a cumulative memory, based on what has happened to the species in the past.

"If you make a new compound and crystallize it, there won't be a morphic field for it the first time. Therefore, it may be very difficult to crystallize; you have to wait for a morphic field to emerge. The second time, however, even if you do this somewhere else in the world, there will be an influence from the first crystallization, and it should crystallize a bit more easily. The third time there will be an influence from the first and second, and so on. There will be a cumulative influence from previous crystals, so it should get easier and easier to crystallize the more often you crystallize it. And, in fact, this is exactly what does happen. Synthetic chemists find that new compounds are generally very difficult to crystallize. As time goes on, they generally get easier to crystallize all over the world".[12]

---

12   Sheldrake, "Morphic resonance: introduction", http://www.sheldrake.org/research/morphic-resonance/introduction

Through experience there is a build-up of group memory or what Jung in humans called the collective unconscious. Whereas Jung and analytical psychologists rely largely on dream interpretation and the archetypes that appear in dreams, Sheldrake as a biochemist cites laboratory experiments on organisms that indicate experiences contribute to a group memory and are passed along to generations of a species across time and distance. Sheldrake continues:

"There are quite a number of experiments that can be done in the realm of biological form and the development of form. Correspondingly, the same principles apply to behaviour, forms of behaviour and patterns of behaviour. Consider the hypothesis that if you train rats to learn a new trick in Santa Barbara, then rats all over the world should be able to learn to do the same trick more quickly, just because the rats in Santa Barbara have learned it. This new pattern of learning will be, as it were, in the rat collective memory - in the morphic fields of rats, to which other rats can tune in, just because they are rats and just because they are in similar circumstances, by morphic resonance. This may seem a bit improbable, but either this sort of thing happens or it doesn't.

"Among the vast number of papers in the archives of experiments on rat psychology, there are a number of examples of experiments in which people have actually monitored rates of learning over time and discovered mysterious increases. In my book, *A New Science of Life*, I describe one such series of experiments which extended over a 50-year period. Begun at Harvard and then carried on in Scotland and Australia, the experiment demonstrated that rats increased their rate of learning more than tenfold. This was a huge effect - not some marginal statistically significant result. This improved rate of learning in identical learning situations occurred in these three separate locations and in all rats of the breed, not just in rats descended from trained parents".[13]

Sheldrake suggests the inheritance of acquired characteristics that are imparted through ways other than by DNA. As we have seen,

---

13 Ibid.

epigenetics is arriving at similar conclusions. Sheldrake states:

> "I am suggesting that heredity depends not only on DNA, which enables organisms to build the right chemical building blocks - the proteins - but also on morphic resonance. Heredity thus has two aspects: one a genetic heredity, which accounts for the inheritance of proteins through DNA's control of protein synthesis; the second a form of heredity based on morphic fields and morphic resonance, which is nongenetic and which is inherited directly from past members of the species. This latter form of heredity deals with the organization of form and behaviour".[14]

If we more specifically allude in human terms to races and *ethnoi*, and to history and collective experiences shared over generations, and reinforced by customs, legends, ethics, institutions and religions, which we collectively call "culture", a theory of race-formation through epigenetics and formative causation emerges. These theories converge also with Jungian psychology of the collective unconscious. Sheldrake comments on the application of his theory to Jung's:

> "Jung thought of the collective unconscious as a collective memory, the collective memory of humanity. He thought that people would be more tuned into members of their own family and race and social and cultural group, but that nevertheless there would be a background resonance from all humanity: a pooled or averaged experience of basic things that all people experience (e.g., maternal behaviour and various social patterns and structures of experience and thought). It would not be a memory from particular persons in the past so much as an average of the basic forms of memory structures; these are the *archetypes*. Jung's notion of the collective unconscious makes extremely good sense in the context of the general approach that I am putting forward. Morphic resonance theory would lead to a radical reaffirmation of Jung's concept of the collective unconscious..."[15]

---

14   Ibid.

15   Sheldrake, http://www.sheldrake.org/research/morphic-resonance/part-i-mind-memory-and-archetype-morphic-resonance-and-the-collective-unconscious

Soil and Race Formation

Race formation and landscape are linked through diet. The changes via what is eaten are conveyed epigenetically. A population cluster attached its *ecological niche*, to use Gumilev's term, is formed over generations epigenetically through what grows in the soil on which one lives, cultivates and harvests or gathers. Because of the generations that are born and die, invest their labour and often their blood for the soil, there is a spiritual connection that shapes an *ethnos*.

A race that has not been rendered soulless by materialism will be deeply attached to the soil; to one's native land; the land of one's ancestors and of one's descendants. Such an outlook will build up as morphic resonance and be passed along to generations epigenetically. Such hitherto mystical concepts as race-soul and archetype might now be explained with empirical evidence.

Eminent Japanese soil scientist Katsuyuki Minami, of Kitasato University, considers the importance of soil on the moulding of culture and *ethnos*, in reference to the way which the health of soil is being destroyed. He makes an interesting point in giving the etymology for the word "culture" as originally meaning "cultivating the soil and raising crops":

> "Culture is therefore inseparable from soil. Over time, the concept became more abstract and began to include both the physical, intellectual and spiritual products derived from altering nature. Therefore, culture includes not only food, clothing and shelter, but also technology, academia, art, morality, religion, politics, and other livelihood-shaping modes".[1]

Professor Minami, coming from a civilisation that has retained some health, as distinct from Western rationalist academics, recognises the bond between a people and the land, including the "spirits of the land". Minami states that "Every ethnic group or region has its own characteristics and great 'spirits of the land'. When people are totally

---

1   Katsuyuki Minami, 2009.

colored by these land spirits, it is proof that they are indigenous to that place".[2]

The Japanese write this as *tsuchi*, *chi* meaning "spirit", and *tsu* meaning "place", hence the Japanese conception of the "genius loci". *Tsuchi* in Japanese tradition signifies something spiritual in the soil. *Chi* also means "blood",[3] indicating the connexion between blood, soil, and spirit. Rites continue to be performed to the spirits of the land by Shinto.

A vestige of the bond between man and soil is alluded to in *Genesis*, when man was formed from soil by God and God's spirit was breathed into him. Here again the etymology of words is instructive: "human" derives from "humus" (soil), and when the human organism dies it returns to the soil, "for dust thou art, and unto dust thou shalt return".[4]

Minami cites the scientist Tukuyaki Fujiwara on the connexion between soil and civilisation, which he calls "cultural soil science"; Minami explaining "that the different types of soil distributed throughout the world have fostered different cultures". Minami quotes Fujiwara's book *Soil and Ancient Japanese Culture: In Search of the Roots of Japanese Culture — An Exploratory Discussion on Cultural Soil Science*: "Because soil is the embodiment of the environment, I believe that cultures come into being with soil as the underlying factor". Fujiwara classifies cultures according to their manner of land cultivation: "rice paddy soil cultures" (China, Japan, India, Thailand); loess cultures (Han Chinese – barley, wheat millet); "oasis soil cultures" (fruit trees, vegetables); grassland soil cultures (Mongols – livestock); "coral limestone soil cultures" (coconut palms, breadfruit trees, banana trees); "laterite soil cultures" (tropical rain forests, savannahs: taro, yams); "red-yellow soil cultures" (slash-and-burn, South East Asia, dry rice, millet, mulberries); "brown forest soil cultures "volcanic ash soil cultures" (slash-and-burn, south East Asia); "podsol cultures" (sub-polar, Siberian *ethnoi* such as Buryats).[5]

---

2   Ibid.
3   Ibid.
4   Genesis 3: 17.
5   Katsuyuki Minami.

The Decline and Fall of Civilisations

Soil degradation has been a factor in the decay of numerous civilisations. Plato wrote in *Critia* of the deforestation of Attica: "as in the case of small islands, all the richer and softer parts of the soil having fallen away, and the mere skeleton of the land being left". The megalithic culture on Easter Island collapsed through deforestation, tree trunks having been used to roll into place the *Maoi* statues. The Mayans decimated the hill side forests causing erosion.[6] Today we should add the deforestation of the Amazon and other environments through the Western economic imperative; likewise with China, and the destruction of soil nutrients through chemical contamination. The careless treatment of the soil returns us to our thesis: the destruction of soil has frequently occurred when a civilisation has reached its cycle of decay when civilisation is disconnected from the cosmic order. Minami comments: "Modern Western society and societies that have adopted its philosophy are consuming precious plant nutrients from the soil at a tremendous rate … in North America, in Asia's river basins, in the broad expanse of Russia, and in almost every other place in the world, the soil is being lost".[7] This crisis of Western civilisation is alluded to by Minami:

> "Because of the many processes and tools used in the real world of agriculture of which most of us are unaware, we have become alienated from the soil and the land. People no longer have a living relationship with the soil and land that produced us. Many of us think of the land as nothing more than a space between the cities that produces crops".[8]

Zoological interpretations of race classified by skull measurements, bone density, and genetic clusters, are insufficient to understand the character of race. Such classification is the product of 19th century materialism, and is a reflection of the *Zeitgeist* of which Britain was the primary harbinger. Measuring and weighing displaced the prior conceptions of race as soul and spirit of the German Idealists such as Herder, Goethe, and Fichte. Ironically Hitlerian racism was influenced more by British and French than by German conceptions. Creativity began to be measured by tests devised by Alfred Binet, for France, and championed by Francis Galton, father of eugenics, in Britain.

---

6   Ibid.
7   Ibid.
8   Ibid.

Soil and Race Formation

The insufficiency of materialistic criteria for the determination of race can be discerned from the agonising statistical work that took place for years in an effort to identify "Kennewick man", originally thought to have been a Caucasoid, and eventually found to be Ainu/proto-Polynesian.[9] Indeed, both Ainu and Polynesian were long regarded as "archaic Caucasians" on the basis of statistical analyses. The disparity between the facial angles of Negroids and Caucasians is still regarded as a measure of evolutionary disparity. However, Polynesians have a facial angle that is vertical,[10] which by such criterion would define them as superior to the Caucasian in a zoological hierarchy.

Physical anthropology fails to sustain racial-materialism as a viable doctrine for studying culture and history. The recourse to Dr. Carleton S. Coon, who stated in his *Origin of Races* that there is an evolutionary lag of 200,000 years between Caucasians and Africans, fails, even when cited by a writer as erudite as Carleton Putnam.[11] Coon, president of the Amercian Association of Physical Anthropologists, saw races as adaptations to changing environments in a series of "phases" of history. He regarded Western technology as having transcended the need for geographical adaptation, thereby making "race" redundant as a survival mechanism. He wrote of the present "phase four" that mankind "is starting to become a single cultural community…"[12] What Coon saw was "a vision of paradise", as he entitled his final chapter, pre-empting Francis Fukuyama's "end of history". He envisaged a world order. The much-maligned "Communist-Jew", Franz Boas, with his cultural studies, is of more value to an appreciation of *ethnos* than Carleton Coon's physical anthropology.

---

9   Douglas Presston, 2014.
10 Philip Houghton, 39-60.
11 Carleton Putnam, 1967, 32-34.
12 Carleton S. Coon, 1957, 406.

Part III

Rise and Fall

I.Q. and Creativity

The decline of civilisations because of *dysgenics*, or down-breeding through the proliferation of those who are of lower I.Q., is often, but not invariably, associated with the mixing of races (*miscegenation*). Hence, *eugenics*, or up-breeding, is the means by which civilisation can be not only maintained but advanced. Eugenics was particularly prominent in Victorian England, founded as a movement by Sir Frances Galton,[1] side-by-side with Darwinism, and found its way to Germany and especially to the USA, where sterilisation laws were enacted in many states to prevent breeding by the "feeble minded". Hitler's Germany was a latecomer in the field. Books such as *Applied Eugenics* became bestsellers in the USA.[2] Eugenics continued to have prominent proponents after World War II, such as Dr. Elmer Pendell,[3] and the Nobel Laureate, physicist Dr. William Shockley. As one would expect the Leftist opposition to eugenics as something suggestive of Hitlerism or as implicitly "racist" has generally been hysterical rather than scholarly. Conversely, eugenics originally had its advocates among the Left, such as the American geneticist Dr. H. J. Muller, who urged Stalin to adopt eugenics to achieve Soviet world superiority,[4] Dr. J. B. S. Haldane in Britain, and Fabian socialists such as playwright George Bernard Shaw.

The Right has remained the diehard champion of eugenics and the importance of hereditary I.Q. in determining the destiny of a civilisation. It is a legacy of the biological materialism that has dominated the Right, while the Left found it opportune to change to an adversary position, and claim to be the champions of disaffected racial minorities. Hence, for the Right the maintenance of civilisation is reduced to a matter of preserving the purity of the "white race", and protecting the racial gene pool from contamination by inferior, non-white genes. Such biological reductionism, like the economic reductionism of Marxism, intends to explain all historical phenomenon

---

1   Francis Galton, Hereditary Genius.
2   Paul Popenoe and Roswell H. Johnson, Applied Eugenics.
3   Elmer Pendell, 1977.
4   H. J. Muller, letter to Stalin, 1936,

I.Q. and Creativity

around a single focus, which in turn is based on the assumption that the white race alone creates civilisation. Hence, if Caucasian mummies are found in China or South America this will be assumed as evidence that even these civilisations were created by whites.

With genetic explanations for the lowering of intelligence as the cause for cultural decline and fall one returns to the counting and measuring fixation of the 19th century.

The highest I.Q. clusters are among north east Asian nations, the lowest among sub-Saharan nations. Can one therefore suppose that the most creative cultures exist among those peoples with the highest average I.Q.s? Statistical analysis of intelligence does not show the élan of a people, or the creativity which is always based on small culture-bearing strata. Those north east Asian states that have the highest I.Q.'s correlated with high GDPs have long since stagnated culturally. They are economically animated by Western technology and a hard work ethic.

Race does not correlate with I.Q. and creativity. The average I.Q. for Greece is 92, which places the Greeks at 15th on a world I.Q. ranking of 43, along with racially-pure Ireland. Italy ranks 5th with an average I.Q. of 102, higher than most other white nations, despite the supposition among race-materialists that Rome fell through miscegenation. Spain is 9th at 98 I.Q. points, and Portugal, 12th at 95.[5]

Where there are significant regional variations, such as that of southern Italy with a lower I.Q. average than the North, race-materialists posit heavy miscegenation for the south, to the extent of occasionally referring to Sicilians (average I.Q. 89) as "niggers", but they are only 3 I.Q. points lower than Ireland. The regional I.Q. variations between north and south in Italy are assumed to reflect the lower economic development of the south. However, during the Classical and the Medieval eras of Italy's history, the development of southern Italy was superior to that of the north. Up until the destruction of the Kingdom of the Two Sicilies during the latter part of the 19th century, the southern kingdom was a glowing example of Western civilisation;[6]

---

5   I.Q. Research, https://iq-research.info/en/page/average-iq-by-country
6   Bolton, "Suppressed Identity: The Kingdom of the Two Sicilies".

yet since these eras there have not been significant genetic shifts.[7] Hence, the current backwardness of southern Italy and the lower average I.Q. cannot be explained by miscegenation or other genetic factors. The Negroid element even in Sicily is marginal at around 2%. The I.Q.'s of the Nordic states are average, Denmark having the same I.Q. as Spain. (Norway 100, Sweden 99, Denmark 98).[8]

It seems that little can be determined from I.Q. as the result of miscegenation. While the highest I.Q. clusters are in Asia and the lowest in sub-Saharan Africa, the multitude of mid-scoring states are not racially consistent. For example, Switzerland, Iceland and Mongolia have the same average I.Q. of 101, placing them near the top of the world I.Q. scale at 6th.[9] Even if it were accepted that Greece was inundated by African genes, that does not explain the same I.Q. score for Ireland. Miscegenated Argentina at 93 is above Ireland, Greece and Bulgaria.

While the Irish in Eire score 92 I.Q. points, Irish-Americans score 99.7. Graeco-Americans score 99, while the average I.Q. score in Greece is 92. However, Dutch-Americans score 95.9, in comparison to their cousins in The Netherlands who score 100. Spanish-Americans score 92.4 compared with the 98 points of their kin in Spain. U.S. American Indians at 91.2[10] are on par with Greeks and Irish. The Hungarian average I.Q. is 98, or 9th on a world scale, but Hungaro-Americans score 101.6.[11]

Brazil with an average I.Q. of 87 has been regarded as a primary example of the consequences of miscegenation. Brazil's self-image is that of a "coloured" nation, while Argentina is regarded as "white". Brazil is regarded by race–materialists as an example of the careless attitude Portuguese had towards preserving their race and a propensity to breed with Negro slaves. One racial theorist asked why Brazil, with such a large land mass, having been settled by the Portuguese since the 16th century and with an abundance of mineral wealth, has remained

---

7   Vittorio Daniele, Paolo Malinima, 844-852.
8   I.Q. Research, op. cit.
9   Ibid.
10   Anatoly Karlin, "Hamburgers and Rednecks: I.Q. Estimates of U.S. Ethnic Groups".
11   Ibid.

stagnant? The answer, it is assumed, lies in race contamination, the Portuguese having from prehistoric times included non-Europoid elements that populated the lower Iberian Peninsula, mixed by both Moorish invasions and Negro slaves, but "revitalized" by "a Teutonic resurgence from the north".[12]

> "Brazil has been for over 400 years a veritable maelstrom of races, a cauldron of multiracialism. No other country in the world has had such a large number of white, black and red races thrown together in such close physical contact… the general result has been the debasement not only of the national racial strain, but to the holding down of economic standards of living of a very low level".[13]

With the advance of genetics mapping we can now understand the racial dynamics of Brazil better than such assumptions. There is no non-European basis to the Portuguese, and subsequent incursions of Moors and Negro slaves have affected the Portuguese only marginally. This will be examined below. The self-identification of Brazilians is often incorrect. Many "white Brazilians" who assume themselves to be "very mixed" were found to have very little African and Indian descent.[14] Dark complexion in Brazil is often the result of U.V. levels rather than genetics. A comprehensive genetic study of Brazilians found that:

> "Once such a correction was performed on the basis of the relative proportion of Amerindian, European and African ancestries, there emerged a higher level of uniformity than expected. In all regions studied the European ancestry was predominant, with proportions being ranging from 60.6% in the Northeast to 77.7% in the South. The African proportion was highest in the Northeast (30.3%), followed in decreasing order by the Southeast (18.9%), South (12.7%), and North (10.9%). On the other hand, the Amerindian proportion was highest in the North (19.4%), while relatively uniform in the other three other regions".[15]

---

12   Seth Adamson, 4-5.
13   Ibid., 8.
14   M. *Helena, L. P. Franco, Tania A. Weimer, F. M. Salzano, 127–132.*
15   Sergio D. J. Pena, et al., 2011.

On the push for a "Black identity" the authors of the 2011 genetic study state:

> "Our results have considerable sociological relevance for Brazil, because the race question presently figures prominently in Brazilian political life. Among the actions of the State in the sphere of race relations are initiatives aimed at strengthening racial identity, especially 'Black identity' encompassing the sum of those self-categorized as Brown or Black in the censuses and government surveys. The argument that non-Whites constitute more than half of the population of the country has been routinely used in arguing for the introduction of public policies favoring the non-White population, especially in the areas of education (racial quotas for entrance to the universities), the labor market, access to land, and so on. Nevertheless, our data presented here do not support such contention, since they show that, for instance, non-White individuals in the North, Northeast and Southeast have predominantly European ancestry and differing proportions of African and Amerindian ancestry".[16]

A study of Brazil cited by Lynn and Vanhanen found that despite the comparatively low mean I.Q. Brazil has the same cluster of talented individuals at public universities as those nations with high mean I.Q.s. The authors state that the cognitive performance of those in Brazil's universities is not lesser to those in the developed nations. The conclusion is that national mean I.Q. is not a good indicator of potential. The estimate is that there are 20 million Brazilians with the top human potentials (10% of the population) and this rivals the quality and magnitude of "human capital in developed countries".[17]

Mensa India, undertaking a research programme to identify unrecognised genius among children, estimate that 5,000,000 with genius level I.Q.s are dwelling in slums.[18] Slums are the abode of India's lowest castes and where according to race-materialists one

---

16 Ibid.
17 Carmen Flores-Mendoza, Keith F. Widaman, Marcela Mansur-Alves, José Humberto da Silva Filho, Sonia Regina Pasian, Carlos Guilherme Marciel Furtado Schlottfeldt, "Considerations about IQ and Human Capital in Brazil", Temas em Psicologia, 2012, Vol. 20, No. 1, 133.
18 C. Weitenberg, "India's Beautiful Minds".

would expect to find the highest concentration of "inferior" Dravidians, whose "blood" contaminated the Aryans and caused the decay of civilisation.

The correlation between creativity and I.Q. has been studied since the early 20th century, pioneered by the educational psychologist Lewis Terman. The genius children in Terman's large sample groups were notable for their contributions to the sciences or arts, whereas several subsequently eminent individuals who missed the minimal I.Q. of 130 for inclusion in the group included Nobel Laurate William Shockley, who became a noted exponent of eugenics.

Inspirare

The attempt to measure creativity statistically is another symptom of the materialistic *Zeitgeist*. Traditional societies recognised that creativity is a reflection of the divine in man. The etymology of "inspiration" comes from the 14th century: Middle English *enspire*, from Old French *inspirer*, from Latin *inspirare*: "breathe or blow into," from *in-* "into" +" *spirare*": "breathe." The implication is one of *spirit*. The word originally described a divine or supernatural being that would "impart a truth or idea to someone," as defined by the *Oxford English Dictionary*. To the Christians inspiration comes from the Holy Spirit, to the Greeks it is imparted by the muses and the Gods Apollo and Dionysus, and to the Norse by Odin.

The Greeks referred to the *daemon* and the Roman to *genius*, as spirits who guided the artist. The American poet Ruth Stone described her inspiration this way:

> "As [Stone] was growing up in rural Virginia, she would be out, working in the fields and she would feel and hear a poem coming at her from over the landscape. It was like a thunderous train of air and it would come barrelling down at her over the landscape. And when she felt it coming... because it would shake the earth under her feet, she knew she had only one thing to do at that point. That was to, in her words, "run like hell" to the house as she would be chased by this poem. The whole deal was that she had to get to a piece of paper fast enough so that when it thundered through her, she could collect it and grab it on the

page. Other times she wouldn't be fast enough, so she would be running and running, and she wouldn't get to the house, and the poem would barrel through her and she would miss it, and it would 'continue on across the landscape looking for another poet'".[19]

The Renaissance epoch destroyed the idea of the divine spark by substituting humanism for religion, the individual who is a "genius" rather than *having* a "genius." Art became a reflection of the individual ego rather than a reflection of the divine, and degraded into narcissism,[20] and in our modern world into psychosis and the degenerate; the projection of the twisted mind of the artist onto canvas, into clay and stone, as architecture and in literature, screen and play scripts, patronised by business interests for profit instead of by aristocrats wanting to promote excellence.

Those such as Ruth Stone who retain that divine spark of creativity recognise that they are mediums for the divine. Flashes of inspiration come over them, and their creativity comes easily and without complex calculations as if flowing through them from an outside source. Max Planck, father of quantum theory, wrote that the pioneer scientist must have "a vivid intuitive imagination, for new ideas are not generated by deduction, but by artistically creative imagination."

In a 1994 study of interviews with Nobel Laureates in the hard sciences, it was found that 18 of 72 interviewees stated that intuition feels different from reasoning and cannot be rationally explained. In an anecdote about the nuclear physicist Fermi, when questioned on why he disagreed with two colleagues who were arguing about a calculation, he shrugged his shoulders and said "my intuition tells me so".[21]

August Kekulé had been contemplating how the atoms in benzene are arranged, the ratio of carbon and hydrogen atoms being different to other hydrocarbon compounds. One night in 1865, having contemplated the problem without success, he fell asleep in his chair. He began dreaming of atoms dancing, gradually forming into the shape of a snake, which

---

19 Related by Elizabeth Gilbert, in "Your Elusive Genius," 2009.
20 Elizabeth Gilbert, Ibid.
21 Larisa V. Shavinina (ed.), 451.

I.Q. and Creativity

circled around and bit its own tail. This image of the widespread motif of the self-devouring serpent, the *ouroboros*, danced before Kekulé's eyes. On waking he realised he was being shown by this image that benzene molecules are composed of rings of carbon atoms. This enabled a new understanding of chemical bonding and opened up a new field of organic chemistry. Kekulé said of the experience:

> "I sat at the table to write my textbook, but ... my thoughts were elsewhere. I turned my chair to the fireplace and began to doze. Again the atoms began to somersault in front of my eyes. This time the smaller groups kept modestly in the distance. My mind's eye, sharpened by repeated visions of this kind, could now distinguish larger structures with different conformations; long lines, sometimes aligned and close together; all twisting and turning in serpentine movements. But look! What is that? One of the snakes had bitten its tail and the way it was whirled mockingly before my eyes. As if it had produced a flash, I woke up. ... I spent the rest of the night to check the consequences of the hypothesis. Let us learn to dream, gentlemen, because then maybe the truth is noticed".[22]

The remarkable mathematician Srinivasa Ramanujan, despite having no formal education in mathematics, produced 3900 equations and other formulae which he said were shown to him in dreams by the Hindu goddess Namagiri. He described one of these dreams:

> "While asleep, I had an unusual experience. There was a red screen formed by flowing blood, as it were. I was observing it. Suddenly a hand began to write on the screen. I became all attention. That hand wrote a number of elliptic integrals. They stuck to my mind. As soon as I woke up, I committed them to writing."[23]

The significance of creativity, like that of "race" is not that it can be statistically measured and quantified, and its origins identified in terms of cerebral fissures, but that it is a reflection of the divine order that transcends materialistic conceptions. The death of a race's *inspirare* is caused by the severing of the nexus with the divine.

---

22 E. Boyd, R. Morrison, 14.3.
23 Belal E. Baaquie, Frederick H. Willeboordse, 38.

Assumptions About Miscegenation

Because the Right, the custodian of tradition within the epoch of decay, has been infected by the spirit of materialism, there is a focus on secondary symptoms of culture disease, such as in particular immigration, rather than primary symptoms such as the banking system, let alone a recognition of *causes*. Additionally, "race" becomes a matter of skull measuring, rather than spirit and élan. Hence the character of a civilisation and of a people is discerned via the types of bone and skull found amidst the ruins. History then becomes a matter of statistics. How feeble such attempts remain is demonstrated by the years of controversy surrounding the racial identity of Kennewick Man.

Trotsky called "racism" "Zoological materialism". As an "economic materialist", that is, a Marxist, he did not explain why his own version of materialism is a superior mode of thinking and acting than the other. Tradition does not see history as unfolding according to material forces, but by metaphysical forces acting on the terrestrial. Spengler, like Goethe and Hegel, et al intuited history over a broad expanse as a metaphysical unfolding.

The best known exponents of racial determinism were of course German National Socialists, the reductionist doctrine being expressed by Hitler: "…This is how civilisations and empires break up and make room for new creations. Blood mixture, and the lowering of the racial level which accompanies it, are the one and only cause why old civilisations disappear…"[1]

Hitlerism was the coalescing of racial doctrines that were commonplace during the latter half of the 19th century, when a science of race was systemised and popularised by the French diplomat Count Arthur de Gobineau, with his *Inequality of the Human Races*.[2] The hitherto spiritual-moral-cultural foundations of races, their rise and fall, were replaced by a reductionist interpretation based on the premises of blood purity and blood contamination. De Gobineau wrote of this:

---

1 Adolf Hitler, 123.
2 Arthur de Gobineau *The Inequality of the Human Races*.

Assumptions About Miscegenation

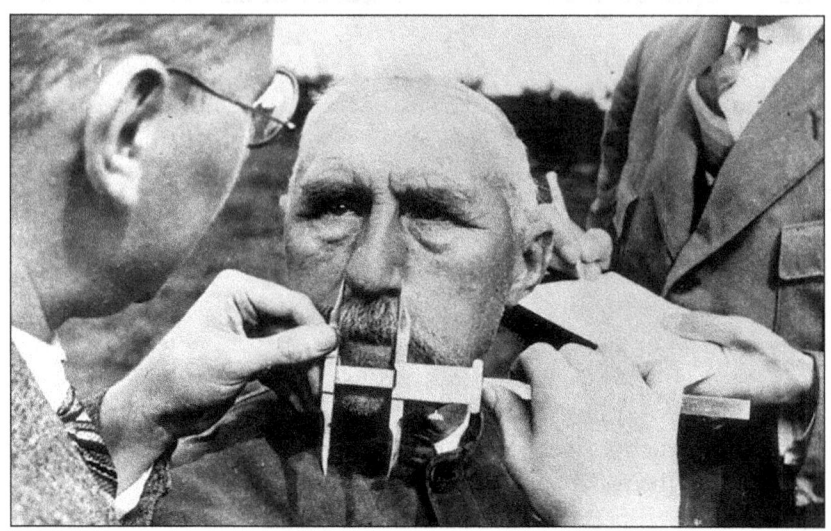

German eugenics scientists measuring facial features.

"I return now to my main subject, which is to show that fanaticism,[3] luxury, corruption of morals,[4] and irreligion do not necessarily bring about the ruin of nations …All these phenomena have been found in a highly developed state, either in isolation or together, among peoples which were actually the better for them – or at any rate not the worse".[5]

Hence, de Gobineau rejected the hitherto moral explanations for the decline and fall of civilisations, despite the recent example in his own country of the French Revolution as the product of moral decay. The racial doctrine was popularised in Germany by an Englishman, Houston Stewart Chamberlain, who already had a significant influence on Wilhelmian Germany with his *Foundations of the Nineteenth Century*. Hitlerian National Socialism was an uneasy mixture of 18th century German Idealism (Fichte, Herder) and of 19th century English Darwinism, brought to Germany by Ernst Haeckel, and Sir Francis Galton's eugenics.[6]

---

3   The example of a society based on "fanaticism" given by de Gobineau is the human sacrifice practised by the Aztecs.

4   The examples given by de Gobineau of nations based around luxury are France, Germany, England and Russia, and other European states, whose vitality he claims did not seem to have been affected. (de Gobineau, *The Inequality of the Races*, Chp. II, 8).

5   Joseph Arthur de Gobineau, Ibid., II, 7.

6   Francis Galton, Hereditary Genius.

In the USA books opposing miscegenation on eugenic grounds, such as Lothrop Stoddard's *Revolt Against Civilization*[7] became best-sellers. Specifically, Stoddard, Madison Grant[8] and other race theorists claimed that the Nordics – "the best of all human breeds",[9] as Stoddard put it - were the primary culture-creators, who are in danger of being genetically swamped as much by non-Nordic Europeans as by Blacks and Asians.[10] Biological racism is primarily an English world-view of the 19th century, which was used to justify capitalism in an economic survival of the fittest, known as Social Darwinism. Karl Marx just turned the same theories upside-down and claimed them for the "proletariat," the uprooted and urbanised former rural class, which had hitherto been secure with cottage, village and Church.

Modernist Versus Traditional Interpretations of History

Dr. Caleb Saleeby, a British physician and prominent public health advocate, was a leading exponent of eugenics who warned against the impact of alcohol, narcotics and lead poisoning on the racial "germ-plasm". His primary concern was however the purity of the racial stock. Saleeby was a genetic determinist who rejected the possibility of the fall of civilisations so long as the racial gene pool remains uncontaminated. Saleeby's comments are worth quoting at length because they summarise the opinion of zoological materialists who reject culture is an organism subject to the same morphological life-cycles as other organisms:

> "Nations, races, civilisations rise, we shall all agree, because to inherent virtue of breed they add sound customs and laws, acquirements of discipline and knowledge. But, these acquirements made, power established, and crescent from year to year—why do they *then* fall? If they can *make* a place for

---

7   Lothrop Stoddard, Revolt Against Civilization, 1922. Stoddard's views on the "resurgence of atavism" among political revolutionaries is a valuable insight which is examined in Bolton, *The Psychotic Left*, 2013.

8   Madison Grant, 1916.

9   Stoddard, *The Rising Tide of Color* , 183.

10 Ibid.

themselves, how much easier should it not be to *maintain* it?"¹¹

Saleeby advocated the widespread perception that gained scientific credibility through the application of Darwinian evolution, Mendelian genetics , and Galtonian eugenics that the rise of civilisations is based on superior races, and the fall of those civilisations is caused by genetic pollution with inferior races. Saleeby rejected the prior theory that the decline and fall of civilisations and nations had been caused by moral decadence, writing: "Two explanations, each falsely asserting itself to be rooted in biological fact, have long been cited and are still cited in order to account for these supreme tragedies of history".[12] What he called "racial senility" Saleeby traced back to the Greek philosophers:

> *"The fallacy of racial senility.*—The first may claim Plato and Aristotle as its founders, and consists of an argument from analogy. Races may be conceived in similar terms to individuals. There are many resemblances between a society - a 'social organism,' to use Herbert Spencer's phrase - and an individual organism. Just, then, as the individual is mortal, so is the race. Each has its birth, its period of youth and growth, its maturity, and, finally, its decadence, senility and death. So runs the common argument".[13]

This will be recognised as the historical-morphology of Spengler writing a decade after Saleeby.

Saleeby believed that the "germ-plasm" (genes) is immortal. However, much more is known about genetics than in Saleeby's time. Life ends through cellular degeneration, just as cultures end by the degeneration of the cellular constitutes of the social organism. Human DNA is degenerating, and every individual contains many harmful mutations that are inheritable. Genetically related diseases are increasing. Dr. John C. Stanford, a geneticist of prominence,[14] contends that from a geneticist's viewpoint, humans are devolving via what he calls

---

11   Caleb Saleeby, Chapter XV, 257.
12   Ibid., 256.
13   Ibid.
14   John Sanford, Connell University, College of Agriculture and Life Sciences, http://hort.cals.cornell.edu/people/john-sanford

"genetic entropy".[15] Interestingly, as we have seen, tradition related for millennia that humankind is devolving from a primordial Golden Age.

Saleeby was typical of the 19th century intelligentsia who assumed that industry and science would assure the immorality of Western civilisation, and English commerce in particular. He drew on the young sciences of heredity and evolution to prove his optimism in regard to the immortality of the race:

> "We must reply, however, that biology, so far from confirming it, declares as the capital fact which contrasts the individual and the race that, whilst the individual is doomed to die from inherent causes, the race is naturally immortal. The tendency of life is not to die but to live. If individuals die, that is doubtless because, as I believe, more life and fuller is thus attained than if life bodied itself in immortal forms: but the germ-plasm is immortal; it has no inherent tendency either to degenerate or to die. Species exist and flourish now which are millions of years older than mankind. 'The individual withers, the race is more and more".[16]

Saleeby states that it is not races that die but empires and civilisations. This is accurate, but the races that persist after the demise of their civilisations are a reflection of the historical and cultural exhaustion of the civilisations and empires that have been exhausted of creative energy. These races are what Spengler referred to as *fellaheen*. As will be shown below, contrary to the assumptions of those who state that civilisations fall through miscegenation, the North African Moslems who created the splendid Islamic civilisation; the Hindu Indians; and the American Indians whose ancestors created the Olmec, Aztec, Incan, exhausted their historical and cultural possibilities. They are genetically the same race as their ancestors. The Chinese, having gone through many "dynastic cycles" within the context of an enduring Chinese Civilisation, are reanimated not be a renaissance of Chinese culture, whose possibilities seem exhausted, but through the adaption of Western technics. As Saleeby states, the Jews have persisted, but they have done so by grafting on many races, maintaining their *ethnos* not through the purity of

---

15   John Sanford, *Genetic Entropy*, 2014.
16   Caleb Saleeby, 257.

the gene pool, but through the strength of their religious and mythic tradition. Saleeby is also correct in pointing out that British (and other white) babies still come into the world physically healthy. He correctly lamented that pollutants such as alcohol and tobacco were poisoning the gene pool. He stated that the assumption of "racial senility" is in particular disproved by the continuing healthy birth and fertility rates, yet if Saleeby were alive today he would note that the white races have indeed become increasingly infertile. The statistics for abortion provide a more accurate view of the senility of a civilisation than statistics for mixed marriages. Saleeby had written of these matters:

"It may be added that, in historical instances, civilisations have, on the one hand, persisted, and, on the other, fallen, despite change, and even substitution, in the races which created them: and, on the other hand, the most conspicuously persistent of all races in the historic epoch, the Jews, have survived one Empire after another of their oppressors, but have never had an Empire of their own. Thus, so far as the historian is concerned, it is not races at all that die, but civilisations and Empires. Plato's argument from the individual to the race is therefore irrelevant, as well as untrue. The fatalistic conception to which it tempts us, saying that races must die, just as individuals must, and that therefore it is idle to repine or oppose, is utterly unwarrantable and extremely unhealthy. To take our own case, despite the talk about our own racial decadence, nearly all our babies still come into the world fit and strong and healthy - the racial poisons apart. We kill them in scores of thousands every year, but this infant mortality is not a sign that the race is dying, but a sign that even the most splendid living material can be killed or damaged if you try hard enough. The babies do not die because races are mortal, but because individuals are, and we kill them. The babies drink poison, eat poison, and breathe poison, and in due course die. The theory of racial senility, inapplicable everywhere because untrue, is most of all inapplicable here.

If a race became sterile, Plato and Aristotle would be right. There is no such instance in history, apart from well-defined external, *not inherent*, causes, as in the case of the Tasmanians. Dismissing this analogy, we may also dismiss, as based upon nothing better, the idea that the great tragedies of history were necessary events at all. We must look elsewhere than amongst the inherent and necessary factors of racial life for the causes which determine these tragedies; and we shall be entitled to assume as conceivable the proposition that, notwithstanding the consistent fall of all our predecessors, the causes are not inevitable, but, being external and environmental, may possibly be controlled: man being not only creature but creator also".[17]

Precisely what Saleeby is assuming to have been disproven by genetics in his time, in our time is beign reaffirmed by epigenetics:

"The Lamarckian explanation of decadence. - The second of the two false interpretations of history in terms of biology is still, and always has been, widely credited. When historians have paid any attention to the breed of a people as determining its destiny, they have invariably added to the fallacy of racial senility this no less fecund error. It is that, in consequence of success, a people become idle, thoughtless, unenterprising, luxurious, and that these *acquired characters are transmitted* to succeeding generations so that, finally, there is produced a degenerate people unable to bear the burden of Empire - and then the crash comes. The historian usually introduces the idea already dismissed by saying that a 'young and vigorous race' invaded the Imperial territories - and so forth. The terms 'young' and 'old,' applied to human races, usually mean nothing at all.

"The reader will recognise, of course, in this doctrine of the transmission to children of characters acquired by their parents, the explanation of organic evolution advanced by Lamarck rather more than a century ago. It is employed by historians for the explanation of both the processes they record, progress and retrogression. Thus they suppose that for many generations a race is disciplined, and so at last there is produced a race with discipline in its very bone; or for many generations a nation finds it necessary to make adventure upon the sea, and so at last there is produced a generation of predestined sailors with blue water in its blood. And in similar terms moral and physical retrogression or degeneration are explained.

---

17   Ibid, 257-258.

"Let us consider the contrast between the interpretation which accepts the Lamarckian theory of the transmission of acquired characters and that which does not. Consider the babies of a new generation. According to Lamarck, these have in their blood and brain the consequences of the habits of their ancestors. If these have been idle and luxurious, the new babies are predestined to be idle and luxurious too. This, in short, is a 'dying nation.' But, if acquired characters are not transmitted, the new generation is, on the whole, not much better, not much worse, than its predecessors - so far as this supposed factor of change is concerned. Each generation makes a fresh start, as we see in the babies of our slums to-day. It does not begin where the last left off - whether that means beginning at a higher or at a lower level than that at which the last started: but it makes a fresh start where the last did.

"Now, in general, we have seen that Lamarck's theory is discredited. The view of Mr. Galton is accepted, that acquired characters are not transmitted, either for good or for evil. If there are no other factors of racial degeneration or racial advance, then races do not degenerate or advance, but make a fresh start every generation: and Empires rise and fall without any relation to the breed of the Imperial people - an incredible proposition".[18]

Races do indeed "degenerate or advance", as is our thesis, but they do so not in accordance with eugenics or dysgenics, but from being subjected to the life-cycles of social organisms, if not already having succumbed to environmental changes or invasions. As we now know through the comparatively new revolutionary science of epigenetics, acquired characteristics can be inherited, although not in the terms assumed by Lamarck or his Soviet counterpart Lysenko. Epigenetics does not repudiate genetics but explains an added dimension to inheritance, as we have seen. Contrary to Saleeby, each generation does not make a "fresh start," and does indeed inherit the experiences of its forebears.

Saleeby follows with the eugenicist argument that only genetic degeneration, whether through miscegenation, or the proliferation of the worst among the same race, can cause the permanent fall of a race:

---

18   Ibid, 259.

"Some historical instances. - In the face of certain facts of contemporary history I do not for a moment assert that there are no other causes of Imperial failure than the arrest or reversal of selection. But I do assert that if this is not the cause, then, in the absence of the transmission of acquired characters, the race has not degenerated, and is capable of reasserting itself. Only by the arrest or reversal of selection can a race degenerate - apart from the racial poisons [alcohol, tobacco, etc.]. If, then, a civilisation or Empire has fallen through causes altogether non-biological - through carelessness, or neglect of motherhood or alteration of ideals - the changes in character so produced are not transmitted to the children, and the race is not degenerate but merely deteriorated in each generation. For instance, we have been brought up to believe that there is no possible future for Spain; it is a dying nation, a senile individual, a people of degenerates; it has had its day, which can never return. The historian explains this by the false analogy between a race and an individual, and by the false Lamarckian theory of heredity. To these the biologist retorts with comments upon their falsity, and with the conviction that since Spain, even allowing for the anti-eugenic labours of the Inquisition, has not been subjected to the only process which can ensure real degeneration—viz., the consistent and stringent selection of the worst—she is yet capable of regeneration. Regeneration is not really the word, because there has been little real degeneration, but only the successive deterioration of successive and undegenerate generations. The new generation is found to be potentially little worse and little better than its predecessors of the sixteenth century. There has been no national or racial degeneration. The environment is modified for the better, i.e., so as to choose the better, and Spain, as they say in misleading phrase, 'takes on a new lease of life.' The historian of the present day, knowing as a historian what qualities of blood have been in the Spanish people, and basing his theories upon sound biology, must confidently assert that that blood, incapable, as he knows, of degeneration by any Lamarckian process, may still retain its ancient quality and will yet make history".[19]

Again the assumption, legitimate for Saleeby's time, and until

---

19 Ibid., 267-268.

quite recently, that acquired characteristics cannot be passed on to subsequent generations, is the basis for the dogma that so long as the gene pool remains healthy there is no reason that a race that has undergone societal or national collapse cannot regenerate. As will be seen below it has been argued, incorrectly, that Spanish, Portuguese, Italians, Greeks and other whites did collapse through miscegenation. Likewise, as Evola, pointed out, Swedes remain Nordic genetically, but show no sign of reviving former greatness, because they fulfilled their national-mission as allotted to them within a specific historical era.

Other than Britain, the home of the eugenics movement, where industrialism provided the British with an optimism for the assumption of never-ending progress, the USA provided a large share of racial theorists of the early 20th century, whose conception of the rise and fall of civilisations was based on zoology, and in particular on the superiority of the Nordic not only above non-white races, but above all sub-races of the white, such as the Dinaric, Mediterranean and Alpine.

Senator Theodore G. Bilbo of Mississippi wrote a book championing the cause of segregation, and more so, the "back-to-Africa" movement, stating that miscegenation with the Negro will result in the fall of white civilisation. He briefly examined some major civilisations. Bilbo wrote that Egyptian civilisation was mongrelised over centuries, "until a mulatto inherited the throne of the Pharaohs in the Twenty-fifth dynasty. This mongrel prince, Taharka, ruled over a Negroid people whose religion had fallen from an ethical test for the life after death to a form of animal worship". This should be "sufficient warning to white America!"[20] Because Sen. Bilbo had started from an assumption, his history was flawed. As will be shown below, it was Taharka and the Nubian dynasty that renewed Egypt's decaying culture, which had degenerated under the white Libyan dynasties. Sen. Bilbo proceeded with similar examinations of Carthage, Greece, and Rome.

Another gentleman of the Old South tradition, Lt. Colonel Earnest S. Cox, after travelling the world and studying race relations, wrote a popular book defending racial separatism, published in 1923, *White America*.[21] Cox, like Senator Bilbo, and others of the Old South, had a paternalistic attitude towards Blacks, not one of hatred or contempt.

---

20   Theodore G. Bilbo, 14.

21   Ernest S. Cox, White America.

The Decline and Fall of Civilisations

They regarded total geographic racial separation – not just segregation – as necessary, and deplored the exploitation that pitted Black labour against White. Hence like Bilbo, Cox worked with Black nationalists such as Marcus Garvey, and supported the "Back-to-Africa" movement among the Blacks. Nonetheless, Cox, like Bilbo and others, predicated their race doctrines on dogmatic assumptions around the mixing of blood (miscegenation). Cox stated the basis of this:

"Scientific research has done much toward establishing the following propositions:

The white race has founded all civilizations.
The white race remaining white has not lost a civilization
The white race become hybrid has not retained civilization".[22]

From such assumptions the conclusion is that whenever a non-white civilisation has arisen it can only have been from a small white culture-bearing stratum. The assumption is that since non-whites cannot create a civilisation, when a civilisation appears among non-whites they cannot have originated it. The argument is circular. Hence, for example the millennia of Chinese civilisation must have been derived from the proto-Celtic Tocharians at the Tarim Basin, the mummified remnants being of much interest to ethnologists in recent years.[23]

For Cox, et al, the Chinese showed "high sustaining qualities" for civilisation, when derived from whites, and he referred to Chinese accounts of Caucasian tribes.[24] However, the Chinese like most highly cultured races encountering other races for the first time, regarded the Caucasian peoples of Central Asia as hairy and "backward", not as awe-inspiring culture-heroes. Cox wrote that the earlier epochs of Chinese civilisation were more impressive than the later because China would have had a Caucasian culture-bearing stratum that eventually succumbed to miscegenation.[25] This assumption, which is also applied to Egypt, Oceania and South and Central America,[26] relegates the

---

22   Ibid., 11.
23   Elizabeth Wayland Barber, 1999.
24   Cox, 81-82.
25   Ibid., 82.
26   Ibid., 80.

ebbs and flows of history to a reductionism as simplistic as Marx's historical theory of "class struggle".

These are assumptions that can no longer be justified by "science", yet continue as the primary argument of the "Right", and particularly the Anglophone Right. Hence the belief continues that whenever there are traces of blondism even among the darkest of races, there was an ancient "Nordic" presence. The blondes occasionally seen among Australoids and Melanesians were assumed to be evidence of white, blond culture-bearers sojourning into far-flung lands, and imparting whatever rudiments of culture primitive races were able to retain. However, the blondness is the result of a specifically Oceanic genetic mutation expressed as the TYRP 1 gene, that is not related to the blondism of Europeans.[27] When a 9,000 year old skull was found near Washington and dubbed "Kennewick man" there was difficulty in determining the race.[28] A Eurocentric assumption was widely made that Kennewick man was the remnant of a white culture-bearing stratum that had been exterminated by the Indians; for example:

> "The long-cherished victim status of Native Americans would be weakened—or worse, reversed. Suppose an archeological dig at Kennewick revealed a whole community of people with Caucasian DNA? Suppose it found dozens or hundreds of Euro-American skeletons, most with Native American arrowheads in their backs, victims of a pogrom-like massacre? If a Caucasoid Kennewick Man and his tribe roamed the Cascade rain-shadow dry interior of Washington State 9,000 years ago, we must then ask a painful question: what happened to them? Why did they vanish while Native American tribes took over the land that once was theirs? Did white-skinned early Americans lack the skill or luck to survive? Or were they killed off by darker-skinned invaders in an act we today would define as racism and genocide (especially if its victims were not of European ancestry)?"[29]

So we have a circular argument in assuming that miscegenation is the primary – often the only – cause for culture decay on the basis

---

27 S. N. Bhanoo, 2012.
28 Morten Rasmussen, et al, 455-458.
29 Lowell Ponte, *Politically Incorrect Genocide*, 1999.

for example that a "mulatto", Teharka, became pharaoh of Egypt in 688B.C. From here it is assumed that this is evidence for the cause of Egyptian collapse through the influence of Black Nubia.[30] We shall examine the decline of Egypt below. The image of the Nubian as coming to Egypt as a "docile, subservient workman and soldier"[31] is an assumption far from correct, given the vibrancy of Nubia and its maintenance of Egyptian civilisation long after Egypt itself had decayed. However, the Nubian culture also eventually decayed. The same assumptions are made about the decay of "Aryan India" through miscegenation.[32] Again, this is not borne out by genetic studies. The decay of India is much more complex than a matter of miscegenation, and will also be examined below.

---

30   Cox, 44-45.
31   Ibid., 55.
32   Ibid, 67-79.

Civilisations That Died

Mesopotamia

The Fertile Crescent, enriched by the Tigris and the Euphrates rivers, was the centre of the earliest known Civilisation. Over the course of thousands of years several civilisations rose and fell in this region. The reasons for decline vary.

The civilisation of Sumer (3000-2000 B.C.) laid the foundation for subsequent civilisations in the region. The basis of the social structure was an alliance of city states. The rivers were central to the civilisation to the extent that the priesthood helped direct the irrigation and collective agriculture, and the temples also stored crops and seeds. Agricultural organisation prompted the development of cuneiform writing to keep records and advanced mathematics, which in turn assisted with advances in engineering of the type required for the sustenance of such a civilisation, such as the building of canals, dams and walls. In particular Sumer had a commendable legal code. Many of these laws were based on restorative justice rather than on revenge. The rights of women, including slaves, and children were encoded. [1] Sumerian proverbs indicate the ethos:

> "An unjust heir who does not support a wife, who does not support a child, has no cause for celebration". "As long as you live you should not increase evil by telling lies". "Hand added to hand, and a man's house is built up. Stomach added to stomach, and a man's house is destroyed". "He who owns many things is constantly on guard. Or: He who acquires many things, he must keep close watch over them". "Ignoramuses are numerous in the palace". "Strength cannot keep pace with intelligence". "The elephant spoke to himself: 'There is nothing like me!' The wren answered him: 'But I, in my own small way, was created just as you were!'" "The honest man will earn his pay".[2]

---

1   Code of Ur-Nammu (circa 2100 B.C.).
2   "Sumerian Proverbs", "Selected Proverbs", http://oaks.nvg.org/sumer-proverbs.html

Ruins of Sumerian city-state of Ur in ancient Mesopotamia.

The unity achieved between feuding city-states by Sargon (circa 2300 B.C.) created the Sumerian empire. However, Sargon's successors were not equal to the task; there were rebellions against corrupt rulers. The nomadic Guti invaded and Sumer was fractured as a unified state. Ur Nammu, an official of the city-state of Ur, overthrew the Guti and re-established unity and stability. The system of weights and measures he introduced thwarted the corrupt practices of merchants that had become far-reaching. Ur Nammu, gaining the trust of the city-states, was named King of Sumer and Akkad.

Conquest by Amorites established Babylon as the centre of a new empire. Like the Romans vis-à-vis Greek civilisation, and the Nubians vis-à-vis Egypt, the Amorites sought to continue rather than to destroy the Sumer culture. Hammurabi, circa 1750 B.C. re-established a unified imperial state. The famous legal code of Hammurabi was again one of high ethos. These Babylonians surpassed the Sumerians in science and literature, epitomised by the *Epic of Gilgamesh*. However, the Babylonian empire began stagnating circa 1550 B.C. After Hammurabi there was a notable decline in the arts. The distinctive cylinder-seals failed to make progress, and are part of the "general decline of power and civilisation and even the workmanship", which became "careless".[3] As we shall consider, the decline of workmanship is a significant symptom of decay.

The conquering Kassites did not provide an impetus for renewal. "The old 'land' had lost its force of reaction and recovery".[4] The impact of the Kassites is hardly discernible other than from King-lists; "they have no history".[5] The slope of decline was "uniformly long and undisturbed", "an age sinking slowly into decline and spinning itself out only because there was no neighbour with enough force to cut even so thin a thread", until interrupted by the sudden sacking of Babylon by the Hittites.[6]

Circa 1000 B.C. the Assyrians from northern Mesopotamia, a militaristic people, conquered Babylonia. In contrast to the restorative justice of the Sumerian and Babylonian laws, the legal code of the Assyrians was based on blood retribution, mutilation and death. It is a notable feature of the difference in culture that women were treated harshly under the Assyrian laws:

> "Married women must be veiled, as must a concubine accompanying her mistress. But a harlot shall not be veiled; her head must be uncovered, and (if not) she shall be beaten fifty stripes with rods and pitch poured over her head".

> "Leaving aside the penalties for a man's wife which are inscribed on the tablet, a man may flog his wife, he may pluck her hair, he may strike and damage her ears. There is no guilt involved in this".

> "If a man divorces his wife, if it is his will he may give her something; if it is not his will, he shall not give her anything and she shall go out in her emptiness".[7]

---

[3] I. E. S. Edwards, C. J. Gadd, N. G. L. Hammond, E. Sollberger (eds.), *The Cambridge Ancient History*, Vol. II, part I, 218.

[4] Ibid., 224.

[5] Ibid., 225.

[6] Ibid., 226.

[7] The Code of Assura, ca. 1075 B.C.

Civilisations That Died

Such was the hatred the Assyrians aroused among subject peoples that when they in turn succumbed to invasion their capital Nineveh was sacked in 621B.C. by a coalition of Babylonians, Persians, Medes, and Scythians, and obliterated without trace.

Among the conquerors of the Assyrians circa 600B.C. were the Chaldeans. Nebuchadnezzar revived the greatness and the ethos of Babylon prior to the Assyrians. He returned to the laws and the religion of Hammurabi's Babylon. However the later extent of decay is indicated by the last king, Belshazzar: as the Persians were advancing on Babylon he offered no defence other than to trust the walls of the city to keep the armies at bay, hoping that Persians would long be delayed by other conquests before they reached Babylon. The capital fell without resistance. The Greek historian Herodotus, who travelled to Babylon and described its splendour and customs, said of the Persian occupation:

> "Owing to the vast size of the place, the inhabitants of the central parts (as the residents at Babylon declare) long after the outer portions of the town were taken, knew nothing of what had chanced, but as they were engaged in a festival, continued dancing and revelling until they learnt the capture but too certainly. Such, then, were the circumstances of the first taking of Babylon".[8]

The Ming court displayed the same moral bankruptcy in China when faced with Manchu armies. The glitter of palace opulence blinded the rulers to unpleasant realities. The Chaldeans rebelled against Persian rule; Babylon was besieged by Darius for nineteen months. Herodotus records the depravity to which the Babylonians had sunk:

> "Babylon revolted. The revolt had been long and carefully planned; indeed, preparations for withstanding a siege had been going quietly on all through the reign of the Magian [Persians] and the disturbances which followed the rising of the seven against him, and for some reason or another the secret never leaked out. When the moment finally came to declare their purpose, the Babylonians, in order to reduce the consumption of food, herded together and strangled all the women in the city each man

---

8   Herodotus, *The History of the Persian Wars* (circa. 430 B.C.) I: 191. The event is recorded in The Book of Daniel 5.

exempting only his mother, and one other woman whom he chose out of his household to bake his bread for him".[9]

The Chaldean-Assyrian-Babylonian rabble had sunk into irredeemable depravity. The Mesopotamian civilisation was displaced on the world stage by Persia, followed by Alexander's Greece. A long period of chaos followed Alexander's death at Babylon in 323B.C. By the time Roman emperor Trajan entered Babylon in 115A.D. he found "nothing but mounds, and stones and ruins".[10]

Persia

The Persian Empire by the time of the Greek invasion, was regarded by the Hellenes as opulent, and "feminised". The role of the eunuchs in corruption of the empire at the royal court is reminiscent of the corruption of China's dynasties. The deterioration of Persia had been noted after the death of Cyrus the Great, Xenophon writing in *Cyropaedia* "everything began to deteriorate" while Cyrus' sons squabbled and provinces revolted.[11] During the reign of Cambyses, Plato remarked, the royal heirs had "a womanish rearing by royal women lately grown rich. ..."The sons of Cyrus "were without training in their father's craft, which was a hard one, fit to turn out shepherds of great strength, able to camp out in the open and to keep watch and, if need be, to go campaigning. He overlooked the fact that his sons were trained by women and eunuchs and that the indulgence shown them as 'Heaven's darlings' had ruined their training".[12]

> "So when, at the death of Cyrus, his sons took over the kingdom, over-pampered and undisciplined as they were, first, the one killed the other, through annoyance at his being put on an equality with himself, and presently, being mad with drink and debauchery, he lost his own throne at the hands of the Medes, under the man then called the Eunuch, who despised the stupidity of Cambyses".[13]

---

9   Herodotus, *Histories*, 3.150-160
10 Casius Dio, Roman History 63:30; Markham J. Geller, 329.
11 Xenophon, *Cyropaedia*, 8.8.2.
12 Plato, *The Laws of Plato* (University of Chicago Press, 1980), 3. 694.
13 Ibid., 3. 695.

Revived by the heroism of Darius, the empire regressed to decay after his death, under the reign of Xerxes, according to Plato, who commented that Darius unlike his successor, had not been raised in luxury. "Since then there has hardly ever been a single Persian king who was really, as well as nominally, 'Great'".[14]

If Persia was a decaying remnant of its former glory it was also the outer enemy that served as a catalyst for the alliance of the Greek city states. In the *Panegyricus* (380 B.C.) Isocrates exhorted Greeks to unite and defeat Persia. Hellas regarded the Persians with contempt, looking upon them "as effeminate and unversed in war and utterly degenerate from luxurious living".[15]

Commenting on the degenerated character of the once glorious Persian army, Isocrates stated that,

> "it seems to me that in every quarter the Persians have clearly exposed their degeneracy; for along the coast of Asia they have been defeated in many battles, and when they crossed to Europe they were duly punished, either perishing miserably or saving their lives with dishonour; and to crown all, they made themselves objects of derision under the very walls of their King's palace".[16]

Isocrates explained that this decay of the Persian ethos was part of a process of decadence that had reduced the Persians to a "mob" without fortitude:

> "And none of these things has happened by accident, but all of them have been due to natural causes; for it is not possible for people who are reared and governed as are the Persians, either to have a part in any other form of virtue or to set up on the field of battle trophies of victory over their foes. For how could either an able general or a good soldier be produced amid such ways of life as theirs? Most of their population is a mob without discipline or experience of dangers, which has lost all stamina

---

14   Ibid.
15   Isocrates , Panegyricus , 124 in: George Norlin, Isocrates , 1980.
16   Ibid., 4.149.

for war and has been trained more effectively for servitude than are the slaves in our country".¹⁷

Recent DNA studies show that Iranians have remained mainly "western Eurasian", "with a very limited contribution from eastern Eurasia, South Asia and Africa".¹⁸

Greece

The Hellenic civilisation is often ascribed by racial theorists as being the creation of a Nordic culture-bearing stratum. The same has been said of the Latin, Egyptian, and others. This theory is illustrated by depicting sculptures of ancient Hellenes of "Nordic" appearance. Such depictions upon which to form a theory are unreliable: the ancient Hellenes were predominantly Dinaric-Alpine-Mediterranean. The skeletal remains of Greeks show that from earliest times to the present there has been remarkable uniformity,¹⁹ according to studies by Sergi,²⁰ Ripley,²¹ and Buxton,²² who regarded the Greeks as an Alpine-Mediterranean mix from a "comparatively early date." American physical anthropologist Carlton S. Coon stated that the Greeks remain an Alpine-Mediterranean mix, with a weak Nordic element, and are "remarkably similar" to their ancient ancestors.²³

American anthropologist J. Lawrence Angel, in the most complete study of Greek skeletal remains starting from the Neolithic era to the present, found that Greeks have always been marked by a sustained racial continuity.²⁴ Angel cites American anthropologist Buxton who had studied Greek skeletal material and measured modern Greeks, especially in Cyprus. He concludes that the modern Greeks "possess physical characteristics not differing essentially from those of the former

---

17   Ibid., 4. 150.
18   M. Derenko, et al. , 2013.
19   The following sources are cited from D. Pontioks, "Racial Type of the Ancient Hellenes", http://dienekes.110mb.com/articles/hellenes/
20   G. Sergi, 1901.
21   W. Z. Ripley, 1900.
22   L. H. D. Buxton, *The Inhabitants of the Eastern Mediterranean*, Biometrika, Vol. 13, Issue 1, 92-112, 1920.
23   C. S. Coon, 1939.
24   J. Lawrence Angel, 1944.

[ancient Greeks]".[25] The most extensive study of modern Greeks was conducted by anthropologist Aris N. Poulianos,[26] concluding that Greeks are and have always been Mediterranean-Dinaric, with a strong Alpine presence. Angel states that "Poulianos is correct in pointing out ... that there is complete continuity genetically from ancient to modern times".[27] Nikolaos Xirotiris did not find any significant alteration of the Greek race from prehistory, through classical and medieval, to modern times.[28] Anthropologist Roland Dixon studied the funeral masks of Spartans and identified them as of the Alpine sub-race.[29] Although race theorists often state that Hellenic civilisation was founded and maintained by invading Dorian "Nordics", Angel states that the northern invasions were always of "Dinaroid-Alpine" type. A recent statistical comparison of ancient and modern Greek skulls found "a remarkable similarity in craniofacial morphology between modern and ancient Greeks."[30]

If miscegenation and the elimination of an assumed Nordic (Dorian) culture-bearing stratum cannot account for the decay of Hellenic civilisation, what can? The Roman historian Livy observed:

> "The Macedonians who settled in Alexandria in Egypt, or in Seleucia, or in Babylonia, or in any of their other colonies scattered over the world, *have degenerated into Syrians, Parthians, or Egyptians*. Whatever is planted in a foreign land, by a gradual change in its nature, degenerates into that by which it is nurtured".[31]

Here Livy is observing that occupiers among foreign peoples "go native", as one might say. The occupiers are pulled downward, rather than elevating their subjects upward, not through genetic contact but through moral and cultural corruption. The Syrians, Parthians and Egyptians had already become historically and culturally passé, or *fellaheen*, as Spengler puts it. The Macedonian Greeks in those colonies succumbed to the force of etiolation. Alexander even encouraged this

---

25 J. Lawrence Angel, 1946.

26 Aris N. Poulianos, 1961. Poulianos, 1999.

27 *Aris N. Poulianos, 1962.*

28 N. Xirotiris, "*Rassengeschichte von Griechenland*", 157-183, in I. Schwidetzky, (ed.),*Rassengeschichte der Menschheit*. Volume 6. R. Oldenbourg Verlag, Munich, 1979.

29 J. Boardman, 1989.

30 E. Argyropoulos, 195-204.

31 Livy (Titus Livius), *The History of Rome,* 33: 17.

The Decline and Fall of Civilisations

in an effort to meld all subjects into one Greek mass, which resulted not in a Hellenic civilisation passed along by multitudinous peoples, but in a chaotic mass from which Greece did not recover, despite the Greeks staying racially intact. The Greeks, Romans and other conquerors lost the strength of tradition to maintain themselves among alien cultures. Dr. W. W. Tarn stated of this process:

> "Greece was ready to adopt the gods of the foreigner, but the foreigner rarely reciprocated; Greek Doura (the Greek temple in Mesopotamia) freely admitted the gods of Babylon, but no Greek god entered Babylonian Uruk. Foreign gods might take Greek names; they took little else. They (the Babylonian gods) were the stronger, and the conquest of Asia (by the Greeks) was bound to fail as soon as the East had gauged its own strength and Greek weakness".[32]

Spengler pointed out to our own Late West that a primary symptom of decay is depopulation. Polybius (born circa 200B.C.) observed this phenomenon of Hellenic Civilisation:

> "In our time all Greece was visited by a dearth of children and generally a decay of population, owing to which the cities were denuded of inhabitants, and a failure of productiveness resulted, though there were no long-continued wars or serious pestilences among us. If, then, any one had advised our sending to ask the gods in regard to this, what we were to do or say in order to become more numerous and better fill our cities,—would he not have seemed a futile person, when the cause was manifest and the cure in our own hands? For this evil grew upon us rapidly, and without attracting attention, by our men becoming perverted to a passion for show and money and the pleasures of an idle life, and accordingly either not marrying at all, or, if they did marry, refusing to rear the children that were born, or at most one or two out of a great number, for the sake of leaving them well off or bringing them up in extravagant luxury. For when there are only one or two sons, it is evident that, if war or pestilence carries off one, the houses must be left heirless: and, like swarms of bees, little by little the cities become sparsely inhabited and weak. On this subject there is no need to ask the gods how we are to be relieved from such a curse: for anyone in the world

---

32   W.W. Tarn, Vol. VI, 301-302.

will tell you that it is by the men themselves if possible changing their objects of ambition; or, if that cannot be done, by passing laws for the preservation of infants".[33]

Greek historians were very conscious of the corrupting role of wealth and luxury in the decay of a culture, as we have seen in regard to their observations on Persia. They sought to draw lessons for their own civilisation. The warning was that the imperial stage of a civilisation is wrought with dangers caused by contact with foreigners. The victors are liable to be corrupted by those who were already too decadent to defend themselves.[34] The Greek historians regarded Persian civilisation as the continuation of the Median civilisation conquered by Cyrus in 550B.C. To Strabo the feminised attire of wealthy Persians came from the Medes.[35]

The Greek elite eagerly embraced Persian extravagance. Persian dress, art, products and aesthetics were associated with cultural status. This attitude seeped downward among the masses. While Herodotus and others tried to warn of the Orientalisation of Greek culture, there were many Greek poets and writers who referred admiringly to Oriental extravagance.[36] Xenophon satirised the way Persian austerity was given up to gluttony, drunkenness, and ease even among the military.[37] With the empire of Alexander the Great came a policy of multiculturalism, including intermarriage,[38] Alexander affecting Persian dress and symbols[39] in an effort to achieve ethnic harmony in the forming of a new world order.

Sparta

If any culture was ideally placed to resist the forces of internal decay it was Sparta. This came closest to Plato's ideal state. Iconic as the epitome of austerity and discipline, where the hardest course was

---

33 Polybius, Histories, 37.9.

34 "Herodotus on the character of Persian imperialism", in A. Fitzpatrick-McKinley (ed.), 2014.

35 Strabo, Geography, XI.13.9.

36 Erich S. Gruen, 11.

37 Xenophon, Cyrus, 8.8.

38 Given that the Persians were at this time Aryans, as were the Medes (Strabo referring to them in his Geography as Ariana) while the Greeks were mainly Dinaric-Alpine-Mediterranean, this does not seem to support the theory that miscegenation with an inferior race brought the collapse of Greek Civilisation.

39 Erich S. Gruen, 69.

embraced as the best, women were esteemed as mothers, and men as soldiers. Luxury was eschewed, foreign influences rejected, and the accumulation of wealth was prohibited. There was no cash nexus to influence politics. Gold and silver were prohibited. Coins were made of heavy iron, which was worthless for trading. Mercantile activities were forbidden. Nothing was imported. Meals were communal, each Spartan being assigned to a table to which s/he contributed food from their own generous allotment of land. Black broth was the preferred meal of the older men. Homes were austere and furniture simple. The Spartans were regarded as the custodians of the Greek ethos and the bulwark against Persia. Plutarch wrote of the laws of the Spartans as an example for other Greeks. He noted that Sparta regarded booty from conquest as a corrupting influence:

"It was forbidden them to be sailors and to fight on the sea. Later, however, they did engage in such battles, and, after they had made themselves masters of the sea, they again desisted, since they observed that the character of the citizens was deteriorating sadly. But they changed about again, as in all else. For example, when money was amassed for the Spartans, those who amassed it were condemned to death; for to Alcamenes and Theopompus, their kings, an oracle had been given: 'Eager desire for money will bring the ruin of Sparta'".[40]

The founding laws of Lycurgus (circa 800-900B.C.) were eroded over centuries. The small Spartan strata was denuded by continual warfare, until during the last days of Sparta there were just 700 Spartans remaining. Plutarch states of the decline:

"Yet, nevertheless, when Lysander had taken Athens, he brought home much gold and silver, and they accepted it, and bestowed honours on the man. As long as the Spartan State adhered to the laws of Lycurgus and remained true to its oaths, it held the first place in Greece for good government and good repute over a period of five hundred years. But, little by little, as these laws and oaths were transgressed, and greed and love of wealth crept in, the elements of their strength began to dwindle also, and their allies on this account were ill-disposed toward them. But although they were in this plight, yet after the victory of Philip

---

40   Plutarch, The Ancient Customs of the Spartans (42).

of Macedon at Chaeroneia, when all the Greeks proclaimed him commander both on land and sea, and likewise, in the interval following, proclaimed Alexander, his son, after the subjugation of the Thebans [335BC], the Spartans only, although they dwelt in an unwalled city, and were few in number because of their continual wars, and had become much weaker and an easy prey, still keeping alive some feeble sparks of the laws of Lycurgus, did not take any part in the campaigns of these or of the other kings of Macedon who ruled in the interval following, nor did they ever enter the general congress or even pay tribute. So it was, until they ceased altogether to observe the laws of Lycurgus, and came to be ruled despotically by their own citizens, preserving nothing of their ancestral discipline any longer, and so they became much like the rest, and put from them their former glory and freedom of speech, and were reduced to a state of subjection; and now they, like the rest of the Greeks, have come under Roman sway".[41]

Rome

Another often cited example of the fall of civilisation through miscegenation is that of Rome. However, despite the presence of slaves and traders of sundry races, like the Greeks, Italians now are substantially the same as they were in Roman times. Arab influence did not occur until Medieval times, centuries after the "fall of Rome".

The genetic male influence on Sicilians is estimated at only 6%. The predominant genetic influence is ancient Greek.[42] The African Haplogroup L have a less than 1% frequency throughout Italy other than in Latium, Volterra, Basilicata and Sicily where there are frequencies of 2% to 3% .[43]

Sub-Saharan, that is, Negroid, mtDNA have been found at very low frequencies in Italy, albeit marginally higher than elsewhere in Europe, but date from 10,000 years ago. A genetic study shows, "....mitochondrial DNA studies show that Italy does not differ too

---

41 Ibid.
42 Cornelia Di Gaetano, et al., 91–99;
43 Ibid.

The Decline and Fall of Civilisations

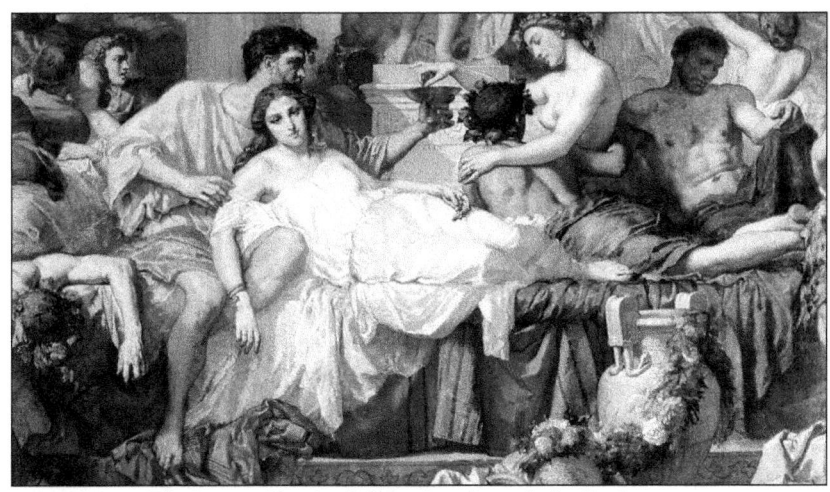

The Roman Empire falls to decadence in its final years.

much from other European populations". Although there are small regional variations, "The mtDNA haplogroup make-up of Italy as observed in our samples fits well with expectations in a typical European population".[44]

Hence, an infusion of Negroid or Asian genes during the epoch of Rome's decline and fall is lacking, and the reasons for that fall cannot be assigned to miscegenation. What slight frequency there is of non-Caucasian genetic markers entered Rome long before and long after the fall of Roman Civilisation. There was no "contamination of Roman blood", but of Roman spirit and élan.

Alien immigration introduces cultural elements that dislocate the social and ethical basis of a civilisation and aggravate an existing pathological condition. The English scholar Professor C. Northcote Parkinson, writing on the fall of Rome, commented that the Roman conquerors were subjected "to cultural inundation and grassroots influence". Because Rome extended throughout the world, like the present Late Western, the economic opportunities accorded by Rome drew in all the elements of the subject peoples, "groups of mixed origin and alien ways of life". "Even more significant was what the

---

44 F. Brisighelli, et al., "Uniparental Markers of Contemporary Italian Population Reveals Details on Its Pre-Roman Heritage".

Romans learnt while on duty overseas, for men so influenced were of the highest rank". Parkinson quotes Edward Gibbon's *Decline and Fall of the Roman Empire*, referring to the Roman colony of Antioch:

> "...Fashion was the only law, pleasure the only pursuit, and the splendour of dress and furniture was the only distinction of the citizens of Antioch. The arts of luxury were honoured, the serious and manly virtues were the subject of ridicule, and the contempt for female modesty and reverent age announced the universal corruption of the capitals of the East..."[45]

Roman historian Livy wrote of the opulence of Asia being brought back to Rome by the soldiery:

> "...it was through the army serving in Asia that the beginnings of foreign luxury were introduced into the City. These men brought into Rome for the first time, bronze couches, costly coverlets, tapestry, and other fabrics, and - what was at that time considered gorgeous furniture - pedestal tables and silver salvers. Banquets were made more attractive by the presence of girls who played on the harp and sang and danced, and by other forms of amusement, and the banquets themselves began to be prepared with greater care and expense. The cook whom the ancients regarded and treated as the lowest menial was rising in value, and what had been a servile office came to be looked upon as a fine art. Still what met the eye in those days was hardly the germ of the luxury that was coming".[46]

The Greek historian Polybius (200-118 BC), his own civilisation having decayed into what the Romans regarded with contempt, noted how Rome's wealth and success was affecting young Romans:

> "some of [the young Roman men] had abandoned themselves to love affairs with boys and others to consorting with prostitutes, and many to musical entertainments and banquets and all of the extravagances that they entail ... infected with Greek weaknesses during the war with Perseus. So great in fact was the

---

45 Edward Gibbon, Vol. II, Ch. 24.
46 Livy, The History of Rome, 39. 6

permissiveness and hedonism among young men that some paid a talent for a male lover and others three hundred drachmas for a jar of caviar.

"... This aroused the indignation of Cato, who said once in a public speech that it was the surest sign of deterioration in the republic when pretty boys fetch more than fields, and jars of caviar more than ploughmen. It was just at the period we are treating of that this present tendency to extravagance declared itself, first of all because they thought that now after the fall of the Macedonian kingdom their universal dominion was undisputed, and next because after the riches of Macedonia had been transported to Rome there was a great display of wealth both in public and in private".[47]

Here we see from Polybius' description a Rome full of *hubris*, self-assured through its material comforts that the old Roman ethos was no longer required, with a few such as Cato and Scipio who sought to warn of collapse.

There was no sudden collapse of Rome, no apocalyptical invasion by "barbarians" that resulted in its death. As is typical of the cycles of decline and fall the process is long, and therefore only really even noticeable by the particularly perceptive, whose warnings are typically unheeded or ridiculed, as in our own Late West.

---

47   Polybius, The Histories, IX: 24: "Affairs of Italy".

Civilisations That Died

The Collapse of Rome

Rome was in an advanced state of decay by the end of the second century; over two hundred years before the official "end" of the Empire in 476 A.D. As an imperial power Rome was abandoning provinces, beginning with Dacia and parts of Germany. Cities were declining. There was no further significant construction of the great monuments of Roman power after the end of the second century.

The Rome of this epoch is more notable for constantly collapsing, poorly built high rise tenement slums. These *insulae*, rising five, six, seven, and some eight and nine storeys high, homed most of the one million inhabitants of Rome by 150 A.D. Juvenal commented of the *insulae*:

> "We're living in a city that's propped up with little more than matchsticks: and they're the only way the rent-man can keep his tenants from falling out, as he plasters over the gaps in the cracks and tells them not to worry when they go to bed (even if the place is just about to fall around them!). It's wrong for people to have to live in fear of house-fires and buildings collapsing all the time. Right now your next-door-neighbour is calling for the fire-brigade and moving his bits and pieces while your own wee garret is smoking and you doing nothing about it. If the folk at the bottom of the stairs panic, the chap who's trapped and the last to burn is the one in the top attic just under the roof that keeps the rain off himself and the pigeon's nest..."[48]

Augustus established building codes, and Nero, after the great fire of 64 A.D., also used the opportunity to establish strict building regulations and paid for the reconstruction himself. By the fourth century there were about 46,600 *insulae* in Rome and only about 1,800 private houses, while the population had declined to around 700,000.

The decline in architectural style and methods of construction is a dramatic feature of the final epochs of civilisation that have been noted by archaeologists from Indus Valley to Mesoamerica.

---

48   Juvenal, Satires, i. 3. 193ff.

No More Romans

Professor Hugh Trevor-Roper comments of this epoch undergoing "a fundamental structural change which the great emperors at the end of that century, and Constantine himself at the beginning of the next, did but stabilise".[49] From the third century the empire had lost its moorings, and the capital was no longer Rome but "wherever warring emperors kept their military headquarters: in the Rhineland, behind the Alps or in the East; in Nicomedia or Constantinople, in Trier, Milan or Ravenna".[50]

The moral decay of Rome resulted in the displacement of Roman stock, not by miscegenation, but by the falling birth-rate. Such population decline is itself a major symptom of culture decay. The problem that it signifies is that a people has so little consciousness left as to its own purpose that its individuals do not have any responsibility beyond their own egos. Augustus, who sought to reverse the population decline, addressed the Roman nobles:

> "How otherwise shall families continue? How can the commonwealth be preserved if we neither marry nor produce children? Surely you are not expecting some to spring up from the earth to succeed to your goods and to public affairs, as myths describe. It is neither pleasing to Heaven nor creditable that our race should cease and the name of Romans meet extinguishment in us, and the city be given up to foreigners,—Greeks or even barbarians. We liberate slaves chiefly for the purpose of making out of them as many citizens as possible; we give our allies a share in the government that our numbers may increase: yet you, Romans of the original stock, including Quintii, Valerii, Iulli, are eager that your families and names at once shall perish with you".[51]

Tacitus remarked that regardless of state efforts to encourage the birth-rate, "childlessness prevailed."[52] At the beginning of the second century

---

49   Hugh Trevor-Roper, 27.
50   Ibid.
51   Cassius Dio, Dio's Rome (Kessinger Publishing, 2004), Book IV, 86.
52   Tacitus, Annals of Imperial Rome, iii, 25.

Pliny the Younger wrote that his was "an age when even one child is thought a burden preventing the rewards of childlessness." Plutarch observed that the poor had lost the confidence to sire children.[53] By the middle of the second century Hierocles stated that "most people" seemed to regard children as interfering with their lifestyle.[54] Marriage was no longer regarded as a crucial institution and was considered another burden to a hedonistic existence. As early as 131 B.C. the Roman Censor Quintus Caecilius Metellus Macedonicus proposed to the Senate that marriage be made compulsory, as so many males were opting to remain unmarried. A century later Augustus Caesar quoted Quintus in proposing his own marriage laws, but met no more favour in the Senate than had the Censor. Prostitution was so widespread it became a substitute for marriage. Roman cities also abounded with male prostitutes as homosexuality and bi-sexuality had become common.[55]

These attitudes seem very "modern" and very familiar to our own present Western societies, with the abortion and birth control that have resulted in no Western societies having a birth-rate above replacement levels; where aging populations are replenished with immigrants from Africa and Asia to augment the workforce and maintain the taxation levels, while natural birth increases that do take place within Western states are from migrant families. There is presently no reason to suppose that the second and third generation children from migrant parents are acculturating as French, German, English, etc. They settle as elements foreign to the culture organism.

Professor Tenney Frank, foremost scholar on the economic history of Rome, also considered the results of population decline, from the top of the social hierarchy downward:

> "The race went under. The legislation of Augustus and his successors, while aiming at preserving the native stock, was of the myopic kind so usual in social lawmaking, and failing to reckon with the real nature of the problem involved, it utterly missed the mark. By combining epigraphical and literary references, a fairly

---

53 Plutarch, Moralia, Book iv.
54 Stobaeus, iv, 24, 14.
55 Rodney Stark, 117.

full history of the noble families can be procured, and this reveals a startling inability of such families to perpetuate themselves. We know, for instance, in Caesar's day of forty-five patricians, only one of whom is represented by posterity when Hadrian came to power. The Aemilsi, Fabii, Claudii. Manlii, Valerii, and all the rest, with the exception of Comelii, have disappeared. Augustus and Claudius raised twenty-five families to the patricate, and all but six disappear before Nerva's reign. Of the families of nearly four hundred senators recorded in 65 A. D. under Nero, all trace of a half is lost by Nerva's day, a generation later. And the records are so full that these statistics may be assumed to represent with a fair degree of accuracy the disappearance of the male stock of the families in question. Of course members of the aristocracy were the chief sufferers from the tyranny of the first century, but this havoc was not all wrought by delatores and assassins. The voluntary choice of childlessness accounts largely for the unparalleled condition. This is as far as the records help in this problem, which, despite the silences is probably the most important phase of the whole question of the change of race. Be the causes what they may, the rapid decrease of the old aristocracy and the native stock was clearly concomitant with a twofold increase from below; by a more normal birth-rate of the poor, and the constant manumission of slaves".[56]

While allusions to "race" by Professor Frank are enough for "zoological materialists" to spin a whole theory about Rome's decline and fall by the miscegenation of the "white race" with blacks and Orientals, we now know from genetics that despite the invasions over centuries, the Italians, like the Greeks, have retained their original racial composition. What Frank is describing, by an examination of the records that show a disappearance of the leading patrician families, is that Rome was in a spiritual crisis, as all civilisations are when they regard child-bearing as a burden. As Julius Evola pointed out the "secret of degeneration" is that a civilisation rots from the top downward, and as Spengler pointed out, one of the primary signs of that rot is childlessness. That there were Roman statesmen with the wisdom to understand what was happening is indicated by Augustus' efforts to raise the birth-rate, but to no avail. Of this symptom of moral decay, Professor Frank wrote:

---

56 Tenney Frank, 1916, 704-705.

"In the first place there was a marked decline in the birth rate among the aristocratic families. ... As society grew more pleasure-loving, as convention raised artificially the standard of living, the voluntary choice of celibacy and childlessness became a common feature among the upper classes. ..."[57]

Even the emperors had ceased to be of the founding lineage. Tacitus commented that "emperors could be made elsewhere than in Rome. By the third century A.D. they were generally made elsewhere." Trevor-Roper states that "there were not only military emperors from the frontier: there were also Syrian, African and half-barbarian emperors; and their visits to Rome became rarer and rarer".[58] By 100 A.D. the population of the Empire began to contract. Provinces of the Empire such as Dacia and Germany could not be held. With the population decline of Romans those defending the Empire were drawn increasingly from the "barbarians"; Gauls, Illyrians, Germans, and Sarmatians. By 400 A.D. most of the Empire's towns and cities had contracted to half the size they had occupied in 150 A.D. From the end of the second century to the fifth the rural population also declined.[59] The urban centres were in a continual state of population flux from newcomers compensating for the shortage of Romans. Stark comments that the Graeco-Roman cities "were populated by strangers".[60]

So far as Roman marriage existed the numbers of children sired were small. Infanticide was widespread. Children were left in the streets for any passers-by, but more often the infant would die from the elements or from preying animals. The state aim of three children per family, despite inducements, could not be reached. The excavation of a villa at the port city of Ashkelon found the remains of 100 new-born babies thrown into a sewer.[61]

Abortion was common. Many women died as a result, and many became infertile. [62] Despite the dangers, women resorted to abortion

---

57 Ibid.
58 H. Trevor-Roper, 47.
59 Richard Hodges and William Whitehouse, 40-42.
60 Rodney Stark, 156.
61 Ibid., 118.
62 Ibid., 119.

frequently to dispose of the offspring of an illicit liaison; poor women due to economic limitations, and wealthy women to avoid too many heirs to the estate. Philosophers including Aristotle and Plato justified abortion to prevent overpopulation; and their intellectualising rationalised under-population.[63] Just as there were many techniques of abortion there were also many methods for birth control. Anal intercourse was a popular method.[64]

By contrast the Christian and Jewish communities continued to uphold marriage. Hence, they remained the only fertile communities.[65] When Christianity gained the ascendency and laid the foundation of Western civilisation on the ruins of Rome, it did so because it had maintained its vitality. So far from Christianity being responsible for Roman decline and fall, as contended by Edward Gibbon, Nietzsche and others, Rome had been in a state of decay for centuries. Its final collapse cleared the way for the Western.

Urbanisation, the magnetic pull of the megalopolis, the depopulation of the land and the proletarianism of the former peasant stock as in the case of the West's Industrial Revolution, impacted in major ways on the fall of Rome. A. M. Duff wrote of the impact of rural depopulation and urbanisation:

> "But what of the lower-class Romans of the old stock? They were practically untouched by revolution and tyranny, and the growth of luxury cannot have affected them to the same extent as it did the nobility. Yet even here the native stock declined. The decay of agriculture ... drove numbers of farmers into the towns, where, unwilling to engage in trade, they sank into unemployment and poverty, and where, in their endeavours to maintain a high standard of living, they were not able to support the cost of rearing children. Many of these free-born Latins were so poor that they often complained that the foreign slaves were much better off than they, and so they were. At the same time many were tempted to emigrate to the colonies across the sea which Julius Caesar and Augustus founded. Many went

---

63 Ibid., 121.
64 Ibid., 121.
65 Ibid., 127.

away to Romanize the provinces, while society was becoming Orientalized at home. Because slave labour had taken over almost all jobs, the free born could not compete with them. They had to sell their small farms or businesses and move to the cities. Here they were placed on the doles because of unemployment. They were, at first, encouraged to emigrate to the more prosperous areas of the empire to Gaul, North Africa and Spain. Hundreds of thousands left Italy and settled in the newly-acquired lands. Such a vast number left Italy leaving it to the Orientals that finally restrictions had to be passed to prevent the complete depopulation of the Latin stock, but as we have seen, the laws were never effectively put into force. The migrations increased and Italy was being left to another race. The free-born Italian, anxious for land to till and live upon, displayed the keenest colonization activity".[66]

The foreign cultures and religions that came to Rome from across the empire changed the temperament of the Roman masses who were uprooted and migrating to the cities; where as in the nature of the cites, as Spengler showed, they became a cosmopolitan mass. Frank writes of this:

"This Orientalization of Rome's populace has a more important bearing than is usually accorded it upon the larger question of why the spirit and acts of imperial Rome are totally different from those of the republic. There was a complete change in the temperament! There is today a healthy activity in the study of the economic factors that contributed to Rome's decline. But what lay behind and constantly reacted upon all such causes of Rome's disintegration was, after all, to a considerable extent, the fact that the people who had built Rome had given way to a different race. The lack of energy and enterprise, the failure of foresight and common sense, the weakening of moral and political stamina, all were concomitant with the gradual diminution of the stock which, during the earlier days, had displayed these qualities. It would be wholly unfair to pass judgment upon the native qualities of the Orientals without a further study, or to accept the self-complacent slurs of the Romans, who, ignoring

---

66   A. M. Duff, 200-201.

certain imaginative and artistic qualities, chose only to see in them unprincipled and servile egoists. We may even admit that had these new races had time to amalgamate and attain a political consciousness a more brilliant and versatile civilization might have come to birth".[67]

What is notable is not that the Romans miscegenated with Orientals, but that the uprooted, amorphous masses of the cities no longer adhered to the traditions on which Roman civilisation was founded. The same process can be seen today at work in New York, London and Paris. Duff wrote of this, and we might consider the parallels with our own time:

"Instead of the hardy and patriotic Roman with his proud indifference to pecuniary gain, we find too often under the Empire an idle pleasure-loving cosmopolitan whose patriotism goes no further than applying for the dole and swelling the crowds in the amphitheatre".[68]

The Roman Traditional ethos of severity, austerity and disdain for softness that Emperor Julian attempted to reassert was greeted by "fashionable society" with "disgust".[69] Parkinson remarked that "there is just such a tendency in the London of today, as there was still earlier in Boston and New York".[70] These "world cities" no longer reflect a cultural nexus but an economic nexus. In the Late West, during the time of the Industrial Revolution, and the rise of the bourgeoisie, it is what "old wealth" was calling with disdain the "new rich", who did not have the sense of *noblesse oblige* that had been passed on through landed families for centuries; who, as we might say, lacked "class", no matter what their wealth.

---

[67] Frank, 705.
[68] Duff, 205-206.
[69] C. Northcote Parkinson,), 100-101.
[70] Ibid., 100.

India

India is the most commonly cited example of a civilisation that decayed through miscegenation, the invading Aryans imposing a High Culture on India and then forever falling into decay because of miscegenation with the low caste "blacks", or Dravidians. However, genetic research indicates that the higher castes have retained a predominately Caucasian genetic inheritance:

> "As one moves from lower to upper castes, the distance from Asians becomes progressively larger. The distance between Europeans and lower castes is larger than the distance between Europeans and upper castes, but the distance between Europeans and middle castes is smaller than the upper caste-European distance. ... Among the upper castes the genetic distance between Brahmins and Europeans (0.10) is smaller than that between either the Kshatriya and Europeans (0.12) or the Vysya and Europeans (0.16). Assuming that contemporary Europeans reflect West Eurasian affinities, these data indicate that the amount of West Eurasian admixture with Indian populations may have been proportionate to caste rank."

> "As expected if the lower castes are more similar to Asians than to Europeans, and the upper castes are more similar to Europeans than to Asians, the frequencies of M and M3 haplotypes are inversely proportional to caste rank."

> "In contrast to the mtDNA distances, the Y-chromosome STR data do not demonstrate a closer affinity to Asians for each caste group. Upper castes are more similar to Europeans than to Asians, middle castes are equidistant from the two groups, and lower castes are most similar to Asians. The genetic distance between caste populations and Africans is progressively larger moving from lower to middle to upper caste groups"... "results suggest that Indian Y chromosomes, particularly upper caste Y chromosomes, are more similar to European than to Asian Y chromosomes."

> "Nevertheless, each separate upper caste is more similar to Europeans than to Asians."[71]

---

71 Michael Bamshad, et al., 994–1004.

Citing further studies, "...admixture with African or proto-Australoid populations" is "occasional".[72]

The chaos that afflicted India was of religio-cultural type rather than racial. Despite the superficiality of dusky hues, the Indian ruling castes have retained their Caucasian identity to the present. There was no genetic destruction of Indian Civilisation by miscegenation with "blacks".

The Real Meaning of *Varna*

The caste system introduced by the Aryans was based on their social hierarchy prior to entering India. Among themselves there were priests, warriors and commoners. To these were added the *sudra*. Because the word caste, *varna*, also means "colour", it was assumed by 19th century Indologists in Europe that this referred to race, and that the breakdown of the race-based caste system caused the collapse of Indian civilisation. *Varna* is the symbolic (heraldic) colour applied to the castes. While sudra (labourers) were "black", the colour was symbolic of unenlightenment; one might say, "being in the dark". By contrast the brahmana priests were "white". The warrior, ksatriya caste was symbolised as red, the colour often associated with the martial ethos in numerous cultures, after the identity of the "red planet", Mars. The vaishya, or merchants, were symbolised with yellow (gold).[73] Hindu tradition describes *varna* symbolically:

> *Sattwa*, white colour, shining, wisdom, light;
> *Rajas*, red colour, reflecting energy, motion;
> *Tamas*, black colour, covering ignorance, darkness.

Varna derives from the root word *Vṛtra* वृत्र, meaning essence or quality. This would be apt in describing the traditional meaning and purpose of castes of a hierarchical society: to maintain character. It is not traditionally a "colour bar" in terms of preventing miscegenation. The colour or *varna* symbolised the character of the caste one was born into. It is based on the maintenance of "race" as understood by tradition, defined by Oswald Spengler as "duration of character", and of "having race", as having a certain élan. To the brahmanic civilisation

---

72   Ibid.
73   David Frawley, 261-62.

"having race" was fulfilling one's *dharma* or cosmic duty and ensuring ones ritual purity by correctly performing the prescribed rites of purification, embodied to the highest degree by the brahman caste. This is explained in the *Bhagavad Gita*, the primary Hindu text:

> "The duties of the Brahmins, Kshatriyas, Vaishyas, and Shudras— are distributed according to their qualities, in accordance with their guṇas (and not by birth).
>
> "Tranquillity, restraint, austerity, purity, patience, integrity, knowledge, wisdom, and belief in a hereafter—these are the intrinsic qualities of work for Brahmins.
>
> "Valour, strength, fortitude, skill in weaponry, resolve never to retreat from battle, large-heartedness in charity, and leadership abilities, these are the natural qualities of work for Kshatriyas.
>
> "Agriculture, dairy farming, and commerce are the natural works for those with the qualities of Vaishyas. Serving through work is the natural duty for those with the qualities of Shudras.
>
> "By fulfilling their duties, born of their innate qualities, human beings can attain perfection. Now hear from me how one can become perfect by discharging one's prescribed duties.
>
> "By performing one's natural occupation, one worships the Creator from whom all living entities have come into being, and by whom the whole universe is pervaded. By such performance of work, a person easily attains perfection.
>
> "It is better to do one's own *dharma*, even though imperfectly, than to do another's *dharma*, even though perfectly. By doing one's innate duties, a person does not incur sin.
>
> "One should not abandon duties born of one's nature, even if one sees defects in them, O son of Kunti. Indeed, all endeavours are veiled by some evil, as fire is by smoke".[74]

---

[74] Bhagavad Gita, 18: 41-48.

The Decline and Fall of Civilisations

With reference to the Sanskrit gunas गुण (18: 41) which means the quality or character of something, one sees the ethical and moral basis of *varna*. The *Mahabharata*, of which the *Bhagavad Gita* is a part, reiterates that sudra are those who are not in accord with the *dharmic* law of the cosmos, regardless of their birth:

> "The devotees of the Lord are not Shudras; Shudras are they who have no faith in the Lord whichever be their caste. A wise man should not slight even an outcaste if he is devoted to the Lord; he who looks down on him will fall into hell".

> "A man does not become a Brahman by the mere fact of his birth, not even by the acquisition of Vedic scholarship; it is good character alone that can make one a Brahman. He will be worse than a Shudra if his conduct is not in conformity with the rules of good behaviour".

The *Mahabharata* states of Krishna's warrior companion, Arjuna the archer, that he "put his dark arm" around the river goddess Ganga to console her.[75] *Tulsidas Ramayana* relates that when Sita is asked by village women "which of the two men is your husband", she answers, "the dark one [Rama] is my husband, the fair one is my brother in law". Vyasa, who composed the *Mahabharata*, was the son of a fisherwoman and a brahman father. Valmiki, author of the epic *Ramayana*, was a hunter who became a brahman through his wisdom. Aitareya, who wrote the *Aitareya Upanishad*, was the son of a sudra woman.

It is apparent that the caste system designed to assure a hierarchy based on character, allowed for social mobility. The assumption among those who see miscegenation resulting in the decay of Indian civilisation is that this was caused by the undermining of a race-based caste system. Earnest S. Cox for example, wrote of the "Hindu religion which gave its sanction to caste to preserve the Caucasian", but that "the illegitimate mixed breeds in India twenty-five centuries ago had increased until they were more numerous that the whites", giving rise to Buddhism, which stripped Brahminism of caste and sought to "level the races".[76] To the contrary, the caste system became ossified during India's cycle

---

75 Vyasa, Mahabharata "The Lonely Encounter", 215.
76 Cox, 79.

of decline, when character no longer determined status. As has been seen, genetic studies show India is racially much as it has been since Vedic times, so miscegenation cannot account for the decay of her civilisation, and Buddhism was very quickly absorbed into a resilient Hinduism without impacting the castes.

The Indus Valley

Supposedly a civilisation that succumbed to Aryan invasions from Afghanistan, the civilisation of the Indus Valley, primarily in what became Pakistan, was a vast culture region extending across 30% of the Indian landmass, whose trade relations extended to Sumerian. Skeletal evidence from Indus indicates "proto-Mediterranean" with a "Negroid" element, "broad nosed" with a large brain case.[77] A "Veddid or Australoid ethnic strain appears to be at the base of the Indus people".[78] The widespread Aryan invasion of Indus, and the skull-cracking of its natives,[79] is a long-held but now discredited myth. The Aryans appear to have been contemporaneous with the proto-Mediterranean and Indus *ethnoi* rather than later intrusions. The brahmanic religion that became Hinduism is likely to have had its roots in the Indus civilisation rather than having been introduced by Aryan invaders. The *Vedic* literature could reach as far back as before 3000 B.C.[80]

Settlements of cultivators in the Indus Valley date to 7000B.C. The Indus Valley civilisation extends through 2500 B.C. to 1900 B.C., although the civilisation had decayed by 1300.[81] What might be called the "Spring epoch" in Spengler's scheme, occurred for the Indus around 2600 B.C. The features of the Indus High Culture include: well-crafted seals with animal motifs; town planning including, drainage; a system of weights and measures; distinctive ceramic and figurine styles, and the emergence of a social hierarchy.[82]

---

77 A. Ghosh (ed.) An Encyclopaedia of Indian Archaeology, Vol. 1 "Skeletal Remains", 317-318.

78 S. S. Sarakar, "Aboriginal Races of India", Bulletin of the Anthropological Survey of India, Calcutta, 1964 (i), cited by Ghosh, 318.

79 Anthony Esler, 1992; William McNeill, 1997; 1989.

80 Navaratna S. Rajaram, 1995.

81 M. N. Vahia and N. Yadav, 2011, 27-28.

82 Ibid., 31.

The Decline and Fall of Civilisations

The decay of the Indus Valley civilization cannot be ascribed to the influence of a "Negroid" element. Negroids had been a component of the Indus Valley race in its primordial beginnings. Despite the rise and fall of the Indus Valley civilisation the biological race from prehistory to the present day has remained stable. In general the Indus race was "tall, long-headed and broad-nosed".[83] "The population of the Indus Valley appears to have remained more or less stable from the Harrapa times to the present day".[84] Physical anthropologist and archaeologist Kenneth R. Kennedy, who examined the skeletons from Harrapa city, states that he "recognizes a biological continuum of many of their morphometric variables in the modern populations of Punjab and Sindh".[85]

Vahia and Nadav of the Tata Institute of Fundamental Research, suggest a pattern for the life-cycle of civilisations when seeking an explanation for the decline of Indus. They state that when a civilisation reaches a certain phase of development it must expand, whether territorially and/or technology or contract and collapse.[86] History testifies through time and place, from Rome and Central and South America to Tonga, recent Japan, Britain, and the current de facto world empire of the USA, empire-building is the usual end-product of a civilisation or state that has reached a critical mass in balance between resources and population. "[A]t the peak of the exploitation of its current capabilities, a society is essentially in a self-contradictory course. It not only enjoys highest level of prosperity, but also must quickly come up with the next level of rise to avoid a collapse in near future".[87]

As Spengler pointed out, empire is the last stage of civilisation. However, there is a self-destruct mechanism within the imperial cycle that ends with the over-extension of borders and conversely the importation of alien subjects, and with them alien ideas, that more often lead to decay rather than to invigoration.

---

83   Ghosh, 317.
84   Ibid., 318.
85   Kenneth R. Kennedy, "Skulls, Aryans, and Flowing Drains: The Interface of Archaeology and Skeletal Biology in the Study of the Harappan Civilization", in Possehl, 291.
86   M. N. Vahia and N. Yadav.
87   Ibid., 38.

Civilisations That Died

While the common explanation for the decline and depopulation of the Indus cities is that of environmental changes due to changes in monsoon patterns, Vahia and Yadav do not concur:

> "However, the changes seem to be small and cannot fully account for the fall of the civilisation. It seems that the fall of the civilisation seems to have been triggered by internal reasons rather than external factors.[88]

> "As the society becomes ever richer, it finds it increasingly difficult to meet the increasing expectations of its population and heads to chaos. If the technological breakthrough does not come at its scheduled time, the chaos ensuing from the inability to meet the increasing demands and expectations may actually result in a fall in the standard of living…"[89]

By 1300 B.C. Harrapa was overcrowded, and the hitherto orderly streets were being encroached on by houses and workshops.

> "The fact that this was a decay rather than destruction is highlighted by Kenoyer[90] (2008). Discussing the environmental evidence, he concluded that there was no substantial evidence of change in weather pattern. He also shows that the decay was gradual, at least in Harappa where signs of overcrowding, decay beginning with loss of the elite along with the disappearance of signs of complex mercantile activities such as weights and seals".[91]

The decline in the quality of brick manufacturing, a key feature of the Indus civilisation, at Harrapa during the "Late Phase", is an important indication of cultural decay. "[T]he decline in baked brick manufacturing is not merely a loss of one specific technology, but also represents a considerable loss of symbolism". The quality of brick manufacturing indicated a central authority ensuring that there was standardisation of brick dimensions, which had a precise ration of 4:2:1, with standardised moulds in use from 4000 to 3600 B.C. During the "Late Phase" there

---

88   Ibid., 33.
89   Ibid., 38.
90   J. M. Kenoyer, 2008, 183-208.
91   M. N. Vahia and N. Yadav, op. cit., 33.

was a deviation from the so-called "Indus proportion". The change in style and quality of brick manufacture is a significant indicator of transformation in Indus or at least Harrapan society:

> "Beyond the molds, the standards are also preserved in the craftsmen's tradition and in social norms. The deviation from the standard in the Harappan Late phase could therefore point to a changed social norm, or to the lack of craftsmen to keep up the traditional brick manufacture".[92]

During the "Late phase", there was not only a decline in trade but a change in religion. The change in the belief system is indicated by a change in burial methods, which also implies a change in the ruling elite.[93] Khan and Lemmen also do not agree that environmental changes were sufficient to cause the collapse of the civilisation.[94] Environmental changes could have exacerbated the culture-crisis with an inability of the new social structure to maintain flood protection.[95]

They ask, "what do bricks tell us about these social changes?" Up to five changes in brick proportion suggest shifts in architectural preference and lack of control by those responsible for urban planning. The urban centres seem also to have been experiencing a reversal in population, including the loss of craftsmen, with the disintegration of cities into villages.[96]

This suggests what was being played out was the process of decline that Spengler stated leads to a people becoming *Fellaheen*, unless being pushed into new historical directions, as indeed occurred with the rise of the brahmanic-Hindu Civilisation after the Indus.

---

92 A. Khan and C. Lemmen, 5.
93 Ibid., 6.
94 Ibid., 7.
95 Ibid.
96 Ibid.

Civilisations That Died

Maurya

The Mauryan Empire united much of India, and under Asoka a practical unifying ethos of *Dhamma* was formulated by combining elements of Buddhism and Hinduism that was "pragmatic and intensely ethical". A moral discipline was imposed by Asoka's *Dhammic* edicts, prohibiting excessive feasting and drinking, animal fights and sacrifices.[97] Family was the social foundation.[98] Theft was rare, laws were straightforward, resources and food were abundant, metallurgy, manufacturing textiles, and carpentry, including boat-building, were widespread and impressive, according to Greek observers.[99] Typical of the High Culture cycle, economic activity was organised through guilds. Merchants were forbidden excessive profits and subjected to laws protecting the public from poor quality goods.[100] Mauryan India was noted for the excellence of its stone monuments and buildings, initiated by Asoka. In particular the Mauryan stone columns, crowned with colossal animal sculptures, were considered without equal in the world.[101]

In contrast to Asoka, his fourth successor, Salisuka, was noted for his cruelty and injustice.[102] Like Sargon's Mesopotamia, Darius' Persia, Alexander's Greece, and others, subsequent generations of the ruling class did not have the stamina of their forebears. Stagnation followed a succession of rulers circa 150 B.C. Professor Sen comments: "The successors of Asoka proved unequal to the task of maintaining intact the mighty fabric of the emporia or to arrest the forces of decay". There followed a "woeful tale" of "divided loyalty and the dismemberment of the provinces from central moorings". The dismembering of the empire was encouraged by the political alliances of the Greek invaders in 206 B.C. "A succession of feeble rulers" after Asoka could not maintain the unity of the state. There was a quick succession of kings, and with each there were changes in the state bureaucracy. Despite the social ethos of Asoka's *Dhamma*, an Indian national consciousness was lacking, and in the absence of a strong king such as Asoka, provincialism dismembered the empire.[103]

---

97   Sailendra Nath Sen, 148.
98   Ibid., 150.
99   Ibid., 158.
100 Ibid., 159-160.
101 Ibid., 166.
102 Ibid., 152.
103 Ibid., 154.

The Decline and Fall of Civilisations

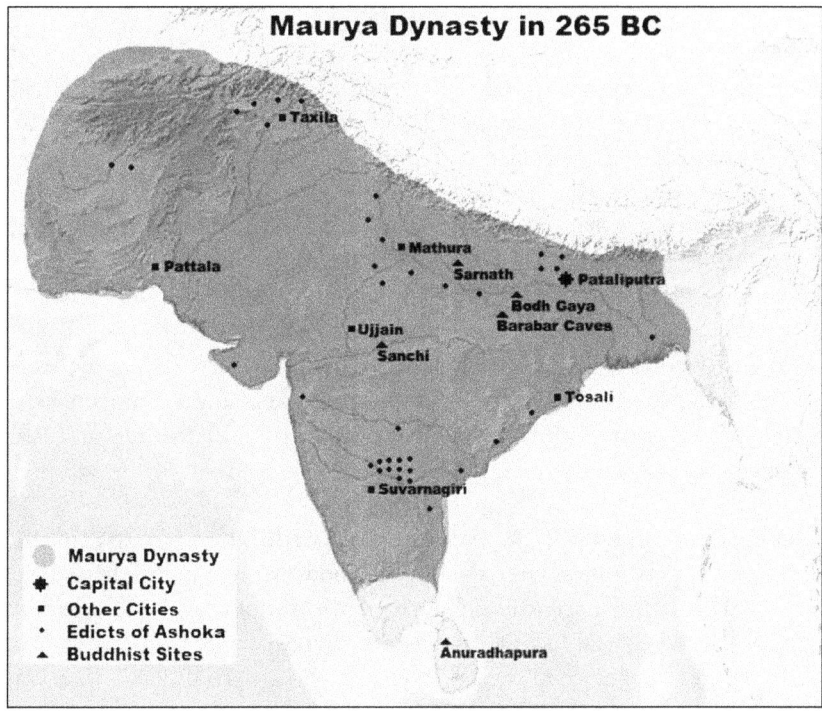

Extent of the Mauryan Empire in 265 B.C.

The Mauryan ruler Vasumitra succumbed to hedonism, and "afforded a welcome opportunity to the forces of disintegration to set in". While watching a theatrical performance he was murdered by Kosala, whose rule provided an opportunity for the unitary Mauryan state to succumb to the separatism of local princes. Mauryan India lingered until circa 185 B.C., when the last Maurya, Brihadratha, a weak ruler unable to resist Greek invaders, was assassinated, and the Sunga dynasty emerged.[104] Devabhuti, assuming the Sunga rulership in 82 B.C., "was a dissolute king", overthrown after a ten year reign, and a new dynasty was formed, the Kanvayana.[105]

---

104 Ibid., 168.
105 Ibid., 171.

Gupta India

Centuries of foreign invasions, dynastic ebbs and flows, and provincial rivalries, acceded to the rise of another great empire in 320 A.D., the Gupta, "the last great empire builders"[106] of India. Samudragupta is remembered as the "Indian Napoleon" for his establishment of a unitary state covering much of India.[107] Under the Guptas India experienced two hundred years of "unexampled moral and material progress, under a resurgent Brahminism and decline in Buddhism.[108] Like the Mauryans, Gupta subjects were honest, and the priests and warriors lived simply. The guilds, self-governing, were again the basis of the social economy. Relations between workers and employers were subjected to state arbitration. Metallurgy, manufacturing and the sciences, especially chemistry, advanced.[109]

Dissension both among the provinces and within the dynasty, and the brief rise of Yashodharman, chief of Mandasor, who had defeated the Hunas (Huns), caused the collapse of the Gupta, and independent kingdoms were established. The Gupta dynasty was eclipsed by 550 A.D. Professor Sen[110] notes again that it was internal decay that was the foundation of the collapse of the Gupta Empire:

> "The Guptas in the last days of their sovereignty experienced a veritable decay when dissensions in the imperial family itself sapped the vitality of the empire. ... The influence of religion cannot altogether be ignored in discussing causes of the decline of the Gupta empires that had been the case of the Maurya Empire when the people lost the virility due to the teaching on non-violence, an essential ingredient of Buddhism. While the earlier Guptas were staunch followers of Brahminism, the later Gupta rulers... had Buddhist leanings".[111]

---

106   Ibid., 227.
107   Ibid., 209.
108   Ibid., 227.
109   Ibid., 241.
110   Emeritus Professor of History, University of Calcutta, Senior Research Fellow, Indian Council of Historical Research.
111   Sailendra Nath Sen, 223.

The Decline and Fall of Civilisations

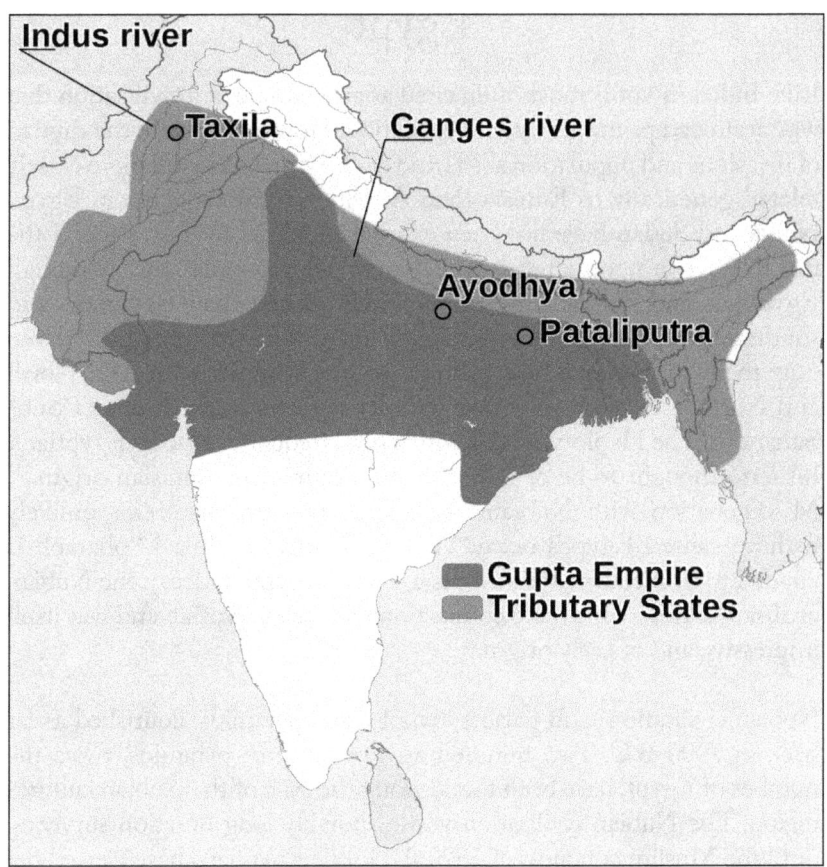

The Gupta Empire - 320-550 A.D.

Goyal states that the unity of the Gupta Empire, relying on the assertiveness of the emperor, with inspiration from the energy of the Vaishnava doctrine "gradually ebbed down due to the influence of the life-negating and world-renouncing esoteric doctrine of the later Buddhism. It eventually sucked the Gupta emperors dry of their martial fervour and capacity for administering subordinates with strength and determination".[112] The Gupta era is considered the "golden age of Indian history".[113] "The post-Gupta period is noted for the state of confusion and confrontation in the history of northern India".[114]

---
112 S. R. Goyal, *A History of the Imperial Gupta* (1967), 368, quoted by Sen, 223.
113 Ashvini Agrawal, 264.
114 P. N. Chopra, 174.

Civilisations That Died

Egypt

Like India, Egypt is most often cited as an example of a civilisation that was destroyed primarily by miscegenation. However, despite the myriad of invasions and population shifts, today's Egyptians are still more closely related genetically to Eurasia than Africa. Migrations between Egypt, Nubia and Sudan have not been extensive enough to "homogenise the mtDNA gene pools of the Nile River Valley populations", although Egyptians and Nubians are more closely related than Egyptians and southern Sudanese. However, significant differences remain.[115] Even now, today's Egyptians have primary genetic affinities with Asia, North and Northeast Africa. The least affinity is to the populations of Sub-Sahara.[116] The Haplotype M1, with a high frequency among Egyptians, hitherto thought to be of Sub-Saharan origin, is of Eurasian origin.[117] Miscegenation with Nubian "slaves" and mercenaries seems unlikely to have caused Egypt's decay. While a Nubian or "black" pharaoh is alluded to by racial-materialists as a sign of Egyptian decay, the Nubian civilisation had an intimate connection with the Egyptian and was itself impressive and of early origin.

Nubian civilisation with palaces, temples and pyramids, flourished as far back as 7000 B.C. Two hundred an twenty-three pyramids, twice the number of Egypt, have been found along the Nile of the Nubian culture-region. The Nubian civilisation was of notably long duration surviving until the Muslim conquest of 1500 A.D. The Egyptians have viewed the Nubians either as a "conquered race or a superior enemy". Hence, Egyptian depictions of shackled black slaves give an inaccurate impression.[118]

Nubians became the pharaohs of Egypt's 25th dynasty, providing stability where previously there had been ruin caused by civil wars between warlords, circa 700 B.C. The Nubians were the custodians of Egyptian faith and culture at a time when Egypt was decaying. They regarded the restoration of the faith of Amun as their duty. It was the Nubian dynasties (760-656 B.C.), especially the rulership of Taharqa, which revived and purified Egyptian culture and religion. It was under

---
115 Matthias Krings, et al, 1173.
116 L. L. Cavalli-Sforza, et al, 1994.
117 Ana M. Gonzalez, et al., 8: 223.
118 Johanna Granville, 472.

The Decline and Fall of Civilisations

Egyptian Pharaoh Taharqa, of the 25th Dynasty.

the white rule of the Libyan pharaohs of the 21st dynasty (1069-1043 B.C.) that Egypt began a sharp decline. Ptolemaic (Greek) rule (332-30 B.C.) under Ptolemy IV (222 to 205 B.C.) brought to the rich and sumptuous pharaohs' court "lax morals and vicious lifestyle" ending in "decadence and anarchy".[119] Byzantine rule (395 to 640 A.D.) wrought destruction on the Egyptian heritage, which was succeeded by Islam.

Of the long vicissitudes of Egypt's rise and fall, it was the Nubian dynasty that had restored Egyptian cultural integrity. References to Nubians on the throne of the pharaohs tell no more of the causes of Egypt's decay than if historians several millennia hence sought to ascribe the causes of the USA's culture retardation to Obama's presidency as a "black".

We see in Egypt as in Rome, the Moorish civilisation, India and others, the causes of culture decay and fall as being something more than miscegenation. The contemporary Western should look for answers beyond this if only because he can see for himself that the West's decay has no relationship to miscegenation. The number of Americans

---

119 Fayid Atiya, 2006.

describing themselves as "mixed race" was just under 9 million in 2010. The USA did not become the global centre of culture-pestilence because of its mixed race population. What is more significant than the percentages of miscegenation, are the percentages of population decline caused by such factors as abortion. Twenty-one percent of all pregnancies in the USA are aborted.[120] These are the factors that indicate the pathogenic state of a civilisation.

Of Egypt's chaos contemporary sages observed the disintegration of authority, traditional religion, and the founding ethos. Egypt was often subjected to invasions and to natural disasters. These served as catalysts for cultural degeneration. The papyrus called *The Admonitions of an Egyptian Sage*, credited to Ipuwer, states that after invasions and class war, Egypt fell apart, there was family strife, the noble families were dispossessed by the lowest castes, authority was disrespected and overthrown, lawlessness and plunder were the norm, and the nobility was attacked: "A man looks upon his son as an enemy. A man smites his brother (the son of his mother)". Craftsmanship has become degraded: "No craftsmen work, the enemies of the land have spoilt its crafts". There is rebellion against the Uraeus or Re. "A few lawless men have ventured to despoil the land of the kingship". It appears that the foundations of traditional society, god, monarch, family and land, have been caste asunder. "Asiatics" have seized the land from the ancestral occupiers, and have so insinuated themselves into the Egyptian culture that one can no longer tell who is Egyptian and who is alien: "There are no Egyptians anywhere".[121] "Women are lacking and no children are conceived".[122] The political and administrative structure has collapsed, with "no officers in their place". The laws are trampled on and cast aside. "Serfs become lords of serfs". The writings of the scribes are destroyed.

What is being described is not a sudden upheaval, although the allusion to natural disasters and Asiatic invasion would imply this. The breakdown of regal authority, civil authority, depopulation, laws, family bonds, religious faith, agriculture and the social structure, imply an epoch of decline into chaos. The social structure has been reversed,

---

120 R. K. Jones and J. Jerman, 2014, 46(1):3–14.
121 A. H. Gardiner, 9.
122 Ibid., 10.

as though a communistic revolution had occurred. "He who possessed no property is now a man of wealth. The prince praises him. The poor of the land have become rich, and the possessor of the land has become one who has nothing. Female slaves speak as they like to their mistresses. Orders become irksome. Those who could not build a boat now possesses ships. "The possessors of robes are now in rags". "The children of princes are cast out in the street".[123]

With this inversion of hierarchy has come irreligion and the degradation of religion. The ignorant now perform their own rites to the gods. Wrong offerings are made to the gods.[124] "Right is cast aside. Wrong is inside the council-chamber. The plans of the gods are violated, their ordinances are neglected… Reverence, an end put to it". [125]

Ipuwer's admonition was not only to rid Egypt of its enemies but to return to the traditional ethos. This meant the reinstitution of proper religious rites, and the purification of the temples. "A fighter will come forth," Ipuwer prophesises, to "destroy the wrongs". "Is he sleeping? Behold, his might is not seen".[126] The Egyptians await an avatar, the personification of the Sun God Ra (which tradition states was the first of the Pharaohs). Ipuwer avers to Egypt having previously gone through such epochs, alluding to his saying nothing other than what others have said before his time.[127]

The Pharaoh is castigated for allowing Egypt to fall into chaos, with his authority being undermined, and without taking corrective actions.[128] The Pharaoh as God-king had not maintained his authority as the nexus between the earthly kingdom and the divine. The Pharaoh had caused "confusion throughout the land". Certainty of the social hierarchy, crowned by the God-king, is the basis of traditional societies. It seems that Egypt had entered into an epoch of what a Westerner could today identify as scepticism and secularism.

---

123 Ibid., 11.
124 Ibid., 11.
125 Ibid/, 102.
126 Ibid., 13.
127 Ibid., 97.
128 Ibid., 8.

Nefer-rohu warned Pharaoh of similar chaos. Likewise there would be "Asiatic" invasions, natural disasters, Ra withdrawing his light, and again the inversion of hierarchy:

> "The weak of arm is now the possessor of an arm. Men salute respectfully him whom formerly saluted. I show thee the undermost on top, turned about in proportion to the turning about of my belly. The top man will make wealth. It is the paupers who eat the offering bread, while the servants jubilate. The Heliopolitan Nome, the birthplace of every god, will no longer be on earth". [129]

It is notable, again, that Nefer-rohu identifies the chaos with the breaking of the nexus with the divine and the inversion of hierarchy. Also of interest is that Nefer-rohu refers to a redeemer, who has a Nubian mother, uniting Egypt and driving out the Asiatics and the Libyans (the whitest of races of the region) and defeating the rebellious. Chaos resulted not from race-factors but from a falling away of the regal and religious authority. The race-factor was that of the Nubians being the custodians of culture during periods of Egyptian decay.

Arabia

Islam had its Golden Age, centred in Morocco, and extending into Spain. The cultures that flourished in Morocco, both Islamic and pre-Islamic, were Berber. The Islamic civilisation they established with the founding of the Idrisid dynasty in 788 A.D. was ended by the invasion of the Fatimids from Tunisia ca. 900 A.D. Chaos ensued. Although there was a revival of High Culture during the 11th and 14th centuries, dynasties fell in the face of tribalism. The 16th century saw a revival initiated by al-Ghalin, several decades of wars of succession after his death in 1603, and continuing decline under Saadi dynastic rule during 1627 to 1659.

Caucasoid mtDNA sequences are at frequencies of 96% in Moroccan Berbers, 82% in Algerian Berbers and 78% in non-Berber Moroccans. The study of Esteban et al found that Moroccan Northern and

---

[129] "The Prophesy of Nefer-rohu", translated by John A. Wilson, 1973.

Southern Berbers have only 3% to 1% Sub-Saharan mtDNA.[130] Although difficult to define, since "Berber" is a Roman, not an indigenous term, the estimate for present day Morocco is 35% to 45% Berber, with the rest being Berber-Arab mixture.[131] The primary point is that the Moroccan civilisation had ruling classes, whether pre-Islamic or Islamic, that remained predominantly Berber-Caucasian for most of its history, whether during its epochs of glory or of decline. Miscegenation does not account for the fall of the Moorish civilisation.

The High Culture of Spain was brought to ruin and decay not by miscegenation between "superior" Spaniards" and "inferior" Moors but by the overthrow of the Moorish ruling caste. Stanley Lane-Poole refers to the decay that descended on Moorish Spain:

> "Andalusia, at all events, could not dispense with her leaders; and the instant her leader died, down fell the State. When 'great Cæsar fell,' then 'I and you and all of us fell down,' not so much for sympathy as incapacity. The multiplicity of mutually hostile parties and factions made anything resembling a settled constitution impossible in the dominion of the Moors. Only a strong hand could restrain the animosity of the opposing creeds and races in Andalusia; and those who have considered the character and history of Ireland, and the irreconcilable enmity which prevails between the north and the south in that island of factions, will allow that the Arabs were not the only people who found mixed races and religions impossible to govern with the smoothness of a homogeneous nation.

> "Each revolution brought its fresh crop of horrors. The people of Cordova, who had greatly increased in numbers, had also nourished those independent sentiments which the immense development of trade and manual industry, and the consequent creation of a prosperous artisan class, generally promote; and when they overturned Almanzor's dynasty, the mob broke out in the usual manner of mobs, and wreaked their vengeance by pillaging the beautiful palace which the great Minister had built in the neighbourhood of the capital for the use of himself

---

130 E. *Esteban, et al., 2004, 31(2): 202–212.*
131 Steven L. Danver, 23.

and the government officials. When they had ransacked the priceless treasures of the palace, they abandoned it to the flames. Massacres, plundering, and assassination went on unchecked for four days. Cordova became a shambles. Then the Berbers had their turn; the imperious Slav guards, who had won the cordial detestation of the people, were succeeded by the brutal Berbers, who rioted in the plunder of the city. Wherever these barbarians went, slaughter, fire and outrage followed. Palace after palace was ransacked and burnt, and the lovely city of Ez-Zahrā, the delight of the Great Khalif, was captured by treachery, sacked, and set on fire, so that there remained of all the exquisite art that two khalifs had lavished upon its ornament nothing but a heap of blackened stones. Its garrison was put to the sword; its inhabitants fled for refuge to the mosque; but the Berbers had neither scruples nor bowels, and men, women, and children were butchered in the sacred precincts".[132]

What is most significant is the rise to prominence of what in Western terms was a bourgeois class, resulting in a mob revolt. It seems analogous to the West's epochal event: the French Revolution of 1789, that eliminated the final vestiges of tradition. Most significantly Lane-Poole refers to the decayed condition of the once vigorous Berbers, who had established the Moorish civilization in North Africa and Spain:

"What had happened to the Romans and the Goths now happened to the Berbers. They came to Spain hardy rough warriors, unused to ease or luxuries, delighting in feats of strength and prowess, filled with a fierce but simple zeal for their religion. They had not been long in the enjoyment of the fruits of their victory when all the demoralization which the soft luxuries of Capua brought upon the soldiers of Hannibal came also upon them. They lost their martial habits, their love of deeds of daring, their pleasure in enduring hardships in the brave way of war—they lost all their manliness with inconceivable rapidity. In twenty years there was no Berber army that could be trusted to repel the attacks of the Castilians; in its place was a disorganized crowd of sodden debauchees, miserable poltroons, who had

---

132 Stanley Lane-Poole, 1886, X.

drunk and fooled away their manhood's vigour and become slaves to all the appetites that make men cowards. Instead of preserving order, they had now become the disturbers of order; brigands, when they could pluck up courage to attack a peaceful traveller; thieves on all promising opportunities". [133]

The Muslims had become effete. The scene was set for their displacement by those who had retained their robustness of character by eschewing moral and material corruption:

"Though descended from an older kingdom, the northern states had most of the qualities of new nations. They were rude and uncultivated; few of their princes possessed the elements of what could be called education, and they were too poor to indulge in the refined luxuries of the Moorish sovereigns. The Christians were simply rough warriors, as fond of fighting as even their Moslem antagonists, but even better prepared by their hard and necessarily self-denying lives for the endurance of long campaigns and the performance of desperate deeds of valour". [134]

The lesson of the Moors is the same as that of other civilisations far and wide: "Every nation, it appears, has its time of growth and its period of efflorescence, after which comes the age of decay. As Greece fell, as Rome fell, as every ancient kingdom the world has known has risen, triumphed, and fallen, so fell the Moors in Spain". [135]

Ibn Khaldun (1332-1406), a well-travelled sage, grappled with the same problems confronting Islamic civilisation as those Spengler confronted in regard to The West. A celebrated scholar, political adviser, and jurist, Ibn Khaldun's domain of influence extended over the whole Islamic world. His major theoretical work is *Muqaddimah* (1377) intended as a preface to his universal history, *Kitabal-Ibar*, where he sought to establish basic principles of history by which historians could understand events. His theory is cyclic and morphological, based on "conditions within nations and races [which] change with

---

133 Ibid.
134 Ibid., XI.
135 Ibid., XII.

the change of periods and the passage of time".¹³⁶ Like Evola¹³⁷ he was pessimistic as to what can be achieved by political action in the cycle of decline, writing that the "past resembles the future more than one drop of water another".¹³⁸

Ibn Khaldun stated that history can be understood as a recurrence of similar patterns motivated by the drives of acquisition, group co-operation, and regal authority in the creation of a civilisation, followed by a cycle of decay. These primary drives become distorted and lead to the corrupting factors of luxury and domination, irresponsibility of authority and decline.

Like Spengler, in regard to the peasantry,¹³⁹ Ibn Khaldun traced the beginning of culture to group or familial loyalty starting with the simple life of the desert. The isolation and familial bonds lead to self-reliance, loyalty and leadership on the basis of mutual respect. Life is struggle, not luxury. According to Ibn Khaldun, when rulership becomes centralised and divorced from such kinship, free reign is given to luxury and ease. Political alliances are bought and intrigued rather than being based on the initial bonds and loyalties. Corruption pervades as the requirements of luxury increase. The decadence starts from the top, among the ruling class, and extends downward until the founding ethos of the culture is discarded, or exists in name only.¹⁴⁰ Ibn Khaldun begins from the organic character of the noble family in describing the analogous nature of cultural rise and fall, caused by a falling away of the original creative ethos with each successive generation:

> "The builder of the family's glory knows what it cost him to do the work, and he keeps the qualities that created his glory and made it last. The son who comes after him had personal contact with his father and thus learned those things from him. However, he is inferior to him in this respect, inasmuch as a person who learns things through study is inferior to a

---

136 Muhammad Ibn Khalud, The Muqaddimah, Franz Rosenthal, 24.
137 Julius Evola, 2003.
138 M. Ibn Khalud, 12.
139 Oswald Spengler, The Decline..., Vol. II, p. 184.
140 M. Ibn Khaldun, 366.

The Decline and Fall of Civilisations

Ibn Khaldun historian and sociologist, 1334-1406 A.D.

person who knows them from practical application. The third generation must be content with imitation and, in particular, with reliance upon tradition. This member is inferior to him of the second generation, inasmuch as a person who relies upon tradition is inferior to a person who exercises judgment.

"The fourth generation, then, is inferior to the preceding ones in every respect. Its member has lost the qualities that preserved the edifice of its glory. He despises those qualities. He imagines that the edifice was not built through application and effort. He thinks that it was something due to his people from the very beginning by virtue of the mere fact of their descent, and not something that resulted from group effort and individual qualities. For he sees the great respect in which he is held by the people, but he does not know how that respect originated and what the reason for it was. He imagines it is due to his descent and nothing else. He keeps away from those in whose group feeling he shares, thinking that he is better than they".[141]

For Ibn Khaldun's "generation" we might say with Spengler "cultural epoch". Ibn Khaldun addresses the *causes* of this cultural etiolation, leading to the corrupting impact of materialism. Again, his analysis is remarkably similar to that of Spengler and the decay of the Classical civilisations:

---
141 Ibid., 107.

"When a tribe has achieved a certain measure of superiority with the help of its group feeling, it gains control over a corresponding amount of wealth and comes to share prosperity and abundance with those who have been in possession of these things. It shares in them to the degree of its power and usefulness to the ruling dynasty. If the ruling dynasty is so strong that no-one thinks of depriving it of its power or of sharing with it, the tribe in question submits to its rule and is satisfied with whatever share in the dynasty's wealth and tax revenue it is permitted to enjoy. ... Members of the tribe are merely concerned with prosperity, gain and a life of abundance. (They are satisfied) to lead an easy, restful life in the shadow of the ruling dynasty, and to adopt royal habits in building and dress, a matter they stress and in which they take more and more pride, the more luxuries and plenty they acquire, as well as all the other things that go with luxury and plenty.

"As a result the toughness of desert life is lost. Group feeling and courage weaken. Members of the tribe revel in the well-being that God has given them. Their children and offspring grow up too proud to look after themselves or to attend to their own needs. They have disdain also for all the other things that are necessary in connection with group feeling.... Their group feeling and courage decrease in the next generations. Eventually group feeling is altogether destroyed. ... It will be swallowed up by other nations."[142]

Ibn Khaldun refers to the "tribe" and "group feeling" where Spengler refers to nations, peoples, and races. The dominant culture becomes corrupted through its own success and its culture becomes static; its inward strength diminishes in proportion to its outward glamour. Hence, the Golden Age of Islam is over, as are those of Rome and Athens. New York, Paris, and London are in the analogous cultural epochs of these fallen city-states. The "world city" becomes the focus of a world civilisation that ends as cosmopolitan and far removed from its founding roots. The Muslim determination of what is "progress" and what is "decline" has a spiritual foundation:

---

142 Ibid.

"The progressiveness or backwardness of society at any given point of time is determinable in relative terms. It can be compared to other contemporary societies [like the Spenglerian method] or to its own state in the past. ... for Muslim society although economic progress is not frowned upon, it is placed lower on the order of priorities as compared to other factors; e.g. the acquisition of knowledge or the provision of justice. There is also a tradition (*Hadis*) of the Holy Prophet that lists the symptoms of society that is in a pathological state of decline. These outward symptoms point to an underlying malaise in the society but can also provide a useful starting point for corrective actions for stopping or reversing the onset of decline. The high and low points of Muslim civilisation can be identified as those of a 'Golden Age' or of an 'Abyss'".[143]

The Islamic *Hadith* states that those in a decaying society would be corrupted, while others might resist within themselves:

"There will be soon a period of turmoil in which the one who sits will be better than one who stands and the one who stands will be better than one who walks and the one who walks will be better than one who runs. He who would watch them will be drawn by them. So he who finds a refuge or shelter against it should make it as his resort".[144]

Hebrew

A traditionalist "race", conscious of its nexus with the divine as the basis of culture, endures regardless of contact with foreigners because of its inward strength. This allows it to accept foreigners not only without weakening the cultural organism but even strengthening it; because it accepts foreign input on its own terms, as synthesis or symbiosis. A traditional "race" surviving over the course of millennia without succumbing to the cyclical laws of decay is the Jewish. They are the traditional "race" *par excellence*. No better example can be had than this people that has maintained its nexus with its divinity as the basis of survival, whose religion is a race-founding and race-sustaining mythos.

---

143   Misbah Islam, 2008, 45.
144   Hadith 54: 13.

Contrary to the beliefs of certain racial ideologues, including extreme Zionists and ultra-Orthodox Jews, this survival is not the result of bans on miscegenation. The Jewish law as embodied in the *Torah*, the first five books of the Old Testament, is based not on zoological race but on a race mythos. The Mosaic Law demands "race purity" in the traditional sense; that of a community of belief in a heritage and a destiny. Phineas killed an Israelite and a Midianite for copulating, not for reasons of race purity, but because of the threat to Israelite culture from marriages with Midianites at the time. Moses had married the daughter of a Midianite priest.[145] Where marriages with Hittites, Amorites, and Canaanites were prohibited it was to prevent cultural and religious corruption.[146] However, in the same *Book of Deuteronomy*, where the Israelite war code is being established, when a city has been defeated the adult males are to be eliminated, and the women and children are to be taken to be grafted on to Israel.[147] The commandments for this type of "scorched earth policy" were based on preventing foreigners from teaching Israel their religions.[148] There are precise laws on marrying non-Israelitish captive woman, who after a month of mourning for the deaths of her family, will have the marriage consummated and thereby become part of Israel.[149]

Jeremiah (circa 600 B.C.), son of the high priest Hilkiah, was one of the most significant voices against culture-decay, analogous to Ipuwer the Egyptian sage, Cato the Censor, and our own Spengler, Evola and Guénon. Jeremiah warned that Israel would prosper while tradition was maintained, but would fall if it weakened that tradition. Jeremiah saw the destruction of the Temple of Solomon and the carrying into Babylonian captivity of Judah.

The first cause of Israel's corruption was the subversion of its founding religion, quickly proceeded by invasion. Hence, Jeremiah warned that invasion was imminent as a punishment for Israel's departure from the traditional faith: "I will pronounce my judgments on my people because of their wickedness in forsaking me, in burning incense to

---

145 Exodus 18.
146 Deuteronomy 7.
147 Ibid., 20:14.
148 Ibid., 20:18.
149 Ibid., 21:10-14.

The Prophet Jeremiah painted by Michelangelo for the Sistine Chapel.

other gods and in worshiping what their hands have made".[150] From their being a holy people, they had fallen from the oath of their forefathers, Jeremiah admonishing: "The priests did not ask, 'Where is the LORD?' Those who deal with the law did not know me; the leaders rebelled against me. The prophets prophesied by Baal, following worthless idols. 'Therefore I bring charges against you again,' declares the LORD. 'And I will bring charges against your children's children'".[151]

Jeremiah stated that the priesthood has become corrupt, from whence the rot proceeded downward. "The prophets prophesy lies, the priests rule by their own authority, and my people love it this way. But what will you do in the end?" [152] Specifically, all of Israel had become motivated by greed. The admonition was to stand at the "crossroads" as to what paths to follow, and to choose "the ancient paths":

"From the least to the greatest, all are greedy for gain; prophets

---

150 Jeremiah 1: 16.

151 Ibid., 2: 8-9.

152 Ibid., 5: 31.

and priests alike, all practice deceit. They dress the wound of my people as though it were not serious. 'Peace, peace,' they say, when there is no peace. Are they ashamed of their detestable conduct? No, they have no shame at all; they do not even know how to blush. So they will fall among the fallen; they will be brought down when I punish them,' says the LORD. This is what the LORD says: 'Stand at the crossroads and look; ask for the ancient paths, ask where the good way is, and walk in it, and you will find rest for your souls. But you said, 'We will not walk in it'".[153]

The perennial survival of the Israelites is based on their adherence to tradition. Prophets such as Jeremiah are the Jews' perennial warning to stay true to their "ancient paths" or destruction will result. The Jews have maintained unity by a strong tradition based on a coming King-Messiah, Jerusalem as their *axis mundi*, and the Mosaic Law, with attendant rites such as Passover and Purim, as a universal code wherever they are. These axial points have formed and maintained them as a metaphysical race.

Their tradition has enabled them to supersede the organic laws of decay, while being the carriers of culture pathogens among other civilisations in such forms as Marxism. However, foreign culture pathogens cannot infect a healthy culture organism; and are therefore an effect, not a cause, of decay. As considered above, Israel itself was able to synthesise foreign elements due to its own inner strength, rather than succumbing to them. The USA through lack of a traditional foundation, was unable to do so. Foreign culture pathogens can only enter a culture organism when that organism is already in a state of decline; when its immunity or antibodies (the attitudes condemned as "xenophobia", "racism", "anti-Semitism") are weak. When alien pathogens do enter the host culture, it is susceptible to what Lev Gumilev called "zigzagging", in being diverted from its normal life-cycles.

---

153 Ibid., 6: 13-16.

The Decline and Fall of Civilisations

Mesoamerican and Andean

The High Culture of the Americas began in Mesoamerica, with the Olmec. Although obscure, and usually ascribed to epidemics introduced by Spanish invaders, dynastic rivalries, civil wars, and ecological disasters uprooting entire High Cultures such as the Chimú, the life-cycles of certain cultures within the American civilisation share analogous features to those of the Old World.

Among the seminal Civilisations of Mesoamercia was Teotihuacan, whose decline proceeded through several centuries (700A.D. to 900). Teotihuacan, whose "Middle Horizon" epoch (200A.D. to 650) is analogous to the West's Gothic or early Medieval epoch, the period of cultural flowering, centred on a well-planned city of about 125,000 inhabitants, as the commercial and political nexus of Mesoamerica.

Mass manufactured ceramics and obsidian tools were exchanged for raw materials and foodstuffs. Teotihuacan was the London, Rome, Athens and Babylon of Mesoamerica. The far-flung commercial relations declined perhaps due to overextension, bureaucratic inefficiency or the rise of commercial rivals. In what is called the "Metepec Phase" there seems to have been a revolt during which temples and other public buildings were burnt on the Street of the Dead and elsewhere.[154]

The decline of the traditional order seems to have started from circa 550A.D. when "destructive events in the central area of the capital marked a violent end to its governing apparatus. More than a hundred centrally located structures were burned, sculptures were smashed and scattered, and the institutions of state showed no signs of recovery afterward". These events are referred to by some archaeologists collectively as the "Big Fire," which they place at 550 ± 25. The events were the culmination of a long period of "sociopolitical instability and decline". [155]

Although Teotihuacan remained a major centre the burning of its religious and political symbols indicate a fracturing of its ethical foundations of the type that herald the beginning of culture decline,

---

154 Richard A. Diehl, 1989, 11.
155 Sarah C. Clayton, 2016, 107.

Sculpture unearthed at the Teotihuacan archeological site in Mexico.

analogous to the Reformation in Western Christendom, or Buddhism in Brahmanic India; and a challenge to the traditional hierarchy, analogous to Cromwell's Revolution against the English monarchy or the Jacobin Revolution in France. That there was a revolution against the elite and its traditional hierarchy, that permanently altered the course of the civilisation, is suggested when Diehl comments that the most logical reason for the abandonment of the Street of the Dead, after its torching, was that "the area was associated with the discredited Middle Horizon elite and their social system".[156]

While Teotihuacan had been the largest city in the Mexican Basin, from 700A.D. to 850 the population declined by 76% from 125,000 to 30,000.[157] A change of ceramic styles from Metepec to Coyotlatelco suggests also a change of character of those remaining. While dwellings were maintained, new construction stopped. Population within the Teotihuacan Basin declined from 250,000 to 175,000. However, some communities grew, suggesting that the original inhabitants were slowly being replaced by outsiders. Diehl cites studies indicating that the city underwent a period of decay, with poor sanitation, crowding, water supplies, infectious diseases and low life expectancy. During the latter

---

156 Richard A. Diehl, 14.
157 Ibid., 12.

The Decline and Fall of Civilisations

phase of its decline, the city relied on rural migration to supplement its population, as deaths seem to have outnumbered births.[158]

Diehl comments that the migrants that entered the city during the Coyotlatelco period reflect "cultural and artistic poverty". Diehl poses the question as to whether this is the result of migrants from socially and culturally marginal areas outside the Basin, but if they were descendants of the Metepec phase, "and direct heirs to the great Teotihuacan cultural tradition, they experienced one of the most dramatic episodes of deculturation ever documented in Pre-Columbian America". Diehl asks why these inhabitants of the formerly great culture centre remained, and "whether they attempted to preserve their established traditions?"[159] It has been suggested that the Coyotlatelco style originated from outside the Basin.[160] Therefore the inhabitants of the city in its last phase were not the heirs of the culture's founders. The city became the centre for the dispersal of another, debased, style over the region. Diehl states that although Teotihuacan long continued as a city culture,

> "it apparently lacked an architectural tradition, large public construction efforts, monumental art, and even a definable art style. We cannot even detect an elite, although it surely existed. Apparently the ideology and power that held together the Teotihuacan world for so many centuries ceased to exist and was not replaced. Perhaps their absence led to the total decay of Teotihuacan's economic and political structure by the end of the Coyotlatelco period. Whatever happened, by A.D. 850 the birthplace of Mesoamerican urbanism had passed into the shadows of Nahuatl myth…"[161]

What can be said of the people of Teotihuacan over the course of centuries is that while the *ethnoi* seems to have changed and the city was turned into a multicultural society, the race in a zoological sense did not change. It is an example of the deleterious impact of multicultural dynamics, where there was neither a successful symbiosis nor synthesis. The murals depicting the types at Teotihuacan remain of the

---

158 Ibid., 13.
159 Ibid.
160 Ibid., 14.
161 Ibid., 16.

same race-type; distinctively Indian.¹⁶² Teotihuacan decayed and died through the disruption and distortion of its founding ethos.

Inca

Andean civilisation is generally regarded as one of historical continuity¹⁶³ stretching over millennia, and incorporating many High Cultures, each one succeeding another, until ending with the Inca.

It has been contended by some that the Central and South American civilisations must have been the products of white culture-heroes. Remnants of blond and red hair among American mummies, and the bearded, white god-king Viracocha are adduced to prove this, in ways similar to the presence of the Tocharians in China. However, the sculptures of the Olmec are decidedly Chinese, although Afrocentrists assert that they are depictions of Blacks.¹⁶⁴ It seems that several races, and not just the Amerindian, were present in the culture region. Recently there have been claims for a Polynesian presence,¹⁶⁵ reversing Thor Heyerdahl's contention that Polynesia was settled from America.¹⁶⁶ Indeed, some of the evidence from Heyerdahl seems more Mongolian than Caucasian, such as the "Clay head from Vera Cruz, Mexico.¹⁶⁷ Whatever the remnants of sundry races, for millennia the overwhelming majority of Central and South Americans were Indians, including their god-kings and leadership strata.

Local lords retained control of their ethnic communities in an imperial federation that constituted an efficient culture organism, with a common ethos based on a solar religion, albeit with local variations, but unified with veneration for Viracohca, who had been a widespread culture-hero prior to the Inca.

---

162   See for example, fig. 7 (c and q), "The Glyphic Corpus in the Cacaxtla Murals", Janet Berlow, "Early Writing in Central Mexico", in Richard A. Diehl, Teotihuacan during the Coyotlatelco Period, 24.
163   William T. Sanders et al, "Pre-Columbian Civilizations: Andean Civilization".
164   Paul Barton, "Black Civilizations of Ancient America".
165   Based on the genetic affinities between South American and Polynesian chickens, more recent DNA studies have shown the theory to be incorrect. Roff Smith, "Chick DNA Challenges Theory that Polynesians Beat Europeans to the Americas", 2014.
166   Thor Heyerdahl, 1952.
167   Heyerdahl, plate XX: 1, "clay head from Tres Zapotes, Vera Cruz, Mexico."

The Decline and Fall of Civilisations

The Olmecs (1500-400 BC) were the first major civilization in Mexico.

"Pachacuti Inca Yupanqui invented a state religion based on the worship of a creator-god called Viracocha, who had been worshiped since pre-Inca times. Priests were appointed, ceremonies were planned, prayers were prepared, and temples were built throughout the empire. He also expounded the view that the Inca had a divine mission to bring this true religion to other peoples, so that the Inca armies conquered in the name of the creator god. His doctrine was a relatively tolerant one. Conquered groups did not have to give up their own religious beliefs; they merely had to worship the Inca god and provide him and his servants with food, land, and labour".[168]

Sun temples were erected in each newly conquered land to serve as the axis for local veneration, with the central axis existing at the great Sun Temple at Cuzco, where the chief priest, as important as the king, performed rituals to assure the continuing connexion between the terrestrial and the divine. Another great Sun Temple existed at Vilcashuman, the geographic axis of the empire. These centres of worship were connected metaphysically by *huacas* (sacred sites) throughout the empire, of which Sanders et al write:

---

168 William T. Sanders et al.

"Along with the shrines and temples, *huacas* (sacred sites) were widespread. A *huaca* could be a man-made temple, mountain, hill, or bridge, such as the great *huacachaca* across the Apurímac River. A *huaca* also might be a mummy bundle, especially if it was that of a lord-Inca. On high points of passage in the Andes, propitiatory cairns (*apacheta*, 'piles of stones') were made, to which, in passing, each person would add a small stone and pray that his journey be lightened".[169]

The highly centralised, efficient system that had kept the great empire functioning for three centuries, fell apart when the royal succession was disputed. Circa 1483 the Chanca, another High Culture, attacked the Inca, having subdued the Quechua. At the same time, at Cuzco, there was dispute over who would succeed Virachocha Inca (not to be confused with the mythic culture-hero) between Inca Urcon and Cusi Inca Yupanqui, latter the choice of the military. As the Chanco approached Cuzco, Inca Urcon and his father Viracocha Inca, withdrew, while Inca Yupangqui and a small group of military and noble backers stayed to resist. Inca Yupangqui defeated the Chanca, but his efforts to negotiate with his father and brother failed. He assumed rulership taking the title Pachacuti, retaining his centre at Cuzco, while the faction under Virachocha and Urcon ruled from Calca. Pachacuti Inca Yupangqui entered into an alliance with the Chanca. However, shortly after Viracocha Inca died and Urcon was killed in a battle against Cuzco. The Inca Empire was reunited under Pachacuti Inca Yupangqui. While fighting now resumed between the Inca and the Chanca, Pachacuti Inca Yupangqui and his brother Capac Yupangqui, came into conflict, resulting in the extension of the empire, and the conquering of the Chimú. Sanders et al comment: "The rapid expansion of the empire, however, created a number of problems concerned with sustaining themselves and governing a large number of diverse ethnic groups".[170] Among the reforms initiated by Pachacuti Inca Yupangqui, a ruler could not inherit property from his predecessor. This meant that each new ruler would have to extend the empire. Ethnic groups from newly conquered lands were resettled and replaced with those who had been raised under the Inca.

---

169 Ibid.
170 Ibid.

The Decline and Fall of Civilisations

This period is analogous to the Late or Winter civilisation cycle. The focus was on military conquest and trade, and many *ethnoi* were incorporated into the Inca *superethnos*. Topa Inca Yupanqui's death in 1493 prompted a power struggle between his sons, with Huayna Capac taking the kingship with only minor bloodshed, expanding territory into Ecuador. Smallpox or measles entered from Bolivia, and Huayna Capac was among those who succumbed to the epidemic in 1525, leaving another struggle for the kingship, Huayna Capac's principal wife having been childless. A successor to the throne was chosen by the chief priest, but without the prerequisite ceremony. The empire divided into regions led by contenders. A devastating civil war ensured between Huascar in the south, holding Cuzco, with Atahuallpa controlled Ecuador and parts of northern Peru. Atahuallpa's forces won, ignominiously killed Huascar's family, took Huascar before Atahuallpa, and even burned the mummy of the revered Topa Inca Yupanqui. This final conflict led by Atahuallpa occurred while the Spaniards were proceeding.[171]

Atahuallpa seems to have been in revolt against tradition. Although the chief priest had bypassed ceremonial, he had supported the chosen successor of Topa Inca Yupanqui, whose venerated memory was desecrated by the followers of Atahuallpa, who was captured and killed by the Conquistadors in 1533.

The Inca (1200A.D. to 1533) are the end of a long line of High Cultures in the Americas; albeit the best known because they succumbed to Western conquest. The Inca had conquered the long-enduring Chimú High Culture (900A.D. to 1470) when the Chimú had succumbed to the challenges of the environment and had been fractured. Chimú arts, sciences engineering, imperial organisation and hierarchical government, provided the foundations for the Inca civilisation. However, the Incan victory was short-lived, as they had entered an epoch of decline, culminating in the Spanish invasion. While smallpox and other diseases brought by Spaniards decimated the Inca population, a civil war for the line of royal succession added to the ease with which a small contingent of Spaniards was able to triumph over the Incan empire.

As with the character of empires, which are necessarily multi-ethnic and multi-cultural, if a strong axis of central administration is fractured,

---

171 Ibid.

the constituent parts of the imperial organism fall apart. "The centre cannot hold" as W. B. Yeats poetically referred to such a situation, and the divinity of the god-king must become doubtful, such as when a Chinese Emperor was said to have "lost the Mandate of Heaven". Sanders[172] et al state of this epoch of the Inca:

> "The rapid incorporation of so many mountain and coastal desert polities before 1532 calls for explanation. It is tempting to view such expansion in the context of the instantaneous breakup in 1532, when some of the same forces were likely to have been at work: dispersed territories, interlocked with some belonging to other powers in the region, and multiethnic and polyglot agglomerations in neighbouring valleys. Each political unit - as eventually was the case with the Inca state itself - was likely to share pastures, cultivated terraces, and beach installations; hegemonies shifted according to local and regional circumstances. The Early, Middle, and Late Horizons were temporary concatenations, and none lasted for very long. The Spanish invasion interrupted these alternations: a player had entered the field who ignored the local rules and who did not fathom the true sources of Andean wealth, which was not silver but an intimate familiarity with local conditions and possibilities and the ability to pool vastly different geographic and ecological tiers into single polities".[173]

The Inca hierarchy that had held various complementary regional *ethnoi* together in a symbiosis had fractured. Foreign invasion exploited the situation and provided the final death blows.

---

172 William T. Sanders (1926-2008), was pre-eminent in the field of Mesoamerican archaeology. See: Joyce Marcus, 2011; http://www.nasonline.org/publications/biographical-memoirs/memoir-pdfs/sanders-william-t.pdf
173 William T. Sanders et al, op cit.

Japan

The corrupting influence of money and mercantilism has been a traditional Japanese concern. As in China, the cyclic unfolding of history has followed dynastic lines. The Tokugawa dynasty saw the necessity to address two primary issues to prevent cycles of decay: restrictions on the accumulation of wealth, and the restoration of a rural population as the foundation of a healthy society. Guilds, the social basis of traditional societies as a reflection of the divine cosmic order, were re-established. However, because of the prosperity and development of Japan under the Tokugawa dynasty, the efforts to overcome the laws of decay were insufficient.

> "Although government heavily restricted the merchants and viewed them as unproductive and usurious members of society, the samurai, who gradually became separated from their rural ties, depended greatly on the merchants and artisans for consumer goods, artistic interests, and loans. In this way, a subtle subversion of the warrior class by the *chonin*[174] took place".[175]

The warrior caste had been compromised and subordinated to commerce, beginning the process of the inversion of hierarchy. The migration of the rural population to the cities, was prompted by famine. While many families became landless tenant farmers, others became a new rich class of landowners. Many samurai became destitute and became wage-earners. Incursions from Russians and British were resisted. Peasant revolts increased into the 19th century. Attempts were made to stop the decline by trying to revive the martial ethos, restrict foreign trade and associated influences, suppress the *Rangaku*[176] and eliminate luxury among bureaucrats and samurai.[177]

> "A struggle arose in the face of political limitations that the shogun imposed on the entrepreneurial class. The government ideal of an agrarian society failed to square with the reality of commercial distribution. A huge government bureaucracy had

---

174 Town merchants.
175 Ronald E. Dolan and Robert L. Worden, 1994, "Togukawa".
176 Scholars of Dutch learning.
177 Dolan and Worden.

A group of Samurai, pose for hand coloured photograph 1890s.

evolved, which now stagnated because of its discrepancy with a new and evolving social order. Compounding the situation, the population increased significantly during the first half of the Tokugawa period. Although the magnitude and growth rates are uncertain, there were at least 26 million commoners and about 4 million members of samurai families and their attendants when the first nationwide census was taken in 1721. Drought, followed by crop shortages and starvation, resulted in twenty great famines between 1675 and 1837. Peasant unrest grew, and by the late eighteenth century, mass protests over taxes and food shortages had become commonplace. *Newly landless families became tenant farmers, while the displaced rural poor moved into the cities. As the fortunes of previously well-to-do families declined, others moved in to accumulate land, and a new, wealthy farming class emerged.* Those people who benefited were able to diversify production and to hire laborers, while others were left discontented. *Many samurai fell on hard times and were forced into handicraft production and wage jobs for merchants*".[178] [Emphasis added].

---

178 Ibid.

Following a peasant uprising in 1837, although only lasting a day, the state attempted again to restore tradition. Attempts were made to restore the martial ethos, and to oppose the corrupting influences of trade and luxury among bureaucrats and samurai. American overtures were rebuffed until 1854, with the Treaty of Peace and Amity (or Treaty of Kanagawa), allowing ships to enter two ports and the presence of an American consul. In 1859 a further treaty allowed the extension of trade. The Dutch and other Western influences increased, including the translation of foreign books. In 1868 the Tokugawa dynasty was overthrown.[179]

The Meiji regime sought to change the traditional social structure. Although there was a move towards democratisation, the aim was to establish the Emperor as the axis of Japan, and to restore Shinto as the focus of belief. However, the foreign influences increased. The Tokugawa hierarchy of samurai, farmer, artisan, and merchant was abolished by 1871.[180] The samurai ethos continued to be undermined, with many becoming merchants and bureaucrats. Feudal land was replaced by market capitalism. Taxes were paid with cash rather than in kind. Industrialisation proceeded from the 1870s. "The Meiji leaders also modernized foreign policy, an important step in making Japan a full member of the international community".[181] Despite constitutional changes, and parliamentary government, with increasing party influence, the Japanese eschewed both Westminster and U.S. constitutional systems, maintaining a very limited franchise. The Emperor remained the ultimate authority.

The Meiji constitution remained in force until 1947,[182] then democratisation was imposed by the occupying powers. As in Germany, the ruling strata of several hundred thousand were purged and 700 were executed. "State Shinto was disestablished", and Hirohito was obliged to repudiate the divine status of the Emperor.[183]

Despite the foreign imposition of the post-1945 epoch the great

---

179 Ibid.
180 Ibid., "The Meiji Restoration".
181 Ibid., "Foreign Relations".
182 Ibid., "The Development of Representative Government".
183 Ibid., "World War II and the Occupation".

strength of the Japanese continues to be their concept of social relations based on traditional religions of Shinto and Zen Buddhism. "Harmony, order, and self-development are three of the most important values that underlie Japanese social interaction".[184]. The individual is a constituent part of a social organism.

> "Japanese children learn from their earliest days that human fulfilment comes from close association with others. Children learn early to recognize that they are part of an interdependent society, beginning in the family and later extending to larger groups such as neighbourhood, school, community, and workplace. Dependence on others is a natural part of the human condition; it is viewed negatively only when the social obligations it creates are too onerous to fulfil".[185]

Despite superficial appearances, the Western Liberalism that sanctifies individualism and the Free Market has been rejected and the social organism maintained. Hierarchy also remains strong; based on Confucianism, which maintains the social organism.

> "Confucianism emphasizes harmony among heaven, nature, and human society achieved through each person's accepting his or her social role and contributing to the social order by proper behavior. An often quoted phrase from the Confucian essay *Da Xue* (The Great Learning) explains, 'Their persons being cultivated, their families were regulated. Their families being regulated, their states were rightly governed. Their states being rightly governed, the whole kingdom was made tranquil and happy'".[186]

"This view implies that hierarchy is natural";[187] that is to say, it is an organic view of society.

How much longer Japan can be maintained as one of the few remaining traditional societies is problematic, given that it is a culture within the orbit of the decaying West, and particularly with its role

---

184 Ibid., "Values and Beliefs".
185 Ibid.
186 Ibid., "The Public Sphere Order and Status".
187 Ibid.

in globalisation. Any other people-culture-nation-state would have succumbed within a few years of enforced democratisation, pacifism, equality, and market-economics. Religion, Emperor and Family remain the foundations that have allowed Japan to endure. The Japanese have a unique quality of being able to synthesise what is useful from other cultures into their own without infecting their culture-soul. This is not proof for "enrichment" through "multiculturalism". To the contrary, there has been nothing "multicultural" about Japan. The Japanese have amalgamated aspects of other cultures into their own on their terms. Amaury de Riencourt, an expert on Asia who, like Spengler, wrote of history as organic, stated of this process:

> "For more than a thousand years, every element of Chinese Civilisation seeped into Japan, and yet the Japanese character remained unimpaired in its essence. What the Japanese did later on with Western Civilisation they did at this early stage with Chinese forms and ideas, and in such a way that other people known to history have ever been able to adapt themselves so promptly and readily without at the same time destroying their own personality.
>
> "The essence of their peculiar character was already well shaped in these early days and it has not changed since. The Japanese were and are neither creators nor imitators but exploiters and adapters".[188]

The Japanese "enters into organic relations" with an alien culture form through an "instinctive but always creative metamorphosis". The Japanese were able to adopt Chinese forms, "yet preserve their inner, instinctive self…"[189] A most eminent teacher of Zen Buddhism, D. T. Suzuki, explained how Japan had been able to absorb foreign elements, to enable the strengthening of the Japanese culture:

> "Zen typifies Japanese spirituality. This does not mean Zen has deep roots within the life of the Japanese people, rather that Japanese life itself is 'Zen-like.' The importation of Zen provided the opportunity for Japanese spirituality to ignite, yet the

---

188 Amaury de Riencourt, 112.
189 Ibid.

constituents themselves which were to ignite were fully primed at that time. Zen arrived in Japan riding the wave of Chinese thought, literature, and art, but Japanese spirituality was by no means seduced by these trappings. It was nothing like the entrance of Buddhist literature and thought that took place during the Nara period (646-794). The Buddhism of the Nara and Heian [794-1185] periods was merely tied conceptually to the life of the upper classes, whereas Zen put down its roots in the midst of the life of the Japanese samurai. It was cultivated and it budded in that which existed at the depths of the samurai's seishin. These buds were not foreign clippings but developed from the very life of the Japanese warrior. I said it put down roots, but that is not quite the correct expression. It would be better to say that spirituality of the samurai was on the verge of breaking through to the surface, and that Zen removed all the obstacles from its path… Thereupon, although the Zen Sect of Japan was content to allow the supremacy of Chinese literature, the Zen life of the Japanese came to full flower in Japanese spirituality".[190]

With the militarily defeat, foreign elements were imposed on Japan, not absorbed and harmonised. A dichotomy is at work which is coming into ever sharper focus. The Japanese character of thoroughness has combined with Faustian technics, and the Japanese ethos of "harmony" has been lost. As in China, Faustian technics is destroying the land, and in so doing the soul of Japan. Japanese thoroughness and efficiency is pushing society into a faster rate of destruction than even that of the West. The particularly insightful Japanologist, Alex Kerr, has written of the destructive process:

"Writers on Japan today mostly concern themselves with its banks and export manufacturing. But in the greater scheme of things, for a wealthy nation does it really matter so much if its GNP drops a few percentage points or the banks falter for a few years? The Tang dynasty poet Du Fu wrote, 'Though the nation perishes, the mountains and rivers remain.' Long before Japan had banks, there existed a green archipelago of a thousand islands, where clear mountain springs tumbled over mossy stones and waves crashed along coves and peninsulas lined with fantastic

---

190 D. T. Suzuki, Japanese Spirituality 18-19.

rocks. Such were the themes treasured ... in everything that defined Japan's traditional culture. Reverence for the land lies at the very core of Shintoism, the native religion, which holds that Japan's mountains, rivers, and trees are sacred, the dwelling place of gods. So in taking stock of where Japan is today, it is good to set economics aside for a moment and take a look at the land itself.

When we do, we see this: Japan has become arguably the world's ugliest country. ... the native forest cover has been clear-cut and replaced by industrial cedar, rivers are dammed and the seashore lined with cement, hills have been leveled to provide gravel fill for bays and harbors, mountains are honeycombed with destructive and useless roads, and rural villages have been submerged in a sea of industrial waste.

"Similar observations can be made about many other modern nations, of course. But what is happening in Japan far surpasses anything attempted in the rest of the world. We are seeing something genuinely different here. The nation prospers, but the mountains and rivers are in mortal danger ...

"During the past fifty-five years of its great economic growth, Japan has drastically altered its natural environment in ways that are almost unimaginable to someone who has not traveled here.

"Across the nation, men and women are at work reshaping the landscape. Work crews transform tiny streams just a meter across into deep chutes slicing through slabs of concrete ten meters wide and more. Builders of small mountain roads dynamite entire hillsides. Civil engineers channel rivers into U-shaped concrete casings that do away not only with the rivers' banks but with their beds. The River Bureau has dammed or diverted all but three of Japan's 113 major rivers. ... Meanwhile, Japan's Construction Ministry plans to add 500 new dams to the more than 2,800 that have already been built. ...It is not only the rivers and valleys that have suffered. The seaside reveals the greatest tragedy: by 1993, 55 percent of the entire coast of Japan had been lined with cement slabs and giant concrete tetrapods ..."[191]

---

191 Alex Kerr, 2002, Chapter I.

Japan's organic destiny lay in China. American interests prevented Japan from following its life's course. Japanese expansion in China was seen as a threat to the USA's global markets.[192] To use Gumilev's term, the life-course was "zigzagged" by foreign intrusion. Japan still has the inner strength to rebel, if that strength can be directed back toward tradition. However, Japan after the trauma of the world war, and the foreign occupation, adopted the Faustian impulse without synthesising and harmonising this in the manner that had for millennia been, like the Jews and the Chinese, Japan's strength. The Faustian impulse has instead been a poisonous intrusion. Animism, the pervasiveness of spirit throughout nature, is the basis of Japanese religiosity. The Faustian intrusion is a perpetual raping and killing of the Japanese soul.

Afrikaner

The collapse of the Afrikaner civilisation in South Africa is an example of a culture that decayed through internal weakening, while also being an example, like the Hebrews, of race-formation beyond genetics. Afrikaner civilisation is referred to because it constitutes a unique cultural organism within Western civilisation. It was a "Moonlight Civilisation", reflecting the glow of Western Civilisation, a term used by Amaury de Riencourt in describing the Korean and Japanese "Moonlight Civilisations" vis-à-vis the Chinese. Afrikaner civilisation existed outside the mainstream of the diseased Western civilisation as a conscious effort to preserve a cultural vitality amidst the West's decay. It was the last of the Western cultures to maintain rural values and something of the ethos that had expired in Europe centuries previously. The Afrikaner collapse was the result of succumbing to Western pathogens.

The assumption that the Afrikaner, due to apartheid, and before that, anti-miscegenation laws, must be among the purest of races is incorrect. While Virginia and other U.S. states had the "one drop of blood" anti-miscegenation law, there was no such rigid criterion among the Afrikaners. If one looked "white" one was "white". The racial test consisted of skull measurement and complexion. The proportion of non-white genes within the Afrikaner ranges from 5% to 7%. J.A. Heese, studying the Afrikaners of the period 1657–1867 concluded the genetic composition to be: Dutch 34.8%, German 33.7%, French 13.2%, British

---

192 K. R. Bolton, "Origins of the Japanese-Amercian War: A Conflict of Free Trade vs. Autarchy".

The Decline and Fall of Civilisations

5.2%, Other European 2.7%, Non-White 6.9%, Unknown 3.5%.[193] G.F.C. de Bruyn found the non-European genetic composition to be 5.4%, and Unknown to be 3.9% .[194] From an early period there were marriages between the European settlers and Coloured women. From parish records Heese, found that by 1807 between 7.2% and 10.7% of the Afrikaners had African and Asian descent. The approximately 2000 emigrants from Holland, Germany and France, who founded the Afrikaner colony in 1650 intermarried with the Khoi and the San "relatively frequently". They were augmented by Indian traders and Malayo-Negroid hybrids from East Africa and Madagascar.[195]

Afrikaners have a higher non-Caucasian genetic inheritance than Berbers and Brahmin. Afrikaners have a larger proportion of sub-Saharan DNA than Portuguese who have the highest proportion of sub-Saharan genes of any European population, albeit still low, and whose decline is assumed by racial materialists to be the result of miscegenation.[196] However, here too the number of African slaves imported into Portugal at a time when many Portuguese males were departing for Brazil, has been exaggerated. The American physical anthropologist Carleton S. Coon, often quoted by racial materialists, stated of the Portuguese:

- "Non-Mediterranean elements in the Portuguese population are rare and of little importance. A few Nordics are scattered throughout but are particularly concentrated in the north. Traces of Dinaric blood, as we have already seen, may likewise be found on the northern coast. ... On the whole, the absorption of Negroes by the Portuguese has had no appreciable effect on the racial composition of the country. Portugal remains, as it has been since the days of the Muge shell-fish eaters, classic Mediterranean territory".[197]

Returning to the Afrikaners, if one objects to migration to European lands on the basis of genetics then the Afrikaner must be of lesser desirability than many elements from India and North Africa.

---

193 J. A. Heese, 1971.
194 J.S. Bergh (ed.), R. T. J. Lombard, 1988.
195 M. J. Kotze, 2001.
196 For example, Dr. William L. Pierce, "The Black Man's Gift to Portugal", 1971.
197 Carleton S. Coon, 1939, XI: 15.

Boer soldiers relaxing during the war with Great Britain.

The strength of the Afrikaner had not been from genes but from race-forming myths of the Great Trek, and the Battle of Blood River. The "had race", in the Spenglerian sense, as the strongest races have it, through factors other than biological. They had sworn a holy oath to God on 16 December 1838. They had made a covenant with God for victory against the Zulus, every much as significant as Abraham's covenant is for the Jews. It is such a mythos, such as the celebration of the Day of the Oath, and the celebrations at the Voortreker Monument, that made the Afrikaners as immune from culture disease as the Hebrews, Japanese and Chinese, and for the same reasons, with a sense of their own holy mission, for which apartheid was significant above all as a symbol. Afrikaners have their equivalents of the Jewish Passover and Purim as holy celebrations of the *volk*. It is this mythos that formed the Afrikaner "race"; not DNA.

Infection by Western pathogens via Liberalism caused the decay of the Afrikaner culture organism. The culture pathogens entered the Afrikaner culture organism as early as the 1960s. Even in 1949 the Christian-based Afrikaner world-view was being undermined. The theologian professor Ben Keet argued against a scriptural justification for apartheid[198] that was the premise of the Reformed Church and the spiritual foundation of the Afrikaner culture. The Reformed Church was as important in forming and sustaining the Afrikaner folk as Judaism is for the Jews, Hinduism for the Indians, Confucianism for the Chinese, Shintoism for the Japanese, and Eastern Orthodoxy for the Russians. As the Israelite prophets knew, religious purity is more significant for the maintenance of a race than "blood" purity. The Afrikaner was destroyed by subverting his Church.

Another primary factor in culture decay was industrialization, undermining the peasant ethos of the Boer, which had, like the Amish in Pennsylvania, made them an anomaly in the Western world. The Anglo-Boer wars and the ongoing ill-will directed towards the Boers from the outside world was a culture conflict between "Money and Blood" to use Spengler's term. Donald Akenson refers to an Afrikaner "rural cosmology".[199] This enabled the Afrikaner to maintain order amidst the chaos of the fast-changing pace demanded by industrialism. The rural population in England during the Industrial Revolution had no such "rural cosmology," since the Reformation had destroyed the traditional social order of the rural communities. The English and German-Jewish traders, the so-called *Uitlanders* or "Outsiders" that the Boers had fought to keep at bay, served as the carriers of the culture-pathogen of industrialisation. Historian Professor LeRoy Vail wrote of this modernisation:

> "What was common for all the region's peoples – the blacks and whites alike – was that many of them were gradually losing control over their lives and control over that most basic factor of production, the land, slipped from their grasp. No longer were rural communities – whether black of white – able to exist autonomously beyond the reach of capitalism and colonial administration... for white Afrikaners, land ownership was also important, kept alive as the ideal Afrikaner way of life even among the poor whites of the cities and towns".[200]

Akensen comments that "within Afrikaner society what was developing

---

198 Charles Bloomberg, 1990, 221.
199 D. H. Akensen, 1992, 80.
200 Quoted by Akensen, 80.

was a contest between a rural, pre-capitalist covenantal cultural grid, and the material reality of modern industrial capitalism, and all this was taking place within the context of the decline of the second British Empire."[201] Afrikaner solidarity was undermined by an alliance of money between the Jewish, English and Afrikaner bourgeoisie and upper classes. This also contributed to breaking Afrikaner cultural hegemony. Afrikaners were "increasingly awash with a tidal wave of foreign films (most of U.S. origin) and television (which was introduced in South Africa only in 1975). Despite efforts at restriction, "these media gave access to a world of international values that Afrikaner society previously had been able to keep at bay".[202]

Most importantly, Afrikaner "covenantal cosmology" was undermined by culture-pathogens subverting the Afrikaner churches. Self-doubt eroded the belief-system that had maintained the Afrikaner for several centuries. Akensen refers to this "belief in their own corporate personality every bit as vivid as that shown by the ancient Hebrews".[203] During 1969-90 three of the Dutch Reformed churches that had hitherto been united in support of Afrikaner identity, took three different courses. The NHK maintained its traditional position. The Gereformeerde Kerk repudiated the formative idea of the Afrikaner as a covenant *volk*. The main body of the Dutch Reformed faith in South Africa, the NGK, maintained a traditional position until backing down in the face of world condemnation in its 1986 theological document *Kerk en Samelewing* ("Church and Society"), which Akensen describes as "confused" and "contradictory", in trying to justify an about-face. The document "completely destroyed the religious basis of everything that the Afrikaner culture had developed during the previous 125 years".[204] The Afrikaner was no longer a "convent people" above all others. The trinity between state, *volk* and church was discarded. The focus on the Old Testament, that had scripturally justified apartheid, was dropped. "Thus did the leading Dutch Reformed Church effectively declare the covenant dead". [205]

---

201 Ibid.
202 Akensen, 303.
203 Ibid., 73.
204 Ibid., 308.
205 Ibid.

The Decline and Fall of Civilisations

Such contentions paved the way for the cultural and spiritual subversion of the 1960s. The intelligentsia had its Sixties movement (*Sestiger*), some of whom had worked in France. They wrote of Afrikaner self-doubt. Such was the decay of the Afrikaner cultural Establishment, once infected, that in 1964 the *Akademie vir Wetenskap en Kuns* ("Science and Art"), "guardian of Afrikaner culture", awarded the annual Hertzog prize to Etienne le Roux for the novel *Sewe Dae by die Silbersteins*, "a parable on the failure of the nationalist mission". Afrikaner "cultural hierarchy" had been "fractured".[206] By the 1970s, the Broederbond, the mainstay of Afrikaner political and cultural hegemony, had opened dialogue with the African National Congress. In 1990 the Broederbond had prepared a memo in which apartheid was described as detrimental to Afrikaner interests. Professor Pieter de Lange, the chairman of the Broederbond since 1984, said: "Some of us became convinced that Afrikaner interests had become so entwined with everyone's interests in South Africa and internationally that you couldn't promote Afrikaner interests in isolation. You had to promote everyone's interests".[207]

---

206 William Beinart, 2001, 190.

207 Christopher S. Wren, "A Secret Society of Afrikaners Helps to Dismantle Apartheid", 1990.

China

The annals of China's imperial courts record the decadence that resulted in the mythic loss of the "Mandate from Heaven", which justified the overthrow of successive dynasties. Much of this decadence revolves around the influence of the caste of eunuchs whose corruption infested the imperial court. China succumbed to decadence centuries ago, dynasty after dynasty. The Maoist interregnum has only reanimated a corpse by the use of Western technics and economic models. Nonetheless, Chinese civilisation endured for two and a half millennia. Of the epochs of decline, Backhouse and Bland wrote in their study of the Chinese annals:

> "Amongst such morals and conclusions as the reader may draw from study of these three centuries of Chinese history, one of the most obvious is to be found in the persistent coincidence of periods of demoralisation in the State with the ascendancy of eunuchs at Court. The Chinese have always realised the truth of this matter; scholars, historians and moralists never fail to declare that the Empire's crisis of private corruption and public disorder, the decline and fall of dynasties, have been caused or greatly hastened by the interference and intrigues of these Court menials in affairs of State. The first Manchu rulers perceived clearly the evils of a eunuch-ridden Court, and took wise precautions against them. In the fate of the Mings, the lesson was writ plain for them to learn, adding one more to the many warnings of history against the insidious dangers of the Court's excessive polygamy and the atmosphere of debauchery and enervation thereby created. They could see for themselves to what a pitiful state the Throne and Court had been brought by the tyrannous cruelty, treachery and greed of the eunuchs who infested the Forbidden City and projected the 'poisonous miasma' of their influence to the farthest frontiers of the Empire. ..."[208]

After the decay of the Ming dynasty, the Manchus re-invigorated China with military vitality, administrative efficiency, and civic virtue, purging the eunuch caste. Yet, the authors ask, why was it that from this state of revivification of China under the Manchus that within

---

208 E. Backhouse and J. O. P. Bland, 1914, 17.

The Decline and Fall of Civilisations

Chinese Bowl from the Ch'ien Lung period.

their reign China again reverted to decadence? Backhouse and Bland, writing of Chien-lung (1711-1799), state:

"Studying the history of this great Monarch's long reign, and that of his immediate successors, we perceive that the chief cause of the swift decline and fall of the Manchu power, and of the consequent demoralisation of the whole system of government, lay (as Tzu Hsi[209] admitted on her deathbed) in the corruption of public and private morals which set in, so soon as the 'rats and foxes' of the Court were permitted to interfere in affairs of State. So long as the Palace eunuchs were kept in the place wisely assigned to them by Shun Chih,[210] and debarred from all high offices, the Court retained its virile dignity and the public service its efficiency. The luxury, nepotism and venality introduced during the regime of Ch'ien Lung's favourite, the Grand Secretary, Ho Shen, restored to the Palace eunuchs opportunities which they had not enjoyed since the overthrow of the Ming dynasty. Fifty years later, their ascendancy at Court was completely established. Henceforward, they were able to exercise once more their traditional functions as the tempters of youth, the debauchers of age, in the profound seclusion of the Forbidden City, until gradually the Son of Heaven on his

---
209 Empress Dowager.
210 First Manchu Emperor.

Throne became a defenceless puppet in their supple bloodstained hands". [211]

The last of the Ming dynasty at the middle of the 17th century continued their debaucheries while the Manchus pushed forward.

"Habits and ambitions of luxury, and with the degenerate Mings the lust of perquisites and power, of pomp and circumstance, was not killed by their cataclysmic disasters. For eighteen years, harried from one short-lived capital to another, four successive claimants to the Throne of their dynasty retained some semblance of their regal state and a place in the minds, if not the hearts, of their people. During these years there were times when, had there been a strong man amongst them, their dominion might well have been restored and the Manchus driven back, for the Confucian virtues of faithfulness and loyal devotion ... were not lacking at this period; many a brave soldier, many a stoic philosopher of the mandarins, upheld the proud traditions of their caste, and died rather than submit to the rule of the alien, and many millions of the 'stupid people' went bravely to their graves because of that loyalty to the central idea of the Confucian doctrine. But the Mings were all unworthy, even in adversity. As they had been before the threatening storm, so they remained ... invertebrate, irresolute to the end. Four years after the flight from Peking, when the adherents of Kuei Wang, the last of the Mings, were making a successful stand in the Kuang provinces, when Coxinja was beginning to organise new forces of resistance to the Manchus, and when several rebel forces had taken the field on their own account, a little statesmanship, a little courage, might have won the day. But it was not to be. The little Court in exile kept up its tinsel state, grateful to its loyal adherents only so long as they replenished the Privy purse which paid for its revels; leaving its armies unvictualled whilst it rehearsed some new play, or sent the eunuchs through the country in search of new favourites for the harem of the 'Palace,' that was now a moving tent". [212]

---

211 Backhouse and Bland, 18.
212 Ibid., 166-167.

Again the social degeneration of the culture has started to rot from the head down. Yet the Ming dynasty was not weak militarily. As the Manchus advanced on the Yangtze with a force of 60,000, the Ming emperor lamented mournfully to his eunuchs that "there is not in all my court an actor worthy of the name". General General Shih K'o-fa, a brave soldier and a scholar, asked to be given control of the 80,000 strong forces at the Emperor's disposal and to lead them without the interference of courtiers and civil officials, but the Emperor refused, and "he continued to squander money on revels and banquets, while the troops in the field were left insufficiently fed and clad".[213]

Amidst Court intrigues, General Shih addressed his Emperor in Spring, 1645:

"Whilst Your Majesty is banqueting on choice viands and quaffing wine from beakers of jade, it behoves you to remember your starving servants in the North. If, in spite of all his efforts, the late Emperor was unable to ward off disaster, how much more should you, inferior to him in ability, tremble as one who stands on the brink of a precipice. If you perform your duties with zeal and vigilance, it may be that your ancestors' spirits in Heaven will intercede with the Almighty on your behalf, and that your heritage may be regained. But if you remain in idle dalliance in Nanking, lavishing favours on sycophants and forgetful of the welfare of your troops, if you proclaim our secret plans from the housetops and fail to distinguish between loyal devotion and treason, if you show yourself so lacking in dignity that the worthy men about you are constrained to retire from official life, and the brave hesitate to serve you, then assuredly your ancestors will regard you as unworthy of their aid, and destruction, inevitable and final, will come upon you".[214]

General Shih awaited supplies that never arrived. His supporters at court were being executed on the advice of corrupt advisers. Shih observed that "fawning eunuchs" intrigued for high office and rewards for themselves and their protégés at Court. Backhouse and Bland comment: "Where the Court is not pure, the army will surely fail in its

---

213 Ibid., 169.
214 Ibid.

duty".²¹⁵ On the inevitable defeat of Nanking by the Manchu forces, Prince Yii spent three days attempting to persuade General Shih to become Imperial Commissioner of the Nanking Province. Yet he would not betray his Emperor and chose beheading.

The ascension of the Manchus under the Emperor Shun Chih, a young man both physically and mentally strong, at first saw the relegation of the eunuchs to that of menials,²¹⁶ and supervision of admission to the priesthood. In 1661 Shun had died or withdrew to the priesthood. Four ministers were appointed as Regents, awaiting the coming of age of Shun's seven year old son K'ang Hsi, a firm but humane ruler under whom there was a flowering of the arts.²¹⁷ However, most of K'ang's twenty-four surviving sons acted with cruelty and ignorance.²¹⁸ In particular the Heir Apparent, Yiin Jeng, was regarded as deranged. Yiin was arrested. K'ang declared that such a man could not be the nexus between heaven and the people, declaring in public:

> "The Classic of History says: 'Heaven sees as my people see; Heaven hears as my people hear. Heaven will surely detest the man whom the people hate.' How can such a man be permitted to perform the ancestral sacrifice or worship the tutelary deities as Emperor?"²¹⁹

K'ang died in 1722, and was succeeded by the least depraved of his sons, Yung Cheng. As under the Ming, the Manchu dynasty was wracked by rival cabals at Court. The acrimony among the Emperor's brothers remained intense, several of whom Yung had executed for rebellious conspiracy. Yung's reign was marked by rebellion throughout the Empire, with increasing references to the "alien" rule of the Manchus. Yung nonetheless left an impressive corpus of scholarly writing and it can be supposed that he would have been a great ruler had it not been for the intrigues of his brothers. In particular, he reduced the Court eunuchs to menial status.²²⁰ The rule of Chia Ch'ing was notably worthy, having

---

215 Ibid., 172.
216 Ibid., 232.
217 Ibid., 239.
218 Ibid., 249.
219 K'an Hsi, "Decree to the Nation", Backhouse and Bland, 261.
220 Backhouse and Bland, 291.

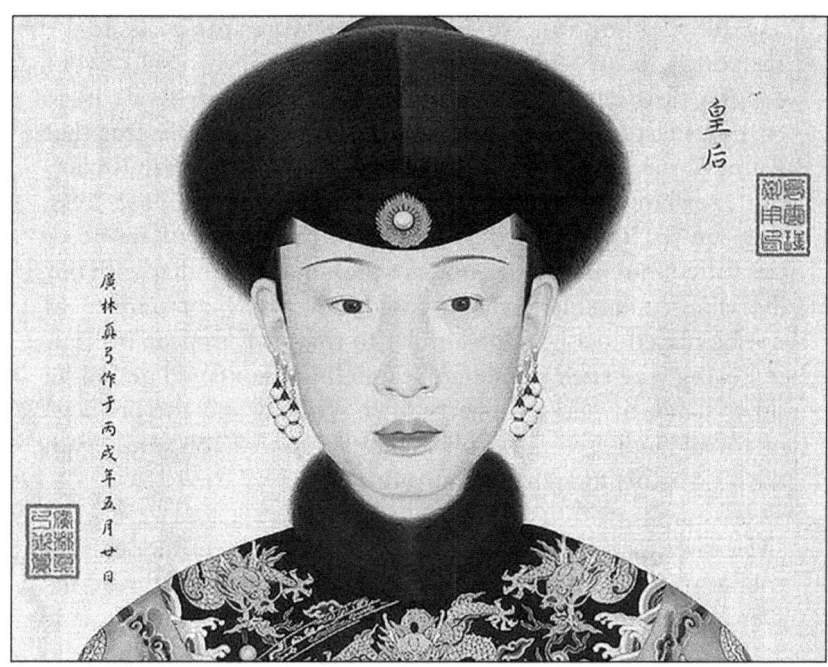

Empress Xiaoyichun (1727-1775) consort of Emperor Ch'ien Lung.

qualities of soldier, statesman and scholar, and eschewing opulence at Court.[221] The rule of Ch'ien Lung for sixty years was also one of nobility, yet his favourite minister, Ho Shen, Grand Secretary, was to be the source of decay for the succeeding regime.[222] "Amongst Chinese historians and scholars there is a common saying: 'A cycle of virtuous rule was brought to nought by Ho Shen : the disastrous century of rebellion and decline which followed was due to him and to him alone'."[223]

Ch'ien also rejected the blandishments of British and other foreign trade and diplomacy, recognising the dangers to China's culture, although Ho Shen tried to counsel a more conciliatory course. Ch'ien referred to the irreconcilability between the cultures, stating that those Europeans who were living in Peking were obliged to blend into the Chinese culture. To King George III, Ch'ien wrote:

---

221 Ibid., 310.
222 Ibid., 319.
223 Ibid.

"As to your entreaty to send one of your nationals to be accredited to my Celestial Court and to be in control of your country's trade with China, this request is contrary to all usage of my dynasty and cannot possibly be entertained. It is true that Europeans, in the service of the dynasty, have been permitted to live at Peking, but they are compelled to adopt Chinese dress, they are strictly confined to their own precincts and are never permitted to return home. You are presumably familiar with our dynastic regulations. Your proposed Envoy to my Court could not be placed in a position similar to that of European officials in Peking who are forbidden to leave China, nor could he, on the other hand, be allowed liberty of movement and the privilege of corresponding with his own country; so that you would gain nothing by his residence in our midst."

"Moreover, our Celestial dynasty possesses vast territories, and tribute missions from the dependencies are provided for by the Department for Tributary States, which ministers to their wants and exercises strict control over their movements. It would be quite impossible to leave them to their own devices. Supposing that your Envoy should come to our Court, his language and national dress differ from that of our people, and there would be no place in which to bestow him. It may be suggested that he might imitate the Europeans permanently resident in Peking and adopt the dress and customs of China, but, it has never been our dynasty's wish to force people to do things unseemly and inconvenient. ... "

"You assert that your reverence for Our Celestial dynasty fills you with a desire to acquire our civilisation, our ceremonies and code of laws differ so completely from your own that, even if your Envoy were able to acquire the rudiments of our civilisation, you could not possibly transplant our manners and customs to your alien soil. Therefore, however adept the Envoy might become, nothing would be gained thereby."

"Swaying the wide world, I have but one aim in view, namely, to maintain a perfect governance and to fulfil the duties of the State: strange and costly objects do not interest me. If I have commanded that the tribute offerings sent by you, O King, are to be accepted, this was solely in consideration for the spirit which prompted you to dispatch them from afar. Our dynasty's majestic virtue has penetrated unto every country under Heaven, and Kings of all nations have offered their costly tribute by land and sea. As your Ambassador can see for himself, we possess all things. I set no value on objects strange or ingenious, and have no use for your country's manufactures. This then is my answer to your request to appoint a representative at my Court, a request contrary to our dynastic usage, which would only result in inconvenience to yourself." [224]

In a second "mandate" to King George, Emperor Ch'ien addresses other concepts central to the traditional state, of which Peking was the *axis mundi*:

"My capital is the hub and centre about which all quarters of the globe revolve. Its ordinances are most august and its laws are strict in the extreme. The subjects of our dependencies have never been allowed to open places of business in Peking".[225]

In point 7 of Ch'ien's second "mandate" to King George, he described the importance of traditional religion as something that cannot be compromised for the sake of "religious freedom":

"(7) Regarding your nation's worship of the Lord of Heaven, it is the same religion as that of other European nations. Ever since the beginning of history, sage Emperors and wise rulers have bestowed on China a moral system and inculcated a code, which from time immemorial has been religiously observed by the myriads of my subjects. There has been no hankering after heterodox doctrines. Even the European (missionary) officials in my capital are forbidden to hold intercourse with Chinese subjects; they are restricted within the limits of their appointed residences, and may not go about propagating their religion. The distinction between Chinese and barbarian is most strict, and your Ambassador's request that barbarians shall be given full liberty to disseminate their religion is utterly unreasonable".[226]

---

224 Imperial Mandate of Ch'ien Lung to King George III [1], Backhouse and Bland, 324-325.

225 Imperial Mandate of Ch'ien Lung to King George III [2], Ibid., 330.

226 Ibid.

Civilisations That Died

To the Celestial Emperor the King of England was no more than the chief of a barbarian tribe, while Peking was the axial centre of the world. The British pleas were called "wild ideas and hopes". The Emperor by his own account had exercised "kindly indulgence" by hearing them. The Emperor had shown the King of England far more regard than others because George had shown his "submissive loyalty" by sending his "tribute mission". It was the King's "bounden duty" to "obey these instructions for all time". Should Britain's "barbarian merchants" attempt to land they would be expelled immediately. "Tremblingly obey and show no negligence".[227] Foreigners could not gain anything even by trying to acquire the "rudiments" of Chinese civilisation. Foreigners had nothing to offer China, least of all the merchants' trinkets.

Ch'ien was a vigorous sportsman, a poet, strong and just, who eschewed luxuries. Of those that brought China to decay following him:

> "As the traveller gazes to-day on the melancholy ruins of Yuan Ming-yuan, or the hunting parks at Jehol and Peking, he cannot but wonder that a race which could produce so wise and so virile a ruler, and send its armies across Asia, should to-day be represented only by the besotted and effeminate creatures who walk so delicately and so uselessly as Manchu Princes".[228]

The reign of Chi'en's son Chia Ch'ing saw an epoch of decline, until his death in 1821. He was succeeded by his son, Tao Kuang. The rebelliousness that had occurred under Chia continued. "The canker worm of effeminacy had already eaten deep into the heart of the Manchu military organisation". [229] The virility had gone from the Manchus as it had from the Ming. Of Tao's successor, his fourth son Hsien Feng, the chroniclers portray him as "a thoroughly dissolute and depraved specimen of humanity, physically and morally contemptible", whose reign saw the invasion of the Forbidden City and its looting, and a rival government of rebels established at Nanking.[230]

---

[227] Ibid., 330-331.
[228] Ibid., 334-335.
[229] Ibid., 390.
[230] Ibid., 405.

"Whatever was left of virility and patriotism at Peking gnashed its teeth in impotent rage, not so much because of the imminence of the danger, as because of the hopeless depravity of the Sovereign and the men whom he delighted to honour. Rome was burning whilst China's Nero not only fiddled, but danced obscenely to his own music. Whilst province after province passed through fire and sword to acknowledge the sway of the Rebel Emperor, the Lord of Heaven busied himself with the provision of new lights for his harem or joined his evil genius, the notorious Minister Su Shun, in orgies of unspeakable debauch in the low haunts of the Chinese quarter".[231]

As Nanking fell (1853) to the Taiping rebels, Hsien's primary concern was the selection of new concubines for his harem, while the decadent power of the eunuchs had become "a conspicuous factor" since the death of Ch'ien Lung.[232] On one occasion, weakened by debauched excesses, the lord of the world was too weak to perform the sacrificial rites at the Temple of Heaven.[233] What more perfect traditional symbolism that the Mandate of Heaven had been removed from the Emperor?

The end of imperial China was overseen by a corrupt chief eunuch, Chang Yiian-fu, around the beginning of the 20th century. Chang arrogated semi-regal functions, lived in over-wrought opulence, spent the public purse lavishly, and was in effect the ruler of China. Chang epitomises the long-sliding decline and fall of the Manchus.[234]

---

231 Ibid., 406.
232 Ibid., 407.
233 Ibid., 409.
234 Ibid., 500-508.

Chiang Kai-shek attempts a Resurgence

General Chiang Kai-shek, the much-maligned leader of China during the war against both Japan and the Red Army, attempted a resurgence, realising the epoch of decay that China had entered over the past century was the finale of Chinese civilisation, and not just another cycle of dynastic decay. He wrote of this:

> "A survey of our long history of five thousand years reveals the alternate rise and fall of states and the survival and extinction of nations. Yet the national decay during the last hundred years reached a point unequalled in our history. The state and the nation became weakened and encountered inner crises in the political, economic, social, ethical, and psychological spheres, until the basis of rebirth and recovery was almost destroyed".[235]

Chiang ascribed the unprecedented humiliation of China by foreign-imposed treaties as a symptom of decay. The Manchus had defeated the Ming dynasty due to the latter's moral decay. The Confucian system of scholarly excellence as the basis for state service declined. "Social corruption and academic degeneration became more pronounced each day". The Manchus, far from working to harmonise China as a cultural totality, sought to keep the clans divided.[236] China no longer possessed the health of an organism capable of withstanding foreign pathogens. The Han Chinese ideal was of the farmer-soldier, the peasant in traditional China being esteemed above the merchant in the social hierarchy. However, the Manchu soldiers came to abjure work. The Manchu,

> "did not recognize that when soldiers are not also farmers, they become loafers and hoodlums. Although every male Manchu was a soldier, the final result was that all the Manchus became parasitic loafers. By the time of the T'ai-p'ing Rebellion, the Banner Troops as well as the Green Battalions were degenerate and useless. It was then that the Hsiang [Hunan] Militia and the Hwai Militia [from northern Anhwei] earned fame as the beginning of local armed forces [i.e., farmer-soldiers]".[237]

---

235 Chiang Kai-shek, 1947, 42.
236 Ibid., 48.
237 Ibid., 49.

The Decline and Fall of Civilisations

General Chiang Kai-shek sought China's cultural resurgance.

By the time that the foreign powers entered as conquerors through imposed treaties, China was rotting.

> "These domestic policies of the Manchu Government, destructive to others as well as to itself, were pursued throughout the reigns of Tao Kuang and T'ung Chih, until the spirit with which the dynasty was founded became lost, together with its traditional institutions. The result was political disintegration and the deterioration of national defense. A general situation of chaos and collapse developed".[238]

In a situation analogous to the present, while China received the technics and science of the West, it also received the corruption of a rotting corpse animated by money. Chiang vividly described the predicament when confronted with the foreigner:

> "China's ancient philosophy of ethics is based on a careful and thorough study of the interrelations of human society. Although social organization is in a state of constant evolution, yet the principles of the relations between father and son, husband and

---

238 Ibid.

wife, elder brother and younger brother, friend and friend, between higher and lower ranks, the honorable and the humble, men and women, old and young, down to the duty of neighbors to protect each other and care for the sick, have remained the unchangeable ethical rules of social life. During the past hundred years, with the spread of the wanton customs of the concessions, the people not only neglected these ethical principles, but discarded and scorned them. As a consequence, between father and son, husband and wife, brothers, friends, high and low, old and young, neighbors and communities, there was no thought of reciprocal love and reciprocal friendliness, and above all, the virtue of co-operation and sense of unity were lost. Everything was planned for material interest, with a total lack of self-discipline. Duty was shirked in the struggle for profits. The high and the low deceived each other, and the people cheated one another right and left. The old and the weak received no consideration or relief, and the sick received no help. The people treated their own blood relations as strangers, and regarded their fellow countrymen as enemies. And they failed to recognize the error of such unethical and abnormal behavior. They transformed China, a propriety-loving and virtue-respecting country, into a country without modesty or shame. Such was the evil effect of the unequal treaties. If this can be tolerated, then what cannot be tolerated?"[239]

Chiang described the moral and ethical shift resulting physical deterioration:

"The steady deterioration of the people's virtue affected their physical condition, causing them to grow weaker day by day. The physical strength of the countless numbers of unemployed in the cities was, of course, completely exhausted, and as the merchants and ordinary people became accustomed to a life of luxury and dissipation, their health also deteriorated. The most serious danger was the threat to the health of the youth in the schools. Physical training could not include the entire student body, and ethical training had long been neglected by the principals and teachers. A life of luxury and dissipation outside the schools lured the youth and caused them to become physically weak and

---

239 Ibid., 93.

mentally decadent, while contagious diseases and syphilis from the cities further undermined their health. How could these physically and mentally weakened youths, after leaving school, promote scholarship, or reform the people's way of life so that they could assume the responsibilities of the state and develop social enterprises? It was indeed impossible to predict when this degeneration of the state and decline of the nation would end".[240]

The decay of China followed the same rhythm as other civilizations. After several thousand years of dynastic cycles, the entire civilisation, albeit the longest-enduring, succumbed. Wealth drained the stamina of some classes through luxurious decadence, while the great mass of the rest of society could not secure the basics of life, and deteriorated from that end. The youth of the leadership classes became too dissipated to assume their leadership responsibilities.

The great achievements of Chinese civilisation had endured for millennia, while synthesising foreign influences on their own terms. The Chinese rejected foreign blandishments of commerce if this would infect the Chinese culture organism. The subordination of commerce enabled the Chinese to defend their civilisation longer than others. Chiang stated of this adaptation:

> "... The Chinese nation was still able to absorb and adopt foreign culture and learning for its further advancement. And because China could absorb other forms of civilization, her own civilization became even broader and greater. However, China's culture and learning have their own ancient standards. *China was able to absorb other forms of civilization and learning precisely because she had her own standards and her own system by which to judge these other forms of civilization.* Thus, when foreign civilizations were transplanted to China, they became a part of China's national economy and of the people's livelihood, and thus could remain indefinitely as part of China's civilization".[241] [Emphasis added].

---

240 Ibid., 93-94.
241 Ibid., 96-97.

"Harmonising" Elements

This cultural alchemy of absorbing foreign elements is a fine line between acquiring health or death for the culture organism, and China and Japan had mastered it as have few others. This cultural alchemy the Chinese referred to as "harmonising" elements. Analogically one might compare this process to the vaccination of the human organism with a small dose of virus to accentuate the health of the organism; while an incorrect amount of the same virus results in illness and possibly death. China had however reached an epochal point of balance where foreign culture bodies could poison the culture organism rather than invigorate it. Chiang described this process, enabled by the humiliating imposition of foreign treaties that now subordinated China to commerce in a reversal of the traditional ethos. With this opening to foreign trade came foreign doctrines. In prior centuries when Jesuit and Protestant missionaries had entered China, the Chinese eschewed the adoption of Christianity while accepting the Western science that the Jesuits offered, and the only way the Jesuits could interact more successfully than other missionaries was to become Sinified in customs, manners and dress.[242] China absorbed Western science without compromising its moral, ethical and spiritual foundations. The 19th century was a different matter. Chiang stated:

> "On the other hand, during the past hundred years, China's civilization showed signs of great deterioration. This was because, under the oppression of the unequal treaties, the Chinese people reversed their attitude toward Western civilization from one of opposition to one of submission, and their attitude toward their own civilization changed from one of pride to one of self-abasement. Carried to extremes, this attitude of submission [to Western theories] became one of ardent conversion and they openly proclaimed themselves loyal disciples of this or that foreign theory. Similarly, the attitude of self-abasement was carried to such an extreme that they despised and mocked the heritage of their own civilization. We should bear in mind that from the Opium War down to the Revolution of 1911, the unanimous demand of the people was to avenge the national humiliation and make the country strong, and all efforts were

---

242 Amaury de Riencourt, 139-146.

concentrated on enriching the country and strengthening the army. In other words, it was our unwillingness to become slaves that first caused us to study Western civilization. It follows that we should also study Western civilization for the purpose of winning our independence and making China strong. Unfortunately, after the Revolution of 1911, the will to avenge our national humiliation and make the country strong perished with the failure of the Revolution, and the effects of the unequal treaties were further deepened after this failure. Unconsciously, the people developed the habit of ignoring their own traditions and cultivating foreign ways; of respecting foreign theories and despising their native teachings; of depending upon others and blindly following them. Thus, although the Chinese people originally studied Western civilization because of their unwillingness to become slaves, the result was that they unconsciously became the slaves of foreign theories because of their studies of Western civilization".[243]

Liberalism and Communism

The cultural alchemy, the harmonisation of opposites, the *Tao*, that was the basis of Chinese strength succumbed to imbalance. Although Chiang places the cause of this on the imposition of foreign treaties, immunity to foreign toxins had long been deteriorating. Chiang cites the two primary examples: Communism and Liberalism:

"…two types of thought individualistic, Liberalism and class-war Communism, were suddenly introduced among the educated classes and spread throughout the whole country. … As a result, the educated classes and scholars generally adopted the superficial husks of Western culture and lost their own respect and self-confidence and lost their confidence in Chinese culture. Wherever the influence of these ideas prevailed, the people regarded everything foreign as good and everything Chinese as bad".[244]

Chiang saw Liberal ideology being as much a foreign and corrupting influence as Communism:

---
243 Chiang Kai-shek, 97.
244 Ibid., 98.

"As for the struggle between Liberalism and Communism, it was merely a reflection of the opposition of Anglo-American theories to those of Soviet Russia. Not only were such political theories unsuited to the national economy and the people's livelihood, and opposed to the spirit of China's own civilization, but also the people that promoted them forgot that they were Chinese and that they should study and apply foreign theories for the benefit of China. As a result, their copying only caused the decay and ruin of Chinese civilization, and made it easy for the imperialists to carry on cultural aggression. China's theoreticians and political leaders, either directly or indirectly, intentionally or unintentionally, adopted the theories and interests of the imperialists as their own, and forgot their own origin and the purpose of their study. They even maintained this attitude in social propaganda and education, thus causing the people to accept without question the unequal treaties and the aggression and exploitation of the imperialists. This is the greatest single danger of cultural aggression, and the greatest threat to the nation's spirit. ..."[245]

This Liberalism, now more often called "human rights" and "democracy", remains the doctrine by which the USA infects a culture as the prelude to domination. What Chiang saw as cultural imperialism is now called "globalisation." Chiang describes how far-reaching the process was, spreading out from the foreign concessions as entry points of infection:

"When economic conditions in the interior were poor, the people migrated to the cities. But it was difficult to find employment and they were therefore forced to sell their sons and daughters, and fell into the evil habits of prostitution and kidnapping. Thus, during the past hundred years, beautiful and prosperous cities became hells of misery and chaos. As for gambling, its damage was not limited to the rich, but also spread to the poor. The rich lost their fortunes and went bankrupt, and the poor lost their livelihood and met disaster. Once tainted with the habit of gambling, the social order became completely lawless. The people's minds were paralyzed and their morality

---
245 Ibid., 100.

destroyed. Moreover, the practice of gambling was not limited to the gambling dens, but extended from lotteries to speculative activities in the market activities that did not follow the laws of production and exchange, but depended solely on luck to obtain unmerited profits. The concessions became the concentration points for surplus capital, but there were no well-established industries to employ this capital. Consequently, many people, both rich and poor, engaged in gambling, spent money lavishly in houses of prostitution, and became paralyzed with drugs. After having gone bankrupt and broken up their families, they degenerated into thieves and bandits, using the concessions as their hideouts and engaging in all sorts of criminal activities. China's five-thousand-year-old tradition of diligence, thrift, and simplicity, of cotton clothes and a simple diet, of women weaving and men farming, were completely undermined by the opium, gambling, prostitutes, and thugs of the concessions."[246]

The rot starts by the depopulation of the countryside and the migration of the peasantry into the cities to become a rootless proletariat. With this comes the breakdown of generational bonds to family, land, and village. Money thinking dominates in society, high and low. Morals loosen, along with concepts of honour. Capitalism based around speculation replaces craft. The intricate relationships that form a healthy social organism reached crisis point.

Chiang, largely overlooked or ridiculed among Western academics and journalists, betrayed by the USA, which insisted that he accommodate the Communists, fought a heroic struggle. He was fighting a battle against the tides of the Age.

Mao Tse-tung, behind the appearance of a humble peasant, was like the decadent officials, eunuchs and monarchs of the Ming and Manchu dynasties. Mao "led a life of royal self-indulgence, practised at tremendous cost to the country.... as soon as he conquered China".[247] Over his twenty-seven year rule fifty estates were created for him; many never used. They were set in sumptuous locations. His swimming pools were kept heated all year at tremendous cost and waste, should he decide

---

[246] Ibid., 92.
[247] Jung Chang and Join Halliday, 2005, 342.

Civilisations That Died

The Chinese 'Cultural Revolution' 1966-76 resulted in the death of millions and the destruction of countless religious and cultural artifacts.

to swim.[248] For his meals the rice membrane between the husk and kernel had to be meticulously extracted, while Mao exhorted that the peasantry could survive on 140 kg of grain.[249] A notable feature of the Mao regime was the determination to destroy Tradition. In 1966 the Red Guards were unleashed in the "Cultural Revolution". These fanatical youths looted jewellery, antiques and ancient books from private collections for Mao and his entourage.[250] Public monuments to China's ancient past were destroyed, including 4,922 of Peking's 6,843.[251] Statues of Buddha were broken. The home of Confucius in Shandong, an impressive museum, was vandalised by Red Guards.[252] The "Cultural Revolution" was aptly named: it was a revolt against millennia of tradition.

---

248 Ibid., 345.
249 Ibid.
250 Ibid., 540-541.
251 Ibid., 541.
252 Ibid., 542.

Is China the Future?

Affluence does not equate with spiritual, culture and moral health. As we have seen, to the contrary, affluence corresponds with cycles of decay. It is the opulence of the bloated billionaire prior to dying of a heart attack through excess or a "pop star" or "Hollywood celebrity" succumbing to drugs and alcohol. China's economic power, like the USA's, is illusionary. China sees itself, as it always has, as the central focus of world-power. However, China's wealth exists as the reflection of western technics and money-thinking.

As China's economic power expands, so too will the internal market continue to open, not just to Western technics and sciences, but to the culture of decay that goes with it. As we have seen the Chinese emperors were stringent in rejecting any foreign influences that would undermine Chinese culture, including commerce. Chiang Kai-shek also wished to pursue this outlook. Mao's answer in his pursuit of power was to import the foreign doctrine Marxism while pursuing a vigorous policy of destroying Chinese classical culture and Confucianism in particular.

Amoury De Riencourt wrote of China that "what is now missing is a moral code". He saw that moral code as being in a revival of Confucianism, which was "inevitable", and cited Confucianist congresses being held, "pilgrims" that visit Confucius' birthplace as a "national shrine", and of the sage's works being sold "everywhere in bookstores". He considered Confucianism as "one of the most remarkable moral codes ever devised". De Riencourt saw a revival of Confucianism as being "the only means of curbing inevitable corruption".[253] He concluded his updated edition of *The Soul of China*: "A revival of a new form of Confucianism should provide China, in the twenty-first century, with the all-embracing philosophy of life which it lost in the twentieth, when its traditional interpretation collapsed".[254]

That is an option for China's reinvigoration. Regarding the health of China as for the USA or Europe in terms of economic statistics is as meaningful as judging the health of an individual by the affluence of their clothes. Not much can be diagnosed of the collective morality.

---

253 Amaury de Riencourt, 298-299.
254 Ibid., 300.

For that one looks at demographics, abortion rates, marriage and family stability, and the other factors we have considered previously in civilisations. Symptoms of Chinese weakness include:

Ageing Population

Presently, at least 123 million people, or 9% of the population, are over 65. Estimates are that China will become the world's most aged society by 2030. By 2050, senior citizens will comprise over 30% of the population.

Marriage Breakdown

One in five marriages ends in divorce, double the rate a decade ago. In Beijing 39% of all marriages end in separation. This breakdown in marriage is symptomatic of factors that are typically found in civilisations in decay. Shu Xin, founder of Weiqing Divorce Club, Shanghai, a counselling service, stated: "This generation is very self-centred, very independent. And they have high expectations as to cost and return. ... They're revelling in these newfound freedoms, even the freedom to divorce".[255] What Shu sees as a "free generation" Spengler saw as the "last man" and "last woman" of Late civilisation, "liberated" from the bonds of children, marriage and family; affluent and self-absorbed until becoming *Fellaheen*.

Rural Depopulation

Rural depopulation and the urbanisation and proletarianisation of the peasantry is a primary symptom of culture-decay. China's peasantry is declining and urban sprawl is encroaching. The expert projection is that city-dwellers will rise from the present 45% to 70% by 2040. McKinsey Global Institute states that by 2025 many cities will be constructed in rural localities. However, so far from studying such trends as symptoms of decline, such think tanks can only see urbanisation as offering an expanded consumer market.[256] The attitude is itself a symptom of decadence.

---

255 Louisa Lim, 2010.
256 "Preparing for China's urban billion", McKinsey Global Inst., 2009.

The Decline and Fall of Civilisations

Nine Commentaries on the Chinese Communist Party

One of the most insightful works on contemporary China has been undertaken by Chinese traditionalists, with *Nine Commentaries on the Chinese Communist Party*, a series of articles beginning in November 2004 in the U.S.-based Chinese paper *Epoch Times*. Being traditionalists the authors are able to look at China beyond merely analysing statics. Hence, to them the Communist Party is an assault on the Universe itself; a breach of the nexus between Heaven and Earth; the "Way" or *Tao*, on which 5,000 years of civilisation had been based. They describe the character of a culture according to the traditionalist outlook:

> "Culture is the soul of a nation. This spiritual factor is as important to mankind as physical factors such as race and land. Cultural developments define the history of a nation's civilization. The complete destruction of a national culture leads to the end of the nation. Ancient nations that had created glorious civilizations were considered to have vanished when their cultures disappeared, even though people of their races may have survived. China is the only country in the world whose ancient civilization has been passed down continuously for over 5,000 years. Destruction of its traditional culture is an unforgivable crime"[257].

The Chinese civilisation had endured through the maintenance of core spiritual principles:

> "Although the Chinese nation has experienced invasion and attack many times in history, the Chinese culture has shown great endurance and stamina, and its essence has been continuously passed down. The unity of heaven and humanity represents our ancestors' cosmology. It is common sense that kindness will be rewarded and evil will be punished. It is an elementary virtue not to do to others what one does not want done to oneself. Loyalty, filial piety, dignity, and justice have set the social standards, and Confucius' five cardinal virtues of benevolence, righteousness, propriety, wisdom, and faithfulness have laid the foundation for social and personal morality. With these principles, the Chinese

---

[257] Nine Commentaries on the Chinese Communist Party Commentary 6.

culture embodied honesty, kindness, harmony, and tolerance. Common Chinese people's death memorials show reverence to 'heaven, earth, monarch, parents and teacher.' This is a cultural expression of the deep-rooted Chinese traditions, which include worship of god (heaven and earth), loyalty to the country (monarch), values of family (parents), and respect for teachers. The traditional Chinese culture sought harmony between man and the universe, and emphasized an individual's ethics and morality. It was based on the faiths of the cultivation practices of Confucianism, Buddhism, and Taoism, and provided the Chinese people with tolerance, social progress, a safeguard for human morality, and righteous belief".[258]

The ebb and flow of thousands of years of Chinese history culminated with the wilful destruction of its cultural and spiritual foundations by the Communist Party, with its "inherent ideological opposition to traditional Chinese culture. Thus, the CCP's destruction of Chinese culture has been planned, well organized, and systematic, supported by the state's use of violence. Since its establishment, the CCP has never stopped 'revolutionizing' Chinese culture in the attempt to destroy its spirit completely".[259] In China the Marxist process of cultural destruction targeted the family, as in the Soviet Union in its formative stages:

> "Confucianism values family, but the *Communist Manifesto* clearly promulgates abolition of the family. Traditional culture differentiates the Chinese from the foreign, but the *Communist Manifesto* advocates the end of nationality. Confucian culture promotes kindness to others, but the Communist Party encourages class struggle. Confucians encourage loyalty to the monarch and love for the nation. The *Communist Manifesto* promotes the elimination of nations".[260]

Marxism is a revolt against Heaven or the Divine in whatever language it is called.

---

258 Ibid.
259 Ibid.
260 Ibid.

"Traditional Chinese culture believes in God and the heavenly mandate. Accepting the mandate of heaven means that rulers have to be wise, follow the Tao and be attuned to destiny. Accepting belief in God means accepting that authority over humanity rests in heaven. The CCP ruling principle is summarized as, 'Never more tradition's chains shall bind us, arise ye toilers no more in thrall. The earth shall rise on new foundations; we are but naught; we shall be all.'[261] The CCP promotes historical materialism, claiming that Communism is an earthly paradise, the path to which is led by the pioneer proletarians, or the Communist Party. The belief in God thus directly challenged the legitimacy of the CCP's rule".[262]

The Communists sought the destruction of all religion: Confucianism, Tao and Buddhism.

"Soon after the CCP established a government, it began to destroy temples, burn scriptures and forced the Buddhist monks and nuns to return to secular life. Neither was it any softer in destroying other religious places. By the 1960s, there were hardly any religious places left in China. The Great Cultural Revolution brought even greater religious and cultural catastrophe in the campaign of 'Casting Away the Four Olds' — i.e., old ideas, old culture, old customs and old habits".[263]

Other than religious items, traditional culture in general was targeted, including the ancient calligraphic manuscripts and paintings. Piles were burned. Quoting Mao:

"What can Emperor Qin Shi Huang brag about? He only killed 460 Confucian scholars, but we killed 46,000 intellectuals. In our suppression of counter-revolutionaries, didn't we kill counter-revolutionary intellectuals as well? I argued with the pro-democratic people who accused us of acting like Emperor

---

261 From the *Communist Internationale* anthem. The Chinese translation literally means: "There has never been a saviour, and we do not rely on God either; to create human happiness, we rely entirely on ourselves." Footnote 27, Ibid.

262 Nine Commentaries…, Commentary 6.

263 Ibid. Numerous examples are given of the destruction of temples, manuscripts and relics.

Qin Shi Huang. I said they were wrong. We surpassed him by a hundred times."

As we have seen, a culture pathogen such as Marxism or Liberalism cannot infect a culture-organism unless that organism has been weakened. Hence such doctrines as Marxism and Liberalism are not *causes* but *symptoms* that aggravate the weaknesses already present. The authors of the "Nine Commentaries", as traditionalists, recognise the long periods of decline China had undergone before reaching the stage that allowed a doctrine dedicated to the total destruction of tradition to triumph. The destruction of *Tao*, of harmony, and the supremacy of a materialistic, man-centred dogma has had catastrophic effects on the landscape, as it did in other Communist states, and indeed in the Liberal states where economics is also the focus. The air, the water, and the land, have been poisoned through human arrogance in defying the divine. The "6th Commentary" concludes:

> "China started to deviate from its traditional culture in the Song Dynasty (960-1279 AD), and that culture has experienced constant depredation ever since. After the May Fourth Movement of 1919, some intellectuals who were eager for quick success and instant benefit attempted to find a path for China by turning away from the traditional culture toward Western civilization. Still, conflicts and changes in the cultural domain remained a focus of academic contention without the involvement of state forces. When the CCP came into existence, however, it elevated cultural conflicts to a matter of life-and-death struggle for the Party. So the CCP began to exercise a direct assault on traditional culture, using destructive means as well as indirect abuse in the form of 'adopting the dross and rejecting the essence.'

> "The destruction of the national culture was also the process of establishing 'the Party culture.' The CCP subverted human conscience and moral judgment, thus driving people to turn their backs on traditional culture. If the national culture is completely destroyed, the essence of the nation will disappear with it, leaving only an empty name for the nation. This is not an exaggerated warning.

"At the same time, the destruction of the traditional culture has brought us unexpected physical damage.

"Traditional culture values the unity of heaven and humans and harmonious co-existence between humans and nature. The CCP has declared endless joy from 'fighting with heaven and earth.' This culture of the CCP has led directly to the serious degradation of the natural environment that plagues China today. Take water resources for example. The Chinese people, having abandoned the traditional value that 'a nobleman treasures wealth, but he makes fortune in a decent way,' have wantonly ravaged and polluted the natural environment. Currently, more than 75 percent of the 50,000 kilometers (or 30,000 miles) of China's rivers are unsuitable for fish habitat. Over one third of the groundwater had been polluted even a decade ago, and now the situation continues to worsen. ..."[264]

The Nine Commentaries is a remarkable document. It provides insights not only into the Chinese predicament but into the Western, having followed the same path of decay. As these Chinese traditionalists state, life is more than the health of an economic balance sheet in the service of economic theories.

"Culture offers no answers for questions such as how to expand industrial production or what social systems to adopt. Rather, it plays an important role in providing moral guidance and restraint. The true restoration of traditional culture shall be the recovery of humility toward heaven, the earth and nature, respect for life, and awe before God. It will allow humanity to live harmoniously with heaven and earth and to enjoy a heaven-given old age".[265]

---

264 Ibid.
265 Ibid.

Birth of The West

In his study of Rome's social history sociologist Rodney Stark wondered how the Empire survived as long as it did, and came to the conclusion that it did so only through the continual importation of barbarians and semi-barbarians. Far then from being a threat, the "barbarians" were seen as a means by which Rome might make good manpower shortages. The problem was that no sooner had the latter settled within the imperial frontiers than they adopted Roman vices. By the end of the first century, the only groups in the Empire that were increasing by normal demographic process were the Christians and the Jews, and these two were immune from the contagion of Roman decadence.[1]

Rome's adoption of Christianity in the fourth century may have had as one of its major goals the halting of the Empire's population decline. Christians had large families and were noted for their rejection of infanticide and abortion. In legalising Christianity Constantine may have hoped to reverse the population trend, where imperial decrees on marriage and children had not. Constantine was also recognising the inevitable. By the late third century Christians were a majority in areas of the East, particularly of Syria and Asia Minor, and with the Jews were the only groups registering an increase in many other areas. By the fourth century Jews formed up to one tenth of the Empire's population. It would appear that regardless of Christianity's legal status, Rome would inexorably become Christian.

Did Christianisation halt the decline of Rome? Many such as Nietzsche asserted that Christianity destroyed Rome. Christianity is said to have sapped the martial ethos of the Roman, with its doctrine of worldly renunciation and pacifism. Yet when was Christian Rome ever pacifistic and otherworldly? Rome had been in the process of moral decay for centuries, as we have seen. Christianisation was a symptom, not a cause. But did Christianisation as a symptom aggravate the fall of Rome, or place it again at the centre of a new culture that would become just as imperial, just as martial, and would surpass the Classical Roman in its learning, heroism, conquest, and arts, marching behind Constantine's motto: "In hoc signo vinces"?

---

1   Robert Stark, 1996.

Birth of The West

Although Rome was sacked by the Goths and by the Vandals, by 476 A.D. the Western Empire was officially dissolved, neither sought to destroy the culture they had found despite the connotations of the word "vandal". By this time, over the course of a century, Germanic tribes comprised the majority of the Roman legions, the officer corps and many of Rome's citizenry. Eroc (Crocus), chief of the Alamanni, put his formidable forces behind the proclamation of Constantine as Emperor. During the mid-6th century, two decades of war between Byzantines and Goths reduced Rome to ruins, and even the surrounding countryside was uninhabitable.

By 579 the Senate had ceased to function. Commerce had stopped. Rome "had become a village housed in the vast and crumbling ruins of antiquity, a village ministering to the wants of its bishop, the custodian of an immense historical museum living on the trade of pious tourists who, as the centuries wore on, began flocking to the eternal city from the wilds of the newborn West".[2] The Germanic Lombards settled in multitudes, and established a northern kingdom, while the Franks established their authority over Gaul. These would become the foundation for The West. Clovis, the King of the Franks, converted to Catholicism. In 751 Pepin's claim to the throne of the Franks was recognised by Pope Boniface. He became the first "king of Europe".

Already under Charles Martel (686-741) the Christian armies fighting the Arabs in 732 AD were being called "European" in the *Chronicle of Isidore of Spain*. The empire of Charlemagne (AD 768-814) is named "Europe" by the contemporary chroniclers. In 755 the priest Cathwulf praised Charlemagne as chosen by God, and ruling over "the glory of the empire of Europe".[3]

In 799 Angilbert, Charlemagne's son-in-law and the Court poet, described the Emperor as "the father of Europe" – *Rex, pater Europae*.[4] The "Kingdom of Charles" was called "Europa" in the *Annals of Fuld*. Alcuin (735-804), master of the palace school, theologian and Court rhetorician, called this "the continent of faith".

---

2   Lawrence R. Brown, 1963, 307.

3   Denis de Rougemont, 1966, 46.

4   Angilbert, Monumenta germ.Poet.Carol. I, 368. Quoted by Denis de Rougemont, 46.

Christian Visigothic Spain became a centre of High Culture. Christianity provided the catalyst for a Romano-Gothic and Frankish synthesis from which emerged Western Culture. This Western Culture was not Roman or Jewish; it was a unique, self-contained, independently flowering culture-organism, fertilised on the prior Roman and Gothic landscape, but growing up as a new species.

Because of the fracturing of Western thinking during the Renaissance, since that time we have been taught that the "progress of man" has struggled to overcome the superstition of the so-called "Dark Ages". The Western Medieval or "Gothic" era is regarded as a low-point in "human history", overcome by the Enlightenment, thanks to Greek, Roman, Arab, and Chinese learning. Very little of merit is accorded to Western originality. Indeed, the "Gothic" era was so named during the Renaissance because the Goths were regarded as primitives. As we have seen, Giambattista Vico, writing during the "Age of Enlightenment", pointed out that the "reasonable man" as he called the rationalist mentality emerging during his time, worshipped his "reason" at the expense of the imaginative that was the creative impulse in man. Hence, what is disparaged as the "Dark Age" of superstition was in reality the formative stage of the "Spring epoch", the High Culture of The West, during which the imaginative impulse flourished.

Western Civilisation was synonymous with Christendom, as was "Europe". The Faith defined one's identity vis-à-vis "the other" – Jew, Mongol, Muslim. Any such concept as "Judaeo-Christianity" was an unthinkable blasphemy. As Hilaire Belloc wrote: "Europe is the faith".[5] The Christianity that leavened the tribes of Europe shaped a unique ethos, art, architecture, and science that is not a hybrid of anything. What was unique about all of this was that it aspires heavenward, its symbol pure, infinite space, described by Oswald Spengler as the Westerner's "Faustian soul": the spires of its Gothic Cathedrals, the soaring of its sacred organ music, the perspective of its landscape painting, its exploration, its astronomy, its calculus...

The figure of the Gothic Christ was not that of the "pale Galilean" of Swinburne's imagination.[6] He was a warrior-king. The warrior Christ

---

5 Hilaire Belloc, *Europe and the Faith*.
6 Algernon Charles Swinburne, "Hymn to Proserpine", 1866.

was at the beginning of the Western culture-organism, depicted in the 8th century Anglo-Saxon poem "Dream of the Rood," where the self-sacrificing hero hangs upon the "rood" (rod, crucifix or tree) Odin-like for the sake of others:

> …The young hero stripped himself – he, God Almighty –
> strong and stout-minded. He mounted high gallows,
> bold before many, when he would loose mankind.
> I shook when that Man clasped me. I dared, still, not bow to
> earth, fall to earth's fields, but had to stand fast.
> Rood was I reared. I lifted a mighty King,
> Lord of the heavens, dared not to bend.
> With dark nails they drove me through: on me those sores are
> seen, open malice-wounds. I dared not scathe anyone.
> They mocked us both, we two together.
> All wet with blood I was, poured out from that Man's side,
> after ghost he gave up.
> Much have I born on that hill of fierce fate.
> I saw the God of hosts harshly stretched out.
> Darknesses had wound round with clouds the corpse of the
> Wielder, bright radiance; a shadow went forth, dark under
> heaven.
> All creation wept,
> King's fall lamented. Christ was on rood. …

The following century the metamorphosis of Christianity had proceeded to the extent that the Gospels were placed in a European setting. The Galileans became the "Northern people", the Jews of Jerusalem the evil "Southern people". This was the *Heliand*, the earliest German epic, an account of the "Saxon saviour". With Jesus as the son of a warrior chief, and his band of twelve warriors, *Heliand*, states the translator, Professor G. Ronald Murphy, "created a unique cultural synthesis between Christianity and Germanic warrior society – a synthesis that would plant the seed that would one day blossom in the full-blown culture of knighthood and become the foundation of medieval Europe".[7] Here the key word is *synthesis* in making the Gospels the "foundation of medieval Europe"; the Europe of Gothic High Culture. The Lord's Prayer in *Heliand* appeals to "good

---

7   G. Ronald Murphy (translator) , 198, 51-52.

Chieftain". The betrayal by Judas "is made more serious by making it an act of betraying one's own family chieftain, to whom one was bound by blood and absolute loyalty".[8]

Interpreting the Gospel of Luke on the taking of Jesus in Gethsemane by the Romans, Christ's followers are warriors, willing to lay down their lives for their chieftain. However Jesus must fulfil his fate or *wyrd*. Simon Peter, a mighty, noble swordsman cannot restrain his anger at the "enemy clan" and strikes their priest:

> "Christ's warrior companions saw warriors coming up the mountain making a great din
> Angry armed men. Judas the hate filled man was showing them the way.
> The enemy clan, the Jews, were marching behind.
> The warriors marched forward, the grim Jewish army, until they had come to the Christ.
> There he stood, the famous chieftain.
> Christ's followers, wise men deeply distressed by this hostile action
> Held their position in front.
> They spoke to their chieftain, "My Lord chieftain", they said, "if it should now
> Be your will that we be impaled here under spear points
> Wounded by their weapons then nothing would be so good to us as to die here
> Pale from mortal wounds for our chieftain".
>
> Then he got really angry
> Simon Peter, the mighty, noble swordman flew into a rage.
> His mind was in such turmoil he could not speak a single word.
> His heart became intensely bitter because they wanted to tie up his Lord there.
> So he strode over angrily, that very daring Thane, to stand in front of his commander
> Right in front of his Lord.
>
> No doubting in his mind, no fearful hesitation in his chest he drew his blade

---

8   Ibid., 147-148.

The Ruthwell Cross - An 8th century Anglo-Saxon cross carved with runic inscriptions from one of the first English poems.

And struck straight ahead at the first man of the enemy with all the strength in his hands
So that Malchus was cut and wounded on the right side by the sword.
His ear was chopped off.
He was so badly wounded in the head that his cheek and ear burst open with the mortal wound
Blood gushed out, pouring from the wound.
The men stood back; they were afraid of the slash of the sword.[9]

This was the era of Charlemagne, when The West was born, under one Emperor and one Faith. The ethos was Chivalry, born from the *synthesis* of Gothic Christianity, and celebrated in epic literature. *The Song of Roland*, an 11th century saga of the battles of Charlemagne in the 8th century, is regarded as the foundation of the ethos, with the duties of a Knight enunciated:

To fear God and maintain His Church
To serve the liege lord in valour and faith
To protect the weak and defenceless
To give succour to widows and orphans
To refrain from the wanton giving of offence
To live by honour and for glory
To despise pecuniary reward
To fight for the welfare of all
To obey those placed in authority
To guard the honour of fellow knights
To eschew unfairness, meanness and deceit
To keep faith
At all times to speak the truth
To persevere to the end in any enterprise begun
To respect the honour of women
Never to refuse a challenge from an equal
Never to turn the back upon a foe.[10]

This epoch from the 7th century was the birth and blossoming of the Western culture-organism; not Jewish, Arab, Roman, or Greek, but a unique life-form making its own impress on ethics, mathematics, physics, architecture, music, and warfare.

---

9   Ibid., 158-161.
10 Cindy Wood, 166.

Romanesque & Gothic Styles

"Romanesque" was the first properly Western style of architecture. It was so named due to its use of Roman classical columns and arched vaults. Again, this emphasising of outside influences on Western culture obscures the unique and self-contained character of cultures. The implication is that today's civilisation is the sum total of preceding cultures in a procession, each handing the torch of civilisation on to the next in line culminating in the Late West, which some such as Francis Fukuyama even call "the end of history" because they cannot envisage anything more prefect than Late Western liberal-democracy and capitalism.

Lessay Abbey, Normandy, France.

Western civilisation is regarded as the descendent in particular of the Graeco-Roman, with major input from the Arab, Indian and Chinese. Such similarities are superficial. The Western perspective is not Greek, Roman, Indian, Arab or Chinese, any more than the Russian is Western. The Western perspective of infinite space that Spengler called "Faustian" informed every aspect of its High Culture including those elements that were adapted from others, such as the column and the arched vault; becoming the purely Western-Faustian "Gothic" style.

The "Romanesque", despite the name being applied to it centuries later (19th century), seeks escape from the earth-bound solidity of the Classical Roman Temple, while the Western soul finally soars unbound several centuries later with the Gothic. The Romanesque sought communion with the body of Christ, and with the representation of the heavenly Jerusalem on earth. Jerusalem for Western Christendom became as much the *axis mundi* as for Judaism and Islam. It is a spiritual axis and again to compare the outlook of the Westerner with that of the Jew or Muslim is not only fallacious but harmful.

The portal of the Romanesque church represented the metaphor of Christ that he is "the door".[11] The Romanesque portal guided the entry from the secular to the spiritual into the interior of the church. The portal lead the way of the faithful as symbolic of Christ leading the way. The development from Romanesque to Gothic was away from the Church as a material representation and towards transcendence from the earthly plain to spirit. The monk Bernard of Angers, writing of the Abbey of Sainte-Foy of Conques in 1013 described the allegorical character of the architecture, with the basilica comprised of three forms by the division on the roofs, "but on the inside these three forms are united across their width to shape the church into one body", thus representing the trinity.[12]

Romanesque: Cathedral of Pisa, Italy.

---

11   John, 10: 9.
12   Calvin B. Kendall, 13.

Gothic: Milan Cathedral, Italy.

From the 12th century, starting in France, the uniquely Western style started manifesting in its most recognisable form: Gothic. The Gothic Cathedral was the purest expression of the Western "Faustian" soul. The theologian Nicole Oresme (1320-1382) referred to this religious world-feeling towards infinity, writing that there is "Beyond the cosmos an infinite void that reflects the infinity and immensity of God".[13] While the "imaginative" faculty of the Western mind in its formative stage strived towards the infinity of God; in the Late civilisation epoch of rationalism, the Faustian imperative continues, no longer in the name of God, but of science, reaching out towards the infinity of space with rocketry. Both Gothic spire and spaceship symbolise the Faustian imperative; one of High Culture, the other of Late civilisation.

The genius of Gothic man is shown in an architecture and engineering that is alone Western.

---

13 Edward Grant, 552.

The Decline and Fall of Civilisations

"The whole scheme of the building is determined by, and its whole strength is made to reside in a finely organized and frankly confessed framework rather than in walls. This framework, made up of piers, arches and buttresses, is freed from every unnecessary incumbrance of wall and is rendered as light in all its parts as is compatible with strength — the stability of the building depending not upon inert massiveness, except in the outermost abutment of active parts whose opposing forces neutralize each other and produce a perfect equilibrium. It is thus a system of balanced thrusts in contradistinction to the ancient system of inert stability. Gothic architecture is such a system carried out in a finely artistic spirit".[14]

"Interiors induce a sense of infinity by making the beholder aware of the unending variety and limitlessness of God's creation, the *Andachtsbilder* induced a sense of infinity by permitting the beholder to submerge his being in the boundlessness of the Creator Himself".[15]

The restlessness of spirit, which well describes the Faustian imperative, is recognised as Gothic across the arts and sciences:

"This compulsion and lack of peace characterize the Gothic in all forms, preventing relaxation and the lapse into partial awareness. Gothic nervousness quickens the senses as more of the mind becomes awake to more of the world. Even in its embryonic state, Gothic art displayed the type of agitation that would continue to appear in Gothic architecture and literature".[16]

---

14   Charles H. Moore, "Development and Character of Gothic Architecture", I 8.
15   Ibid., G 19.
16   Linda Bayer-Berenbaum, "The Relationship of Gothic Art to Gothic Literature", in The Gothic Imagination: Expansion in Gothic Literature and Art, 1982.

Comparative Culture Styles

Islamic architecture: Dome of the Rock Mosque, Jerusalem, Israel.

While the Gothic Cathedral expresses infinite space, the Arab dome symbolises the vault of heaven. A Koranic verse states: "And we have made the sky a roof withheld (from them). Yet they turn away from its portents".[17]

> "The dome is, of course, a cosmic symbol in every religious tradition; and symbolically, in Islam the dome represents the vault of heaven in the same way as the garden prefigures Paradise."[18]

This contrasts to the Gothic, Islamic architecture reflecting,

> "Enclosed space, defined by walls, arcades and vaults, [as] the most important element of Islamic architecture. The tendency to an infinite repetition of individual units (bays, arches, columns, passages, courtyards, door-ways, cupolas) and the continuous

---

17 Koran, 21.32.
18 James Dickie, Allah and Eternity: Mosques, Madrases and Tombs, in Architecture of the Islamic World, George Michell (ed.), 33.

merging of spaces without any specific direction or any specific centre or focus. And if a definite spatial limit is reached, such as a terminal wall, the surface that should stop the progress of anyone moving through the building will be decorated with patterns that repeat themselves, leading on visually beyond the given limit of the wall, surface, vault or dome".[19]

Russia is not part of the Western civilisation despite the attempts of Peter the Great (*Petrinism*), Catherine the Great, Lev Trotsky, Boris Yeltsin and sundry others in both Russia and the West to make it so. Russia is its own distinct culture-organism. Remaining with architecture as an example of the expression of different race-souls, the dome is here as with the Arabic, the focus of symbolism, representing the celestial space. The product of the Eastern Church of Byzantium, the "dome of Byzantine churches represents the firmament covering the earth like a lid."[20]

The Russian theologian Sergei Bulgakov explained this contrast of soul-feeling between the Gothic and the Byzantium:

> "...whether it is the dome of St. Sophia in Constantinople, which so admirably represents the heaven of Divine Wisdom reflected on earth, or whether it is the cupola of stone or wood of a Russian village church full of sweetness and warmth — the impression is the same. The Gothic temple rises in pride toward the transcendent, but in spite of the unnatural feeling striving toward the heights, there is always the feeling of an insurmountable distance, yet unattained. Under the Orthodox dome, on the other hand, one has the sense of a bowed humility which assembles and reunites; there is the feeling of life in the house of the Father, after the union between divine and human was created". [21]

The Faustian urge is one of ever striving for the unattainable divine in the cosmos. For the Russian an inner unity with the divine: hence, the mystical character of the Russian soul that endures despite hardship; in contrast to the restless spirit of the Westerner. Instead of the

---

19 Ernst J. Grube, 1995, 13.
20 Evgenii Trubetskoi, "A World View in Painting", in *Icons: Theology in Color*, 16-17.
21 Sergei Bulgakov, 1997, 150-151.

Russian Orthodox Church: Christ the Saviour Cathedral, Moscow.

heavenward Gothic spire there is the upward pointing flame atop the dome of the Russian church reaching towards God. The difference between the Gothic spire and the Orthodox flame is that,

> "It is through the flame that heaven descends to earth, enters the church, and becomes the ultimate completion of the church, the consummation, in which the hand of God covers everything earthly, in a benediction from the dark blue dome".[22]

In the West, Faustian humanity aspired to ascend to Godhead; in Orthodox humanity the Russian seeks the descent on Earth of the Holy Spirit.

Chinese architecture reflects the insularity of the Chinese, is earthbound, symmetrical and defensive. The buildings were traditionally of a common height; social hierarchy was symbolised instead in the expanse. The upward curves of the roof are gently pointing heaven-ward. The focus of architecture was to connect geologically. Even reaching heavenward man must remain earthbound,

---
22   Trubetskoi, "A World View in Painting", 16.

mountain-like. Heaven and earth were within, Confucius stating: "Heaven and earth grow within me simultaneously and all things become one with me".[23]

One can discern the gulf between the souls of the Chinese and Gothic-Faustian, which are now obscured by China having adopted the economic paradigm of the Late West; obscured but not obliterated. The Chinese sought to merge with the landscape; the Faustian to dominate. "In traditional Chinese architecture, by contrast, the building merges with the site. There is a reciprocal penetration and permeation between the natural environment and the manmade environment".[24] Traditional Chinese construction does not seek to dominate the landscape but to meld with it, creating a spatial sequence that connects heaven and earth through the medium of man.[25] Space is seen inwardly, as a void to be utilised,[26] where the Faustian sees infinity. China, after repudiating its tradition, and adopting the Western economic model via Marxism, now seeks conversely to dominate the landscape to the extent of self-destruction. It is an attempt to adopt the Faustian imperative for economic gain that will cause ruin to China as it is to the Late West, because the spiritual impulse is lacking in both, and both have a world outreach beyond any previous empire.

What we see in architecture as profound differences in race-soul between Western, Arabic, Russian and Chinese, manifested in every other area of culture: there was an Arabian, Chinese Gothic, Roman, Indian, physics, metaphysics, mathematics, art, music, engineering, all reflecting different race-souls. There was not one universal "truth", but what was true for the life-cycle of each culture. In the present epoch of the Late West there is the push towards a universal aesthetics, or "globalisation", where all traditions of distinctive race-souls are repressed or distorted to reflect the primacy of money. It was Communism that bought the Late Western economic model to China, as it had to Russia in 1917. The despoliation of the land, pollution of rivers and the air is not a legacy of China's race-soul but the excrescence of a decaying Late West spreading its culture-pathogens world-wide in the name of "progress".

---

23   Shun-xun Nan and Beverly Foit-Albert, 2007, 4.
24   Ibid., 3.
25   Ibid., 7.
26   Ibid., 8.

Western Science

Likewise, Western science is not Greek, Arabic, Indian, Muslim, or Chinese; it is *Western*. While the modern Westerner might assume that there is only one objective, scientific method of looking at nature, each culture has its own perspective innate to itself. This does not mean that any one of them is "false".

Again, we are taught that Western science prior to the Renaissance, or revival of Graeco-Roman learning, was not much more than superstition, and it was only through the rediscovery of Classical learning that true science became known to Western civilisation, while in the meantime the Chinese, Arabs and Indians were showing their intellectual superiority. Hence modern mathematics is ascribed even by scholars to the Greeks, developing that of the Egyptians and Phoenicians from the time of Thales, 600 B.C., to the capture of Alexandria by the Muslims in 642 A.D.

From the Arabs are ascribed algebra and numeration. Europe supposedly remained "dark" until the "Renaissance" a thousand years later. This fits nicely with the "world line of progress" theory, to be able to establish a continuous chain of learning from Greek to "modern". Thereby, the organic life-cycle of cultures is obscured in favour of a "world culture" that has reached its apex with the present, according to historians such as Francis Fukuyama. The Greeks, Indians, Arabs, Westerners and Chinese saw the same things in nature from different perspectives, thereby determining the differences in thinking.

The Classical conception of numbers was that of integers or whole numbers. The Classical cultures were based on perceptions of the solid body, as one sees in their architecture, and the sensuality of their sculpture. Likewise with the Classical conception of atoms as indivisible. The Greek and Roman principles that supposedly founded Western science were known as fragments or as poor translations during the Medieval epoch. Western theoretical mechanics was established in the 13th century by Jordanus Nemorarius with the publication of *Elementa super demonstrationem ponderis*, accurately discovering the law of the lever. He did not owe his theories to Archimedes or other Classical sources. Other geniuses of the Medieval era have been obscured or forgotten by the Renaissance, such as William Heytsbury, working on the law of acceleration of falling bodies; Richard Swineshead, working on continuous change of the variable; Jean Buridan, student of Occam, whose theories on motion repudiate the Aristotelian.

The inability of Classical man, chained to sensory perception, to perceive the infinity of numbers, and the focus of Renaissance scholars on Archimedes, retarded the development of mathematics during the Renaissance epoch. The question of infinity, the basis of the Faustian outlook, had been addressed by Medieval scholars but was discarded by Renaissance mathematicians.

While Classical and Arabian mathematics had become static, the Western, in keeping with the Faustian impulse, is without limit, reflected in such Faustian concepts as the mathematics of continuous change, and differential calculus. This supposed "dark age" of burning heretics, inquisitions, and book burnings was rather one in which bishops and friars experimented and calculated; when universities such as Oxford were built, teaching new concepts such as phenomenal causality, terrestrial and celestial mechanics, change as a mathematically expressible relation, mathematics freed from typically Classical limitations of sense perception.

The physicist Pierre Duhem, having studied the Medieval epoch at a time when the it was discounted as an intellectual void, concluded that "the mechanics and physics of which modern times are justifiably proud to proceed, by an uninterrupted series of scarcely perceptible improvements", derive from "doctrines professed in the heart of the medieval schools".[27] His discovery of the then forgotten Jordanus Nemorarius prompted Duhem's to write extensively on what became the establishment of the history of medieval science. He showed that Western science derives from the Medieval epoch, not from the Classical via the Renaissance:

> "When we see the science of Galileo triumph over the stubborn Peripatetic philosophy of somebody like Cremonini, we believe, since we are ill-informed about the history of human thought,

---

27   David C. Lindberg, Robert S. Westman (eds.) P. Duhem, (1905), "Preface", Les Origines de la statique 1 (Paris: A. Hermman, 1905) iv, in "Conceptions of the Scientific Revolution from Bacon to Butterfield", Reappraisals of the Scientific Revolution , 14.

that we are witness to the victory of modern, young science over medieval philosophy, so obstinate in its mechanical repetition. In truth, we are contemplating the well-paved triumph of the science born at Paris during the fourteenth century over the doctrines of Aristotle and Averroes, restored into repute by the Italian Renaissance.

"The role that impetus played in Buridan's dynamics is exactly the one that Galileo attributed to *impeto* or *momento*, Descartes to 'quantity of motion,' and Leibniz finally to *vis viva*. So exact is this correspondence that, in order to exhibit Galileo's dynamics, Torricelli, in his *Lezioni accademiche*, often took up Buridan's reasons and almost his exact words.

"Nicole Oresme attributed to the earth a natural impetus similar to the one Buridan attributed to the celestial orbs. In order to account for the vertical fall of weights, he allowed that one must compose this impetus by which the mobile rotates around the earth with the impetus engendered by weight. The principle he distinctly formulated was only obscurely indicated by Copernicus and merely repeated by Giordano Bruno. Galileo used geometry to derive the consequences of that principle, but without correcting the incorrect form of the law of inertia implied in it".[28]

Duhem's rediscovery of Medieval science was not well received by other French scientists because it demonstrated the place of metaphysics in an era where secularism and atheism were the vogue.

During the 13th century a medical corpus was being created based on case studies, which classified diseases and their symptoms. The physician Theodoric Borgognoni, who became Bishop of Cervia, wrote the four volume *Cyrurgia* ("Surgery"). He used anaesthetics for surgery, comprising an inhalation of opium, mandrake, hemlock, mulberry juice, and ivy soaked in a sponge. He wrote on the prevention of the festering of wounds by the use of wine as a disinfectant; a

---

28 Pierre Duhem *Mémoires de la Société des Sciences Physiques et naturelles de Bordeaux* (1917) cited in Roger Ariew and Peter Barker *(eds.)*, 1996, 193-196. See: Roger Ariew, "Pierre Duhem", *The Stanford Encyclopedia of Philosophy* (Fall 2014 Edition), Edward N. Zalta (ed.), https://plato.stanford.edu/archives/fall2014/entries/duhem/

technique used by his father. This lost knowledge did not become part of medical procedure again until the antiseptic techniques of Joseph Lister during the 1860s. Until then allowing wounds to fester was regarded as a healing process, based on Greek and Arabic procedure, on which he wrote: "For it is not necessary that bloody matter (pus) be generated in wounds - for there can be no error greater than this, and nothing else which impedes nature so much, and prolongs the sickness". This treatment was in vogue up until World War II when a U.S. surgeon, Eldridge Campbell, on duty in Italy, was introduced to the "revolutionary method of wound treatment" used by Theodoric seven centuries previously.[29] Borgognoni's test for shoulder dislocation, by being able to touch the opposite ear or shoulder with the hand of the affected arm, remains in use.[30]

Henry de Mondeville, chief surgeon to the armies of Philip the Fair and Louis X, using Borgognoni's method to disinfect wounds, surgical incisions, needles, thread and dressings, wrote a treatise on the results.

Gilbert Anglicus wrote on the contagious nature of smallpox, and advice to travellers to only drink distilled water, and to sea voyagers to eat fruit; practices that were not rediscovered until the 18th century. Such was the knowledge of medicine in the Medieval epoch until 1498 when Niccolo da Reggio translated the Greek text of Galen into Latin, which was soon translated throughout Europe into the 16th century. A regression ensued for centuries. The knowledge of anatomy was discarded as were the antiseptic methods of Borgognoni and Mandeville.

The accurate maps of the coasts of Europe, North Africa and the Near East and Mediterranean that were widely distributed from the 13th century were discarded for the mythic geography of Ptolemy, which was translated from Greek in 1409. Again, Western learning had been retarded by recourse to the Greek. Fortunately, Western sea-craft that had been developing since the Medieval epoch, overcame by practice retrogressive theories, and the Age of Discovery ensued regardless.

---

29   A. J. Popp, "Crossroads at Salerno: Eldridge Campbell and the Writings of Theodorico Borgognoni on wound healing", 1995, 174-179.

30   Michael Rogers McVaugh, 159.

Decline of The West

The Renaissance and the Enlightenment were eras of great advance, but nonetheless part of the West's aging, not its youth: where there were great material advances, there was also a spiritual decline. The manner by which the so-called "Gothic" era was disparaged as "barbaric" and the Medieval as "superstition", that is to say, the epoch of Western High Culture, is indicative of the renunciation by the Western intelligentsia of its own origins, and its revival of what it thought was the pre-Western Graeco-Roman culture, in referring to a "renaissance". As we have seen, the origins of the Western sciences and arts were uniquely Western, not Classical or Arab. The name Gothic applied to Medieval culture originated during the Renaissance, and was adopted from the Romans who called the "barbarian" tribes "Goths", circa 250 A.D. The fallacy persists.

To recognise the splendour of the Gothic era, of an epoch supposedly steeped in superstition and ignorance, would imply the honouring of an epoch based on Faith and the Church as custodians of learning. Such an admission has for centuries been unacceptable to the intelligentsia. A consideration of the High Culture of the Gothic era might also imply that the "imaginative" faculties, as Vico pointed out during the Renaissance, are more conducive to High Culture than the "reasonable", that is, the rationalistic. This implies, as Vico insisted, the embracing rather than the repression, of the religious character.

The Reformation was more destructive to the Western culture-organism than any political ideology could be. The English Reformation under Henry VIII, in the name of "freedom" from "popery", fractured the Western culture-organism with petty-state nationalism, and destroyed the counter-balance of the Church, delivering the "people" in the name of "freedom" into the soulless embrace of a rising oligarchy. In the Spenglerian sense, this was an epoch where the forces of "money" fought the forces of "blood"[1] (what we more mundanely call "new money" and "old money"). Henry's revolution was like all such revolutions in the name of "the people": against tradition. Adrian Pabst, lecturer in

---

1   Spengler, The Decline…, Vol. II, 506-507.

politics at the University of Kent, cogently wrote of the epoch:

> "To the mind of many, Henry's tumultuous rule stripped corrupt Catholicism of power and wealth in favour of England's sovereign Church and her free people. In reality however, the break with Rome and the dissolution of the monasteries at home eliminated key pillars of resistance against the forces of nationalism, absolutism and capitalism. As such, this key historical moment holds important lessons for religion, politics and economics today.
>
> "...The violent dissolution of the monasteries in the second half of the 1530s consolidated monarchical absolutism and created the conditions for capitalism. By handing over expropriated land to barons in exchange for their political support, Henry did not simply reinforce the Crown vis-a-vis the Church. He also weakened and destroyed the network of trans-local monastic orders which since the Norman Conquest had helped create and uphold the complex space of intermediary associations that tended to diffuse central power and mediate between individuals and the state, including localities, guilds and agrarian communities. By eliminating the monasteries and cutting ties with the papacy, Henry established a monarchical power vertical that commanded unprecedented fiscal control and military might – the basis for his foreign policy adventurism which further isolated England from the rest of Europe...
>
> "Crucially, the dissolution of the monasteries under Henry VIII and his son Edward VI redistributed one quarter of national wealth at the expense of the peasantry. The endowment of monasteries, including landed property, was transferred to the newly created Court of Augmentations – an early modern precursor of quangos, charged with overseeing monastic expropriation. The triple effect was to curb the social and educational functions of monastic orders, channel wealth and income to the Crown and concentrate land ownership in the hands of the nobility, local magnates and the newly landed gentry.
>
> "Coupled with the forced expropriation of free peasant proprietors by feudal lords during the 'enclosure movement' throughout the

16th century, land ceased to be commonly owned and became privatised. This process ... created the surplus wealth that was used for financial speculation abroad. The ruling classes diverted resources for their own enrichment and self-aggrandisement. As such, the perennial sanctity of life and land was subordinated to secular sacrality of the national state and the transnational market. Thus capitalism was born. Curiously, Henry's quest for national sovereignty made England more dependent on foreign markets than ever before.

"By contrast, elsewhere in Europe the papacy and the monasteries provided a counterweight to secular national monarchs and their vassals. In this sense, the Church retarded the advent of capitalism. Despite widespread corruption and inefficiency, monastic orders preserved a complex space which was not governed by the secular logic of commodification and speculative profit but instead by the religious imperative to support the locality and practice charity.

"...By removing the mediation of the church and other associative institutions, the central state and the free market came to collude at the expense of civil society, local communities and personal welfare".[2]

This for Western civilisation was the birth of international capitalism, free trade, the fracturing of the social organism by the elimination of the monastic orders and the guilds, and the sundering of the West as a culture-organism bounded by a common spiritual outlook and a religious nexus. The Reformation throughout the rest of Europe extended the facture of the West and the rise of oligarchy. Protestantism provided a religious justification for capitalism, and for the excesses of oligarchic exploitation that marked the industrialised West. Max Weber in his seminal study of Protestantism and capitalism writes of the attitude that was to destroy the traditional Western ethos:

"Waste of time is thus the first and in principle the deadliest of sins. The span of human life is infinitely short and precious to make sure of one's own election. Loss of time through

---

2   Adrian Pabst, "Henry VIII and the Birth of Capitalism".

sociability, idle talk, luxury, even more sleep than is necessary for health, six to at most eight hours, is worthy of absolute moral condemnation. It does not yet hold, with Franklin, that time is money, but the proposition is true in a certain spiritual sense. It is infinitely valuable because every hour lost is lost to labour for the glory of God. Thus inactive contemplation is also valueless, or even directly reprehensible if it is at the expense of one's daily work. For it is less pleasing to God than the active performance of His will in a calling".[3]

Hence, working women and children to excessive hours, with the menfolk, where during the Medieval epoch the eight hour day or less was enshrined in guild charters, became an act of piety. The new ethos was justified by the statement of Saint Paul: "He who will not work shall not eat". According to Puritanism, unwillingness to work is symptomatic of the lack of grace. Weber contrast this with the Medieval spiritual ethos that placed work in context:

"Here the difference from the medieval viewpoint becomes quite evident. Thomas Aquinas also gave an interpretation of that statement of St. Paul. But for him labour is only necessary *naturali ratione* for the maintenance of individual and community. Where this end is achieved, the precept ceases to have any meaning. Moreover, it holds only for the race, not for every individual. It does not apply to anyone who can live without labour on his possessions, and of course contemplation, as a spiritual form of action in the Kingdom of God, takes precedence over the commandment in its literal sense. Moreover, for the popular theology of the time, the highest form of monastic productivity lay in the increase of the *Thesaurus ecclesie* through prayer and chant".[4]

Protestantism Judaised Christianity with its focus on the Old Testament, hence grievously subverting the Western psyche and ethos that had made Christianity synonymous with the West for a thousand years. Weber wrote of this:

---

3 Max Weber, 1905, Chapter V, "Ascetism and the Spirit of Capitalism".
4 Ibid.

"But all the more emphasis was placed on those parts of the Old Testament which praise formal legality as a sign of conduct pleasing to God. They held the theory that the Mosaic Law had only lost its validity through Christ in so far as it contained ceremonial or purely historical precepts applying only to the Jewish people, but that otherwise it had always been valid as an expression of the natural law, and must hence be retained. This made it possible, on the one hand, to eliminate elements which could not be reconciled with modern life. But still, through its numerous related features, Old Testament morality was able to give a powerful impetus to that spirit of self-righteous and sober legality which was so characteristic of the worldly asceticism of this form of Protestantism.

"Thus when authors, as was the case with several contemporaries as well as later writers, characterize the basic ethical tendency of Puritanism, especially in England, as English Hebrews they are, correctly understood, not wrong. It is necessary, however, not to think of Palestinian Judaism at the time of the writing of the Scriptures, but of Judaism as it became under the influence of many centuries of formalistic, legalistic, and Talmudic education. Even then one must be very careful in drawing parallels. The general tendency of the older Judaism toward a naive acceptance of life as such was far removed from the special characteristics of Puritanism. It was, however, just as far – and this ought not to be overlooked – from the economic ethics of mediaeval and modern Judaism, in the traits which determined the positions of both in the development of the capitalistic ethos. The Jews stood on the side of the politically and speculatively oriented adventurous capitalism; their ethos was, in a word, that of pariah-capitalism. But Puritanism carried the ethos of the rational organization of capital and labour. It took over from the Jewish ethic only what was adapted to this purpose".[5]

Another significant result of the Reformation was the hitherto despised practice of usury; the lending of money at interest. The traditional religions, including Islam, Catholicism, Buddhism, Hinduism, had all condemned usury. Zwingli, Luther and Calvin, undermined the

---

5   Ibid.

traditional prohibitions on usury by stating that there were circumstances in which it is justified. Other authors of the Reformation such as the 16th century French jurist Molinaeus wrote a justification, *Treatise on Contracts and Usury*, which as banned by the Church. The 18th century Classical English economists Adam Smith, Jeremy Bentham, David Ricardo, and John Stuart Mill, defended usury.[6] This provided the mechanism of insertional finance for the perpetual rule of money: plutocracy. There are few nations not in its grip.

The ascetics of Puritanism came into conflict with King Charles I. Allowing popular amusements on Sunday caused particular outrage. After conflicts with some of the merchants of the City of London an alliance was formed among Puritans and merchants which culminated in regicide and Cromwell's Parliamentary dictatorship. Interestingly, the Puritans identified with Renaissance scientism, which provided them with a further weapon against Catholicism. Weber stated that "the great men of the Puritan movement were thoroughly steeped in the culture of the Renaissance".[7]

However, there remained a fanatical aversion to the arts, which were as much an ungodly waste of time as the sports, taverns and dancing that Charles had allowed on the Sabbath. Weber stated that,

> "the situation is quite different when one looks at non-scientific literature and especially the fine arts. Here asceticism descended like a frost on the life of 'Merrie old England'. And not only worldly merriment felt its effect. The Puritan's ferocious hatred of everything which smacked of superstition, of all survivals of magical or sacramental salvation, applied to the Christmas festivities and the May Pole and all spontaneous religious art".[8]

How the arts could flourish in Holland, despite Cavlinism, was explained by Weber. There was "room in Holland for a great, often uncouthly realistic art". The Calvinist "authoritarian moral discipline" was not able to completely stifle "the joy in life" among prominent circles, "after the short supremacy of the Calvinistic theocracy had

---

6   K. R. Bolton, *Opposing the Money Lenders*, 1-4.
    Brooks Adams, *The Law of Civilization and Decay*, passim.

7   Max Weber.

8   Ibid.

been transformed into a moderate national Church". Calvinism consequently "had perceptibly lost ... its power of ascetic influence".[9] Returning to Puritan England:

> "The theatre was obnoxious to the Puritans, and with the strict exclusion of the erotic and of nudity from the realm of toleration, a radical view of either literature or art could not exist. The conceptions of idle talk, of superfluities, and of vain ostentation, all designations of an irrational attitude without objective purpose, thus not ascetic, and especially not serving the glory of God, but of man, were always at hand to serve in deciding in favour of sober utility as against any artistic tendencies. This was especially true in the case of decoration of the person, for instance clothing".[10]

This Puritan outlook became a foundation of the capitalist ethos with, "That powerful tendency toward uniformity of life, which today so immensely aids the capitalistic interest in the standardization of production".[11] Here we see the formative stages of globalism. The Puritan ethos also provided religious rationalisation for the inequities of capitalism that were to mark the social revolution overturning the traditional Christian beneficence that the emerging oligarchies found so restrictive. Inequities exist because it is part of Divine pre-destination, the concept giving the Puritan merchant;

> "the comforting assurance that the unequal distribution of the goods of this world was a special dispensation of Divine Providence, which in these differences, as in particular grace, pursued secret ends unknown to men. Calvin himself had made the much-quoted statement that only when the people, i.e. the mass of labourers and craftsmen, were poor did they remain obedient to God. ..."

> "Now naturally the whole ascetic literature of almost all denominations is saturated with the idea that faithful labour, even at low wages, on the part of those whom life offers no other opportunities, is highly pleasing to God. In this respect

---

9 Ibid.
10 Ibid.
11 Ibid.

Protestant Asceticism added in itself nothing new. But it not only deepened this idea most powerfully, it also created the force which was alone decisive for its effectiveness: the psychological sanction of it through the conception of this labour as a calling, as the best, often in the last analysis the only means of attaining certainty of grace. And on the other hand it legalized the exploitation of this specific willingness to work, in that it also interpreted the employer's business activity as a calling".[12]

While the traditional societies had the notion of "divine calling" in regard to work, as we have seen this was as part of a social organism, where each "calling" at its duties and obligations, including the merchants, who had their own guilds, as did artisans. These imposed duties and obligations on craft and trade. The traditional social order was far removed from the Free Trade ideology that developed especially in England as a secularised Puritanism.

In the American colonies the Pilgrims and the Puritans saw the Promised Land. Those who became the Pilgrim Fathers of the American colonies regarded themselves as "English Israelites, like the Chosen People leaving Egypt". A British merchant, Thomas Weston, formed from a congregation of English Puritan exiles in Leiden, Holland, the "Saints" to establish their Promised Land in the New World.[13] The Puritans had detached themselves from England and from the Western culture-organism. The USA became a "messianic" nation with a world-mission, profit having been sanctified and forming what has become the "American Dream", to which all nations are expected to convert in the name of Liberal-Democracy. The Masonic ideal of a "new secular order" was a formative influence on American messianism. Hence even the "second religiousness" that Spengler stated was a feature for the revitalisation of a Late civilisation[14] has, to use a Gumliev term, "zig-zagged": instead of a resurgent Western spirituality we have the "prosperity gospel" that declares personal "finances" to be the primary blessing of God, and the masses by their millions are inspired by this message from the holy men of the Late West.

---

12   Ibid.
13   Nichoals Hagger, 4-5.
14   Spengler, The Decline...; Vol. II, 455.

Decay of the Megapolis

As we have seen Late civilisation is marked by depopulation, after a period of overpopulation has resulted in the decay of the cities. These occurrences fulfil a pattern of culture-pathology.

Konrad Lorenz, saw in the overpopulation of the cities one of the "deadly sins" of "civilised man" resulting in the unique ability of the human organism to "suffocate itself". The noblest traits defining what it is to *be* human are the first to perish, Lorenz stated. The more people are obliged to live closer together the more antagonism increased among them.

> "When there is daily and hourly contact with fellow humans who are not our friends, we continually try to be polite and friendly, our state of mind becomes unbearable. The general unfriendliness, evident in all large cities, is clearly proportional to the density of human masses in certain places. For example, in large railway stations and at the bus terminal in New York City, it reaches a frightening intensity".[15]

"Crowded together in our huge modern cites", wrote Lorenz, "in the phantasmorgia of human faces, superimposed on each other and blurred, we no longer see the face of our neighbor". "Neighborly love", or what we might here extrapolate as a sense of kinship, "becomes so diluted by a surfeit of neigbors that, in the end, not a trace of it is left". Lorenz makes the very pertinent comment that "we are not so constituted that we can love all mankind, however right and ethical the exhortation to do so may be".[16] The more we are exhorted to "brotherly love" for all "humanity" the less our humanity becomes. "Emotional entropy" ensues, as we try to find substitute kinship bonds among the nebulous city masses. The greater the crowding the more the individual becomes emotionally detached; the more "urgent the need not to get involved". "…[T]hus today in the largest cities, robbery, murder and rape take place in broad daylight, and in crowded streets, without the intervention of any passer-by".[17] Lorenz regarded as "a

---

15 Lorenz, 14.
16 Ibid., 13.
17 Ibid.

dangerous madness" efforts to create by "conditioning" "a new kind of human being",[18] that "madness" being the ultimate objective of the presently dominate ideologies in the West and China.

Lorenz regarded "the fast-spreading alienation from nature" of the man of Late civilisation as a symptom of "the increasing aesthetic and ethical vulgarity that characterizes civilized man". Detachment from nature, from the awe of nature, which in traditional societies, as we have seen, is an awe and connexion with the cosmos, results in this "aesthetic vulgarity". Culture as an expression of the neurotic city-dweller rather than as symbolic of the healthy organic rhythms of a young culture, becomes a grotesquery of what we call "modern art", and more broadly aesthetics in general, whether as architecture, music or fashion. Lorenz wrote of this epoch:

> "How can one expect a sense of reverential awe for anything in the young when all they see around them is man-made and the cheapest and ugliest of its kind. For the city-dweller even the view of the sky is obscured by sky scrapers and chemical clouding of the atmosphere. No wonder the progress of civilization goes hand in hand with the deplorable disfigurement of town and country'.[19]

Lorenz used an organic analogy to explain the process:

> "If we compare the older centre of any European town with its modern periphery, or compare this periphery, this cultural horror, eating its way into the surrounding countryside, with the still unspoiled villages, and then compare a histological picture of any normal body tissue with that of a malignant tumor, we find astonishing analogies".[20]

Lorenz explains that the cell of the malignant tumour differs from the normal body cell in that it lacks the genetic information required to fulfil is function as a useful member of the "body's cell community". The malignant cell multiplies "ruthlessly", "so that the tumor tissue

---

18 Ibid., 14.

19 Lorenz, 20.

20 Lorenz, 21.

infiltrates the still healthy neighoring tissue and destroys it". He compares the "structurally poor tumor tissues" with the modern suburb of "monotonous houses" "designed by architects without much art, without much thought, and in the haste of competition".[21] As Spengler said, "money wills in Late civilisation", and here in Lorenz's analogy of modern, utilitarian architecture, resulting is "aesthetic vulgarity", money dictates style, because of "commercial consideration", mass production, and "mass dwellings", "unworthy of the name 'houses'", but "at best batteries for 'utility people'", as units that are "anonymous and interchangeable".[22] Yet in the cramped conditions of multi-story apartments, alienation increases as an effort to maintain individuality.[23] The equilibrium between individual identity and social kinship does not exist. Importantly, Lorenz concludes from this:

> "Aesthetic and ethical feeling appear to be closely related, and people who are obliged to live under the conditions described above obviously suffer from an atrophy of both. It seems that both the beauty of nature and the beauty of cultural surroundings created by man are necessary to keep people mentally healthy. The complete blindness to everything beautiful, so common in these times, is a mental illness that must be taken seriously for the simple reason that it goes hand in hand with insensitivity to the ethically wrong".[24]

This lack of aesthetic sensibility allows the man of Late civilisation to have such disregard for ecology. Again "money will", as Spengler said. Here ethics are atrophied. "Cold calculation dictates" Lorenz perceptively observed. The "overwhelming majority" only value whatever brings "commercial gain". "Utilitarianism, with its destructive influence, may be defined as mistaking the means for the end. Money is a means…" As Lorenz states, few today would understand that "money by itself does not represent any value".[25] Here Lorenz, the zoologist, has discovered a great truth that few economists can conceive, but striking at the root of the money-system of Late civilisation, where money

---

21   Ibid.
22   Ibid.
23   Ibid., 22.
24   Ibid. 23.
25   Ibid., 26.

becomes a commodity, when in youthful cultures usury is outlawed and regarded as a hell-spawned sin.[26]

* * *

The decay of the cities is accompanied by a loss of technical ability and craftsmanship. The USA as the citadel of the Late West is experiencing the collapse of its cities. Like Rome's tenements, buildings are falling apart. Like the Indus and Mesoamercia large sections of the USA are becoming uninhabitable, and inner cities are being left vacant.

Adam Forman wrote an article aptly titled "New York City is Crumbling". Citing a report from the Center for an Urban Future, for which he is a research associate, he wrote that,

> "a significant portion of New York City's bridges, water mains, sewer pipes, school buildings, and other essential infrastructure is more than 50 years old and in need of repair. Throughout the city, 1,000 miles of water mains, 170 school buildings and 165 bridges were constructed over a century ago. The city's public hospital buildings are 57 years old, on average, and 531 public housing towers were built prior to 1950".[27]

In 2013, there were 403 water main breaks. In 2014 a major water main break in Manhattan flooded the street and nearby subways. In 2013, subways in south Midtown were flooded. In 2012, 11% of the bridges across New York City were structurally deficient. Forty-seven of these were reported as "fracture critical," meaning they are prone to collapse. "Approximately 4,000 miles of sewer pipe across the city are made of vitreous clay, a material susceptible to cracking and blockage. One and a half thousands of 2,600 public housing buildings do not comply with local standards for exterior and façade conditions."[28] Of the public schools, over 370 of the city's 1,200 public school buildings predating the Great Depression, have "temperamental heating and cooling systems, leaky roofs, and broken elevators".[29] Forman cites

---

26 Bolton, *Opposing the Money Lenders*, 1-3.
27 Adam Forman, "New York City in Crumbling".
28 Ibid.
29 Adam Forman, et al, Caution Ahead: Overdue Investments for New York City's Aging Infrastructure, 5.

The Decline and Fall of Civilisations

Elliot Sander, President and CEO of the New York architectural and engineering firm, The HAKS Group, and former Commissioner of the New York City Department of Transportation:

> "If our infrastructure is not advanced to an acceptable level and then maintained, these systems will degrade. We know from the 1980s that these systems will fall apart. It came very close to killing the city and region. You probably need to double the investment to both bring all the elements up to a state of good repair and to deal with the added demand from the growth we have had, and then put it on a regular replacement cycle. We also need to get more for our money. It will be difficult to do all of this financially and politically. But if we continue on the current course, it is likely New York will be substantially diminished as a global leader, with enormous environmental, social, political, and financial implications that far outweigh the cost."[30]

The concern is for New York City as the financial capital of the world, yet while its Wall Street banks are lenders to the world, it is unable to fund its own infrastructure. The recourse is for the expenditure of billions in debt, backed by taxation. There is no credit lending facility to invest without recourse to debt and taxes. The global financial system devours itself, and its world centre, New York City will crumble, amidst "enormous environmental, social, political, and financial implications". The cycle is set for crumbling buildings and broken utilities, such as one sees in the "Third World", *fellaheen* states, where the jungle or the desert encroach progressively.

A report on Washington referred to "a loose chunk of concrete" that "plummeted onto a woman's car as she drove under the Capital Beltway. It broke loose from a decades-old bridge in Morningside, Maryland". "The Arlington Memorial Bridge is emblematic of the nation's infrastructure challenges". In 2014 the National Park Service stated that the bridge would need to be "shut down by 2021 for safety reasons". "Its facade appears elegant on the outside, but the bridge's innards are withering away".[31]

---

30   Elliot Sander in Forman et al, Ibid., 7.
31   Dave Dildine, "Crumbling Capital".

Decline of The West

That is the character of a Late civilisation in its terminal state: The tenements of Rome were constantly falling down onto the streets while the Roman Empire seemed to flourish. A tourist might one day walk through the streets of New York or Washington and write of its decay like travellers walking through the streets of Morocco, once the centre of a great civilisation: "Above these old broken walls upon which the devouring noontide sun now falls, appear once more the weed covered roofs of the palaces of ancient sultans ... and beyond the more distant medley of terraces, mosques, minarets, and cracked and crumbling walls.[32]

The U.S. Military regards what are called "megacities" (populations of 10,000,000 or more) as an approaching problem of world instability, with the finite capacity of resources, and the cosmopolitan, multi-ethnic character of megacities that will cause conflict. A report by the U.S Army Strategic Studies Group, states that there are currently over 20 megacities in the world; by 2025 there will be around 40. With their growth there are increasing problems of sustainability. The U.S. Army comments that megacities are a unique environment that they "do not fully understand".[33]

The report gives a picture of proliferating criminal networks and underground economies, natural disasters and the inability of decaying infrastructures to withstand the stressors. A feature is predicted to be the breakdown of civic order through ethnic and religious conflict among groups that are forced increasingly together to share diminishing resources and utilities.

> "As resources become constrained, illicit networks could potentially fill the gap left by over-extended and undercapitalized governments. The risk of natural disasters compounded by geography, climate change, unregulated growth and substandard infrastructure will magnify the challenges of humanitarian relief. As inequality between rich and poor increases, historically antagonistic religions and ethnicities will be brought into close proximity in cities. Stagnation will coexist with unprecedented development, as slums and shanty towns rapidly expand alongside modern high-rises. This is the urban future".[34]

---

32   Pierre Loti, 286.
33   Colonel Marc Harris, et al., 2014, 4.
34   Ibid.

"Regardless of the fragility or resilience of the city, their stable functioning is dependent on systems of finite capacity. When these systems, formal or informal, real or virtual experience demand which surpasses their capacity, the load on the city's systems erode its support mechanisms, increasing their fragility. These systems are then more vulnerable to triggers which can push the city past its tipping point and render it incapable of meeting the needs of its population. Some dynamics of friction are observable in all megacities to varying degrees. Population growth and migration, separation and gentrification, environmental vulnerability and resource competition, and hostile actors are all present in some fashion within every megacity".[35]

The military report comments on the increasingly heterogeneous populations inherent in a megacity as potentially "explosive". However, the imposition of a multicultural, cosmopolitan society proceeds apace, with active encouragement from the U.S. State Department, and a myriad of U.S.-based think tanks and NGOs, for cities across the world, as part of the globalisation process. Again, it is a self-destruct system; an inherent characteristic of Late civilisation to rely on the continuation of suicidal tendencies in the name of "progress" and "economic growth". Rome needed workers and soldiers from its provinces until there were few Romans left. The Late West needs migrant workers.

"One of the hallmarks of megacities is rapid hetero and homogeneous population growth that outstrips city governance capability. Many emerging megacities are ill-prepared to accommodate the kind of explosive growth they are experiencing".[36]

"Radical income disparity, and racial, ethnic and sub cultural separation are major drivers of instability in megacities. As these divisions become more pronounced they create delicate tensions, which if allowed to fester, may build over time, mobilize segments of the population, and erupt as triggers of instability".[37]

---

35 Ibid., 12.
36 Ibid.
37 Ibid.

Demographic Suicide

In conjunction with the overpopulating of "megacities" there is a depopulation trend of the native builders and sustainers of the original culture. It has become innervated and exhausted, and on its way to becoming *fellaheen*. In the meantime, the *fellaheen* from other regions flock to the decaying megacities, accelerating the process of cultural decay. This is the process described in the above quoted U.S. Army report, which it "does not fully understand". It is a process that was described nearly a century ago by Spengler:

> "the last man of the world city no longer wants to live – he may cling to life as an individual, but as a type, as an aggregate, no... That which strikes the true peasant with a deep and inexplicable fear, the notion that the family and the name may be extinguished, has now lost its menacing. ... and the destiny of being the last of the line is no longer felt as a doom..."[38]

With this is the rise of the "modern woman", where "instead of children she has soul-conflicts, and marriage is a craft-art for 'mutual understanding'".[39] Augustus made desperate attempts through laws to raise the birth-rate of Romans, but to no avail; such was their hedonism that children became a burden. Buggery and abortion became the preferred options of Romans.

In the custodian of the Late West, the USA, a study published in the *Proceedings of the National Academy of Sciences* "found that middle-aged, white Americans have been getting sicker and dying in greater numbers, even as the rest of the world is living longer and healthier... The authors of that study attributed the trend to what we called 'despair deaths': mainly suicides, drug overdoses, and alcohol-related liver disease.... between 1999 and 2014, mortality rates in the U.S. rose for white Americans aged 22 and 56. Before that, death rates had been falling by nearly 2 percent each year since 1968".[40]

Of particular significance is the drop of fertility rates. A study of the trend in the USA shows:

---

38   Spengler, *The Decline* ..., Vol. II, 103-104.
39   Ibid., 105.
40   Olga Khazan, "Why are so Many Middle Aged White Americans Dying?"

The Decline and Fall of Civilisations

"Fertility rates have dropped to their lowest ever recorded in America, a new CDC [Center for Disease Control] report reveals. In the first quarter of 2016, the birth rate is 59.8 babies born to every 1,000 women. That means for every 100 fertile women, fewer than six will give birth at least once. The staggering statistics follow the steady trend of decline since records began in 1909, when the birth rate was 126.8 babies per 1,000 mothers. Research shows a key driving factor in this trend is the increasing numbers of women delaying childbirth to a point where they experience more fertility problems".[41]

Another major problem is the low health stamina of women: "Now, the biggest problem appears to be underlying health conditions - such as high blood pressure, diabetes, and cardiovascular disease - which the mothers had before giving birth".[42]

The modern Western economic system has not encouraged large families; it has encouraged women to become integrated production units. Feminism and socialism have assisted greatly.[43] Now, after generations of promoting birth control, abortion and female labour, there is panic that aging populations will destroy the economy:

"Initially, reduced child dependency rates were actually beneficial to economic growth. By delaying childbirth, men and women could gain an education before starting a family. This was important in a shifting labor market where smaller, family-run businesses were in decline and a more skilled and specialized labor force was in demand. Men and women could also choose to start their careers before having families, while paying more in income taxes and enjoying the benefits of a higher disposable income. Increased spending power creates demand, which stimulates job growth – and the economy benefits in the short-term... As this large aging population exits the workforce, most of the positive trends that were spurred by declining fertility rates will be reversed, and economic growth will face a significant burden. ... Worldwide fertility rates began to fall substantially in the mid-1960s".[44]

---

41   Mia de Graaf, "Fertility Rates Drop to Lowest EVER in America", 2016.

42   Ibid.

43   Bolton, *Revolution from Above*, 160-181.

44   Caitlin Cheadle, "Fertility Rates Keep Dropping, and it's going to hit the economy

In 2005, Catholic theologian George Weigel, Distinguished Senior Fellow at the Ethics and Public Policy Center, posed pertinent questions in his book *The Cube and the Cathedral*.[45] He was invited to speak to members of the European Parliament. He made what he called "rather obvious points" which, however, are not obvious to those masses, whatever their position in society, who lack historical perspective. Weigel stated:

1. Europe is committing demographic suicide, systematically depopulating itself in what British historian Niall Ferguson has called 'the greatest sustained reduction in European population since the Black Death in the 14th century'.

2. This unwillingness to create the future in the most elemental sense, by creating new generations, is at the root of many of Europe's problems, including its difficulties assimilating immigrants and its fiscal distress.

3. When an entire continent—healthier, wealthier, and more secure than ever before—deliberately chooses sterility, the most basic cause for that must lie in the realm of the human spirit, in a certain souring about the very mystery of being".

Whether "Europe", or Late Western civilisation is "healthier" is debatable. People are living much longer, but is this not a reflection of mass medication rather than healthier lives? With environmental toxins, chemical additives, loss of soil nutrients, and mass food processing, the quality of food is hardly comparable to what it was during the much-maligned Medieval epoch, as shown by William Cobbett.[46] The contention that we of the Late West are "more secure and wealthier than before" might itself be an answer as to why there has been "a certain souring about the very mystery of being". Indeed, the answer, as Weigel states, "must lie in the realm of the human spirit".

The ease of modern Western life in the material realm has meant a loss of the tension of polarities that Carl Jung regarded as essential

---

hard".

45 George Weigel, 2005.
46 William Cobbett, 1824.

to the release of the *libido*, or psychical energy. In the matter of the history of an *ethnos* we might hypothesise this to be an entropic loss of focused collective *libido*. No longer are there the challenges that spur the creative faculties. Ease is sought as a measure of success, and estimated at one's material comfort. A nation's health is measured by the statistics of its Gross National Product and balance of payments.

Returning to the demographic problem, again we might see how children become a burden, as they did with the last of the Romans. Yet this ease of life does not allow for genuine fulfilment, as reflected in the rates of suicide, alcoholism, and drug addiction that seem to increase, along with feelings of pointlessness, as material comfort and security increase. "A certain souring about the very mystery of being", wrought by the triumph of "reason" over faith, has resulted in precisely the opposite of what is intended: the Liberal ideal of the "happiness of the greatest number" becomes ever-more elusive, and no more so than in those who are the wealthiest and most "successful" in Western societies.

Degenerative Culture

"You'd have to be a recent immigrant from Outer Mongolia not to know of the role that people with Jewish names play in the coarsening of our culture. Almost every American knows this. It is just that most gentiles are too polite to mention it … The sad fact is that through Jewish actors, playwrights, and producers, the Berlin stage of Weimar Germany linked Jews and deviant sexuality in all its sordid manifestations just as surely as Broadway does today. Much of the filth in American entertainment today parallels that of Germany between the wars". — Rabbi Daniel Lapin, *Toward Tradition*, January 2005.[47]

One thinks of a "hero" in terms of Thomas Carlyle's study on the role of the heroic individual in shaping history,[48] what has been called "heroic vitalism". In former generations the hero was typically a saint, soldier, empire builder, someone who lived or died for a higher purpose than the self. The definition is that of transcendent self-sacrifice.

---

47   Daniel Lapin, "Jews have Debased American and Jewish Culture".
48   Thomas Carlyle, 1840.

The state of cultural decay is indicated by the types who are elevated into the status of today's "role models", especially for the young. They are Anti-Heroes. The definition is the antithesis of the Hero. The Anti-Hero one of lives for him or herself alone. Hedonism is the lifestyle, narcissism the temperament. The outlook benefits consumer capitalism, as it translates economically into a never-ending thirst for acquisition. This situation is concomitant with the general degradation of social morality, where self-indulgence is elevated into virtue, and immediate gratification is expected.

Paradoxically, this heralding of selfishness as the path to "happiness" as the purpose of life has resulted in a contagion of drug addiction, alcoholism, suicide, and mass medication and therapy for psychiatric disturbances. The self-quest for happiness has resulted in nothing but dissatisfaction and unfulfilled searches for meaning. The most discontented, the drug, pill and alcohol ridden, neurotic and narcissistic, are heralded as role models who symbolise and epitomise "success" in the Late West: the movie and music "stars". It is no coincidence that they also happen to be overwhelmingly "liberals", eagerly jumping on the bandwagon of every transient "feel-good" cause, while Hollywood has from its founding been one of centres for the spread of global spiritual-syphilis.

Hollywood has for generations defined "American culture", which through globalisation has long become synonymous with "Western culture". However, "Western culture" has been deconstructed and redefined by a foreign culture-organism. Hollywood is what Jewish commentators have referred to as "their empire", where Jewish movie moguls were from the start of the motion picture industry able to define the "American Dream".[49] In the realm of music Sumner Redstone's Viacom and MTV are at the apex.

The character of the USA was redefined by Emma Lazarus, whose poem, "The New Colossus" (1883) adorns the Statue of Liberty, to greet "The wretched refuse of your teeming shore", and by Israel Zangwill with his play "The Melting Pot" (1908). Both were ardent Zionists who did not endorse multiculturalism among Jews. That is for Western consumption.[50]

---

49 Neal Gabler, 1988.
50 K. R. Bolton, *Babel Inc.*, 135-147.

The Decline and Fall of Civilisations

Such influence is not a "conspiracy"; it is a natural occurrence when one wilful, vital culture exists within another, whether it is the British in India or the Spanish in Peru. Whether such an influence is positive or negative, symbiotic and complementary or destructive, depends on the culture organisms involved. Gumilev regarded the Jewish culture-organism as a perennially foreign element[51] whose influence causes the "zig-zagging", or distortion, of a culture's life-path.

The Jews as a nomadic people, albeit unified across the world by a traditional *axis mundi* (Jerusalem) and religion, have been a catalyst for the breakdown of national consciousness among other peoples. Their nomadism makes them natural agents for internationalist ideologies, whether of the capitalist or socialist varieties. Other nomads, such as the steppes peoples of Russia and central Asia, have an *ecological niche* and have the potentiality to form nations and empires. Jews do not have an ecological niche, and remain wanderers, which is not to say that Jews per se are innately incapable of being absorbed into Western culture. Such absorption however has been fanatically resisted by the rabbinate and more recently by Zionism, as explained by the heretical Jewish scholar Dr. Israel Shahak.[52]

When traditional dynastic states were broken down and capitalism arose, eroding the authority of the landed aristocracy and the Church, Jews became "harbingers of political and economic change".[53] The "court Jew" became a feature of the rulership of Europe. There were "several hundred", who shaped the emerging capitalist economies, according to Mendes-Flohr and Reinharz,[54]. The Reformation and the English Revolution accelerated the process. Of the latter, Rabbi Menasseh ben Israel, leader of Jewish community in The Netherlands, addressed an appeal for the re-admission of the Jews to England to Oliver Cromwell, whose Puritans had established their tyranny in the name of "liberty". England would gain by Jewish migration because of "Profit". "It is a thing confirmed, that merchandizing is, as it were, the proper profession of the Nation of the Jews". Because God had taken the Jews from Israel, as a "chastisement", and they were a people

---

51   Lev Gumiliev, Dreviania Rus' I veliaia step', 2004. See Mark Bassin, *The Gumilev Mystique*, passim.
52   Israel Shahak, 1994.
53   Paul R. Mendes-Flohr and Jehuda Reinharz (ed.) 1980, 7.
54   Ibid.

without a land, their protection was in their "Riches and possessions", which they could put at the disposal of a nation's ruler.[55] From Italy, Germany, Holland, Poland, Turkey, Egypt, etc., the Jews had profited those places through their international commerce. Hence the Jews are "a Plant worthy to be planted in the whole world, and received into Populous cities…"[56]

The Jewish people thrive during the Late civilisation epochs where Money and City have displaced Faith and Land. While Jews, despite allegations throughout history to the contrary, are not the *cause* of this culture-crisis, it is the Late epoch during which they are positioned to take advantage, which is why we see Jews in prominence especially in the USA, reshaping politics, economics and culture as a people of four thousand years duration amidst a state of 240 years duration.

That the Jewish culture-organism is foreign to the Western culture-organism should be axiomatic and stated without accusations of "anti-Semitism". Theodor Herzl founded Zionism precisely on the assumption that Jews are unable, and indeed must not, assimilate into Western society, or any other. Although the Old Testament shows that foreign culture-organisms assimilated into the Hebrew this was undertaken entirely on Israelites terms, as conquerors. No "zig-zagging" of the Israelite culture-mission and identity was tolerated.

As an unassimilated foreign body the Jewish intelligentsia deconstructs Western culture. When Carl Jung broke with his mentor Sigmund Freud, this was a conflict between antithetical world-views: the Western and the Jewish. Laurens van der Post wrote of the breach:

> "Sex, however important was only part of the story. From there arose his [Jung's] first great and ineradicable difference with Freud. To illustrate it at its most immediate and simple level, he could no more see a great Gothic spire, soaring above the finest of medieval cathedral achievement's, as merely a phallic symbol, than mistake a horse for a mule".[57]

---

55 Menasseh ben Israel "To His Highnesse the Lord Protector of the Commonwealth of England, Scotland and Ireland (1655)"; in Mendes-Flohr and Jehuda Reinharz, 9.

56 Menasseh ben Israel, Ibid., 10.

57 Laurens van der Post, *Jung and the Story of our Time.*

The Decline and Fall of Civilisations

Eminent Jewish historian Dr. Howard Sachar, wrote that the primary motivation of pioneer Freudians was,

> "the unconscious desire of Jews to unmask the respectability of the European society which closed them out. There was no more effective way of doing this than by dredging up from the human psyche… sordid and infantile sexual aberrations… Even Jews who were not psychiatrists must have taken pleasure in the feat of social equalisation performed by Freud's 'new thinking.' The B'nai B'rith Lodge of Vienna, for example, delighted in listening to Freud air his theories …"[58]

When the Frankfurt School of Critical Theory in Weimar Germany synthesised Freud with Marx into the "sex-pol" ("sexual politics") ideology and were sponsored as Jewish refugees from Hitlerism to relocate to Columbia University, and to the Institute of Social Research, New York, their doctrine under various permutations promptly became a primary method for the deconstruction of Western culture, and particularly of Western man.[59]

---

58   H. Sachar, 1991, 400-401.
59   K. R. Bolton, "'Sex Pol' Ideology: The Influence of the Freudian-Marxist Synthesis on Politics and Society", 329-355.

Cultural Pathology as Geopolitical Strategy

If the premise is accepted that Western civilisation is in an advanced state of decay, and that the USA is the self-chosen and universally acknowledged leader of the rotting West, America's identity as the primary carrier of worldwide cultural contagion will be the logical conclusion. The process by which this contagion is taking place is called "globalisation". With economic globalisation comes cultural globalisation.

While prior Late civilisations such as the Alexandrian sought to control the "known world" what is unique today is that the outreach of the Late West literally does impact on every corner of the world due to Western technics. There cannot remain any remote area, any hill tribe, any desert nomads, that are secure from the cultural pathology of the Late West. On this Alexander Stille commented:

> "Globalisation may well raise the standard of living and introduce democratic reforms to countries around the world, but it is also bringing about an unprecedented homogenisation of culture that will almost certainly accelerate the disappearance of thousands of ... distinct cultures."[1]

The Catholic, palaeoconservative writer, the late Joe Sobran, wrote of America's global outreach:

> "Anti-Americanism is no longer a mere fad of Marxist university students; it's a profound reaction of traditional societies against a corrupt and corrupting modernization that is being imposed on them, by both violence and seduction. The very word *values* implies a whole modern culture of moral whim, in which good and evil are matters of personal preference and sodomy and abortion can be treated as 'rights.' Confronted with today's America, then, the Christian Arab finds himself in unexpected sympathy with his Muslim enemy".[2]

---

1   Alexander Stille, 2003, xiv.
2   Joe Sobran, 2001.

Cultural Pathology as Geopolitical Strategy

American strategists acknowledge the USA's cultural pathology as a weapon by which the entire world can be infected and so weakened as to succumb to the money-empire. This is the moral, spiritual and cultural equivalent of bacteriological warfare. U.S. strategists during the Cold War realised that cultural contagion could be used as a weapon to subvert and destroy the moral fabric of enemy states. In 1949 the CIA recruited disaffected anti-Stalinist Bolsheviks, Trotskyites and Mensheviks into the Congress for Cultural Freedom to try and subvert the Soviet bloc and impose "American" values over the world in the name of "freedom of artistic expression." Their favoured media were Abstract Expressionism and jazz.[3] The Congress for Cultural Freedom (CCF) was established under the presidency of Marxist intellectual Professor Sidney Hook, a "lifelong Menshevik", who was awarded the Congressional Medal for Freedom by President Ronald Reagan for his services to American internationalism. Hook had been Trotsky's leading defender in the West when Stalin had purged him from the USSR. The same year the CCF was formed, 1949, the Stalinists launched their counter-offensive against "rootless cosmopolitanism" in the arts.[4]

While the CCF was dissolved, having been thoroughly exposed and discredited as a CIA front, the cultural offensive against the world did not dissipate. The favoured music of the purveyors of cultural contagion is no longer jazz of course, but hip hop, which is promoted by the U.S. State Department, especially among disaffected migrant youth in Europe. Such a cultural offensive is seen as a means of harnessing youth to the "American Dream", rather than becoming anti-American.[5]

Perhaps the most cogent and frank explanation on the use of culture-pathogens to infect states as a geopolitical weapon is provided by Major Ralph Peters, subsequently lieutenant colonel, a prominent military strategist who served with the Office of the Deputy Chief of Staff for Intelligence. Peters wrote in *Parameters*, journal of the U.S. Army War College, "We are entering a new American century, in which we

---

3   Frances Stonor Saunders, 1999.
    Also see the CIA website: "Cultural Cold War: Origins of the Congress for Cultural Freedom, 1949-50"; https://www.cia.gov/library/center-for-the-study-of-intelligence/kent-csi/docs/v38i5a10p.htm#rft1

4   K. R. Bolton, *Stalin: the Enduring Legacy*, 28-54.

5   K. R. Bolton, *Babel Inc.*, 189-199.

will become still wealthier, culturally more lethal, and increasingly powerful. We will excite hatreds without precedent". Peters stated that the "global information empire" led by the USA is "historically inevitable".

> "It is fashionable among world intellectual elites to decry 'American culture,' with our domestic critics among the loudest in complaint. But traditional intellectual elites are of shrinking relevance, replaced by cognitive-practical elites–figures such as Bill Gates, Steven Spielberg, Madonna, or our most successful politicians–human beings who can recognize or create popular appetites, recreating themselves as necessary. Contemporary American culture is the most powerful in history, and the most destructive of competitor cultures. While some other cultures, such as those of East Asia, appear strong enough to survive the onslaught by adaptive behaviors, most are not. The genius, the secret weapon, of American culture is the essence that the elites despise: ours is the first genuine people's culture. It stresses comfort and convenience – ease – and it generates pleasure for the masses. We are Karl Marx's dream, and his nightmare".

> "Secular and religious revolutionaries in our century have made the identical mistake, imagining that the workers of the world or the faithful just can't wait to go home at night to study Marx or the Koran. Well, Joe Sixpack, Ivan Tipichni, and Ali Quat would rather 'Baywatch.' America has figured it out, and we are brilliant at operationalizing our knowledge, and our cultural power will hinder even those cultures we do not undermine. There is no 'peer competitor' in the cultural (or military) department. Our cultural empire has the addicted – men and women everywhere – clamoring for more. And they pay for the privilege of their disillusionment."[6]

Peters lauds the "cultural power" that will addict the masses throughout the world. America's "lethal culture", exported to the world, is that of "comfort and convenience – ease – and pleasure". This is precisely the ingredient for the decay of cultures and the regression of character. The military role is contingent: "The de facto role of the U.S. armed forces

---

6   Ralph Peters, "Constant Conflict", 4-14.

will be to keep the world safe for our economy and open to our cultural assault. To those ends, we will do a fair amount of killing". He calls this "constant conflict". Peters states that "American culture is infectious, a plague of pleasure, and you don't have to die of it to be hindered or crippled in your integrity or competitiveness. The very struggle of other cultures to resist American cultural intrusion fatefully diverts their energies from the pursuit of the future".[7]

Peters uses the terminology of cultural pathology, with words such as "plague" and "infectious". He sees this as America's strength. A parasite only lives as long as its host, and America seeks to kill its hosts – the entirety of the rest of the world. America's "plague" across the world is from its own infection. The USA is not a quarantined purveyor. It spreads infection from its own terminal disease. The USA deludes itself, like a psychotic with AIDS, that it is strong because it can infect and kill others, but it must succumb to its own illness.

Dr. Michael Ledeen, who has been a consultant for the U.S. National Security Council, Defense and State Departments, has referred to the USA as inherently revolutionary and its globalist ideology as "creative destruction". In defending this ideology from a critique by Congressman Ron Paul in 2003 Ledeen wrote:

> "He conveniently leaves out the context, which is a discussion of the basic conflict between us and the terror masters: a conflict between freedom and tyranny. I argue, as I argued during the Cold War with regard to Communism, and as I argued in my books on fascism earlier, that the conflict between America and tyrants is inevitable. It stems from the very nature of America, from our unique freedom and creativity, which has often been described as 'creative destruction.' Every serious writer about America has noticed the amazing speed with which we scrap old ideas, technologies, art forms and even the use of the English language. And it's obvious that more rigid societies, particularly those governed by tyrants, are frightened by the effects and the appeal of freedom on their own subjects. Our existence threatens them, undermines their legitimacy, and subverts their power".[8]

---

7   Ibid.
8   Michael Ledeen, "Dishonorable Congressman", 2003.

For a traditional conservative, there is no need to quote Ledeen out of context. What he calls "freedom" is nihilism. What he calls "tyranny" is the desire to maintain tradition. Ledeen states that the USA is innately "destructive". This he calls "creative" because it is designed to destroy anything that thwarts the "end of history, as Fukuyama calls it, to remake the world on America's terms.

With this so-called "neoconservatism" there is a fundamental Marxism: In *The Communist Manifesto* Karl Marx called movements that thwarted the "wheel of history" "reactionism". Ledeen uses the word "tyranny". Ledeen, like Peters, unequivocally states that the USA is inherently opposed to traditional cultures; that all must be in a perpetual state of flux, or what Leon Trotsky called the "permanent revolution", when he writes of America's "amazing speed with which we scrap old ideas, technologies, art forms and even the use of the English language". When someone as significant as Russian geopolitical analyst and state adviser Dr. Igor Panarin states that, "Trotskyist ideas won at the end of the 20th century in the USA and brightly manifested themselves in the ideology of the liberal globalism of a part of the contemporary American political elite",[9] we can be encouraged that the political and academic elite in Russia precisely knows the character of the struggle for supremacy between world-views.

---

9   Igor Panarin, 2006.

Rise of Russia

While Russia has the same demographic problem as the West, there is a crucial distinction. For the West the sudden realisation of demographic decline is based on how profits will be impacted by aging populations. The answer for Western states is immigration. Russian President Vladimir Putin has been the only major political leader to understand the historic meaning of population decline, stating in his 2012 election programme:

> "About 40 per cent of global mineral resources are located in Russia, whereas Russia's population makes up a mere 2 per cent of the global population. The implications of this disparity are obvious. Unless Russia implements a long-term comprehensive agenda for demographic development to build up its human potential and develop its territories, it risks turning into a geopolitical "void," whose fate would be decided by other powers'. Putin spoke of firstly, supporting 'families with multiple children [with] measures for mitigating the temporary financial strain that affects many families with three or more children'. Unlike Western states Putin advocates 'a smart migration policy… which would prevent the risks of ethnic or cultural clashes', based on a migrant 'applicant's ability to embrace our culture and our values'. 'We must arrange our … policies to address the task of boosting Russia's human potential. It must serve a long-term strategy with historic implications, not merely a campaign agenda".[1]

With the resurgence of Russia has come a resurgence of population. Britta Sandstroem, a Danish population expert, states that "Contrary to popular belief, Russia's demographic situation is improving as Western fertility rates continue to plummet". The population growth level is at least 2.1 children per woman, but in the European Union it is 1.3. The global population trend is 2.3. Sandstroem refers to the lessons of past civilisations: "This decline in Western fertility rates attracts no interest from Western politicians or mass media. They remain stuck in the short term. This mirrors the attitudes of other societies that fell into

---

1 Vladimir Putin, 2012.

crisis because of low birth rates: the Roman Empire, Etruscan society, the Abbasid Caliphate etc".[2]

A World Bank report states that the Russian birth rate increased from 1.34 in 2009, to 1.54 in 2013 and is currently at 1.60. "This rise is almost unique in Europe", according to Sandstroem. "Since President Vladimir Putin acted to address the problem, Russia has been one of the few countries in the western hemisphere to have registered a stable rise in its fertility rate". Sandstroem comments that while Western population decline is compensated by immigration, "If fertility rates continue to grow in Russia and continue to fall in the West in line with present trends then the future belongs to Russia".[3]

The Western High Culture was over 500 years old when the Russian culture-organism coalesced at the Battle of Kulikovo in 1380. Then Moscow became the focus of a new Russian *ethnos* that had been fermenting since the adoption of Christianity in 988. The defeat of the Mongols by a unified Russian force not only formed the Russian nation but made the Orthodox Church the foundation of Russian culture. Saint Sergy of Radonej had worked among the numerous principalities to gain allegiance to the Principality of Moscow. By the time of Kulikovo he inspired the Russian forces to victory. His Trinity Monastery became the symbol of Russian unity. The first to die in the prelude to battle was a monk, Aleksandr Peresvet, from Sergy's Trinity Monastery, in single combat against the Mongol-Tatar champion, Chelubey.

Russia is Orthodox Christianity, just as Western High Culture was Gothic-Catholicism. Russia became the centre of the Orthodox faith when the Byzantine Empire ceased in 1453. Hence, Russia is called the "Third Rome". It sees its mission as one of universal Christian brotherhood, contra the world-missions of the USA, China, and Israel. Russia appeals to the heart, Islam reaches for the sword, the USA and Israel for the missile, China for the cheque book. Sergey Lavrov, Russian Minister of Foreign Affairs, stated:

---

[2] Britta Sandstroem, "Russia's Baby Boom. Fertility Rate Far Higher Than in EU, Rising Quickly. Unique in Western Hemisphere, Government Programs have Worked".

[3] Ibid.

"We believe that human solidarity must have a moral basis formed by traditional values that are largely shared by the world's leading religions. In this connection, I would like to draw your attention to the joint statement by Patriarch Kirill and Pope Francis, in which, among other things, they have expressed support for the family as a natural centre of life of individuals and society".[4]

Lavrov was expressing the traditional Russian perception of her world-mission: universalism as distinct from "globalisation".

The Soul of Russia

Russia has regarded herself as European, as Asian and as Eurasian. Sitting between Asia and Europe, Russia has been continually subjected to invasions and migrations from East and West. Her life-course has "zig-zagged", as the Russian ethnologist Lev Gumilev calls such history;[5] but Russia has, far from being obliterated, proceeded in vigour. She has done so through *synthesis* and *symbiosis* while rejecting both inner parasitism and outer domination. Russia was formed from the synthesis of Graeco-Byzantine-Rus, as Western culture was formed by a synthesis of Italic-Frankish-Gallic. The Russian is a *superethnos* that has synthesised other *ehtnoi* through complete absorption or symbiosis, revolving around the axis of Faith and Motherland vis-à-vis the challenges of geography and invasion.

Spengler regarded Russians as formed by the vastness of the land-plain, as being innately antagonistic to the machine, as rooted in the soil, irrepressibly peasant, religious, and "primitive". When Spengler wrote of these Russian characteristics he was referencing the Russians as a still youthful people in contrast to the senile West. Hence the "primitive" Russian is not synonymous with "primitivity" as popularly understood in regard to tribal peoples, much less to historically-exhausted *Fellaheen*. To Spengler, the "primitive peasant" is the well-spring from which a race draws its healthiest elements during its epochs of cultural vigour.

---

4   Sergey Lavrov, "Russia's Foreign Policy: Historical Background", 2016.
5   Lev Gumilev, Zigzag Istorii, 2013.

The basis of the Russian soul is not *infinite space* – as in the West's *Faustian*[6] imperative, but is *"the plain without limit"*.[7] The Russian soul expresses its own type of infinity, albeit not that of the Western which becomes *enslaved* by its own technics ,[8] and is destroyed by its *hubris*. It is after this Western decline that Spengler alluded to the next world civilisation being that of Russia.

Nikolai Berdyaev in *The Russian Idea* affirms what Spengler described:

> "There is that in the Russian soul which corresponds to the immensity, the vagueness, the infinitude of the Russian land, spiritual geography corresponds with physical. In the Russian soul there is a sort of immensity, a vagueness, a predilection for the infinite, such as is suggested by the great plain of Russia".[9]

The connections between family, nation, birth, unity and motherland are reflected in the Russian language:

род	[rod]: family, kind, sort, genus
родина	[ródina]: homeland, motherland
родители	[rodíteli]: parents
родить	[rodít']: to give birth
роднить	[rodnít']: to unite, bring together
родовой	[rodovói]: ancestral, tribal
родство	[rodstvó]: kinship

Western-liberalism, rationalism, even the strenuous efforts of Bolshevik dialectal materialism, have not been able to destroy, but at most repress, these conceptions of what it is to be "Russian". Spengler, even during the early period of Russian Bolshevism, already predicted that this would take on a different, antithetical form, to the *Petrine*[10] import of Marxism.

---

6   Spengler, *The Decline* ..., Vol. I, 183.

7   Ibid., I, 201.

8   Ibid., II, 502.

9   Nikolai Berdyaev, 1948, 1.

10 Petrine, Petrinism, named after Peter the Great, refers to efforts to Westernise Russia. Bolshevism was one such effort, insofar as Marxism reflects 19th century English economic theory. The accusations of "Jewishness" obscure the materialist Zeitgeist from which both Marxist and Free Trade theories arose in England. Bolshevism was Russianised by Stalin. See: Bolton, Stalin: The Enduring Legacy.

"Russian Socialism"

Of the Russian soul, the ego/vanity of the Westerner is missing; the persona seeks impersonal growth in service, "in the brother-world of the plain". Orthodox Christianity condemns the "I" as "sin".[11]

A comment by an American visitor to Russia, Barbara J. Brothers, as part of a scientific delegation, states something akin to Spengler's observation:

> "The Russians have a sense of connectedness to themselves and to other human beings that is just not a part of American reality. It isn't that competitiveness does not exist; it is just that there always seems to be more consideration and respect for others in any given situation".[12]

Of the Russian traditional ethos, intrinsically antithetical to Western individualism, Berdyaev wrote:

> "Of all peoples in the world the Russians have the community spirit; in the highest degree the Russian way of life and Russian manners, are of that kind. Russian hospitality is an indication of this sense of community".[13]

Taras Bulba

Russian National literature starting from the 1840s began to consciously express the Russian soul. Firstly, Nikolai Vasilievich Gogol's *Taras Bulba*, along with the poetry of Pushkin, founded a Russian literary tradition; that is to say, truly Russian; distinct from the previous literature based on German, French and English. John Cournos states of this in his introduction to *Taras Bulba*:

> "The spoken word, born of the people, gave soul and wing to literature; only by coming to earth, the native earth, was it enabled to soar. Coming up from Little Russia, the Ukraine,

---

11   Spengler, *The Decline ...*, Vol. I, 309.
12   Barbara J. Brothers, *From Russia with Soul*, 1993.
13   Berdyaev, 97-98.

with Cossack blood in his veins, Gogol injected his own healthy virus into an effete body, blew his own virile spirit, the spirit of his race, into its nostrils, and gave the Russian novel its direction to this very day".[14]

Taras Bulba is a tale on the formation of the Cossack folk. In this folk-formation the outer enemy plays a crucial role.

Their society and nationality were defined by religiosity, as was the West's by Gothic Christianity. The newcomer to a *Setch*, or permanent village, was greeted by the Chief as a Christian and as a warrior: "Welcome! Do you believe in Christ?" —"I do", replied the newcomer. "And do you believe in the Holy Trinity?" — "I do".—"And do you go to church?"—"I do". "Now cross yourself".[15]

Gogol depicted the scorn in which trade is held, and when commerce has entered among Russians, rather than being confined to non-Russians associated with trade, it is regarded as a symptom of decadence:

> "I know that baseness has now made its way into our land. Men care only to have their ricks of grain and hay, and their droves of horses, and that their mead may be safe in their cellars; they adopt, the devil only knows what Mussulman customs. They speak scornfully with their tongues. They care not to speak their real thoughts with their own countrymen. They sell their own things to their own comrades, like soulless creatures in the market-place..... . Let them know what brotherhood means on Russian soil!"[16]

That is "Russian socialism"; far from the dialectical materialism of Marx, the mystic we-feeling forged by the vastness of the plains and the imperative for brotherhood above economics, imposed by that landscape. Russia's feeling of world-mission has its own form of *messianism* whether expressed through Orthodoxy, or by Stalin's

---

14   John Cournos in Nikolai Vasilievich Gogol, *Taras Bulba & Other Tales*.
15   Gogol, Ibid., III.
16   Ibid., IX.

version of "world revolution", which included a revival of Orthodoxy.[17] In both senses, and in the embryonic forms taking place under Putin, Russia is becoming conscious of a world-mission.[18]

Commerce is the concern of foreigners, and the intrusions bring with them the corruption of the Russian soul and culture in general: in speech, social interaction, servility, undermining Russian "brotherhood". The Cossack brotherhood was portrayed by Gogol as the formative process in the building up of the Russian people. This race-formation is not one of biology but of spirit. Gogol described this process among the Russians as an expanding mystic brotherhood under God:

> "The father loves his children, the mother loves her children, the children love their father and mother; but this is not like that, brothers. The wild beast also loves its young. But a man can be related only by similarity of mind and not of blood. There have been brotherhoods in other lands, but never any such brotherhoods as on our Russian soil".[19]

The Russian soul is born in suffering. The Russian accepts the fate of life in service to God and to his Motherland. Russia and Faith are inseparable. When the elderly warrior Bovdug is mortally struck by a Turkish bullet his final words are exhortations on the nobility of suffering, after which his spirit soars to join his ancestors.[20] The mystique of death and suffering for the Motherland is described in the death of Tarus Bulba when he is captured and executed, his final words being ones of resurrection:

> "Wait, the time will come when ye shall learn what the orthodox Russian faith is! Already the people scent it far and near. A czar shall arise from Russian soil, and there shall not be a power in the world which shall not submit to him!"[21]

---

17 K. R. Bolton, "Saint Joseph: Was Stalin a Defender of the Church?"
18 Alexander Dugin, 2015.
19 Golgol, IX.
20 Ibid., IX.
21 Ibid., XII.

Tension of Polarities

Berdyaev wrote that "Russia is a complete section of the world, a colossal East-West. It unites two worlds, and within the Russian soul two principles are always engaged in strife - the Eastern and the Western".[22]

With the orientation of Russian policy towards the West, "Old Russia" was "forced into a false and artificial history".[23] With *Petrinism* Russia was dominated by Late Western culture: "Late-period arts and sciences, enlightenment, social ethics, the materialism of world-cities, were introduced…"[24]

"The first condition of emancipation for the Russian soul", wrote Ivan Sergyeyevich Aksakov, founder of the anti-Petrinist "Slavophil" group, in 1863 to Dostoyevski, "is that it should hate Petersburg with all its might and all its soul". Moscow is Holy, Petersburg Satanic. A widespread popular legend portrays Peter the Great as the Antichrist.

The hatred of the West is the hatred for a civilisation that had already reached an advanced state of decay and sought to impose its primacy by cultural subversion rather than by combat, "poisoning the unborn culture in the womb of the land".[25] Russia was still a land where there were no bourgeois and no true class system but only lord and peasant, a view confirmed by Berdyaev, writing: "The various lines of social demarcation did not exist in Russia; there were no pronounced classes. Russia was never an aristocratic country in the Western sense, and equally there was no bourgeoisie".[26]

The cities that emerged threw up an intelligentsia, copying the intelligentsia of the Late West, "bent on discovering problems and conflicts, and below, an uprooted peasantry, with all the metaphysical gloom, anxiety, and misery of their own Dostoyevsky, perpetually homesick for the open land and bitterly hating the stony grey world into which the Antichrist had tempted them. Moscow had no proper

---

22   Berdyaev, 1.
23   Spengler, *The Decline…*, Vol. II, 193.
24   Ibid., II, 193.
25   Ibid., II, 194.
26   Berdyaev, 1.

soul".²⁷ Berdyaev likewise stated that "Russian history was a struggle between East and West within the Russian soul".²⁸

Russia the *Katechon*

Berdyaev stated that while *Petrinism* introduced an epoch of cultural dynamism, it also placed a heavy burden upon Russia, and a disunity of spirit.²⁹ However, Russia has her own religious sense of universal mission. Spengler quotes Dostoyevsky writing in 1878 that, "all men must become Russian, first and foremost Russian. If general humanity is the Russian ideal, then everyone must first of all become a Russian".³⁰ The Russian messianic idea found a forceful expression in Dostoyevsky's *The Possessed*, where, in a conversation with Stavrogin, Shatov states:

> "Reduce God to the attribute of nationality?...On the contrary, I elevate the nation to God...The people is the body of God. Every nation is a nation only so long as it has its own particular God, excluding all other gods on earth without any possible reconciliation, so long as it believes that by its own God it will conquer and drive all other gods off the face of the earth. ...The sole 'God bearing' nation is the Russian nation..."³¹

This is Russia, the *Katechon*, according to Russian messianism; the nation whose world-historical mission is to resist the son of perdition described by Paul:

> "And now you know what is holding him back, so that he may be revealed at the proper time. For the secret power of lawlessness is already at work; but the one who now holds it back will continue to do so till he is taken out of the way. And then the lawless one will be revealed, whom the Lord Jesus will overthrow with the breath of his mouth and destroy by the splendour of his coming".³²

---

27   Spengler, *The Decline...*, II, 194.
28   Berdyaev, 15.
29   Ibid.
30   Spengler, *The Hour of Decision*, 63n.
31   F. Dostoyevsky, *The Possessed*, II: I: 7, 265-266.
32   2 Thessalonians 2: 6-8.

We are not concerned here about the mundane reality of such beliefs, but about the imperatives of history; the role of myth. This mission as the *Katechon* defines Russia as something more than merely an ethno-nation-state. Even the USSR, supposedly purged of all such notions, under Stalin re-expressed the mission with Marxist rhetoric, which was no less apocalyptic and messianic, against the "decadent West". It is not surprising that the pundits of secularised, liberal Western academia, politics and media could not understand, and indeed were outraged, when Solzhenitsyn seemed so ungrateful when in his Western exile he unequivocally condemned the West's liberalism and materialism and did not present himself as a good democrat, like many of the other "dissidents". A figure who was for so long esteemed as a martyr by Western liberalism transpired to be a traditional Russian and not someone who was willing to remake himself in the image of a Western liberal to for the sake of continued plaudits. He attacked the modern West's conceptions of "rights", "freedom", "happiness", and "wealth", the irresponsibility of the "free press", and "television stupor". He referred to a "Western decline" in courage. He emphasised that this was a spiritual matter:

> "But should I be asked, instead, whether I would propose the West, such as it is today, as a model to my country, I would frankly have to answer negatively. No, I could not recommend your society as an ideal for the transformation of ours. Through deep suffering, people in our own country have now achieved a spiritual development of such intensity that the Western system in its present state of spiritual exhaustion does not look attractive. Even those characteristics of your life which I have just enumerated are extremely saddening".[33]

Spengler's thesis that Western civilisation is in decay is analogous to the more mystical evaluations of the West by the Slavophils, both reaching similar conclusions. Solzhenitsyn was in that tradition. Putin is influenced by it in his condemnation of Western liberalism. Putin recently pointed out the differences between the West and Russia as at root being moral and religious:

> "Another serious challenge to Russia's identity is linked to

---

33 A. Solzhenitsyn, 1978.

The Decline and Fall of Civilisations

events taking place in the world. Here there are both foreign policy and moral aspects. We can see how many of the Euro-Atlantic countries are actually rejecting their roots, including the Christian values that constitute the basis of Western civilisation. They are denying moral principles and all traditional identities: national, cultural, religious and even sexual". [34]

Spengler wrote that *Petrinism* represented by Tolstoy, the precursor of Bolshevism, was "the former Russia"; Dostoyevsky is "the coming Russia". Dostoyevsky does not know the hatred of Russia for the West. Dostoyevsky and the old Russia are transcendent. "His passionate power of living is comprehensive enough to embrace all things Western as well". Spengler quotes Dostoyevsky: "I have two fatherlands, Russia and Europe". Dostoyevsky as the harbinger of a Russian High Culture "has passed beyond both *Petrinism* and revolution, and from his future he looks back over them as from afar. His soul is apocalyptic, yearning, desperate, but of this future he is *certain*".[35]

To the "Slavophil", including Dostoyevsky, Europe is precious. The Slavophil appreciates the richness of European High Culture while realising that Europe is in a state of decay. Berdyaev discussed the attitude of Dostoyevsky and the Slavophils towards Europe, differentiating between *Kultur* and *Zivilisation*:

> "Dostoyevsky calls himself a Slavophil. He thought, as did also a large number of thinkers on the theme of Russia and Europe, that he knew decay was setting in, but that a great past exists in her, and that she has made contributions of great value to the history of mankind".[36]

It is notable that while this differentiation between *Kultur* and *Zivilisation* is ascribed to a particularly *German* philosophical tradition, Berdyaev comments that it was present among the Russians "long before Spengler':

> "It is to be noted that long before Spengler, the Russians drew

---

[34] "Putin Speaking About the Collapse of Western Civilization at the Valdai International Discussion Club", 2013.

[35] Spengler, *The Decline...*, II, 194.

[36] Berdyaev, 70.

the distinction between 'culture' and 'civilization', that they attacked 'civilization' even when they remained supporters of 'culture'. This distinction in actual fact, although expressed in a different phraseology, was to be found among the Slavophils".[37]

Dostoyevsky was indifferent to the Late West, while Tolstoy was a product of it, the Russian Rousseau. Imbued with ideas from the Late West, the Marxists sought to replace one *Petrine* ruling class with another. Neither represented the soul of Russia. Spengler states: "The real Russian is the disciple of Dostoyevsky, even though he might not have read Dostoyevsky, or anyone else, nay, perhaps because he cannot read, he is himself Dostoyevsky in substance". The intelligentsia hates, the peasant does not. He would eventually overthrow Bolshevism and any other forms of *Petrinism*.[38] Here we see Spengler stating that the post-Western civilisation will be Russian. "For what this townless people yearns for is its own life-form, its own religion, its own history. Tolstoy's Christianity was a misunderstanding. He spoke of Christ and he meant Marx. But to Dostoyevsky's Christianity, the next thousand years will belong".[39]

By the time Spengler had published *The Hour of Decision* in 1934 he was stating that Russia had overthrown *Petrinism* (in the guise of Bolshevism) and the trappings of the Late West, and that the orientation of Russia was "a new *Idea*, and an idea with a future too".[40] Russia looks towards the "East", but while the Westerner assumes that "Asia" is synonymous with Mongol, the etymology of the word comes from Greek Ασία, circa 440 B.C., referring to all regions east of Greece.[41] During his time Spengler saw in Russia that,

"Race, language, popular customs, religion, in their present form… all or any of them can and will be fundamentally transformed. What we see today then is simply the new kind of life which a vast land has conceived and will presently bring forth. It is not definable in words, nor is its bearer aware of it. Those who attempt to define, establish, lay down a program,

---

37 Ibid.
38 Spengler, *The Decline…*, II, 194.
39 Ibid.
40 Spengler, *The Hour of Decision*, 60.
41 Ibid., 61.

are confusing life with a phrase, as does the ruling Bolshevism, which is not sufficiently conscious of its own West-European, Rationalistic and cosmopolitan origin".⁴²

Of Russia in 1934 Spengler already saw that "of genuine Marxism there is very little except in names and programs". He doubted that the Communist programme is "really still taken seriously". He foresaw that the vestiges of *Petrine* Bolshevism would be overthrown, to be replaced by a "nationalistic" Eastern type which would reach "gigantic proportions unchecked".⁴³ Spengler also referred to Russia as the country "least troubled by Bolshevism".⁴⁴ The "Marxian face [was] only worn for the benefit of the outside world".⁴⁵ A decade after Spengler's death the direction of Russia under Stalin had pursued clearer definitions, but *Petrine* Bolshevism had been transformed in the way Spengler foresaw.⁴⁶ Dr. Igor Panarin recently pointed this out, stating that Marxism had been thrown out of Russia by Stalin, while taken up by the USA as Trotskyism.⁴⁷

As in Spengler's time, and centuries before, there continues to exist two tendencies in Russia: the (traditional) Old Russian and the *Petrine*. Neither one nor the other spirit is presently dominant, although under Putin Old Russia struggles for resurgence. U.S. political circles see this Russia as a threat, and expend a great deal promoting "regime change" via the National Endowment for Democracy, and many other NGOs, which were shut down by Putin in 2015.

Spengler in a published lecture to the Rheinish-Westphalian Business Convention in 1922 referred to the "ancient, instinctive, unclear, unconscious, and subliminal drive that is present in every Russian, no matter how thoroughly westernised his conscious life may be – a mystical yearning for the South, for Constantinople and Jerusalem, a genuine crusading spirit similar to the spirit our Gothic forebears had in their blood but which we can hardly appreciate today".⁴⁸

---

42 Ibid.
43 Ibid., 63.
44 Ibid.,182.
45 Ibid., 212.
46 D. Brandenberger, 2002). Bolton, *Stalin: The Enduring Legacy*.
47 Igor Panarin, 2006.
48 Spengler, "The Two Faces of Russia and Germany's Eastern Problems", 1922.

Bolshevism destroyed one form of *Petrinism* with another form, clearing the way "for a new culture that will some day arise between Europe and East Asia. It is more a beginning than an end". The peasantry "will some day become conscious of its own will, which points in a wholly different direction". 'The peasantry is the true Russian people of the future. It will not allow itself to be perverted or suffocated".[49]

The arch-conservative, anti-Marxist, Spengler, in keeping with the German tradition of *realpolitik*, considered the possibility of a Russo-German alliance in his 1922 speech. The Treaty of Rapallo was a manifestation of that tradition. "A new type of leader" would be awakened in adversity, to "new crusades and legendary conquests". The rest of the world, filled with religious yearning but falling on infertile ground, is "torn and tired enough to allow it suddenly to take on a new character under the proper circumstances". Spengler suggested that "perhaps Bolshevism itself will change in this way under new leaders". "But the silent, deeper Russia" would turn its attention towards the Near and East Asia, as a people of "great inland expanses".[50]

Spengler foresaw new possibilities for Russia. Putin seems conscious, or at least willing to play his part, in fulfilling Russia's historic mission, messianic and of world-scope. He promotes the "Eurasian" bloc to counter American universalism. He also talks of a Euro-Russian union from Lisbon to Vladivostok.[51] Religious revival is an essential part of this process. Whatever Russia is called outwardly, there is an inner – eternal – Russia that is unfolding.

---

49 Ibid.
50 Ibid.
51 "From Lisbon to Vladivostok: Putin Envisages a Russia-EU Free Trade Zone", Spiegel, 25 November 2010; http://www.spiegel.de/international/europe/from-lisbon-to-vladivostok-putin-envisions-a-russia-eu-free-trade-zone-a-731109.html

Russo-European Symbiosis

Must Europe exhaust its possibilities and succumb to *fellaheen* status? Organic relationships can be *symbiotic* and complementary,[52] or amalgamate through *synthesis*. They need not be parasitic, distorting, or retarding in regard to a culture-organism's life cycle. That is how new *ethnoi* and *super-ethnoi* are formed.[53] Like any mixture, it depends on the qualities and circumstances of what is being mixed as to whether the consequences will be invigorating or pathogenic. A blood transfusion of compatible types might save a life, but will sicken or kill if the blood types are incompatible. A virus can create a vaccine, or it can cause sickness and death, depending on the amount and transformation of the virus.

Dr. Walter Schubart, a Baltic-German convert to Orthodoxy, widely known as an authority on Russia prior to World War II,[54] reaching a similar historical-philosophy to Spengler's, proposed the synthesis of the "Promethean" (Faustian) Westerner and the messianic Russian, each complementing the other. Of the two, Schubart wrote that "Messianic man" "longs to bring the discordant external world to harmony with the image that he carries within him". "He does not love the world for itself but only so that he can build within it the Kingdom of God". The world is "raw material for his mission". "Messianic man" seeks reconciliation; unity.[55] The Kingdom of God must be realised on earth.[56] The Gothic Westerner had a messianic impulse with his Crusades not only to secure the Holy Land from the Moor, but to make Jerusalem the centre of the Kingdom of God.

The contrast now between the West and Russia is that "Promethean" (Faustian) man seeks only to exploit and rule the earth[57], which Spengler saw as the final epoch of the Late West's domination by the

---

52   Lev Gumilev, Ethnogenesis and the Biosphere.
53   Ibid.
54   Schubart was professor of sociology and philosophy at the Latvian state University. Dismissed by the Germans in 1941, he was thought to have died in a Soviet camp.
55   W. Schubart, 72-73.
56   Ibid., 74.
57   Ibid., 80.

machine.[58] The Westerner seeks as an end goal "middle class comfort". The Russian is impelled to sacrifice "in a final dramatic scene".[59] The Russian is the collective *Katehon*, holding back the Antichrist. The West has become the Antichrist. The Russian is a martyr. He accepts his fate Christ-like. Rather than submit to Napoleon, the Russians set their Holy City, Moscow, ablaze. The sight forever affected Napoleon.[60]

The Russian mission is to liberate the world from the contagion of the Late West, or to liberate Europe from its own terminal Western *hubris*; to "redeem" the West or to "replace it".[61] This sense of mission has long been conscious among Russian thinkers and holy men. In 1852, seventy years before Spengler, Ivan Kireyevsky, the Slavophil philosopher, wrote of the decline of the West: "The spiritual development of Europe has already passed in zenith. In atheism and materialism it exhausted the only powers at its disposal – those of abstract rationalism – and now it is approaching bankruptcy".[62]

Schubart cited ethnologist and philosopher-historian Nikolay Danilevski's *Russia and Europe* (1871) as anticipating Spengler on organic culture cycles, in which the replacement of the West by Russia as the next world-civilisation was part of the ongoing cyclic historical process.[63] Danilevski had also critiqued the Westernisation of Russia by Peter as ill-fated. Foreshadowing Spengler, Danilevski's culture epochs are those of youth, adulthood, and old age. He saw the Slavic as being in the youth phase, and that with its capital in Constantinople, the Slavic would be considered by a decaying world as its redeemer.

With the revival of "Eurasianism", and Dr. Alexander Dugin's blueprint for a multipolar world against American globalisation, achieving influence among the highest echelons of Russian politics and scholarship, the vision of Danilevski and the 19th century Slavophils, and Spengler's prescience on a post-Western Russian

---

58   Spengler, *The Decline...*, XIV, "The Form-World of Economic Life (B) The Machine", Vol. II, 499-507.
59   W. Schubart, 80.
60   Ibid., 83-84.
61   Ibid., 191.
62   Quoted by Schubart, Ibid.
63   Ibid., 192.

world-civilisation are being actualised. Konstantin N. Leontiev at about the time of Danilevski advanced the idea of "the law of cyclicity of historical development". Lev Gumilev's cyclic-ethnology has a great deal of influence in present-day Russia.[64] Russia has therefore had a long tradition of scholarship on culture-morphology.

Schubart believed there was after the crisis of World War I a revival of religion in the West. Spengler also stated that during the epochal crisis of a Late civilisation there is a "second religiousness",[65] Materialism, secularism, rationalism and scientism, do not satisfy an innate religious yearning, and themselves must assume religious forms. Note how zealous atheists and Darwinists are in defending their faith. Now there are a proliferation of cults and religions throughout the West, symptomatic of existential crisis, of a yearning for a return to the nexus with the divine that is lost in the Winter epoch. If the spiritual chaos that marks a culture in decay takes form as a "second religiousness" in the Spenglerian sense, then perhaps Schubart's aborted hope of a re-spiritualised West as the prelude to a Russian symbiosis will eventuate. At the time Schubart saw Western man "approaching closer to the spirit" of Russia. "While the night of decline is descending upon Western culture, which is destined to perish, the dawn of the Millennium is coloring the distant horizon…"[66] "The approaching collapse of Western culture is unavoidable, and we may even ask ourselves whether it would be desirable to avoid it".[67]

Neither Spengler nor Schubart believed it organically possible to return the West to a Spring epoch, any more than it is possible for a geriatric to return to youth, despite whatever cosmetic and medicinal efforts are made. What Schubart did hope for was a chastising of the Late West's *hubris*, which we see in our collapsing societies, and existential angst, that would lead to the liberation of religious feeling without which "no new creation can become possible".[68] In this "apocalyptic age" Schubart saw the promise of "new life", while in Russia a new type emerges that is transforming what is of value in Western culture,

---

64 Mark Bassin.
65 Spengler, *The Decline…*, Vol. II, 455.
66 Schubart, 284.
67 Ibid., 293.
68 Ibid.

without being retarded or distorted by it, despite the conscious efforts of inner and outer enemies. "This new type, while truly Russian, is yet heir to the eternal values of the West".[69] "For although the Russian of today is not yet the Man of the Millennium, yet it is he – and only he – who will succeed in evolving him; the Russian will purify himself until he has attained the height of development necessary to produce him".[70]

Schubart wrote that "The spiritual Russian needs practical qualities; the practical European is in need of a new humanity". Schubart called it a "synthesis".[71] The remaining option is for the Late West to continue as an animated zombie at the call of the USA, as a carrier of culture-pathogens.

> "A new Apocalypse is approaching with a Last Judgement – and a Resurrection! Promethean man already bears upon his brow the sign of Death. Now let the Man of the Millennium be born!"[72]

---

69   Ibid., 295.
70   Ibid., 296.
71   Ibid., 297.
72   Ibid., 300.

Conclusion

Materialism is the product of a Late civilisation in decay. Materialist doctrines whether on economics, sociology, or history can only interpret according to the gross visions of the "last man" of a dying culture, albeit undertaken in the name of "progress". "Progress" is an illusion. History is organic and therefore cyclic. What is called "progress" today has been seen many times before. Yet our Late Western historians assure us that we are in the best of times, at the "end of history," where Utopia is finally achieved as the crescendo of five thousand years of civilisation. All of history has been marching in a straight line inexorably towards the present. Any who resist are "reactionaries".

Any destructive, depraved or pathogenic fad, ideology or policy can be called "progress". Those who express a more "conservative" approach to current contrived "issues" such as feminism, "reproductive rights", multiculturalism or the current fads of "transgender choice", and "refugee migration", are ridiculed as "fossils" with anachronistic views within modern society. "Such a view in this day and age…", we hear continually, to ridicule anyone who objects to what is called "progress". Yet, what we are told is "progressive" and "modern" is a replay of pathogenic symptoms that have been seen during the Late epoch of civilisations over millennia. If a sage from Egypt, India, Israel, China, Greece, Rome, Persia, were to return today and survey the trends and ideologies that are called "progressive" and "modern" he would smirk, frown, laugh or sneer, and cry out "been there, done that". Today's fads and fancies are as "progressive" as a cancer that changes the cells of an organism. Both, after all, are agents of "change".

Those who do realise that the Late West is in a terminal state, rather than at the dawn of a universal era of peace and plenty, often also do so from materialistic assumptions. Like Karl Marx attempting to formulate an anti-capitalist ideology within the materialistic *Zeitgeist* of 19th century England, but instead formulating another version of the same; zoological theories about "race", where a "race" is defined by statistical analyses of skulls, bones, gene clusters, and I.Q.; are as materialistic as defining the worth of a culture by calculating its gross national product. The 19th century *Zeitgeist*, part of a centuries' long process starting in the West about the time of the Renaissance, saw the birth of "modern" race theories alongside the rise of Darwinism, Marxism and Free Trade.

Race-materialism is like any other form of materialism. As with Marxism, it is a symptom of decline; not an answer to it. Assumptions are made about civilisations dying due to miscegenation, which discount the organic rhythms of life and death. The outlook of the race-materialist is the same as that of the Marxist materialist or the Liberal: that if certain laws are followed utopia awaits. The reality of death is called "pessimism", hence the rejection or ignorance of Spengler among much of the "Right". Yet the optimism of the materialist obscures the possibilities of new life, like someone who refuses to prune a tree of dead matter because the dead matter was once colourful and vibrant. The materialistic *Zeitgeist* that now hangs over the entire world thanks to globalisation, obliterates the metaphysical and spiritual connexion that a culture must maintain if it is live.

Race-materialism is part of this process. Enamoured with the new materialistic sciences of Darwinism and Mendelian genetics, the spiritual meanings of race and culture that had been previously in vogue, especially among the German Idealists, were lost. Ironically, Hitlerism adopted English science at the expense of German metaphysics. The wider application of Darwinian evolution to history, sociology and economics enhanced materialistic conceptions. Again, England was the birthplace of this, concomitant with the industrial revolution and the Manchester School of Free Market economics'. Hebert Spencer, the most influential, widely read philosopher of his day, combined Darwinism with Liberal economics. Darwin saw man an animal; Freud saw man as a penis, and Marx saw man as a stomach. All contributed to the existential problems of the Late Westerner.

Those who resist the "spirit of the age" of decay, yet who are caught within it, like Karl Marx, cannot see from the perspective of detachment. Paradoxically, we Westerners might profit by turning to traditional texts from the East, such as the *Bhagavad Gita*. Evola certainly recommended such study. We Westerners are bogged down in a quagmire of decadence that does not allow one to see with detachment. The severing of our connexion with the divine and the fracturing of our collective psyche started centuries ago. The collapse of the West has been imperceptible over the gradual course of centuries. Our course of death is likely to be that of a whimper rather than a bang, to paraphrase T. S. Eliot. Hence what we see as causes are symptoms and often secondary symptoms at that. There is a spiritual malady that lacks diagnosis because the diagnostic tools have been replaced by materialistic methods to examine materialistic pathogens, that are symptoms rather than causes. What is required is a return to the spiritual essence in defining race and history.

There have arisen new developments in science that have reconnected the nature of man with what was once called the metaphysical and the spiritual, which are renewing our traditional perceptions of man's place in the cosmos. Epigenetics and morphic resonance both provide empirical insights into how races and *ethnoi* are formed through history and landscape, and how Jungian race archetypes of the collective unconscious can be passed along, without discounting genetic laws, as per Lysenko.

Once the unpalatable realisation of the inexorability of the West's death is realised and accepted, consideration might be given as to what can follow. The question is whether the Late Westerner enters a phase of what might forever be that of the *fellaheen*, existing outside history, or whether there are elements of the West that might contribute to another culture cycle. After the fall of the Roman Empire the Italic peoples did not become *fellaheen*, they became part of a synthesis with the Gothic and Frankish peoples, enabled by the catalyst of a metamorphosed Christianity, and became a vital part of the new culture cycle: that of the West.

The Westerner has reached, to use Spengler's term, "the hour of decision". As *Fortunae* asks of Boethius, why do we bemoan our fate when the Wheel spins against us, as it eventually must? Will the still vital elements of the West march along the path of death behind U.S. leadership, in the name of "progress", towards "the end of history"? Alternatively, will the West, like the Italic peoples after the collapse of the Roman Empire, enter into new relations of symbiosis or synthesis with what seems to be the only alternative for redemption: Russia. Whether Russia herself can endure, revitalise and lead, and not succumb to the same forces of outer decay and inner treachery that caused the Soviet bloc to implode, remains the question of our time. Meanwhile, China, having adopted the Late Western economic model, awaits with interest.

The ideal of "one world, one race" is not even a desirable dream. For what purpose? "World peace"? "Universal harmony"? "The Brotherhood of Wo/Man"? While Liberalism sees epigenetics as its ideological ally, it points rather to a new understanding on the forming and shaping of races and ethnoi. Historical experience takes race-formation beyond zoology. The Liberal will object that epigenetics allows for the elimination of race by the shared experiences of all "humanity". Such a psychotic vision requires the imposition of universal conformity in every mode of existence, thought and deed. The objective is complete levelling, with all the violence that implies: a communistic regime without precedent, but more likely implemented by plutocrats than commissars; Jacobinism and Bolshevism on a global scale, but in the name of "democracy". The only way to equalise shared experiences would be to reduce mankind to a nebulous, amoebic existence.

Then finally that might be the "end of history". Anything less, and new ethnoi would arise, and new identifies would be formed, requiring prompt suppression. The race concept as a means of transcendence was affirmed by Julius Evola as a "revolutionary idea" in ways that are beyond the comprehension of pseudo-revolutionary bourgeois such as Marxists, liberals and anarchists. Of this Evola wrote that race doctrine is "a healthy a reaction against both democratic and collectivist myths… of quality over quantity, of 'cosmos' over chaos, of form over shapelessness", the prerequisite for "reorganizing those forces which, through the crisis of the modern world, are sinking the in quagmire of a mechanical, collectivistic and internationalistic indifferentiation". Race as a Revolutionary Idea, as Evola called a text, requires reaffirming by today's Right, above materialistic inanities. The Identitarian movement is a step forward.

Bibliography

Adams, B. *The Law of Civilization and Decay* ([1895] London: Black House Publishing, 2016).

Adamson, S. *Brazil: A Study in Racial Integration and National Weakness* (ca. 1960?, second ed. Steven Books, 2005).

Agrawal, A. *Rise and Fall of the Imperial Guptas* (Delhi: Motlial Banarsidass, 1989).

Akensen, D. H. *God's Peoples: Covenant and Land in South Africa, Israel, and Ulster* (New York: Cornell University Press, 1992).

Ambrose, *Aeterne Rerum Conditor,* http://www.preces-latinae.org/thesaurus/Hymni/AeterneRerum.html

Angel, J. L. "A racial analysis of the ancient Greeks: An essay on the use of morphological types", *American Journal of Physical Anthropology*, 1944.

Angel, J. L. "Social Biology of Greek Culture Growth", *American Anthropologist*, 1946.

Argyropoulos, E. "A comparative cephalometric investigation of the Greek craniofacial pattern through 4,000 years", *Angle Orthod*, Vol 5, No. 3, Fall, 1989.

Ariew, R. "Pierre Duhem", *The Stanford Encyclopedia of Philosophy* (Fall 2014), Edward N. Zalta (ed.), https://plato.stanford.edu/archives/fall2014/entries/duhem/

Aristotle. *Politics*, Book III: I. http://www.perseus.tufts.edu/hopper/text?doc=Perseus:abo:tlg,0086,035:2

Assmann, J. *The Mind of Egypt: History and Meaning in the Time of the Pharaohs* (Harvard University Press, 2002).

Atiya, F. *Ancient Egypt* (Giza: Farid Atiya Press, 2006).

Baaquie, B. E. and Frederick H. Willeboordse. *Exploring Integrated Science* (Boca Raton, Fl.: CRC Press, 2010).

Bibliography

Backhouse, E. and J. O. P. Bland, *Annals and Memoirs of the Court of Peking from the 16th to the 20th Century* (New York: Houghton Mifflin, 1914).

Bamshad, M., et al. "Genetic Evidence on the Origins of Indian Caste Populations", *Genome Res.*, Vol. 11, No. 6, June 2001.

Barber, E. W. *The Mummies of* Ürümchi*: Did European Migrate to China 4,000 Years Ago?* (London: Macmillan, 1999).

Barton, P. "Black Civilizations of Ancient America", *Race and History*, http://www.raceandhistory.com/historicalviews/ancientamerica.htm

Bassin, M. *The Gumilev Mystique* (Cornell University Press, 2016).

Baxter, J. H. "Statistics, Medical and Anthropological, of the Provost-Marshal-General's Bureau, Derived from Records of the Examination for Military Service in the Armies of the United States During the Late War of the Rebellion, of Over a Million Recruits, Drafted Men, Substitutes, and Enrolled Men", Vol. 1. (Washington, D.C.: U.S. Government Printing Office, 1875).

Bayer-Berenbaum, L. "The Relationship of Gothic Art to Gothic Literature", *The Gothic Imagination: Expansion in Gothic Literature and Art*, (Rutherford, N.J.: Fairleigh Dickinson University Press, 1982).

Beinart, W. *Twentieth Century South Africa* (Oxford University Press, 2001).

Belloc, H. *Europe and the Faith* ([1920] London: Black House Publishing, 2012).

Berdyaev, N. *The Russian Idea* (New York: Macmillan Co., 1948).

Bhagavad-Gita. http://www.bhagavatgita.ru/files/Bhagavad-gita_As_It_Is.pdf

Bhanoo, S. N. "Island's Genetic Quirk: Dark Skin, Blond Hair", *New York Times*, 3 May 2012; http://www.nytimes.com/2012/05/08/science/another-genetic-quirk-of-the-solomon-islands-blond-hair.html

Bilbo, T. G. *Take Your Choice: Separation or Mongrelisation* ([1947] Decatur, Ga.: Historical Review Press, 1980).

Bliss, W. D. P. *New Encyclopaedia of Social Reform* (New York: Funk and Wagnalls, 1908).

Bloomberg, C. *Christian Nationalism and the Rise of the Afrikaner Broederbond in South Africa* (London MacMillan, 1990).

Boardman, J. *Athenian Red Figure Vases : The Classical Period : A Handbook* (London: Thames and Hudson, 1989).

Boas, F. "Changes in the bodily form of descendants of immigrants", *American Anthropologist*, New Series, Vol. 14, No. 3, July- September, 1912.

Boas, F. "The Instability of Human Types," *Papers on Interracial Problems Communicated to the First Universal Races Congress Held at the University of London*, July 26–29, 1911, ed. Gustav Spiller (Boston: Ginn and Co., 1912).

Boas, F. *Race, Language, and Culture* (New York: Macmillan, 1940).

Boethius, A. M. S. *The Consolation of Philosophy* (524 A.D.)

Bolton, K. R. "Saint Joseph: Was Stalin a Defender of the Church?", *Inconvenient History*, Vol. 9, No. 1, 2017; https://www.inconvenienthistory.com/9/1/4214

Bolton, K. R. " 'Sex Pol' Ideology: The Influence of the Freudian-Marxist Synthesis on Politics and Society", *Journal of Social, Political & Economic Studies*, Washington, Vol. 35, No. 3, Fall 2010.

Bolton, K. R. *Revolution from Above* (London: Arktos Media Ltd., 2011).

Bolton, K. R. "Nietzsche Contra Darwin", in Troy Southgate (ed) *Nietzsche: Thoughts & Perspectives Vol. III* (London: Black Front Press, 2011).

Bolton, K. R. "Spengler: A Philosopher for all Seasons", *Spengler: Thoughts & Perspectives*, Vol. X (Black Front Press, 2012).

Bolton, K. R. *Stalin: The Enduring Legacy* (London: Black House Publishing, 2012).

Bolton, K. R. *Babel Inc.* (London, Black House Publishing, 2013).

Bibliography

Bolton, K. R. *The Psychotic Left* (London: Black House Publishing, 2013).

Bolton, K. R. *Opposing the Money Lenders* (London: Black House Publishing, 2016).

Bolton, K. R. "Origins of the Japanese-Amercian War: A Conflict of Free Trade vs. Autarchy", *Inconvenient History*, Vol. 8, No. 2, 2016, https://www.inconvenienthistory.com/8/2/4165

Bolton, K. R. "Suppressed Identity: The Kingdom of the Two Sicilies", *Thermidor*, http://thermidormag.com/suppressed-identity-the-kingdom-of-the-two-sicilies/

Boyd, E., and R. Morrison, *Organic Chemistry* (Prentice Hall, 1992).

Brandenberger, C. *National Bolshevism: Stalinist Culture and the Formation of Modern Russian National Identity 1931-1956* (Massachusetts: Harvard University Press, 2002).

Briggs, A. (ed.), *The Nineteenth Century: The Contradictions of Progress* (New York: Bonanza Books, 1985).

Brisighelli, F., et al., "Uniparental Markers of Contemporary Italian Population Reveals Details on Its Pre-Roman Heritage", *PLoS ONE* Vol. , No. 12, e50794, doi:10.1371/journal.pone.0050794, http://journals.plos.org/plosone/article?id=10.1371/journal.pone.0050794#pone-0050794-g002

Brothers, B. J. "From Russia with Soul", *Psychology Today*, 1 January 1993.

Brown, L. R. *The Might of The West* (New York: Joseph J. Binns, 1963).

Bulgakov, S. *The Orthodox Church* (St. Vladimir's Seminary Press, 1997).

Buxton, L. H. D. "The Inhabitants of the Eastern Mediterranean", *Biometrika*, Vol. 13, No. 1, 1920.

Carlyle, T. *On Heroes, Hero Worship and the Heroic in History* (1840).

Carmina Burana (Bavaria, 1230).

Carroll J. B. (ed.), *Language, Thought, and Reality: Selected Writings of Benjamin Lee Whorf* (Cambridge: Technology Press of MIT, 1956).

Carus, P. *The Nature of the State* (Open Court Publishing, 1904).

Carus, P. *The Rise of Man* (Open Court, 1907).

Catholic Encyclopaedia, "Guilds", http://www.newadvent.org/cathen/07066c.htm

Cavalli-Sforza, L. L., et al. *The History and Geography of Human Genes* (Princeton University Press, 1994).

Chamberlain, H. S. *Foundations of the Nineteenth Century* (London: John Lane, 1911).

Cheadle, C. "Fertility Rates Keep Dropping, and it's going to hit the economy hard", *Virtual Capitalist*, 25 November 2016; http://www.visualcapitalist.com/fertility-rates-dropping-economy/

Chiang Kai-shek, *China's Destiny and Chinese Economic Theory*, (New York: Roy Publishers, 1947).

Chopra P. N. (ed.), *A Comprehensive History of Ancient India* (New Delhi: Sterling Publishers Private Ltd., 2003).

Christensen, A. J. (translator) *Popul Vuh: Sacred Book of the Quiché Maya People*, http://www.mesoweb.com/publications/Christenson/PopolVuh.pdf

Clart, P. "The Concept of Ritual in the Thought of Sima Guang (1019-1086)", *Perceptions of Antiquity in Chinese Civilization* (Heidelberg, 2008).

Clayton, S. C. "After Teotihuacan: a View of Collapse and Reorganization from the South Basin of Mexico", *American Anthropologist*, Vol. 18, No. 1, March 2016.

Clover, C. *Black Wind, White Snow* (New Haven: Yale University Press, 2016).

Cobbett, W. *A History of the Protestant reformation in England & Ireland* (1824).

Coe, M. D. *The Maya Vase Book*, "The Hero Twins: Myth and Image", http://www.mesoweb.com/publications/MayaVase/Coe1989-OCR.pdf

Bibliography

Coen, E. and R. Carpenter, "The Power Behind the Flower: What Makes a Plant Flower?", *New Scientist*, Vol.134, No.1818, 25 April 1992.

Condorcet, Marie-Jean-Antoine-Nicolas Caritat. *Sketch for a Historical Picture of the Progress of the Human Mind* ([1794] Weidenfeld and Nicolson, 1955).

Coogan, M. D. (ed.) *Illustrated Guide to World Religions*, (London: Oxford University Press, 2003).

Coon, C. S. *The History of Man* (London: Readers' Union, 1957).

Coon, C. S. *The Races of Europe* (MacMillan, 1939).

Cox, E. S. *White America: The American Racial Problem as seen in a Worldwide Perspective* ([1923] Los Angeles: Noontide Press, 1966).

Cremo, M. A. and Richard L Thompson, *The Hidden History of the Human Race* (Los Angeles: Bhaktivedanta Book Publishing, 1999).

Daniele, V. and Paolo Malinima, "Are People in the South Less Intelligent than in the North? I.Q. and the North-South disparity in Italy", *Journal of Socio-Economics*, Vol. 40, No. 6, 2011.

Danver, S. L. *Native Peoples of the World* (London: Routledge, 2015).

Derenko, M., et al. (2013) "Complete Mitochondrial DNA Diversity in Iranian", *PLoS ONE* 8(11): e80673. https://doi.org/10.1371/journal.pone.0080673

Dickie, J. *Allah and Eternity: Mosques, Madrases and Tombs*, in *Architecture of the Islamic World*, George Michell (ed.), (London: Thames and Hudson, 2011).

Diehl, R. A. "A Shadow of its Former Self: Teotihuacan During the Coyotlatelco Pertiod", *Teotihuacan During the Coyotlatelco Period*, (Harvard University, 1989).

Dildine, D. "Crumbling Capital: Amid crumbling infrastructure, potholes serve as warning sign", *Washington's Top News*, http://wtop.com/dc-transit/2016/12/amid-crumbling-infrastructure-potholes-serve-warning-sign/slide/1/

Dio, C. *Dio's Rome* (Kessinger Publishing, 2004).

Dolan R. E. and Robert L. Worden (eds.). *Japan: A Country Study* (Washington: Library of Congress, 1994).

Donnelly, I. *Atlantis: the Antediluvian World* (New York: Harper & Row, 1971).

Dostoyevsky, F. *The Possessed*, ([1880] Oxford University Press, 1992).

Duff, A. M. *Freedmen in the Early Roman Empire* (Oxford University Press, 1928).

Dugin, A. *Putin vs. Putin* (London: Arktos Media Ltd., 2015).

Duhem P. *Mémoires de la Société des Sciences Physiques et naturelles de Bordeaux* (1917) cited in Roger Ariew and Peter Barker *(eds.) Essays in History and Philosophy of Science*, (Indianapolis: Hackett, 1996).

Duhem, P. *Les Origines de la statique 1*(Paris: A. Hermman, 1905) in D. C. Lindberg, and Robert S. Westman (eds.) "Conceptions of the Scientific Revolution from Bacon to Butterfield", *Reappraisals of the Scientific Revolution* (Cambridge: Cambridge University Press).

Edwards, E. S., et al. (eds.) *The Cambridge Ancient History*, (Cambridge University Press, 1973).

Elazar, D. *American Federalism: A View from the States* (New York, 1994).

Eliade, M. *The Sacred and the Profane* (New York: Harcourt Brace, 1959).

Eliot, T. S. *The Hollow Men* (1925).

Esler, A. *The Human Venture: The Great Enterprise: A World History to 1500*, (Englewood Cliffs, New Jersey: Prentice Hall, 1992).

Esteban, E. et al. "Genetic relationships among Berbers and South Spaniards based on CD4 microsatellite/Alu haplotypes", *Annals of Human Biology*, Vol. 3, No. 2, 2004.

Evola, J. "On the Secret of Degeneration", *Deusches Volkstrum*, No. 11, 1938.

Evola, J. *Race as a Revolutionary Idea* (Arabi, Louisiana: Western Unity Research Institute, 1970).

Bibliography

Evola, J. *Revolt Against the Modern World* ([1969] Inner Traditions International, Vermont, 1995).

Evola, J. *Ride the Tiger: A Survival Manual for the Aristocrats of the Soul* ([1961] Rochester, Vermont: Inner Traditions International, 2003).

Evola, J. *The Elements of Racial Education* ([1941] Thompkins and Cariou, 2005).

Evola, J. *The Hermetic Tradition: Symbols & Teachings of the Royal Art* (Vermont: Inner Traditions, 1995).

Fairbank, J. K. *The United States and China* (Harvard University Press, 1983).

Faulk, C. "Lamarck, Lysenko, and Modern Day Epigenetics", University of Michigan, School of Public Health, 2013; http://www.mindthesciencegap.org/2013/06/21/lamarck-lysenko-and-modern-day-epigenetics/

Fitzpatrick-McKinley A. (ed.) *Assessing Biblical and Classical Sources for the Reconstruction of Persian Influence, History and Culture* (Harrassowitz, 2014).

Flores-Mendoza, C. et al. "Considerations about IQ and Human Capital in Brazil", *Temas em Psicologia*, Vol. 20, No. 1, 2012.

Forman, A. "New York City in Crumbling", *Time*, 14 March 2014.

Forman, A., et al. *Caution Ahead: Overdue Investments for New York City's Aging Infrastructure*, 5; Centre for an Urban Future, March 2014; https://nycfuture.org/pdf/Caution-Ahead.pdf

Frank, T. *American Historical Review*, Vol. 21, July 1916.

Frawley, D. *Gods, Sages and Kings: Vedic Secrets of Ancient Civilization* (Salt Lake City: Passage Press, 1991).

Fukuyama, F. "The End of History?", *The National Interest*, Summer 1989, http://www.wesjones.com/eoh.htm

Gabler, N. *An Empire of their own: How the Jews Invented Hollywood* (Crown, 1988).

Gaetano, C. Di, et al., "Differential Greek and Northern African Migrations to Sicily are Supported by Genetic Evidence from the Y Chromosome," *European Journal of Human Genetics*, No. 17, 2009, http://www.nature.com/ejhg/journal/v17/n1/full/ejhg2008120a.html

Galanter, J. M. et al. "Differential methylation between ethnic subgroups reflects the effect of genetic ancestry and environmental exposures", *eLife*, 3 January 2017; https://elifesciences.org/content/6/e20532

Galton, F. *Hereditary Genius* ([1869] London: Watts & Co., 1950).

Gardiner, A. H. *The Admonitions of an Egyptian Sage from an Hieratic Papyrus in Leiden* (Georg Olms Verlag, 1969).

Geller, M. J. *The Archaeology and Material Culture of the Babylonian Talmud* (Brill Publishing, 2015).

Ghosh A. (ed.) *An Encyclopaedia of Indian Archaeology* (New York: E. J. Brill, 1990).

Gibbon, E. *The History of the Decline & Fall of the Roman Empire* (London: Reprint Society, 1961).

Gilbert, E. "Your Elusive Genius," 2009, http://www.ted.com/talks/elizabeth_gilbert_on_genius

Gobineau, A. de. *The Inequality of the Human Races* ([1853] Torrance, California: The Noontide Press, 1983).

Gogol, V. *Taras Bulba & Other Tales*, (1842), http://www.gutenberg.org/files/1197/1197-h/1197-h.htm

Goldstein, M. *Demographic and Bodily Changes in Descendants of Mexican Immigrants, with Comparable Data on Parents and Children in Mexico* (Institute of Latin-American Studies, The University of Texas, 1943).

Gonzalez, A. M. et al., "Mitochondrial Lineage Traces an Early Human Backflow to Africa", BMC Genomics, 2007.

Gould, B. A. *Investigations in the Military and Anthropological Statistics of American Soldiers*, published for the U.S. Sanitary Commission

(New York: Hurd and Houghton, 1869).

Goyal, S. R. *A History of the Imperial Gupta* (1967).

Graaf, M. de. "Fertility Rates Drop to Lowest EVER in America", *Daily Mail Australia*, 11 August 2016.

Graham, L. *Lysenko's Ghost: Epigenetics and Russia* (London: Harvard University Press, 2016).

Grant, E. G. *A Sourcebook of Medieval Science* (Harvard University Press, 1974).

Grant, M. *The Passing of the Great Race* (Charles Scribner's Sons, 1916).

Granville, J. "The Nubians", *Oxford Encyclopaedia of the Modern World* (New York: Oxford University Press, 2008).

Gravlee, C. C., and Bernard Leonard. "Boas's Changes in Bodily Form: The Immigrant Study, Cranial Plasticity, and Boas's Physical Anthropology", *American Anthropologist*, Vol. 105, No. 2, 4 June 2003, http://nersp.osg.ufl.edu/~ufruss/documents/boas.paperII.pdf

Gravlee, C. C., H. Russell Bernard, William R. Leonard. "Heredity, Environment, and Cranial Form: A Re-Analysis of Boas' Immigrant Data", *American Anthropologist* Vol. 10, No. 1, 2003.

Grube, E. J. "What is Islamic Architecture?", *Architecture of the Islamic World* (London: Thames and Hudson, 1995).

Gruen, E. S. *Rethinking the Other in Antiquity* (Princeton University Press, 2011).

Guénon, R. *Crisis of the Modern World* ([1927] Sophia Perennis/ TRSP Publications, 2004).

Gumilev, L. "Pomni o Vavilone", *Istoki*, No. 20;1989.

Gumilev, L. *Ethnogenesis and the Biosphere*, http://gumilevica.kulichki.net/English/ebe2a.htm

Gumiliev, L. *Dreviania Rus' I veliaia step'* ("Ancient Rus and the Great Steppe") (Moscow: Airis, 2004).

Gumilev, L. *Zigzag Istorii* (Tbilsi State University, 2013).

Hagger, N. *The Secret Founding of America* (London: Watkins Publishing, 2007).

Hancock, G. *Fingerprints of the Gods: A Quest for the Beginning and the End*, (London: Mandarin, 1996).

Harris, M. et al., *Megacities and the United States Army: Preparing for a Complex and Uncertain Future*, Chief of Staff of the Army, U.S. Army Strategic Studies Group, June 2014, https://www.army.mil/e2/c/downloads/351235.pdf

Heese, J. A. *Die Herkoms van die Afrikaner 1657-1867* (Cape Town, 1971).

Hegel, G. W. F. *The Philosophy of History* (Ontario: Batoche Biiks, 2001).

Helena, M. et al. "Blood Polymorphisms and Racial Admixture in two Brazilian Populations", *American Journal of Physical Anthropology*, Vol. 58, No. 2, 1981.

Heller, E. *The Importance of Nietzsche* (Chicago University Press, 1988).

Hesiod. *Works and Days*, ca. 700 B.C. B.C.http://www.sjsu.edu/people/james.lindahl/courses/Phil70A/s3/Hesiodworks.pdf

Heyerdahl, T. *American Indians in the Pacific* (London: George Allen and Unwin, 1952).

Hitler, A. *Mein Kampf*, (London: Paternoster Library, London, 1936).

Hodges R. and William Whitehouse, *Mohammed, Charlemagne and the Origins of Europe* (London, 1982).

Bibliography

Houghton, P. *The First New Zealanders* (Auckland: Hodder & Stoughton, 1980).

Hurley D., "Grandma's experiences leave a mark on your genes", *Discover*, May 2013; http://discovermagazine.com/2013/may/13-grandmas-experiences-leave-epigenetic-mark-on-your-genes

Islam, M. *Decline of Muslim States & Societies* (Xlibris, 2008).

Jensen, L. A. *Rethinking Darwin: A Vedic Study of Darwinism and Intelligent Design* (The Bhaktivedanta Book Trust, 2010).

Joe Sobran, "Why?", *Sobran's —The Real News of the Month*, Volume 8, No. 11, November 2001.

Jones R. K. and J. Jerman. "Abortion Incidence and Service Availability in the United States, 2011", *Perspectives on Sexual and Reproductive Health*, Vol. 46, No. 1, 2014.

Josephus, F. *Antiquities of the Jews* http://penelope.uchicago.edu/josephus/ant-3.html

Jung Chang and John Halliday, *Mao: The Unknown Story* (London: Jonathan Cape, 2005).

Jung, C. G. *The Complications of American Psychology* (1930).

Jung, C. G. "Mind and Earth," (1931).

Jung, C. G. *Memories, Dreams, Reflections* (New York: Pantheon Books, 1961).

Jung, C. G. *Civilisation in Transition*, Collected Works Vol. X (London, Routledge, 1964).

Jung, C. G. *Letters*, (Routledge, 1973).

Jung, C. G. *Collected Works* (Princeton University Press, 2000).

Karlin, A. "Hamburgers and Rednecks: I.Q. Estimates of U.S. Ethnic Groups", http://akarlin.com/2012/07/hamburgers-and-rednecks-iq-estimates-of-us-ethnic-groups/

Kendall, C. B. *The Allegory of the Church: Romanesque Portals and their Church Inscriptions* (University of Toronto Press, 1998).

Kennedy, E. *A Cultural History of the French Revolution* (New York Yale University Press, 1989).

Kerr, A. *Dogs and Demons: Tales from the Dark Side of Japan* (Hill and Wang, 2002).

Keyserling, H. *The Recovery of Truth* (New York: Harper's Bros. Publishing, 1929).

Khalud, M. Ibn. *The Muqaddimah*, Franz Rosenthal, ed. (New Jersey: Dawood, Princeton, 1969).

Khan A. and C. Lemmen, "Bricks and Urbanism in the Indus Civilization Rise and Decline", 24 July 2014, https://arxiv.org/pdf/1303.1426.pdf

Khazan, O. "Why are so Many Middle Aged White Amercian Dying?', *The Atlantic*, 29 January 2016.

Kipling, R. "The Stanger" (1908), https://www.poetryloverspage.com/poets/kipling/stranger.html

Konstantinov, F. V. *Istoricheskii materialism* (Moscow, 1950).

Kotze, M. J. "Disease Profiles in the Genetically Distinct Populations of South Africa", *European Journal of Human Genetics*, 9 May, 2001.

Krings, M., et al. "mtDNA Analysis of Nile River Valley Populations: a Generic Corridor or a Barrier to Migration?", *American Journal of Human Genetics*, Vol. 64, 1999.

Kuzawa, C. W. and E. Sweet. "Epigenetics and the Embodiment of Race: Developmental Origins of US Racial Disparities in Cardiovascular Health", *American Journal of Human Biology*, 2008, http://groups.anthropology.northwestern.edu/lhbr/kuzawa_web_files/pdfs/Kuzawa%20and%20Sweet%20AJHB%20early%20view.pdf

Lane-Poole, S. *The Moors in Spain* (1886).

Bibliography

Lao Zi, *Dao De Jing*, http://www.indiana.edu/~p374/Daodejing.pdf

Lapin, D. "Jews have Debased American and Jewish Culture", *Toward Tradition*, 24 January 2005; http://www.rense.com/general62/deb.htm

Lavrov, S. "Russia's Foreign Policy: Historical Background", *Russia in Global Affairs*, 3 March 2016.

Lawrence, D. H. *The Plumed Serpent* (London: Secker, 1926).

Lawrence, D. H. *Studies in Classic American Literature* (Exeter: Shearsman Books, 2011).

Lawrence, D. H. *The Woman Who Rode Away and Other Stories* (London: Secker, 1928).

Ledeen, M. "Dishonorable Congressman", *National Review*, 10 September 2003, http://www.nationalreview.com/article/207982/dishonorable-congressman-michael-ledeen

Leo XIII, *Rerum Novarum*: *Rights and Duties Capital and Labour* (Vatican City, 1891).

Lim, L. "'Lightning Divorces' Strike China's 'Me Generation'", National Public Radio, 17 November 2010, http://www.npr.org/2010/11/09/131200166/china-s-me-generation-sends-divorce-rate-soaring

Lings, M. "Rene Guénon", *Sophia: The Journal of Traditional Studies*, Vol. 1, No. 1.

Lombard, R. T. J. *Die bydrae van die Franse Hugenote tot Suid-Afrika se bevolkingsamestelling* (Herdenkingsjaar, 1988).

Lorenz, K. *Civilized Man's Eight Deadly Sins* (New York: Harcourt Brace Jovanovich, 1974).

Loti, P. *Morocco* (London: Kegan Paul, 2011).

Man, Myth & Magic (London: Purnell, 1970).

Manichev V. and Alexander G. Parkhomenko , "Geological Aspects of the Problem of Dating the Egyptian Great Sphinx Construction", International Conference of Geoarchaeology and Archaeomineralogy, Sofia, 2008; http://mgu.bg/geoarchmin/naterials/64Manichev.pdf

Mansfield, B. "Epigenetic Biopolitics, Race, Population and Environmental Health", *eLife*, 3 January 2017; http://globetrotter.berkeley.edu/bwep/colloquium/papers/Mansfield-EP-EpigeneticBiopolitics-Race.pdf

Marcus J. and J. A. Sabloff (ed.), *The Ancient City: New Perspectives on Urbanism in the Old and New Worlds*, (Santa Fe, N.M.: School for Advanced Research Press, 2008).

Marcus, J. *William Timothy Sanders: A Biographical Memoir*, National Academy of Sciences, Washington, 2011; http://www.nasonline.org/publications/biographical-memoirs/memoir-pdfs/sanders-william-t.pdf

Marx, K. *A Contribution to the Critique of Political Economy* (1859).

Marx, K. *The Communist Manifesto* ([1848] Moscow: Progress Publishers, 1975).

McDougall, W. *Is America Safe for Democracy?* (New York: Charles Scribner's & Sons, 1921).

McKinsey Global Inst., "Preparing for China's urban billion", February 2009, http://www.mckinsey.com/global-themes/urbanization/preparing-for-chinas-urban-billion

McNeill, W. *A History of the Human Community: Prehistory to 1500*, Vol. 1, (Upper Saddle River, New Jersey: Simon & Schuster, 1997).

McVaugh, M. R. *Medicine Before the Plague: Practitioners and Their Patients in the Crown of Aragon* (Cambridge University Press, 2002).

Medvedev, Z. A. *The Rise and Fall of T. D. Lysenko* (New York: Anchor Books, 1971).

Meloni, M. "If we're not careful, epigenetics may bring back eugenic thinking", *The Conversation*, 26 March 2016; http://theconversation.com/if-were-not-careful-epigenetics-may-bring-back-eugenic-thinking-56169

Mendes-Flohr, P. R. and Jehuda Reinharz (ed.) *The Jew in the Modern World* (New York: Oxford University Press, 1980).

Michurin, V. A. "Glossary of terms, and concepts in the theory of Ethnogenesis of L. M. Gumilev", http://gumilevica.kulichki.net/MVA/mva09.htm#para85

Minami, K. "Soil and Humanity: Culture, Civilization, Livelihood and Health", *Journal of the Japanese* Society of *Soil Science and Plant Nutrition*, Volume 55, No. 5, 2009.

Mishima, Y. *Mishima on Hagakure – the Samurai Ethic & Modern Japan* (New York: Basic Books, 1977).

Moore, C. H. "Development and Character of Gothic Architecture", http://www.encyclopedia.com/arts/culture-magazines/visual-arts-and-gothic

Muller, H. J. letter to Stalin, 1936, http://mankindquarterly.org/files/sample/muellersletter.pdf

Murphy, G. R. (translator), *The Saxon Savior*, (New York: Oxford University Press, 1989).

Nietzsche, F. *Untimely Meditations* ([1876] Cambridge University Press, 1997).

Nietzsche, F. *The Gay Science* ([1882] New York: Vintage, 1974).

Nietzsche, F. *Beyond Good and Evil* ([1886] Penguin Books, 1984).

Nine Commentaries on the Chinese Communist Party, http://www.ninecommentaries.com/english-6

Nisbet, R. A. *Metaphor and History: The Western Idea of Social Development* ([1969] New Brunswick: Transaction Publishers, 2009).

Norlin, G. *Isocrates* (London: Harvard University Press, 1980).

Northcote Parkinson, C. *East & West* (London: John Murray, 1963).

Pabst, A. "Henry VIII and the Birth of Capitalism", *The Guardian*, 2 May 2009, https://www.theguardian.com/commentisfree/belief/2009/may/01/religion-henry-vii-monasteries

Panarin, I. "From United Russia to Eurasian Rus", *Cyril and Methodius*, 12 January 2006.

Parker, G. K. *Seven Cherokee Myths* (Jefferson, N.C.: McFarland & Co., 2006).

Patai, R. *The Jewish Mind* (Detroit: Wayne State University Press, 1977).

Pena, S. D. J. et al., "The Genomic Ancestry of Individuals from Different Geographical Regions of Brazil is more Uniform than Expected", 16 February 2011, http://journals.plos.org/plosone/article?id=10.1371/journal.pone.0017063#pone-0017063-g001

Pendell, E. *Sex versus Civilisation* (Cape Canaveral: Howard Allen, 1977).

Peters, R. "Constant Conflict", *Parameters*, Summer 1997, http://ssi.armywarcollege.edu/pubs/parameters/Articles/97summer/peters.htm

Phillips G. and Martin Keatman, *King Arthur – The True Story*, (London: Arrow Books, 1993).

Phillips, K. "Phenotype Plasticity," *The Journal of Experimental Biology*, June 15, 2006, http://jeb.biologists.org/content/jexbio/209/12/i.full.pdf

Pierce, W. L. "The Black Man's Gift to Portugal", *Attack!,* No. 6, 1971; *The Best of Attack and National Vanguard*, http://www.solargeneral.org/wp-content/uploads/library/best-of-attack-and-national-vanguard-tabloid-kevin-alfred-strom.pdf

Pius XI *The Social Order: Quadragesimo Anno* (1931).

Bibliography

Plato, *The Laws of Plato* (University of Chicago Press, 1980).

Plutarch. *Numus Pompilius*, http://classics.mit.edu/Plutarch/numa_pom.html

Ponte, L. "Politically Incorrect Genocide", *Frontpage Mag*, 5 October 1999; http://archive.frontpagemag.com/Printable.aspx?ArtId=22976

Pontioks, D. "Racial Type of the Ancient Hellenes", http://dienekes.110mb.com/articles/hellenes/

Popenoe, P. and R. H. Johnson, *Applied Eugenics* ([1918] Lisbon: Portuguese Institute of Higher Studies in Geopolitics & Auxiliary Science, 2015).

Popp, A. J. "Crossroads at Salerno: Eldridge Campbell and the Writings of Theodorico Borgognoni on Wound Healing", *Journal of Neurosurgery*, Vol. 83, No. 1, July, 1995.

Possehl G. L. (ed.) *Harappan Civilization: A Contemporary Perspective*, (New Delhi: Oxford and IBH Publishing Co., 1982).

Poulianos, A. N. *"The Origin of the Greeks",* University of Moscow, 1961.

Poulianos, A. N. *The Origin of the Hellenes (*Athens: Morphosis Press, 1962*).*

Poulianos, A. N. *The Origin of the Cretans* (Thessaloniki: Kyromanos, 1999).

Preedy V. R. (ed.) *Handbook of Anthropometry*, Vol. I (New York: Springer, 2012).

Presston, D. "The Kennewick Man Finally Freed to Share his Secrets", *Smithsonian Magazine*, September 2014, http://www.smithsonianmag.com/history/kennewick-man-finally-freed-share-his-secrets-180952462/?page=2

Putin, V. "Bringing Justice?: A Social Policy for Russia", *Russia Today*, 13 February 2012; https://www.rt.com/politics/official-word/putin-building-justice-russia-133/

Putin, V. "Putin Speaking About the Collapse of Western Civilization at the Valdai International Discussion Club", 19 September 2013; http://www.paulcraigroberts.org/2017/03/12/putin-speaking-collapse-western-civilization-valdai-international-discussion-club/

Putnam, C. *Race and Reality* (Washington D.C.: Public Affairs Press, 1967).

Rajaram, N. S. *The Politics of History: Aryan Invasion Theory and the Subversion of Scholarship* (New Delhi: Voice of India, 1995).

Rand, A. "Racism", (1963), *Ayn Rand Lexicon*, http://aynrandlexicon.com/lexicon/racism.html

Rasmussen, M. et al. "The Ancestry and Affiliations of Kennewick Man", *Nature*, No. 523, 23 July 2015.

Redbeard, R. *Might is Right* (1896), https://archive.org/stream/MightIsRightByRagnarRedbeard/might-is-right-ragnar-redbeard_djvu.txt

Reilly, K. *The West and the World: A History of Civilization*, Vol. 1, (New York: Harper Collins, 1989).

Ridegway, W. *The Early Age of Greece* (Cambridge University Press, 1931).

Riencourt, A. de. *The Soul of China* ([1958] Honeyglen Publishing 1989).

Rinpoche, P. *Words of My Perfect Teacher* (Maryland: Rowman and Littlefield, 1998).

Ripley, W. Z. *The Races of Europe, a sociological study* (Kegan Paul, Trench, Trubner, 1900).

Rosenberg, A. *The Myth of the Twentieth Century* ([1930] Torrance, Ca., Noontide Press, 1982).

Rougemont, D. de. *The Idea of Europe* (New York: Macmillan, 1966).

Sachar, H. *The Course of Modern Jewish History* (Vintage Books, 1991).

Bibliography

Sagan, C. *Cosmos* (New York: Random House, 2002).

Saleeby, C. *Parenthood and Race-Culture: An Outline of Eugenics*, "National Eugenics: Race-Culture and History" (London: Cassel, 1909).

Sanders W. T., et al. "Pre-Columbian Civilizations: Andean Civilization", *Encyclopaedia Britannica*; https://www.britannica.com/topic/pre-Columbian-civilizations/Andean-civilization

Sandstroem, B. "Russia's Baby Boom. Fertility Rate Far Higher Than in EU, Rising Quickly. Unique in Western Hemisphere, Government Programs have Worked", *Russia Insider*, 22 February 2016; http://russia-insider.com/en/politics/russias-baby-boom-fertility-rate-far-higher-eu-rising-quickly/ri385

Sanford, J. *Genetic Entropy* (FMS Publications, 2014).

Sarakar, S. S. "Aboriginal Races of India", *Bulletin of the Anthropological Survey of India*, (Calcutta, 1964).

Saunders, F. S. *The Cultural Cold War: The CIA and the World of Arts and Letters* (New York: The New Press, 1999).

Schubart, W. *Russia and Western Man* ([1938] New York: Frederick Ungar, 1950).

Schwidetzky, I. (ed.), *Rassengeschichte der Menschheit*. Volume 6 (Munich: R. Oldenbourg Verlag, 1979).

Sen, S. N. *Ancient Indian History and Civilization* (New Delhi: New Age International Publishers, 1998).

Sergi, G. *The Mediterranean Race: a study of the origin of European peoples* (London: 1901).

Sewall, G. S. "Robert Nisbet's Conservativism", *The Amercian Conservative*, 16 September 2016; http://www.theamericanconservative.com/articles/robert-nisbets-conservatism/

Shahak, I. *Jewish History, Jewish Religion: The Weight of Three Thousand Years* (London: Pluto Press, 1994).

Shapiro H. L. and Frederick Seymour Hulse. *Migration and environment: a study of the physical characteristics of the Japanese immigrants to Hawaii and the effects of environment on their descendants* (Oxford University Press, 1939).

Shavinina L. V. (ed.), *The International Handbook on Innovation* (Dept. of Sciences Administration, University of Quebec, Oxford: Elsevier Science, 2003).

Sheldrake, R. "An Experimental Test of the Hypothesis of Formative Causation", *Rivista di Biologia - Biology Forum* 86 (3/4), 1992, http://www.sheldrake.org/research/morphic-resonance/an-experimental-test-of-the-hypothesis-of-formative-causation

Sheldrake, R. "Epigenetics and Soviet biology", http://www.sheldrake.org/about-rupert-sheldrake/blog/epigenetics-and-soviet-biology

Sheldrake, R. "Morphic resonance: introduction", http://www.sheldrake.org/research/morphic-resonance/introduction

Sheldrake, R. "Sheldrake's response to Michael Shermer", http://www.thebestschools.org/sheldrake-shermer-materialism-science-responses/

Sheldrake, R. http://www.sheldrake.org/research/morphic-resonance/part-i-mind-memory-and-archetype-morphic-resonance-and-the-collective-unconscious

Sheldrake, R. *Three Approaches to Biology*, (1981).

Sheldrake, R. *Psychological Perspectives* (Spring 1987).

Sherry, J. *Carl Gustav Jung: Avant-Garde Conservative* (Palgrave Macmillan, 2010).

Shun-xun Nan and Beverly Foit-Albert, *China's Sacred Sites* (Himalayan Institute Press, 2007).

Smith, R. "Chick DNA Challenges Theory that Polynesians Beat Europeans to the Americas", *National Geographic,* 19 March 2014;

Bibliography

http://news.nationalgeographic.com/news/2014/03/140318-polynesian-chickens-pacific-migration-america-science/

Solzhenitsyn, A. "A World Split Apart — Commencement Address Delivered at Harvard University", 8 June 1978.

Sparks, C. and R. Jantz "A Reassessment of Human Cranial Plasticity: Boas Revisited", Proceedings of the National Academy of Sciences, Vol. 99, No. 23, 2002.

Spencer, H. *Social Statics, or the Conditions Essential to Human Happiness Specified, and the First of them Developed* (London: Chapman, 1851)

Spengler, O. "The Two Faces of Russia and Germany's Eastern Problems", *Politische Schriften*, Munich, 14 February, 1922.

Spengler, O. *Spengler Letters 1913-1936* (London: George Allen and Unwin, 1966).

Spengler, O. *The Decline of The West* ([1926] London: George Allen & Unwin, 1971).

Spengler, O. *The Hour of Decision*, (New York: Alfred A Knopf, 1963).

Stalin, J. *Marksizm i voprosy iazykoznaniia* (Moscow, 1950).

Stark, R. *The Rise of Christianity: A Sociologist Reconsiders History* (Princeton University Press, 1996).

Stark, R. *The Rise of Christianity: How the Obscure, Marginal Jesus Movement Became the Dominant Religious Force in the Western World in a Few Centuries* (New York: Harper One, 1996).

Stille, A. *The Future of the Past: The Loss of Knowledge in the Age of Information* (London: Picador, 2003).

Stoddard, L. *The Rising Tide of Color* ([1920] Sussex: Historical Review Press, 1981).

Stoddard, L. *Revolt Against Civilization* (London: Chapman & Hall, 1922).

Suzuki, D. T. *Nihonteki reisei* (Tokyo: Daitō shuppansha, 1944); English translation : Norman Waddell, *Japanese Spirituality* (Tokyo: Japan Society for the Promotion of Science and Japanese Ministry of Education, 1972).

Tarn, W. W. "Hellenistic Culture", *Cambridge Ancient History*, Vol. VI, 1927.

Trevor-Roper, H. *The Rise of Christian Europe* (London, 1966).

Trubetskoi, E. "A World View in Painting", in *Icons: Theology in Color* (New York: Saint Vladimir's Seminary Press, 1973).

Vahia M. N. and N. Yadav. *Social Evolution & History*, Vol. 10 No. 2, September 2011.

Van der Post, L. *Jung and the Story of our Time* ([1977] London: Random House, 2010).

Vico, G. *The New Science of Giambattista Vico* ([1730] Cornell University Press, 1948).

Vishnu Purana (Calcutta: Elysium Press, 1896).

Voegelin, E. *The Collected Works of Eric Voegelin*, (Columbia: University of Missouri Press, 1999).

"Voluspo", *The Poetic Edda*, http://www.sacred-texts.com/neu/poe/poe03.htm

Waddington, C. H. "Genetic assimilation of an acquired character", *Evolution*, Vol. 7, No. 2, June 1953, , http://www.chd.ucsd.edu/_files/winter2009/waddington-assimilation.pdf

Weber, M. *The Protestant Ethic and the Spirit of Capitalism* (1905).

Weigel, G. *The Cube and the Cathedral* (Basic Books, 2005).

Weitenberg, C. "India's Beautiful Minds", SBS, 21 March 2017; http://www.sbs.com.au/news/dateline/story/indias-beautiful-minds

Bibliography

Wiarda, H. J. *Corporatism and Comparative Politics: The Other Great 'Ism'* (New York: M. E. Sharp, 1997).

Widyono, B. *Dancing in the Shadows* (Maryland: Rowman and Littlefield, 2008).

Wilson, J. A. *The Ancient Near East* (Princeton University Press, 1973).

Wood, C. *Studying Late Medieval History: A Thematic Approach* (London: Routledge, 20216).

Wren, C. S. "A Secret Society of Afrikaners Helps to Dismantle Apartheid", *New York Times*, 30 October, 1990.

Yahuda, R. et al., "Holocaust Exposure Induced Intergenerational Effects on *FKBP5* Methylation", *Biological Psychiatry*, Vol. 80, Issue 5, September 1, 2016.

Yeats, W. B. "The Second Coming", 1919, https://www.poetryfoundation.org/poems/43290/the-second-coming

Zotigh, D. "History of the Modern Hoop Dance", *Indian Country Today*, May 30, 2007, http://www.indiancountrytoday.com/archive/28147954.html

www.ingramcontent.com/pod-product-compliance
Lightning Source LLC
Chambersburg PA
CBHW070716160426
43192CB00009B/1206